I0763087

Praise for

DEREK BAXTER

The Forgotten World War

"*The Forgotten World War* shines a bright and entertaining light on a little-known chapter of the American Revolution. Baxter is the perfect travel companion: informed, curious, and funny in all the right places. A serious theme runs through these pages too: Alliances are nothing new to the United States; they are part of our creation story. Read this book and I guarantee you will utter these two words often and enthusiastically: Who knew?"

—Eric Weiner, *New York Times* bestselling author of *The Geography of Bliss*

"Think you know the American Revolution? *The Forgotten World War* reveals the globe-spanning battles, backroom diplomacy, and unlikely players that turned a rebellion into a worldwide war. Mr. Baxter skillfully weaves all these elements together."

—Chuck Schwam, executive director of the American Friends of Lafayette

"Derek Baxter has done it again… This consummate history explorer takes readers on another journey to faraway historic sites to make a case for why the American Revolution was part of a world war. From India to Sint Eustatius in the Caribbean to the Isle of Jersey and even the Rock of Gibraltar and many other unexpected places. If you thought America's War for Independence was confined to the North American continent, think again. Baxter lets his curiosity lead him, and his hands-on approach invites readers to travel along with him as he explores the war's broader context. He connects with interesting people along the way and tells history stories in a way reminiscent of Tony Horwitz. In this special anniversary year, this is a perfect gift for armchair history lovers who seek new angles on America's past. Baxter shows that history is not drawn solely from archives and libraries but also from the places it happened, and the reward for intrepid travelers is the gift of deeper understanding. Bravo to Baxter for another interesting read."

—Tim Grove, author of *The World Turned Upside Down: The Yorktown Victory That Won America's Independence* and *George Washington: A Revolutionary Life*

"Derek Baxter chose wisely when he selected Mercy Otis Warren as his guide to the Revolutionary War. She counted George Washington, John Adams, and Lafayette as firsthand sources, and her history of the war was more insightful and more global than the better-known (male) historians who came after her. Derek follows her international perspective to describe firsthand the locations where American history forever changed—not just Saratoga and Yorktown but also the Spanish town that birthed the hero of Pensacola; the Dutch port that raised the first salute to the new American nation; the French château where Rochambeau's troops trained to fight the British; and the city in India that marked the last battle of the American Revolution. Part travelogue, part academic scholarship, altogether an enjoyable read."

—Larrie D. Ferreiro, Pulitzer Prize finalist and author of *Brothers at Arms: American Independence and the Men of France and Spain Who Saved It*

"America's Revolution had many heroes, and its freedom was won with the help of numerous friends. They, however, too often go unrecognized. In *The Forgotten World War*, historian and author Derek Baxter restores these forgotten allies to their rightful place. In doing so, Baxter takes readers along for a journey, traveling across North America and overseas, capturing with humor and eloquence the true global scope of the Revolution.

Arriving in time for the 250th anniversary of American independence, *The Forgotten World War* is a moving reminder of its many authors."

—Ryan L. Cole, author of *The Last Adieu: Lafayette's Triumphant Return, the Echoes of Revolution, and the Gratitude of the Republic*

In Pursuit of Jefferson

"Every schoolchild knows Thomas Jefferson wrote the Declaration of Independence, but I doubt even the most dedicated reader of travel literature knows he also published a compact guide explaining the architecture, people, food, and (especially) wines of Old World Europe to the citizens of the brand-new United States. This retracing of the Founding Father's life-changing time abroad is a very entertaining book about a very complicated man."

—Mark Adams, *New York Times* bestselling author

"*In Pursuit of Jefferson* is an endlessly intriguing and completely original portrait of a complicated man and the places that formed him. Derek Baxter is the perfect guide, pairing a wry, eager sense of adventure with meticulous research, ever mindful of Jefferson's instruction to 'follow truth, wherever it may lead'—even when those insights reveal a troubling side of the Founding Father and his legacy."

—Doug Mack, author of *The Not-Quite States of America*

"*In Pursuit of Jefferson* is an excellent historical travelogue focused on Thomas Jefferson's unique musings and wanderings across Europe. Derek Baxter is an unabashed fan of the Sage of Monticello and follows him on his journeys as he matures as a politician, naturalist, scientist, and observer of human nature. The glue that holds the book together is found in the timeless parallels of scenery and outlook that the author discovers along the way. Jefferson, though no Mark Twain, turns out to be the quintessential American abroad—a sometimes fumbling Founder infused with gusto, wit, and affection for most everyone and everything he meets."

—Philip G. Smucker, author of *Riding with George*

"In his debut book, *In Pursuit of Jefferson*, Derek Baxter tells the bittersweet story of Thomas Jefferson, or should I say, Baxter's own reckoning with this most revered—and contradictory—figure from American history. In crisp language that is often conversational, Baxter weaves history with geography, food and wine, and science to tell what is ultimately a story of acceptance. It is only after following Jefferson's 'hints' through Europe—not to mention the Paris of North America—that Baxter comes to accept Jefferson for who he really was—a flawed human who might still offer some 'hints' on how best to move forward today. It confronts the uncomfortable but relevant issue of Jefferson's involvement with slavery plainly and with heartfelt honesty. This is a fine work of historical travelogue that will appeal to anyone with an interest in history, geography, science, and self-discovery—an engaging read offering much food for thought."

—Darrin Lunde, author of *The Naturalist*

"Taking their cues from Jefferson's *Hints* to travelers and following in his footsteps, Derek Baxter and his family gained a deeper and more enlightened understanding of a flawed founder's life and enduring legacies. This is travel writing at its best, an impressively researched and well-crafted chronicle of self-discovery and civic engagement."

—Peter S. Onuf, Thomas Jefferson Memorial Foundation
Professor of History, Emeritus, University of Virginia

"This jaunty, inventive approach to an old question—who was Thomas Jefferson?—turns out to be a wise, readable, and altogether satisfying work… An unusually pleasing and affecting guide to Europe through the eyes of two tourists separated by more than 230 years."

—*Kirkus Reviews*, Starred Review

Also by Derek Baxter

In Pursuit of Jefferson

THE FORGOTTEN WORLD WAR

Exploring *the* Secret History *of the* American Revolution, from Spain to India *and* Back Again

DEREK BAXTER

Cover design by Kelly Winton
Cover images © Couder, Louis Charles Auguste/Château de Versailles,
France/Bridgeman Images, Hary/Shutterstock
Map art by Travis Hasenour

Published by Sourcebooks
1935 Brookdale RD, Naperville, IL 60563-2773
(630) 961-3900
sourcebooks.com

Cataloging-in-Publication Data is on file with the Library of Congress.

Printed and bound in the United States of America.
VP 10 9 8 7 6 5 4 3 2 1

To my parents,
Carl and Judy Baxter,
who always wanted to know why

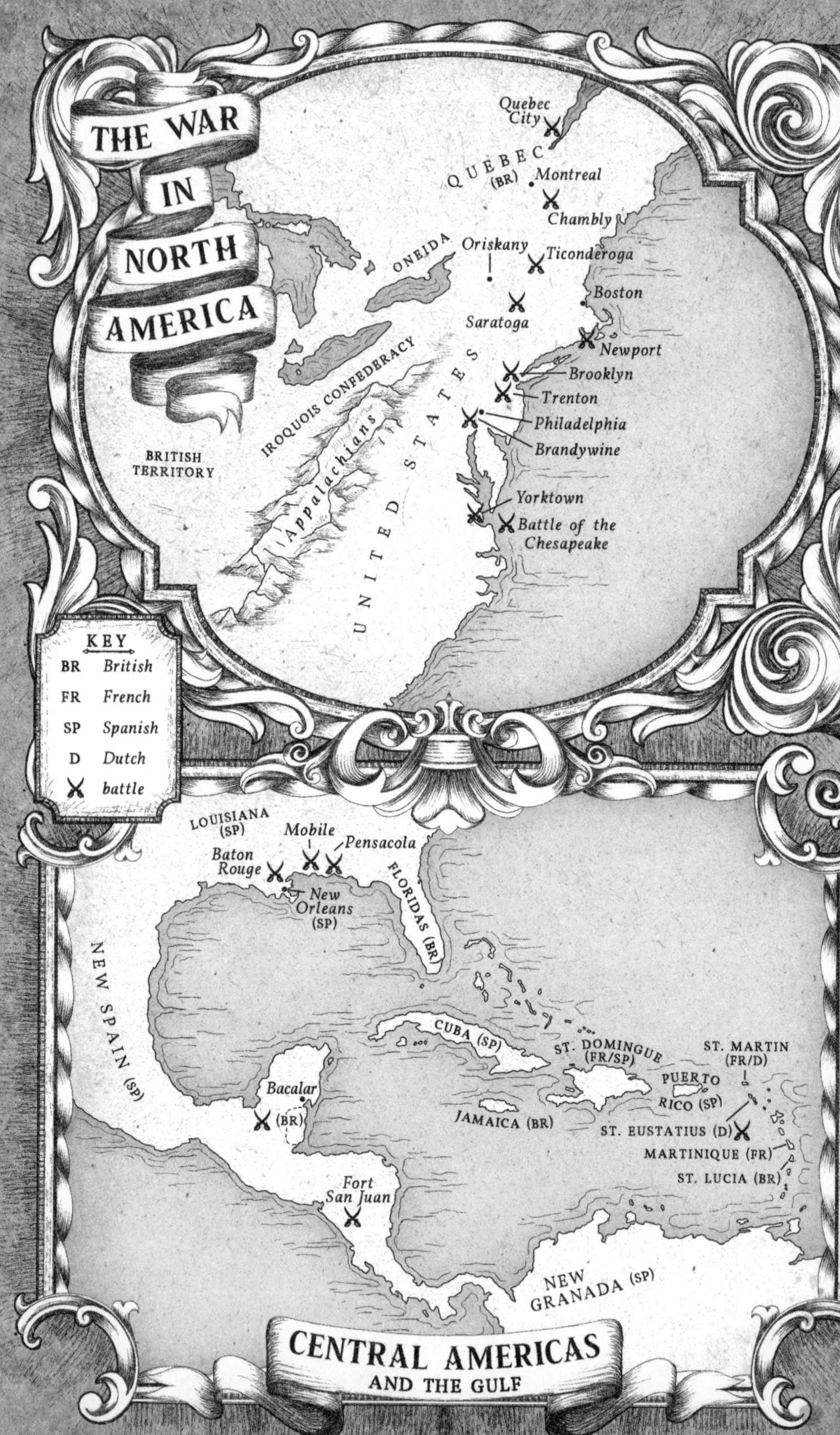
THE WAR IN NORTH AMERICA
Quebec City
QUEBEC (BR)
Montreal
Chambly
ONEIDA
Oriskany
Ticonderoga
Boston
Saratoga
Newport
IROQUOIS CONFEDERACY
Brooklyn
Trenton
Philadelphia
Brandywine
Appalachians
UNITED STATES
BRITISH TERRITORY
Yorktown
Battle of the Chesapeake
KEY
BR British
FR French
SP Spanish
D Dutch
battle
LOUISIANA (SP)
Mobile
Pensacola
Baton Rouge
New Orleans (SP)
FLORIDAS (BR)
NEW SPAIN (SP)
CUBA (SP)
ST. DOMINGUE (FR/SP)
ST. MARTIN (FR/D)
PUERTO RICO (SP)
Bacalar
(BR)
JAMAICA (BR)
ST. EUSTATIUS (D)
MARTINIQUE (FR)
ST. LUCIA (BR)
Fort San Juan
NEW GRANADA (SP)
CENTRAL AMERICAS
AND THE GULF

VESTERN
EUROPE
IRELAND
GREAT BRITAIN
Belle Poule
Jersey
English Channel
St. Malo
DUTCH REPUBLIC
Paris
Versailles
"Hessians"
FRANCE
Burgundy
PORTUGAL
SPAIN
Madrid
Aranjuez
Sagres
Moonlight Battle
Gibraltar
Macharaviaga
INDIA
Delhi
INDIA
BRITISH
Calcutta
Bombay
Arabian Sea
BRITISH
Bay of Bengal
KINGDOM OF MYSORE
Srirangapatna
Pollilur
Madras (BR)
Pondicherry (FR)
Cuddalore
CEYLON (D)

Table of Contents

Introduction

EL CUATRO DE JULIO

The World War We Never Knew Existed

The sound of snare drums echoed from a distant street, growing increasingly louder until the Redcoats marched into the town square. The good guys soon followed, marching in with their black tricorner hats and muskets to polite cheers, while the British soldiers glowered at them. What a way to spend the Fourth of July, I thought, with a good old-fashioned Revolutionary War reenactment. My wife, Liana, smiled at me, while my kids, Miranda and Nico, squirmed in their plastic lawn chairs, waiting for the show.

This celebration had everything you could ask for on the Fourth: a band playing "Yankee Doodle," the American flag flying, kids scarfing down cotton candy and parents pounding hot dogs and beer, waiting for the fireworks to come. If I squinted a little—or finished the drink in my hand—I could have sworn I was in any small-town Independence Day celebration in America. But a sharper-eyed, more sober observer would have found some clues tipping them off that they were not in, say, one of our many Springfields.

The first was that I hadn't seen anyone else in the crowd place their hand over their heart when our national anthem was played.

The next clue had to have been that the reenactment was taking place in front of an ancient church, with its Baroque carvings and mahogany door, centuries older than any church in the States.

The final hint (and this one seemed fairly telling) came when a volunteer ran the gigantic red-and-yellow striped flag of Spain up a flagpole, to lusty shouts of "*Viva España!*"

No, this was a Fourth like no other, celebrated high in the foothills of Andalucia, far, far from home. And the most astonishing part was about to come. Not only was the village of Macharaviaya honoring the national holiday of a country that most villagers had never set foot in, they were also going to reenact a battle of the American Revolutionary War, a battle that I knew nothing about until recently.

The pageant began with scenes recapping the lead-up to the Revolutionary War, described by an offstage narrator. It opened with the Americans in Boston, complaining of their hardships and dreaming of freedom. Many of the arms they carried had come from overseas, from Spanish, French, and Dutch smugglers.

In the next scene, the spotlight found a moon-faced man in a black coat and tri-corner hat. His name was Bernardo de Gálvez. He was responsible for smuggling munitions up the Mississippi River to waiting American armies from his base in New Orleans. Gálvez, as the pageant's narrator told us, was the young governor of Spain's province of Louisiana. In the scene, he had maps spread out over a table as he plotted strategy with Spanish officers.

"I thought Louisiana was French?" Miranda whispered, reasonably enough.

"We had taken it over," Liana responded. By "we," of course, she meant Spain. Although she's Cuban, rather than Spanish, she was brimming with pride at everything that both the Spanish and Latin Americans had done in this war. She was thrilled to find out that her ancestors, too, had played a role in America's origin story.

I had scarcely heard about Bernardo de Gálvez before this trip, but here in his home village, he's a rock star even today. The entire Gálvez family is, for that matter. They had started as shepherds in these foothills and slowly worked their way up to the very heights of the Spanish government and military, with Bernardo's uncle becoming a top minister in the government and his father a noted general.

Yet neither of them could match Bernardo's chutzpah. He fought the powerful British all along the coast of the Gulf of Mexico, taking fort after fort in a surprise campaign before the enemy knew what hit them. The villagers were recreating one of these victories today.

The pageant lights dimmed and came up again on a new scene: Bernardo arguing with his naval officers. He had reached the Bay of Pensacola, the site of Fort George, Britain's chief stronghold in the Gulf. Yet a sandbar near the bay's entrance threatened to strand his ships and expose them to the raking fire of the British guns. The navy was ready to turn around and call it a day. Bernardo's men—a mix of Spanish, French, and free Blacks in Louisiana—looked up at him expectantly.

"I will go alone to get rid of this fear," the actor cried, his voice rising. He held a cannonball high in the air. "I alone! *Yo solo!*"

The men cheered. He would not be alone. Bernardo's sloop cleared the sandbar, and the sheepish naval officers followed him. The pageant mercifully fast-forwarded through the two-month siege that followed (represented by a few offstage *booms!* of the cannons) and reached the climax. A lucky Spanish shot hit the British powder magazine: a tremendous *boom!* Gálvez "sensed death among the defenders," the announcer declared. "It was the most terrible hour." On cue, his soldiers cried out and charged through blue fog pumped out of a smoke machine, with sounds of muskets popping and a stirring song that sounded like an outtake from *Les Mis* filling the air. They screamed and pointed their prop bayonets at the hapless Redcoats. The battle was over, and the crowd cheered. The sky turned bloodred as the sun sank behind the hills of Andalucia.

The narrator recounted how the Battle of Pensacola did much more than prove Bernardo's courage: It played a key strategic role in the lead-up to the 1781 allied victory at Yorktown. For me, that was the most astonishing thing I had learned about this battle. It wasn't a fight between the British and Spanish that coincidentally happened during the time of our Revolutionary War. No, it was *part* of the war, one of many battles fought outside the Thirteen Colonies. The American War of Independence started local but turned into a world war fought between armies in Europe, Latin America, India, and Africa, as well as between navies on countless seas. Bernardo de Gálvez deserves to take his place in the story of the war alongside George Washington, Nathanael Greene, and all the other generals we know so well. So do many others.

The pageant ended to applause, and we settled back to watch the fireworks. "That was crazy," said Miranda. "That was like almost an out-of-body experience. How did they know all this?"

We joined the crowd milling around the plaza. Performers hugged each other and passed around cups of beer; someone realized I was an American and handed me one too. "Everyone is having such a great time," Liana said. "This is one of the best Fourth of Julys that I've ever been to."

Suddenly, like a ghost materializing out of the haze still lingering from the smoke machine, the spitting image of Bernardo de Gálvez walked up to us.

"You look just like him!" Liana blurted out to him in Spanish.

"Yes, I am his relative," the man said, introducing himself as José Gálvez. He had just played the role of Bernardo in the pageant. He beamed when he found out that we were Americans who had come to Spain to learn about his family and their deeds.

"How did you find out about my ancestor?" he asked.

"In an old book," I replied. "One that no one knows about today. That's what sent me here."

The Spaniard looked intrigued. "I invite you to my house next Saturday," he said. "The cast will be there. I'm making a paella. And we can talk." He paused and winked. "And drink!"

"Here, take this and stir," José said to me after we arrived a week later, handing me a long metal spoon. I felt as if I had walked onto the outdoor set of a fancy cooking show on TV: José had placed his massive iron paella pot by his pool in Marbella, an hour's drive south of his ancestral village, with a view of the Mediterranean sparkling blue in the fierce sunlight.

José Gálvez: attorney, reenactor, and paella maker (in no particular order), with his American sous-chef.

As promised, most of the gang from the show was here, in swimsuits this time rather than gowns or tunics. “It’s ready! *A la mesa!*” José cried out. I finished stirring the yellow rice, with chunks of chorizo and small lobsters poking out of it. Cooking this most Spanish of dishes with a relative of Bernardo de Gálvez felt as absurd as making a cherry pie with a descendent of George Washington.

Liana took a long pull on the glass of white wine before her. “This is the best paella I’ve ever had,” she concluded, satisfied.

“Where is the cod?” someone yelled from one end of the table.

“I forgot to cook it,” a shirtless man yelled back, and everyone laughed. But no one went hungry, for someone else swooped in with a heaping platter of shrimp with garlic, while José brought out a slab of tangy *payoya* goat cheese, sweating in the sun.

As everyone ate and drank, and drank some more, our host held forth at the head of the table, wearing a shirt with a picture of Bernardo de Gálvez, emblazoned with his relative’s famous quote: *Yo Solo,* I Alone. José worked as a criminal defense lawyer, but promoting Bernardo seemed as important to him as any of his cases. “Back in March, I had a reenactment event to go to. My girlfriend at the time said she didn’t want to go. I told her I was going with or without her.” He paused for effect. “And so she left!” He burst out laughing, as did everyone around him at the table.

“So it was *yo solo,*” I replied.

“Yes! And I’m too ugly to get another one!” José replied, to even more laughter.

Liana joined the women sitting by the pool, who were making sly comments about the men splashing in the water. Nico threw a beach ball around with other kids. Maybe it was the white wine, but there was something about this lunch that seemed so right. A feeling of easy friendship with people from far away—was this a trait that José had inherited from his long-lost relative?

“He was a true leader,” José said of Bernardo. “His troops loved him a lot. He found ways to cooperate with the French and others and share interests with them. They knew that the English had too much power, they had to be taken down a notch or they would have taken over everything."

"Did you see the cathedral in Málaga?" he asked. I nodded; we had toured it a couple of days prior. "And did you see that it only has one bell tower? We call it the *La Manquita*, the one-armed lady. That's because the parish of Málaga sent so much money to help the Americans during your revolution that we ran out of money and we couldn't finish it. It was my ancestor, the foreign minister," he continued, "who demanded that we help you. We never rebuilt it. Today it reminds us of our sacrifices."

I smiled; I had heard that story as well. We had stood on the cathedral's rooftop and gazed out on the honey-colored south tower, much shorter than its would-be twin to the north, and thought back to the era when the Spanish came to our rescue. A time I still had much to learn about.

José settled back, contented. "Now you must tell me why you came here," he said.

And so I recounted the story, mercifully abbreviated, since my Spanish was rusty (although it seemed to me to be improving with each glass of sangria). Here is the gist.

I had gone to a talk at the Library of Congress about the book collection of Thomas Jefferson, one of my heroes. Jefferson had sold his private library (which he had idiosyncratically organized under the categories of Memory, Reason, and Imagination) to Congress. A devastating fire on Christmas Day 1855 had devoured many of his books, but some still remained.

The curator brought out a few of these survivors. One caught my eye: a modest-looking book entitled the *History of the Rise, Progress, and Termination of the American Revolution*. Published in 1805, it was weathered and had singe marks on the cover, scars from that long-ago fire. Jefferson had filed it under Memory. Surprisingly for the time, it was written by a woman, the poet and political commentator Mercy Otis Warren.

She wrote it even as the war unfolded, for she had unprecedented access to some of its greatest protagonists. Her husband, James Warren, was one of the Patriot leaders in Massachusetts, part of the group pushing for greater liberties in America (and, eventually, independence). Through him, she hosted George Washington, the Marquis de Lafayette, and a Spanish officer who had served at Pensacola. She became close friends with John Adams, who agreed to send her portraits in writing of the personalities he encountered, both at home and abroad. Warren even toured the aftermath of the Battle of Bunker Hill with none other than Martha Washington.

When she finally published her magnum opus, it clocked in at 1,317 pages. President Jefferson wrote that she deserved "high station in the ranks of genius" (today, we'd call that a good blurb) and recommended to his cabinet secretaries that they all purchase it.

Her own story of breaking barriers was incredible enough, but her book told a story that seemed equally fantastic to me. From the beginning, the Americans were desperate for foreign assistance. The Continental Army was dangerously short of ammunition and guns—and was happy to get them via "clandestine assistance" from Dutch merchants, Warren wrote. The French and Spanish even established a front company to more easily send cannons, muskets, gunpowder, and even blankets to the rebels. The Declaration of Independence itself was in part a cry for help—it was drafted to allow Americans to conduct "negotiations with foreign powers" as a self-proclaimed nation, she wrote, for European kings would never sign an alliance with a mere group of rebels.

The French were the first to answer the invitation, allying with the United States in 1778. France went on to assemble a group of allies and partners who all shared a common goal, that of defeating the British, their "hereditary enemy," as Warren put it. The next year, Spain joined the fight—even though it delayed entering into a formal alliance with the Americans, worried that Spanish colonies in Latin America might take the hint and rebel as well.

The Dutch joined in the war as well, fighting the British in the North Sea and the Caribbean. So did the Oneida Indians, who helped the Americans win battles in New York State. The most incredible campaign of all, I learned, was led by the Mysore Kingdom in the south of India. Mysore assembled a huge army of some ninety thousand soldiers (over four times as many as Washington ever put in the field), with some firing iron-cased rockets while others charged on the backs of elephants. They inflicted the single bloodiest defeat that the British suffered during the entire war.

It was far from easy for soldiers to fight alongside others "of a different religion, language, habits, and manners," as Warren put it. Yet they ultimately found a way to make common cause. Americans won independence through their own "prowess and magnanimity," *History* concludes, but always "in conjunction with the armies of their brave allies."

All this almost seemed like an alternative version of the history I had known, as if our Revolution had been fought in a different reality in some strange corner of the multiverse. It certainly wasn't the story I thought I had been raised on—and I had grown up in Virginia as much of a fan of the Revolution as any kid could be. My parents' idea of a good time was dragging the family off on weekends to what my sister called "history houses."

Somewhere on one of those visits to Colonial Williamsburg or Yorktown, I discovered something: I actually liked history houses, especially those connected in some way to the American Revolution, that dramatic struggle for our freedom. One of my ancestors, a lieutenant from North Carolina, even fought in it, a fact that made this long-ago struggle seem even more real to me. And so, while my sister howled about weekends wasted on dead people, I would happily grab my tricorner hat from the closet and join my parents on another trip, touching the Liberty Bell in Philadelphia and walking the Freedom Trail in Boston. I collected crinkly copies of Continental currency from each visitor center I went to and made my own baseball cards out of cardboard—with Revolutionary War heroes on the front.

There were cameos by the French in the tales I grew up on—a grateful tip of the hat to Lafayette, a nod to Rochambeau. But ours remained an American story, of American blood spilled on American soil. Our freedoms, won by ourselves.

Yet now I realized I had learned only half of the narrative, and I needed to learn more about the half that was missing. For even though Jefferson had filed Warren's book under "Memory," our national remembrance of what the allies had done in our war has been mostly forgotten over the years. It seemed bizarre to me that a reader in 1805 would have had a better sense that the American Revolution was a world war than I did as a kid reading my schoolbooks.

And so I resolved to set out on the road to see what else I could uncover. It would be a new version of those travels up and down I-95 I had taken with my parents as a kid. I wanted to search out the foreign versions of Yorktown and Valley Forge, unknown places that played key roles in the Revolutionary War. I wondered if I would see the war any differently by the end. Liana already was feeling new connections to America, which she now knew won its freedom with the help of her own people. What would this trip teach me about who we were when it all started?

I wouldn't have to go it alone. Liana and the kids would be able to accompany me on some of the trips. Even when they couldn't, I had the words of Mercy Otis Warren to help guide me—as well as those of Washington, Franklin, and Adams, all of whom paid close attention to the global dimensions of the war.

Mercy Otis Warren, revolutionary writer.

My goal was to see some of these spots with my own eyes, to pay my respects to places where our independence was won. And, ideally, I hoped to find local experts along the way—reenactors, professors, or historians—who had helped keep the memory of what happened alive, just as José had done here in Andalucia.

His party was winding down. Over by the pool, one of the reenactors—a woman who was a judge in her real life—opened a bottle of Cava with her teeth, to howls of approval from the other partygoers. I clinked glasses with my host.

Soon we'd take our leave. We had other destinations to reach, sites in Spain and beyond with a connection to this history I wanted to uncover. I had a world to explore and an open road before me, with the true story of the American Revolution in my sight.

Part One

A CRY FOR HELP

1775–1778

Chapter One

THE SHOT HEARD 'ROUND THE WORLD

How the Patriots' Need for Munitions Led Them to Look Abroad

April–July 1775

One summer, my history-loving parents took me and my little sister on a swing through New England and New York State, where I discovered some of my favorite stops on our on-again, off-again childhood Revolutionary War tours. (We also learned how to swim in a motel pool, but that's another story.) First came Lexington and Concord in Massachusetts, the site of the Shot Heard 'Round the World in April 1775. I remember walking down the Battle Road Trail, imagining the Redcoats retreating to Boston. They had come out from their headquarters in Boston to seize American war supplies but ended up fleeing back to safety, with bullets singing at them from the woods.

Before we left, Dad bought me a figurine of a determined-looking Minuteman holding his rifle, a miniature version of the famous statue in the park. It stood guard on my dresser next to a miniature Liberty Bell for the rest of my childhood.

Fort Ticonderoga, on the shores of Lake Champlain in New York, was equally evocative. Ethan Allen and the Green Mountain Boys, a militia group from what is now Vermont, along with Benedict Arnold (yes, that Benedict Arnold), dramatically seized the British fort in May 1775. I was impressed by the giant French royal flag flying, with its white background fleur-de-lis, which looked so exotic. The banner made sense—France had built the fort, which the British had taken during the Seven Years' War, 1757–63 (what we in America call the French and Indian War). Even cooler was the ceremonial firing of a cannon in front of Ticonderoga—a boom that couldn't fail to impress a ten-year-old boy.

Our family hike along the Freedom Trail in Boston was another hit, especially for a kid like me who had devoured *Johnny Tremain*, a book about a boy in that port city in those early days of the Revolution. We finally reached the end, where the Bunker Hill Monument, a towering granite obelisk, stood. Nearby, in June 1775, the Patriots famously held their fire in the face of a British attack until they could see the whites of their enemy's eyes, a tale of bravery that stayed with me for years.

Somewhat counterintuitively, all three of these iconic American battles occurred before the United States even existed. We were over a year away from declaring independence yet already were engaged in an undeclared—yet very real—shooting war with Britain. Patriot discontent had been growing for a decade. Americans objected to a series of taxes imposed by Britain (which were intended to pay off the costs of the Seven Years' War). London kept making things worse—taxing tea, sending more troops to the colonies, and closing the port of Boston in response to the unrest. By February 1775, King George had declared Massachusetts to be in a state of rebellion. Three months later, the Second Continental Congress convened in Philadelphia, seeking to forge a consensus on how best to resist this British overreach.

As a kid, I had paid less attention to the underlying causes of the conflict. What captivated me were the individual dramas of each battle, the story of Paul Revere clattering through the streets on horseback, of militiamen waiting resolutely behind stone walls to take their shot. Only recently, reading Mercy Otis Warren's book, did I see a through line to these three battles that I had missed before: They all had something to do with the American need for guns and gunpowder.

British troops at sunrise—who were probably much groggier in real life when the Patriots surprised them at dawn on May 10, 1775.

Lexington and Concord, of course, was about the Patriots trying to keep hold of their stores of muskets and munitions, and fighting back when the British sought to take them. The reason for the assault on Ticonderoga was to seize the British cannon in the fort, which the Americans would use against the British in Boston. And the Americans would have done better at Bunker Hill had they not been so low on gunpowder. That was one reason the Patriots didn't fire until the British were so close to them—the defenders only had what was in their powder horns and thirty additional half-barrels of the stuff to go around.

I should have paid more attention to the other side of my Minuteman figurine, I realized now, to the powder horn slung behind the soldier's back, for that was the key to future victories. If the troops couldn't keep those powder horns full, there would be more Bunker Hills in their future, battles that started out well but ended in retreat when the Patriots ran out of ammo.

Of course, they no longer could get it from Britain. In late 1774, "Parliament actually prohibited the exportation of arms, ammunition, and military stores to any part of America," Warren wrote, "and the king's troops were frequently sent out in small parties to dismantle the forts, and seize the powder magazines or other military stores wherever they could be found."

George Washington arrived in Massachusetts on July 2, 1775, as the first commander in chief of the newly minted Continental Army, which had come into being only a few days before Bunker Hill. The forty-three-year old Virginian was "ignorant," Warren wrote, of just how negligent leaders had been in acquiring "powder, arms, and other warlike stores" before the prohibition set in. What he found when he inspected his troops literally left him speechless—there was only enough gunpowder for each soldier to shoot about nine rounds. When Washington finally found his voice, he swore that "the salvation of the country" was in jeopardy unless more gunpowder could be found.

This shortage, I learned from Warren's *History*, was what first turned the war global. The need to arm at all costs would lead Americans abroad—both to buy guns from foreign smugglers and to seize supplies outside of their own borders. The quest for powder would even turn the Americans from defenders of their own liberties into invaders of another people's homeland.

And so, I made a brief return trip to these battlefields again as an adult. They all looked smaller than I remembered but still left me with something like that thrill I had experienced as a kid, of stepping back into a time when, for America, everything was at stake. My favorite stop this time around was Fort Ticonderoga, which looked almost Hogwarts-like, with stone ramparts set before a placid lake stretching endlessly to the horizon.

"This is a four-pounder," a cheerful reenactor named John, playing the role of a British private in the Royal Artillery, told me in Ticonderoga's powder magazine room. He was cradling the ball, which was swaddled in wool, as if it were a baby. He handed the shot to me so I could get a feel for it. Earlier in the day, John said, he had helped out with a cannon-firing demonstration, and he gave me a quick tutorial on the steps that were involved in shooting off the contraption. In early 1775, Patriots were learning that skill on the fly. And even firing one shot from a small cannon like this, I learned, would require over a pound of gunpowder.

After leaving John, I wandered around the fort and found a row of mortars, squat, toad-like guns pointing at the sky, with whimsical faces and elaborate coats of arms on their tubes. When I peered closer, I saw the inscriptions on their tubes were in French and Spanish—they were European imports. I made my way into the fort museum, which included cases and cases full of guns. Many of those, too, came from Europe: rows of French muskets and sabers and gleaming bayonets. I even came across a cannon with dolphin-shaped handles, with a sign noting that it had been occasionally fired off in front of the fort until a few decades ago. Was that the gun that caught my attention as a kid? If so, it was much smaller than I had remembered. And how intriguing that it came from the Netherlands—which would become our ally in the war.

Before I left, I ran into the museum curator, Matt Keagle, in the fort's courtyard. He looked to be approaching forty and was tall and friendly, sporting an Irish-style cap. I told him about my interest in the role of guns and ammo in the early days of the war and asked if we could talk, say, over coffee. This, it turned out, was like offering a cat a plate stacked with ten pounds of catnip. Matt, I would learn, not only had written his doctorate dissertation on the Revolutionary War period but was also a dedicated reenactor himself—the kind who could distinguish a 1763 model musket from the '66 version quicker than a sommelier could tell you a bottle's vintage.

He was busy with other work duties that day but, conveniently enough, was traveling to the D.C. area, where I lived, not too far in the future and kindly agreed to meet up over coffee.

"The response to Lexington and Concord was that all these militia companies swarmed around the city of Boston," Matt told me, "which of course is very different from Boston today, in that it's almost an island, connected by that narrow neck. All of these provincial militias that were coming in were more than enough to surround the city." The Patriots began what would turn into an eleven-month siege of the port city, which served as the British army's main base.

"One thing we had in abundance in America was people," Matt continued. "But we didn't have the military equipment needed, because we had no standing army of any form prior to the breakout of hostilities. Massachusetts started to create something along those lines, but they lacked ammunition, as well as artillery—that's something that every colonist didn't have lying around, even if they've got a fowling piece to go hunting," he explained. "Americans had very little of a gun-founding base prior to the Revolution. Virtually all of the artillery in America was coming from Europe."

"What about powder?" I asked. "I've heard that was a big problem."

"There was a constant need for gunpowder throughout the war," Matt told me. "It's made from sulfur, saltpeter, and charcoal," he explained. Getting the charcoal wasn't a problem, but sulfur and saltpeter were not commonly mined in America at the time. "America had powder mills but couldn't produce it in an industrial capacity," he continued. "We had to import powder from Britain." Gunpowder, John Adams wrote to Mercy Otis Warren's husband James, was the "one necessary thing" for success.

Surprisingly to me, we needed more guns too. I had in mind that American militiamen all had rifles—that was one of our strengths at the beginning of the war. But the issue was more nuanced, it turned out.

American gun manufactories only turned out a limited supply, Matt told me when we met later. "Those weapons could be made maybe in the hundreds, but we didn't have an industrial base to make them in the thousands that were needed," he told me. Additionally, some of the guns were intended for hunting rather than warfare, and they were many different makes. This would be a huge problem when soldiers had to reload, Matt said, and the cartridges available didn't fit the guns they had at hand.

Given the British prohibitions on exporting guns and ammo, the colonists would have to look for them elsewhere. The Patriots hit on several strategies for overcoming their lack of munitions. The most obvious was finding lightly guarded British forts or supply depots within the Thirteen Colonies, attacking them, and seizing their loot. That's where Fort Ticonderoga came in.

"Ticonderoga was one of the few places captured in the French and Indian War," Matt said. "The British had left artillery there. So American eyes turned to it."

"How did they take the fort?" I asked.

"Two similar expeditions left without knowledge of each other, Benedict Arnold in Connecticut and Ethan Allen of the Green Mountain Boys. They crossed Lake Champlain in boats. They only got eighty or so men across. At 3:30 a.m., they stormed the walls. There was a single sentry there. They didn't know the war had started." The heist yielded some fifty-nine cannon and mortar, which would later prove critical to ending the Siege of Boston.

Ticonderoga was a great success. But there was only so much low-hanging fruit like that, and the British were feverishly moving what stores they had in the interior onto ships offshore.

Another option was to look outside the Thirteen Colonies for places to attack. To my surprise, Matt told me that the conquerors of Ticonderoga didn't stop there—they kept going up to Quebec, about a hundred miles to the north.

"Benedict Arnold had heard that Fort St. Jean in Quebec, at the other end of Lake Champlain, wasn't well-defended by the British," Matt said. "He took a schooner and headed north with fifty men and raided it. It was partly for supplies, to get gunpowder and ammunition, and also because the British government had a sloop there—Arnold knew if you captured that vessel, you cut off the British ability to move freely up and down the lake." The competitive Ethan Allen, suffering from a fear of missing out, sent his own expedition in rowboats, trailing behind Arnold, to try to capture a share of the glory. He was too late, Matt told me. The British, alerted to the attack, had sent reinforcements down from Montreal. "And the Green Mountain Boys went pell-mell into their boats and rowed away back to Ticonderoga."

What a surprising story. Even before the Continental Army existed, we had already taken the fight against the British outside our borders. Washington loved the idea of continuing this. He encouraged an expedition to the Bahamas—which finally occurred in the spring of 1776, when a small American fleet sailed to Nassau and seized two hundred barrels of gunpowder, in the first amphibious assault landing of the newly constituted American marine corps.

The final, most sustainable strategy was to get the needed powder and arms by smuggling them in from European countries that produced them—namely Spain, the Netherlands, and, above all, France.

"The French were undergoing a massive reorganization of their military in all aspects," Matt told me. "They had lost the Seven Years' War pretty catastrophically, and it prompted a great reform of their arms and equipment. When they developed more modern models, they cleared out their arsenals of old weapons that were perfectly serviceable," he explained. "Americans had direct engagements with private merchants, who sold them to us. These were kinds of shady dealings—you couldn't openly send boatloads of weaponry to America; that would be tantamount to declaring war on Britain."

To avoid His Majesty's Navy, the wily Americans sailed with false papers to European ports to load up their cargo. European merchants also shipped the goods to islands in the Caribbean (the Dutch island of Sint Eustatius was a favorite smuggling spot), where small American craft could pick them up, then slip past cruising British ships to drop-off points in hidden coves in New England. The Dutch even sent gunpowder and arms hidden inside chests of tea.

The Spanish did the same. "I've seen some contracts that were made between Massachusetts merchants and Spanish gunmakers in '75 and '76," Matt told me, "particularly from the Basque country, the heart of Spanish gun-making. These were private negotiations," he continued. "They weren't yet enough to tip the scales in the war, to equip whole field armies." Those kinds of shipments would come later, though. In the first couple years of the war, over 90 percent of gunpowder used by the Patriots would be brought in from abroad by smugglers.

"Were Americans thinking of allying with the French or Spanish at the beginning," I asked, "or did they just want their guns?"

"No, they weren't looking at them to be allies at that time," Matt explained, "even though shots had been fired and blood spilled. Many Americans still hoped for reconciliation with England." The Americans were not united—far from it. At this stage in the conflict, the rebels were pressing for greater rights, not independence. In opposition to them, a large contingent of Loyalists had loudly pledged to support the Crown. In 1775, it would have been a bridge too far to actually ask European powers to enter an undeclared war being fought by a government in rebellion.

Besides, the Americans were by no means fans of the French, even as they appreciated *les armes* being smuggled to them. France had fought the British and the colonists in several conflicts in North America, including the Seven Years' War, and hard feelings lingered. Protestant Americans weren't sure how far they could trust these Catholic Frenchmen and Spaniards. These foreigners were "a people of a different religion, language, habits, and manners" than the Americans, Warren wrote, and "ancient prejudices" remained against them. Despite these differences, Americans would eventually plead with France, Spain, and the Netherlands to join the war on their side. All this organized gunrunning helped create relationships that laid the groundwork for that day.

At the very beginning, though, Americans "were not thinking of France the kingdom so much as the French population of *Canada*," Matt told me, "which was much more of a looming concern. The Quebec Act, which Britain passed in 1774, was a deeply upsetting piece of legislation to Americans, who felt that it hemmed in the colonies, that it was a potential path for further British tyranny." The law expanded the boundaries of the province of Quebec far to the south and west, even into what is now Illinois, and also failed to provide for an elected legislature. "Americans thought that this big, Catholic, French-speaking province, which prohibited representative government, could be expanded to increase tyranny across North America. They could be a huge danger to Americans," he said.

"But, Congress thought," Matt continued, "what if we could convince these people that our fight was their fight?"

Incredibly enough, the Continental Congress planned to do just that. It began assembling a force at Fort Ticonderoga in the summer of 1775 that would march into Canada. The goal was "to capture posts as a defensive measure, to protect our forces, and to protect Canadians from the British," Matt said. "Letters went out to Quebec from Ethan Allen encouraging people there to join in the campaign, or at least not directly fight for the British." Americans had only been in the undeclared war for a few months and already wanted to take it outside their own borders.

All this was a lot to digest. I had never fully appreciated the role that powder and arms had in the early strategies of the American forces, or how much we depended on foreign merchants to supply us with munitions in those early years. I knew that ours was a David and Goliath story; who knew that David's sling itself was a foreign import? It didn't make the Minutemen any less brave, but now I understood more about how they and other American soldiers depended on a global web of commerce to get them out into the field. Even in the earliest days of the conflict, the Revolution had an international dimension.

The American obsession with Canada also came as a surprise. We had attacked a fort in Quebec before the Continental Army was even constituted, then planned a full-scale invasion for later in the fall of 1775. I don't remember much at all about these stories from my schoolbooks. Yet, from the very beginning, Patriot leaders were looking internationally as they mapped out the next steps in the war.

I thanked Matt for talking with me and threw out what I thought might be my last question: "How is it that you're both an academic and a reenactor? That doesn't seem all that common."

"Living history is at the heart of my interest, my career arc," he replied. "Seeing people use these objects and being able to engage with them and have a dialogue is really compelling to people. That's how I got into doing historical work myself. It's because I went to living history museums as a kid, places like Old Sturbridge Village in Massachusetts and Colonial Williamsburg. And just that bit of coming alive is just captivating. Something just caught me. I love engaging with history in a tactile way, not just reading about it."

Reenactors making Fort Ticonderoga come alive—including Matt Keagle, portraying a Connecticut sergeant (foreground).

"Why is living history important to your work here?" I asked.

"There are different ways that people learn. Reading is one way, but seeing something, engaging with it, even just smelling and feeling—there's a visceral sensory engagement where it's not even intellectual, it's just an aura. Think of the smell of a campfire, the smell of leather, of wood. And when we do musket demonstrations and there's a firing, you can hear this kind of, 'whoa' from the crowd when the gunpowder smoke drifts across. That sulfur smell, you'll never forget that. It's an emotional response almost, that can spark something in people."

"Where do you get your uniforms?" I asked, my curiosity about his work growing.

"I make them myself, after doing a lot of research." Matt is modest, but when pressed, he allowed that he had made at least a hundred different period uniforms. "What we aim for is that every stitch of clothing, every choice you've made to equip yourself, is effectively an essay. For example, if I make a French uniform and the equipment to go with it, it's effectively a three-dimensional material essay on what a French infantryman looked like in 1780. And with that, we can do what a book of history can't, which is make the footnotes talk."

I had never heard such a moving explanation of living history before. I, too, had loved going to places like Williamsburg as a kid—and the cannon shot I had heard at Ticonderoga stuck with me for years. It hadn't turned me into a reenactor, but at least I was reenactor-adjacent. Seeing the guns and powder and cannon of Ticonderoga, and hearing about their importance from an expert, made the whole subject more real to me. I had discovered what the Patriots needed in 1775, the "necessary thing" for victory that would wind up driving them closer to the European powers they had once mistrusted. And I had learned that the fort I had loved to scramble around in as a kid also served as the staging ground for the invasion of Quebec.

To discover more about that curious episode of the war, I hit the road with the whole family this time, headed north. The Baxters were invading Canada.

Chapter Two

THE ALLIES THAT WEREN'T

America's Doomed Invasion of Canada

August 1775–July 1776

Sunlight sparkled on the rapids of the Richelieu River, its banks lined with maples and fir trees. Liana, the kids, and I drove slowly through the town of Chambly, Quebec, past smart-looking houses with steeply pitched roofs and blueberry patches on their front lawns. "Oh, how pretty," Liana said. "I'd love to live here."

She had just walked into the perfect opening for me. "You know, the Americans tried to do just that," I replied.

It seems strange that America chose to take the war to Canada so many months before they had even declared independence. Why did the Americans choose to go on the offensive? Was there any chance they could have actually succeeded in their plan? Perhaps our visit would give me some insight into this strange early chapter of the war. For taking Fort Chambly—about forty miles north of the New York state line and only twenty miles east of Montreal—was a key part of the invasion strategy.

The stronghold could hardly be in a more picturesque location, overlooking the river, with stone walls around a stone enclosure, watchtowers jutting out at each corner. It might have passed for a small French château. Inside, a guide in her early twenties named Elisabeth gave me a crash course in the fort's backstory. Truth be told, I needed something even more basic—Canadian History 101, which I barely knew anything about.

"Chambly is on an important waterway," she began. "It's on the Richelieu River, which goes north from Lake Champlain in New York to connect to the St. Lawrence River, which is the greatest river in Quebec. And so, people have been living here for many thousands of years."

She walked over to a box, opened it, and brought out some materials that archaeologists had discovered while excavating the fort: first, tools and arrowheads, showing the long-standing presence of the First Nations here, and then a beaver jaw, which illustrated the importance of the fur trade.

"The French came as fur traders and established the colony of New France," she said. "The beaver was very important for the French; the colony depended on the fur trade. And during Lent, you could even eat them, they were considered a fish!"

"No thank you," said Liana.

"There was much competition over the furs and some fighting," Elisabeth went on. "So the French built a log fort here in 1665, later rebuilt it in stone. It was one of five forts protecting Montreal and the trade routes." Elisabeth cheerfully brought out some relics of the French occupation found in digs at the fort—a wine bottle, stylish earthenware, and a two-chambered coffee maker shaped like an hourglass.

"That looks just like ours!" said Liana. It's true; our Italian-manufactured Moka was the spitting image of the one the French used to brew coffee (to go with their beaver).

"The French lost to the English in the Seven Years' War at Quebec City in 1759," Elisabeth said. "The English took over this fort and ruled here for over a century." She brought out a beer bottle—the new residents of Chambly preferred ale to wine, thank you very much. "With the French gone from Canada, the English weren't so worried and didn't keep many troops here. They mostly used the fort as a warehouse for food and ammunition, until the Americans came."

"What can you tell us about the American invasion in 1775?" I asked. From Warren's *History*, I learned that the Americans had sent two different expeditionary forces north in August and September of that year. The main one, under Generals Philip Schuyler (who soon returned home sick) and the Irish-born Richard Montgomery, went north from Fort Ticonderoga. A somewhat smaller force under Benedict Arnold left Massachusetts, taking a secret route north through the wilds of Maine. The two were supposed to converge at Quebec City. Montgomery's men arrived first.

"Here, I'll take you to a place that might be interesting to you," she replied. She led us to a powder magazine. "The Americans tried to take Fort St. Jean, upstream from here, but they couldn't. So, instead they started bombarding Chambly," she said. "The fort couldn't take it; the stone walls weren't thick enough. So, the British surrendered on October 18, 1775.

"The officer who was here messed up. When the fort is taken, you're supposed to throw out the gunpowders," she continued. (Her French accent was so charming, I couldn't bear to tell her the word was singular in English.) "You must throw out the gunpowders, otherwise the enemy would take them. And this officer didn't do that! So the Americans came here and said, 'Oh, that's interesting, a lot of gunpowders.' And they'd take all the gunpowders and use them when they took Fort St. Jean."

"Do you ever get American tourists here?" I asked.

"Oh yes, a lot. We're not far from Montreal. And we mention the American invasion to them. They're normally surprised; they don't really know about it."

"What about the Canadian visitors? Do they know about it?"

"No, not really," she said, laughing softly. "It's not taught in our schools.

They always talk about the French period—even more than they do about the British period. And the American invasion even less. It's just a small part of history. They see it as an anecdote," she said.

In fact, I had stretched Elisabeth's knowledge of the invasion almost to the breaking point. She excused herself, then came back some time later.

"I found this book in the back," she said. "This will tell you more about the battle you're interested in." It was a typewritten monograph, prepared for the Canada parks system in the 1960s. We flipped through its pages, yellowed with age, while Liana and the kids went off to explore the rest of the fort. In it I discovered more about the bounty taken by the Americans from the captured fort—124 barrels of gunpowder, 6,600 cartridges, and 500 hand grenades. They would go a long way in helping the ragged American army as it moved further north. This would be a DIY invasion, with the invaders having to scrounge for military supplies as they went along.

I thanked Elisabeth for going the extra mile. But talk about obscurity! This was Battle Number Four for the Continental Army by my count, an important encounter in the war that founded our nation. Yet you had to do a fair amount of sleuthing to learn about it.

The expedition could have ended like the one at Fort Ticonderoga—the Americans could have returned home with their military loot and called it a day. After all, everyone expected a massive British onslaught in the colonies at some point in 1776, and the Continental Army needed to conserve its forces for it. But mission creep set in. Why stop at Chambly when Quebec could be fully "conquered into liberty," as the Continental Congress had once put it? Back in Cambridge, Washington agreed that "the acquisition of Canada is of unmeasurable importance to the cause we are engaged in."

The operation was taking on more and more of a political dimension. Americans "published a declaration announcing the reasons of this movement," Warren wrote, "inviting the inhabitants of every description to arrange themselves under the banners of liberty, and unite in the common cause of America." Several hundred Canadians did so, even though that number was far fewer than American leaders had expected.

After taking Chambly and Fort St. Jean in November 1775, General Montgomery marched with his forces to Montreal, whose "gates were thrown open," Warren wrote, in the face of the American army and, as I'm now tempted to call it, its gunpowders. The next month, his men began marching the 150 miles east to Quebec City, the province's capital. If all went well, they could take the city's fortress, alongside Benedict Arnold's men.

And then things began to go wrong.

"Watch out, they have bayonets!" the guide called out. Nico had wanted a photo with the two guards standing at the sentry box. To me, they looked like dead ringers for the guards outside Buckingham Palace, with their red jackets and towering bearskin hats. When these guards broke character and spoke, though, it was in French. Canada may still be in the British Commonwealth, but we were a long way from London.

We had driven to Quebec City's Citadel, the sprawling fortress that dominates Cape Diamond, a promontory with three-hundred-foot cliffs. The fortress provided a towering view over both the city and the immense St. Lawrence River below us. Since the fort still serves as the home base for the Royal 22nd Regiment, you can only enter if you sign up for a tour. We gathered with other visitors before a flagpole on a grassy hill, while soldiers in fatigues walked by to their barracks.

"Are there any Americans here?" the guide asked, which took me a little aback. "We were attacked by the Americans."

My family slowly raised our hands. "We come in peace," I offered.

The guide laughed. "It's OK. We don't bear a grudge. We all attacked everyone in the past. You wanted your independence, we wanted ours later."

Despite beginning by warning of the dangers that Americans can pose, she didn't talk about the 1775 invasion during the rest of the tour. Of course, the Citadel itself postdates this battle; it was built in the nineteenth century. Yet the British had some fortifications here at the time of the Revolutionary War. So had the French before them; our guide showed us a French powder magazine from 1750. And the fort's small museum displayed muskets used by British defenders from the American siege. But there wasn't much on the war I was interested in. The failed invasion didn't seem to have made much of an imprint.

At least we got some stupendous views. The fort towered over Quebec City's Upper Town, which was once enclosed by walls. Below that was Lower Town, a place far less protected, where merchants used to store goods. In November 1775, Benedict Arnold advanced on the city, not intimidated in the least by the fortifications bristling with cannon before him.

He was a man who "held in equal contempt both danger and principle," Warren wrote. Arnold had traveled what was definitely not the scenic route, a nearly two-month ordeal through Maine, first up the Kennebec River on leaky boats, then on foot, struggling through "a hideous wilderness" of "woods, mountains, swamps, and precipices," as Warren put it. His men ran out of food and ate tree bark, shoe leather, and anything else semi-edible that they could find. (It was not a good time to be a dog on the expedition.) Disease ran rampant.

"With his little army almost exhausted by hunger and fatigue," Warren continued, Arnold reached Canadian towns near Quebec City. There "[h]e was received in a friendly manner, and a liberal supply of provisions was collected for his relief." The next month, Montgomery showed up, and the two officers planned their attack. And they had to hurry, for soon they wouldn't have any soldiers. "The term of their enlistments was nearly expired," Warren wrote, and on New Year's Day 1776, most of the small army would vanish, as nearly all the soldiers planned to go home.

And so, on December 31, right at the deadline, Montgomery and

Arnold attacked "under the cover of a violent snow storm," as Warren put it. They divided their forces: Montgomery was to lead a party into Lower Town while Arnold and another officer (who was leading a regiment of Canadian volunteers) would create feints to the north. They were then to join together and scale the walls of Upper Town.

But the British were nobody's fools. They had "gained intelligence of these movements," Warren wrote, and repelled each attack. Montgomery led his men deeper into Lower Town but was shot and killed. A nineteen-year-old captain by the name of Aaron Burr tried to pull Montgomery's body out of the snow but had to give up when the gunfire became too hot.

In death, General Montgomery became a martyr for the cause.

As we left the Citadel, I spied, right on the street we were descending, a black granite boulder marking Montgomery's burial site. The British interred him here after the fighting. (Years later, his remains were sent to New York.) In death, he became a martyr for the cause. The defeat had been near total, with nearly half of the American forces becoming casualties or prisoners.

All was not lost from the American perspective, though; they still held Montreal, and a regiment of fresh Continental troops arrived to reinforce them. But, as Washington wrote in a letter to Schuyler, for the Americans to keep campaigning, they would need to receive far more support from their Canadian brethren than they had up to that point. Why hadn't the people of Quebec risen up to join the Patriots in the name of liberty? Better late than never, American leaders decided to try a tactic they hadn't used much yet: diplomacy.

In the spring of 1776, Congress ordered a group of envoys to travel north and actually engage in talks with the population of the city they had conquered. I headed to Montreal to see what I could discover about this trip, one of the first times the new American government had sent emissaries abroad. It might have come on the late side, but the mission did have at least one thing going for it: It was led by one of the greatest diplomats in American history. His name was Benjamin Franklin.

"Here in this building is where Benedict Arnold put on a party for Benjamin Franklin," my guide said, leading me through a hall with walls covered in mahogany paneling. If we had been in Boston or Philadelphia, that statement wouldn't have seemed surprising in the least. But hearing that in a château in Montreal seemed a little bizarre.

I had come to Château Ramezay by myself, while Liana and the kids explored downtown Montreal, to learn about this last, desperate episode of the invasion of Quebec. The guide, Bruno Paul Stenson, was a wiry man with a fine mustache and a fount of knowledge. "This château has been at the belly button of Quebec history for centuries," he told me. It first served as the residence of French governors, I learned, then as a warehouse for a fur trading company. When the Americans took Montreal in late 1775, they commandeered it for the military. After the defeat at Quebec, Arnold made his way back to Montreal to recover from his wounds, taking the sprawling stone château as his own.

"By early 1776, Congress figured out that the army is not good at this, they're screwing it up big time," said Bruno. "They needed to try diplomacy rather than imposing something on the people. Their catastrophic mistake was not understanding who they were trying to get on their side. And that was a big, French-speaking Catholic population.

"The people in the countryside sold goods to the British, and they worried about where they'd find a market if the British left," said Bruno. He knew all about this group—two centuries ago, his own family formed part of it as farmers in the region, part of Quebec's silent majority, weighing their options. Should they throw their lot in with the rebels preaching liberty? Or stick with what they knew, the British? Which one of those two English-speaking, Protestant armies should they trust?

"Congress sent a team of diplomats up here," said Bruno, leading me into another room in the château. "They sent Samuel Chase, a lawyer. He could explain legal issues that had to do with the Revolution. They sent Charles Caroll, a Catholic who had been educated in France, along with a Jesuit priest. He could address French Catholics.

"And they sent this guy, who could talk politics and diplomacy. I think you know him." Bruno paused before a portrait of Franklin looking pensive underneath his flowing gray hair. It took the seventy-year-old diplomat a bone-clattering month to make his way on carriage from Philadelphia to Montreal. He brought with him orders clarifying—some five months after the incursion had begun—that the invaders had only come to help, and that Canadians could choose their own path to freedom.

Franklin also brought a French printer with him to churn out pro-American propaganda, Bruno told me. (The printer wound up starting a paper, the *Montreal Gazette*, that is still published today.) Also tagging along was a twenty-six-year-old French officer named Julien Alexandre Achard de Bonvouloir. Keep your eye on him—although I didn't know it yet, I'd wind up crossing paths with Bonvouloir plenty of times on my journey, sometimes when I'd least expect it. Here in this château, Benedict Arnold threw the party to end all parties, feting the arrival of Franklin and his team with a musical recital and toast after toast.

This was quite a change. Americans were known for their anti-Catholic and anti-French prejudice. Rumors had spread that the Continental Army had even arrested priests. The Patriots now realized that they needed to appeal to this silent majority. The previous fall, General Washington had banned his men from celebrating the anti-Catholic Guy Fawkes Day, which included burning the pope in effigy. The commander recognized that bringing Quebec into the war on the American side "cannot be done so effectually by conquest," he wrote, "as by taking stronghold of the affections and confidence of the inhabitants."

Who knows what this charm campaign might have accomplished had it come the previous fall, back when Americans were demanding loyalty at bayonet point. But nearly six months into the American occupation of Montreal, "it came much too late to do any good," Bruno said. Catholics in Quebec worried whether the Americans would protect their religious freedom; merchants turned their Gallic noses up at the Americans' depreciating paper currency. Plus, after Quebec City, their neighbors to the south were not looking like winners. "The committee returned with little success," Warren wrote. "Words and professions are of little avail when the sword is...lifted for decision."

And soon the rest of the American army was following the diplomats back home. In early May, the British navy forced its way through the ice floes of the St. Lawrence, bringing a rescue mission with them. Nine regiments of Redcoats chased the rebels back to Montreal, then further south. "The American invasion was quite a tale," Bruno concluded. "But it wound up being only a hiccup in history."

"Why isn't it remembered more?" I asked Bruno. That question had been on my mind the whole trip.

"It's just not taught," he said. "What country brags about something they lost?" Neither side came out of the campaign looking good. From Canada's perspective, Montreal had folded far too quickly. From the Americans' side, the Canadians had not risen up en masse to join them and the Patriots had been chased back in disgrace, their army in tatters.

Over twelve thousand Americans marched into Quebec and only nine thousand came back—the rest had died, been taken prisoner, or deserted. "Our misfortunes in Canada," John Adams wrote to Abigail, "are enough to melt a heart to stone." Did the invasion of Canada ever have a chance of succeeding in the first place? Bruno, for one, didn't think so. I wasn't sure. There certainly were plenty of problems with it—the Continental forces were untrained, unpaid, and short on gunpowder. Most of their enlistments expired during the campaign, and the men were only too happy to come home when they did.

Yet for me, the lesson from the Quebec invasion, I thought, was that the Americans had gone about seeking allies in all the wrong ways. They had marched into a foreign land and expected the population to just naturally rise up and join them. They had assumed that Canadians were basically northern, politer versions of Americans. Yet who wants to be conquered into liberty? Maybe if the invaders had spent more time talking to their potential allies and seeing what they had in common, they might have persuaded more people to see the value in taking on the British together. Not coincidentally, after this failed campaign, Congress began commissioning diplomats and giving them instructions on how to negotiate with foreign powers.

Throughout 1776, delegates in Congress dissected the defeat. There was plenty of blame to go around; the causes of the catastrophe ranged from the short enlistments of American troops, to smallpox, to the crash of American paper money. For some, the Canadian debacle reminded them of the many things the American armed forces were lacking—trained troops, ammunition, artillery, enough rifles, military engineers, and a navy (for starters). If, say, France had accompanied the Americans in that expedition, things surely would have gone differently.

His Most Christian Majesty King Louis XVI would never make a deal with a gang of rebels, though. To have a formal relationship with a foreign power, America would need to pronounce itself to be a sovereign nation. At the time of the Canadian campaign, that had not happened yet. If only the United States had declared independence in, say, January 1776, John Adams groused to Abigail later, it would have formed "alliances with foreign states...mastered Quebec and been in possession of Canada."

As spring turned to summer, then, the delegates faced a critical choice. Would the cautionary tale of the Canada invasion lead them to seek some sort of reconciliation with Britain? Or would it lead them to double down and declare independence?

While these debates went on, the reinforced British in Canada were chasing the ragged American army back the way it came. The Americans evacuated Fort Chambly, leaving the graves of fallen soldiers and officers behind (which you can still see today). They fled all the way back to Fort Ticonderoga, the same place many had started out from.

The last group of these soldiers on the run reached Crown Point, a fortification near Ticonderoga, some nine months after the expedition had begun. They were hungry, poorly clothed, and decimated by smallpox. There they had a well-earned, if short, period of recuperation. A few days' rest would surely do them some good. Soon they would be regrouping at Ticonderoga, determined to not retreat any farther and to take a stand. Of course, none of these soldiers had any idea what was going on in Philadelphia, over three hundred miles to their south.

If any of the survivors at Crown Point had access to a calendar after they had caught their breath, they might have noticed the date. It was July 4, 1776.

Chapter Three

SENDING OUT AN SOS

The Year America Cried Out for Help

June–November 1776

What's better than Philadelphia on the Fourth of July? The streets of Old City were already filling up with crowds getting ready for the annual parade, while dancers and marching bands lined up in the side streets, preparing for their entrance. "Philly has to be the best place to celebrate the Fourth," Liana said. "People have come from all over the country to be here. We're here at the mother lode."

I had brought the family up here for Independence Day. But I didn't just want to celebrate, I also wanted to learn more about why we chose that moment in July 1776 to break free from Britain. For my readings of Mercy Otis Warren—bolstered by contemporary research—had clued me into a backstory behind the Declaration that I had never known existed.

"Before we go in Independence Hall, there's somewhere we have to go first," I told my family, to their surprise. We ducked into Carpenters'

Hall, a handsome, two-story Georgian building a few blocks away that had served as the seat of the First Continental Congress in 1774. It played a hidden, now mostly forgotten, role in the lead-up to independence.

Carpenters' Hall, the site of a secret, late-night meeting with an emissary from France.

"Dad, the parade's going to start," said Nico. "What are we doing here, anyway?" I had spent ten precious minutes rummaging through the hall. Finally, I found what I was looking for, a plaque on a staircase roped off to the public, barely visible. But there it was—a recognition that this was the spot where American leaders first met with an emissary from a foreign power.

I had learned about what happened here thanks to the writings of Professor Larrie Ferreiro, one of the leading scholars on the global American Revolution. For years, he had explained, both France and Spain had been sending undercover agents to the Thirteen Colonies to try to figure out how serious the Patriots were about their rebellion.

Would this disturbance provide an opportunity they could use to take revenge on Britain, their hereditary foe?

In late November 1775, some six months before the Declaration was issued, the young French emissary Bonvouloir (whom I also came across during my trip to Montreal) met with Franklin and other members of Congress's new Committee of Secret Correspondence to establish an unofficial connection with France. To throw Loyalist spies off their trail—for many Americans did not want to break with Britain—the rendezvous occurred under the cover of darkness here at Carpenters' Hall. Bonvouloir reported back to Versailles that the Americans had plenty of determination but needed "a good navy, provisions, and money" if they were to win.

Franklin and the other delegates assured the Frenchman of their country's resolve; they and other leaders were ready to "die together rather than surrender." The meeting helped convince Congress that formal French help (in addition to the guns that French merchants were privately smuggling to America) might be forthcoming—but only if the colonies became independent.

We finally reached Independence Hall, just in time. Since all the other time slots that day had been booked, I had reserved a tour while the parade was passing in front of it. The procession started out traditionally enough, with a colonial fife-and-drum band playing. They were followed by a phalanx of Stormtroopers led by Darth Vader (whose connection to the Fourth seems shaky) and then a guy dressed as a Tastykake, that Philadelphia delicacy, throwing cakes to the crowd.

John Adams had gotten it right—he had predicted Independence Day would be celebrated with "Pomp and Parade with Shows, Games, Sports, Guns, Bells, Bonfires and Illuminations from one End of this Continent to the other from this Time forward forever more." Mostly right, that is—he had thought that July 2, when Congress voted for independence, would be the magical day, and he also missed the free Tastykakes.

Inside Independence Hall, the old windowpanes rattled from the pounding music but didn't break—they had been through a lot already. We toured the Assembly Room, where tables draped in green still had quill pens at the ready, as if the ghosts of the Founders might drop in and write away. "It's a lot smaller than I thought," Miranda whispered, as the bands outside launched into "America the Beautiful." A National Park Service guide recounted the lead-up to independence. His talk was wholly focused on the Americans' internal debate, with nary a mention of foreign powers in Europe.

Afterward, a speaker in front of Independence Hall read the entire Declaration of Independence out loud. Cheers went up from the crowd when he got to the money phrase, "life, liberty, and the pursuit of happiness." But I was waiting for what Warren and the leaders in Philadelphia might have seen as the most important line at the time it was written, which came at the end. The new United States, the reader proclaimed, had the "full Power to levy War, conclude Peace, contract Alliances, establish Commerce, and to do all other Acts and things which Independent States may of right do."

For the Declaration, Warren wrote, was intended just as much for foreign audiences as for Americans. With independence formally announced, "Americans could now no more be considered as rebels in their proposals for treaties of peace and conciliation with Britain. They were a distinct people, who claimed the rights, the usage, the faith, and the respect of nations, uncontrolled by any foreign power," she wrote.

"America had been little known among the kingdoms of Europe," Warren continued. "She was considered only as an appendage to the power of Britain... She now appeared in their eyes [as] a new theater, pregnant with events that might be interesting." With independence, America would now have the attention of France, Spain, and the Netherlands, who now saw before them not a set of riled-up colonies but a fellow nation and potential partner. These foreign powers wouldn't automatically join America on the battlefield just because it had declared independence, but the declaration was a necessary first step in laying the groundwork for that to happen.

These revelations flabbergasted me. I had grown up enthralled by Jefferson's words. Now I had discovered that, from the beginning, the Declaration was meant to be translated into other languages (a German version was published only days after it was written). I felt like I needed to learn more about the Founders' interest in foreign powers, for this motivation for independence hadn't shown up in my schoolbooks. It seemed almost subversive to even mention it. So, after my trip I reached out to the scholar Larrie Ferreiro. Conveniently enough, he lived not too far from me in northern Virginia and agreed to meet up for coffee.

Larrie was around sixty, with a dark beard, a Long Island accent, and plenty of enthusiasm for this topic. He had the perfect skill set to research this long-ago world war: He was a trained naval architect, who had designed destroyers and amphibious crafts, so he could fully understand the war at sea. He also had gotten his doctorate on the history of French and Spanish shipbuilding.

"In 1776, the Americans were without a navy, artillery, or gunpowder," he began. "No foreign power would fight alongside us if they saw this conflict as a civil war. They'd only do so if they saw us an independent nation.

"I found a statement in *Common Sense,* by Thomas Paine, on this," he continued. The January 1776 pamphlet was America's first bestseller, galvanizing popular opinion toward independence. "In it, Paine said that petitioning got you nowhere, that a hundred petitions weren't as good as a single declaration of independence. That's the thing that would bring France and Spain into the war. I have no idea why, for two hundred years, history pretty much ignored that statement."

In his research, Ferreiro ferreted out quote after quote from the Founders linking independence to the need for foreign intervention. Richard Henry Lee, the Virginia delegate who sponsored the independence motion in Congress, wrote that it was "not choice then, but necessity that calls for independence, as the only means by which foreign alliance can be obtained." Similarly, John Adams—who was known for being skeptical of Europe, Ferreiro told me—admitted that foreign powers would not acknowledge America until it had "acknowledged ourselves" as independent. Even the famous Mr. Jefferson took note of the debate in Congress that "a Declaration of Independence alone could render it consistent with European delicacy for European powers to treat with us."

The debacle in Canada in the spring of 1776 only hastened Congress's resolve to take the decisive step, for the need for direct foreign help had never been greater, even if it only came in the form of a commercial alliance (as Adams preferred). As for Warren, she couldn't believe Congress had dithered for so long before taking the decisive step. You "should no longer piddle at the threshold," she pointedly wrote to Adams. "It is time to...open every gate that impedes the rise and growth of the American republic."

On June 7, Richard Henry Lee finally marched into what is now known as Independence Hall and made a proposal for the ages. "When Lee introduced the motion for independence, he had a three-part plan," Larrie said. "He wanted Congress to declare independence, write treaties with foreign countries, and establish a confederated government. This is what's going to get us to nationhood." That was the proposal adopted by Congress on July 2.

"The Declaration wasn't for King George; he had gotten the message already," he continued. "It was an engraved invitation for the Kings of France and Spain to help us. The first working day after the text of the Declaration was approved, it was shipped off on the *Dispatch* to bring it to France. That brig was captured by the British, but the intent was there. We were now independent; it was OK for the French and Spanish to openly fight alongside us."

"Why was it so important to get them into the war at that point?" I asked.

"Because of the navy," Larrie replied. "If it's the eighteenth century and you're fighting the British, it's going to be a naval war. Britannia rules the waves. America needed a nation that could protect us from that, a seafaring nation." Naval power, I learned, was essential to eighteenth-century warfare. With many American roads barely passable, it was far easier to transport men and artillery by water. The Patriots had no idea where British warships might land, giving their enemy the perpetual element of surprise. Congress had authorized the building of thirteen frigates, but to truly stand up to His Majesty's Navy, they needed an ally with a powerful fleet.

"How did you become interested in this subject?" I asked as we finished our coffee.

"My kids were in grade school and junior high," he replied. "They were taking history, and I looked at their textbooks. The chapters on the Revolutionary War had very little mention of France, none of Spain.

"I had previously done research on French and Spanish shipbuilding for my PhD. I knew that those countries established a unified navy, and that the first and only time that someone effectively fought and defeated the British navy happened when they did it in the American Revolution. I knew this. I saw nothing about this in my kids' history books.

"So, the question was, what was the role of France and Spain in the war? I went to libraries, museums, there was almost nothing written about it. Even in France and Spain there was very little written about the combined navies. So, if no one else has written about it, I realized, I'm going to have to."

"What has all this taught you about our founding?" I asked.

"I've worked abroad," Larrie said, "and I know that we always work better with our partners than alone. We've always been good at adopting and adapting ideas wherever they come from and making them ours. That's been true since the beginning. We're not a country that bootstrapped its way to independence. When we started, America was at the center of an international alliance."

Larrie smiled. "That's the story I wanted to know. That's the story I tell my children."

The Declaration was a bold step—signers had pledged their lives, fortunes, and sacred honor to the cause. But no one yet knew whether France or Spain would take the claims in it seriously. Would they view the leaders in Philadelphia as the representatives of a brand-new nation or just a bunch of rebels in powdered wigs? And what did this "United States" ultimately want from them—more arms and trade, or a full-fledged military alliance? Either way, France and Spain ran the risk of entering into a protracted war with Britain. If they did join the fight, would the Americans be in it for the long haul, or would they go running back to King George if their defeats mounted? The French and Spanish had some thinking to do. In the meantime, the Americans would be fighting on their own.

The British had evacuated Boston in March 1776, thanks to the cannons brought from Fort Ticonderoga, but they were only regrouping. In the weeks leading up to the Declaration, rumors swirled that the British were sending a huge fleet to America to teach the rebels a lesson. The smart money was that they would try to take New York City. Not only was the city a major port town, but it also was important strategically. If the British seized Manhattan and then moved up the Hudson Valley, they could cut off the rebels in New England from the rest of the country, threatening the very "safety of America," Washington wrote to one of his generals that spring. "We expect a very bloody summer of it," he added in a letter to his brother.

Washington assembled a force of nearly twenty thousand men to protect the city. His troops built fortifications across Brooklyn and two fortresses—Fort Washington and Fort Lee—on either side of the Hudson River, ten miles north of lower Manhattan. At least the

Patriots had gunpowder; some sixty tons had arrived that spring from French, Dutch, and Spanish traders, smuggled from Europe and the Caribbean.

On July 9, Washington ordered officers to read the Declaration to his soldiers. The largest of the readings occurred on the Commons (where city hall in Manhattan is located today). It was "received by three Huzzahs from the troops," one officer recalled. Some inspired troops then surged to Bowling Green, huzzahing all the way, past an iron fence (which still stands to this day) and toppled the statue of King George III (which doesn't). They stuck George's head on a pike in front of a tavern, while the rest of the monarch's body went off to a foundry in Connecticut to become bullets. That way, one witty New Yorker predicted, the Redcoats would have "melted Majesty fired at them."

The British had other ideas. In late June, tens of thousands of Redcoats began to arrive off New York under the command of General William Howe, transported on hundreds of ships led by his brother, Admiral Richard Howe. It was the largest fleet Britain would send anywhere until World War II. It would be a shock-and-awe campaign, designed to batter the rebels into submission. (One noted British historian believed that the British wanted to win the war quickly, before France and Spain had a chance to intervene.) Washington's men were about to attempt to defend an island against the greatest navy in the world. It would be one of his biggest ordeals—and debacles.

It's not that easy to get a sense of the Battle of Brooklyn today. For one thing, obviously, New York City's population exploded over the years—it's over four thousand times greater today than in 1776. Today's landscape looks radically different from how it looked during those revolutionary years too. Over the centuries, hills have been smoothed down, ponds drained, tenements constructed, skyscrapers built. Many of the places where Washington and his men fought are now underneath parking garages or high-rises.

Even so, it surprised me not to find more recognition of the clash, given its importance to our war for independence. Sure, there are a few places and statues related to the Battle of Brooklyn here and there. But unlike, say, in Boston or Philadelphia, in New York you have to work at it—and bring plenty of imagination—to transport yourself back to that time.

On a mild, sunny day, I had come here (solo) to visit a memorial in Fort Greene Park, which I hoped would do just that for me. I walked up a hill that once had been the highest point in Brooklyn, past a fierce pickleball battle raging on a tennis court. I hoped it (the memorial, not the pickleball game) would help answer some questions I had. Why did the war start off so badly for the Continental Army? What were the consequences of the defeat in New York? And why doesn't New York remember its role in the Revolution more?

"At the time, this hill had a fort on it called Fort Putnam," a young man named Seth Johnson told me, pointing out a cannon below us. He was clad in the olive-green uniform of a New York City park ranger, wearing a black hat over his jet-black hair and sporting a shiny silver badge on his chest. "The British first landed on Staten Island," Seth said. "Washington had put most of his men on Brooklyn. General Howe decided to attack at the end of August."

He brought out a map to show me the troop movements, describing how the British managed to flank the Americans, forcing them to retreat. "Here, where we are today, was one of Washington's lines of defense." The Continentals eventually fell back to Brooklyn Heights near the East River. Even this place was not secure. Once the tides and winds were right, His Majesty's Navy could move into place to pulverize Washington's army—perhaps even destroying it in one fell swoop.

"Luckily for the Americans, the fighting stopped after a storm," Seth went on. "Sailors rowed men to safety in Manhattan at night, they dipped their oars in cloth to make no sound. George Washington kept his campfires going onshore. They had to leave their cannons behind, but they escaped." Although the Continental Army lived to fight another day, Washington had nearly lost his entire army in Brooklyn. A couple of weeks later, the British landed on Manhattan and pushed the Americans farther back, to the northern reaches of the island.

The fighting continued into the fall, with the Redcoats handing Washington defeat after defeat. The worst of them all came on November 16. On that day, the British—aided by hired German soldiers known to Americans as "Hessians," for the regions where some of them came from—seized Fort Washington, in what is now Washington Heights in upper Manhattan. Virtually every American defender—some three thousand of them—was killed or taken captive. The British had so many prisoners, they didn't know where to put them all.

"The British decided to 'hulk' ships," Seth told me. "That meant they emptied out the hulls and converted them to prison ships. They put as many people in them as they could. They kept them over at Wallabout Bay, where the Brooklyn Navy Yard is today. These empty ships could maybe fit four hundred people comfortably, and they'd fit a thousand. They say about ten people died a day on those ships from all the worst diseases you could think of—cholera, yellow fever, dysentery."

Seth led me to a most unusual structure at the heart of the park: a granite Doric column soaring nearly 150 feet into the air, with a funeral urn perched on top of it. "The Prison Ship Martyrs' Monument remembers all those who died on those prison ships," he told me. "Here in the park, we say it was about 11,500 people. But I've seen estimates that it was up to 18,000."

"It was incredibly hot in summer and cold in winter on the prison ships," Seth continued. "The men were fed moldy bread and rancid meat. The majority of those who died were only eighteen or nineteen years old. They came from all thirteen colonies. It was so bad on these ships that prisoners would volunteer to help bury the dead; that way they'd at least get off the ship for a few hours.

"There were so many people who had been buried in shallow graves that bones kept washing up in Brooklyn for years later, all throughout the nineteenth century," he went on. "Walt Whitman lived nearby. He wrote about how children would kick skulls around on the shoreline." Whitman helped lead the long campaign to build this memorial, which opened in 1908, Seth told me.

He unlocked the door to the monument, and we stepped inside the shaft, which was lined with bricks. The inside was cool and dark. Drops of water occasionally trickled down and splashed my face. I admired a large plaque on the floor with two iron rings, which read "In Honored Glory/1776/Here Rests our Fallen Soldiers."

"Are they buried under there?" I asked quietly. For some reason, I felt the need to whisper, although no one else was around.

Seth pulled on the rings dramatically and lifted the plaque, which turned out to be a trap door. Underneath, he revealed a shallow pit. It was empty. "No, they put that here for a TV show, and we just left it there because it looks good," he said, smiling. He rapped on it. "It looks like granite, but it's just wood that they spray-painted. It was a crime show. They said that Betsy's Ross flag was buried underneath there, and they wanted something official looking to cover it."

"So where are the bodies?" I asked.

"Further down this hill, past those steps. That's where the crypt is, where many of the bones of the prisoners are buried," he continued. "Only two people have the key to it." I was feeling more and more like I had stepped into a deleted scene from *National Treasure*.

"Have you ever been?"

"Yes, one time. You go down some steps and then come into a room that's about four feet high, ten or fifteen feet long. There are twenty-two caskets, really long ones. Inside, bones from many soldiers are mixed together. They're arranged by type—femurs are together, heads are by heads."

I had never thought much about the fate of these prisoners before.

The Revolutionary War can seem quaint sometimes—all those powdered wigs and silk stockings and quill pens. But this memorial drove home for me how real the suffering was. The British were committing what today would be called human rights violations, I realized, and doing so on a terrifying scale. The war had never seemed more real to me. And in 1776, the Americans were losing it terribly and doing so all alone. The need for allies had never been more critical.

In 1776, France and Spain were still a long way from joining the war, but this memorial would mark the grim fates of many of their countrymen when they eventually did. Seth brought me to the visitor's center, where he pointed out a plaque commemorating a visit by King Juan Carlos of Spain in 1976. "French and Spanish victims were buried here too," Seth said. "Many of them were sailors who were captured by the British later in the war and brought here. They're not included in the official counts of the Americans lost on the prison ships though," he added.

"How many people come to visit the monument?" I asked.

"Not too many," Seth replied wistfully. "It's arguably the largest Revolutionary War crypt in America, but people don't know about it."

A jogger ran by, wearing noise-canceling headphones. In the half hour or so that we had been inside the monument, only one other person had poked their head in.

"Why is that?" I wondered.

"I think it's simple," Seth said. "We want to hear about our victories. We don't want to learn about our losses."

"At no period of the great struggle for independence were the affairs of the United States at so low an ebb," Warren wrote about the period after the fall of New York. "In general, our generals were outgeneraled," John Adams wrote to Abigail following the great defeat. Washington had lost nearly three-quarters of his men, with more deserting by the day.

If there was any good news on the battlefield that fall, it was that the British advance south from Canada had stalled; the Redcoats decided to return to Canada and resume their campaign in spring. Lucky for Washington, for had they swept down upon him from the north, the Continentals might have been done. That was what passed for good news in those dark days of late 1776—the Americans were losing, but at least they weren't losing too quickly.

Washington still found himself in a dangerous situation though. British general Lord Cornwallis was pursuing the remnants of his army south through New Jersey. The Americans "experienced the pains of anxiety, disappointment, and want," Warren wrote, "through a rapid flight from post to post, before a victorious army, who despised their weakness and ridiculed their want of discipline." After the British offered to pardon New Jersey Patriots, thousands suddenly saw the error of their ways and swore allegiance to the Crown. By necessity, Washington committed to a defensive strategy, hoping to keep his army intact, dreaming of better days.

"All was at stake," Warren noted. "Deficient as they were in the means necessary to support a war, against a wealthy and potent nation, they yet stood alone, uncertain whether any other power would aid their cause," she continued. Without foreign help, many thought they may have to "relinquish the contest," as she put it. Yet, so long as Washington's army survived, there was hope.

Congress had already sent a copy of the Declaration of Independence to its representative in Paris, Silas Deane, with orders to send it to the courts of Europe as well. In late October 1776, the brig *Reprisal* set sail on a desperate mission. On board was Benjamin Franklin, carrying another copy of the Declaration along with orders to "use every means in your power" to enter into an alliance with the French. "We only look," Congress wrote, "to heaven and France for succor."

Spain and the Netherlands were also to receive copies of the Declaration, with its language that America was now willing and eager to enter into treaties. News of independence would travel around the world—including to the Oneida Indians and eventually to the Mysore Kingdom in India.

Some of these peoples would enthusiastically embrace the cause of America from the start; others would view the breakaway nation with skepticism and caution. But all of them eventually decided that the Americans' play for independence offered them an opportunity to strike a blow against their common enemy, the British. One by one, each of these groups would join in the loose coalition in support of the rebels, turning the American struggle into a true world war.

And so I set off to discover how, in late 1776, American diplomats and naval commanders sailed on desperate missions, bringing a copy of the Declaration and a plea for help, sending out an SOS to the world. The efforts bore fruit quicker than anyone might have imagined. On November 16—the very same day that British and Hessian soldiers took Fort Washington—a foreign power saluted the American flag for the very first time, recognizing the United States as a free nation. Perhaps surprisingly, this did not occur at Versailles or Madrid, but on a small, volcanic Dutch island in the middle of the Caribbean called Sint Eustatius.

Chapter Four

SIGNS OF HOPE: THE FIRST SALUTE AND THE CROSSING

Why the Dutch in the Caribbean Recognized the U.S. Flag

November–December 1776

We woke up to the crowing of a rooster who had set up shop behind our hotel room. I opened the window and looked out over Gallows Bay. The day was already muggy and warm, and I still didn't have much of an idea of what I'd find in Sint Eustatius (hopefully coffee, for starters).

Liana and I had arrived the night before on a ferry that had bobbed and swayed its way toward the Dutch island for hours, leaving Liana queasy. We disembarked into the pouring rain. No taxis appeared at the port, so we began walking toward our hotel along the side of a road until a van pulled over. I looked at it warily—the side panel said it belonged to a security firm.

"Where are you going?" the driver, a woman named Julia, asked us. She had tattoos running up her arms and a big smile on her face. "I'll take you there."

Sint Eustatius (or Statia, as locals call it) is easy to miss—a small, rocky, teardrop-shaped island in the Leeward Islands of the Caribbean. At only eight square miles, it's a quarter the size of Manhattan, which the Dutch colonized not long before they turned their sights on Statia. It's known for the kindness of its inhabitants, as we quickly found out on our trip to the hotel.

Its population today is only a little over three thousand, far less than what it was in its heyday at the time of the American Revolution. Back then, Statia was one of the main trade hubs of the Caribbean. It even played a role in one of the most remarkable stories of our war for independence. That's what we had come to learn more about. During some of the darkest days of the conflict, how was it that this small island was the one to provide Americans with hope to carry on?

After a breakfast of strong coffee (thank God), Johnny cakes, and salt fish, we began hiking up a path strewn with sea almonds, past bougainvillea and other tropical plants. "This reminds me a lot of Cuba," Liana said as we slowly climbed up. Not surprisingly, the place looked much better in daylight, without baggage to carry in the rain. The island has only one main town, Oranjestad, which is divided in two. Our shambling old hotel, with balconies and verandas surrounded by palm trees, was on a strip near the water known as Lower Town. The main settlement, Upper Town (just like in Quebec City), was at the end of the path.

We stopped at the top, panting heavily. The contours of the island began to take shape: a bay that swept below us, the jagged green cliffs of the island of Saba in the distance, the Quill volcano looming a few miles to our east, and, not far away, the massive stone walls of Fort Oranje standing guard over the scene. We left the path through a wooden gate with a sign that read: "Keep Gate Closed: Don't Let the Goats in No Matter What They Tell You."

We made our way to the town's small museum, where we wandered through the exhibits. There, I pieced together the island's history, beginning with how it was colonized by the Dutch in the seventeenth century.

At the time, the Dutch Republic was the preeminent trading country in the world. Amsterdam's port filled with spices from what are now Sri Lanka and Indonesia, silk from India, sugar from the Caribbean and South America, and much more. The Dutch Republic was famous for being a tolerant country, allowing for more freedom of expression than nearly any other place in Europe. At the same time, it didn't hesitate to engage in the slave trade, a key source of its riches.

After touring the museum, we met a guide, Misha Spanner, out front. Misha had grown up on the island, as immediately became clear since everyone who passed by stopped to say hi or chat briefly with her. She brought us first to a small park.

"The Dutch came in 1636," she began. "The island was uninhabited back then. The French had come before them, but they had left. Statia doesn't have rivers or lakes; it depended on rainfall. Life was hard."

By the time of the American Revolution, the Netherlands' military power had declined greatly from what it had been, but the Dutch were still master traders. Sint Eustatius was their favorite trade depot in the Caribbean, a free port where, unlike on Spanish, French, and British islands, anyone could show up and sell goods.

"Back then, Statia was rich, rich, rich," Misha told us. "Sometimes treasure hunters come here, looking for buried gold or sunken ships." She led us down one of the main streets in Oranjestad, pointing out grand colonial buildings that still stand. "You can tell by the size of some of these houses, many opulent people were living here."

"Why was Statia so important for trading?" I asked.

"Our location was ideal." Statia is placed at an arc of the Leeward Islands, she explained, a natural meeting spot for ships from Europe, Africa, North America, and South America. It was in the center of a chain of islands controlled by the British, Spanish, French, and Danish, and it was open for business.

"Everyone wanted to come," she continued. "They came from many parts of Europe, the Americas, even as far as the Middle East and Asia.

We had a community of Jewish merchants too. When they came to bring stuff to sell, the quality and also the pricing were better than many parts of the world. It also generated the attraction of many people to come here to this big market. And then they had traders from all nationalities, and they'd trade in harmony. Back then, they called Statia the Golden Rock."

Misha Spanner leading us through Upper Town.

Golden, indeed. Sint Eustatius had long been considered, by Europeans and Americans alike, as the best market "of any of the tropical islands," Mercy Otis Warren wrote, with trade and wealth "beyond any calculation." I had learned at the museum how Statia's harbor used to be filled with a hundred ships per day, with sailors and stevedores busy ferrying cargos of trade goods to the shore in boats: tea from India, manufactured goods from Europe, and tobacco, indigo, and lumber from America. The mile-long stretch of warehouses in Lower Town, where the goods were stored for sale, was one of the most valuable pieces of real estate in the world.

Unfortunately, Statia was also a major market for the slave trade. As Misha brought us to Wilhelmina Park at the center of town, she recounted some of the struggles of the enslaved community from the island.

"Here is where slaves were sold," she said as we reached the park. "Our ancestors were auctioned off here. This was also a place of celebration for the end of slavery, in 1863."

"That was so late," I said, "the same as in the U.S."

"Yes, it came here at almost the same exact time as your Emancipation Proclamation," Misha said. "It wasn't easy; the slaves even had to have a revolt beforehand. After the abolishment," she continued, "some slaves threw blue beads off the cliffs."

"Why blue beads?" asked Liana. "Like those in your necklace?"

"Yes, slaves would sometimes get paid for some tasks, especially after the revolt. They would be paid in these beads, which were called "trade beads." They were made in Amsterdam. To marry a wife, a man had to accumulate enough beads to fit around her waist. And after slavery, many threw their beads into the sea to showcase their freedom."

"Where did you get yours?" Liana asked.

"I found them," Misha replied. "You see them sometimes on the ground. It's a tradition here. My younger sister found her first one at age two, even before I found one—we couldn't believe it!

"They say that if you find a blue bead, you will return to Statia one day," she said as we walked—Liana and I now with our heads bowed, scanning the ground for flashes of blue. Sint Eustatius encourages travelers to the island to keep an eye open for them and to even bring a small bead home with them. Although it's said that you don't find the beads, they find you.

Misha led us past a flaming-red flamboyant tree to the ruins of the house of Johannes de Graaf, the Dutch governor of Sint Eustatius during the Revolutionary War. Here is where the American rebels entered the story. "In the olden days, we used to smuggle a lot," she told us. "Everything that was illegal elsewhere was casually legal here. We used to smuggle ammunition. For example, if we're exporting sugar, we'd send it to America with a lot of gunpowder hidden inside. Because of all that ammunition we sent, you were able to fight the war." Statia was one of the principal suppliers of the Continental Army during the early years of the Revolution.

Small, fast American ships would dart down to the Caribbean island and pick up these illicit shipments, trading tobacco, lumber, and indigo in return. The smuggling upset the British, Misha said, but there wasn't much they could do about it. It wasn't officially sanctioned by the Dutch government, which worried that the British would declare war on them if they openly permitted it. But Dutch officials did little to stop it. And so the barrels of gunpowder kept coming—until one bold governor of Sint Eustatius threatened to disrupt this uneasy status quo.

"Johannes de Graaf was born on Statia," Misha told us in front of the remains of his house. "He came from a very wealthy family. By the mid-1770s, he owned 350-plus slaves, and property all over the island."

"If he owned that many people, that speaks to his wealth," said Liana, shaking her head.

"People said he was arrogant. We have a portrait of him in our museum, and you can tell that. He's handsome but looks arrogant, like he's used to getting his way.

"On November 16, 1776, a ship, the *Andrew Doria,* came flying the American flag," Misha continued. "It saluted our fort, and Governor de Graaf decided to return the salute." His country might have been officially neutral, but de Graaf had made up his own mind. He supported the Americans and didn't want to be bound by worrisome bureaucrats back in Holland. His salute of the American flag was the first recognition of the new nation by a foreign power.

"We celebrate November 16 as Statia Day, which is tomorrow." I smiled as she said that—I had long circled it on my calendar and timed our trip to Sint Eustatius to be there for it.

"What's it going to be like?" I asked.

"We'll have music and dancing. Sometimes I perform—I'm an actress and storyteller. But not this time; I just got back from a tour," Misha told us. "That day, you really feel Statia Pride. You can even be enemies, and you'll pass your enemy and they'll hug and greet you and wish you Happy Statia Day!"

We took leave of Misha and thanked her. "We might have been a very small island," she said in parting, "and we have gone through many traumas and struggles. But the First Salute shows that we contributed to a great nation's freedom. That is a blessing and a privilege."

The next morning, Liana and I woke before dawn to our rooster alarm clock and pulled ourselves up the steep, still goat-free path to Upper Town. From the distance, we could make out the faint sound of drums, which grew louder as we reached the fort. It was Statia Day.

Fort Oranje was a sprawling stone structure, festooned for the holiday with balloons, flags, and a huge inflated arch that read "Happy Statia Day." We walked into a large courtyard and took plastic seats not far from a palm tree and a cannon.

"Friends near and far, we give you a warm welcome" a Statia councilwoman said, starting the ceremony right at sunrise. "This is an extraordinary moment, when we remember the rich significance of our own history and honor the vibrant spirit of Sint Eustatius." The Dutch flag was hoisted to a recording of "Het Wilhelmus," followed by the American one to the sounds of "The Star-Spangled Banner." Then Statia's own flag ran up the pole while a man played a song called "Golden Rock" on the steel drums. Dignitaries gave speeches and kids' troupes took turns playing music and performing dance routines. Finally, U.S. Consul General to the Dutch Caribbean John McNamara took the stage.

"I'm from New York City, so it's great to be back in the kingdom," he said to laughter. I guess the Dutch dignitaries in attendance had finally gotten over the loss of Manhattan. McNamara was in his sixties, with a broad straw hat and a deadpan delivery. When the *Andrew Doria* arrived in Statia's waters in late 1776, the U.S. cause was "tenuous," he told the crowd. "If there was offshore betting, I'm sure the odds would have been against the U.S. then."

"Our ambassador is doing stand-up!" I whispered to Liana.

He was right, of course. As we have seen, the very day the ship came to Statia, the British were in the process of taking Fort Washington in the northern end of Manhattan. The Continental Army was in shambles; the cause had never looked bleaker. Several ships—including the *Reprisal*, with Franklin on board—had been dispatched to foreign shores carrying a copy of the Declaration of Independence and a plea for help. The *Andrew Doria*, a 175-foot-long brig under the command of Captain Isaiah Robinson, was one of the first to reach its destination. It flew what's now called the Grand Union Flag: a banner with a miniature British flag in its upper-left-hand corner (where the stars would later go), coupled with thirteen red-and-white stripes.

"On this day, on this spot, Gov. Johannes de Graaf made a decision, a decision that helped change history," McNamara continued. "He decided to return the salute of the U.S. warship *Andrew Doria*, in which the U.S. ship presented thirteen gunshots. This was the very first recognition of the United States of America by a foreign power. The very first." Liana and I looked at each other and smiled. It was still hard to believe that this small volcanic island was the place where another country first acknowledged the United States as a sovereign power.

"This came at one of the most dangerous moments in our history," the consul general continued, "as we sought to gain our independence. We're losing battles, we were up against a very, very powerful force, and the government's recognition of us went a long way to instilling more confidence in our people to drive on and finally achieve our independence."

The First Salute was a great morale boost. However, it didn't immediately bring the Dutch into the war, for Governor de Graaf's bosses in the Netherlands were not amused by his gesture. The British ambassador to The Hague was apoplectic about the incident, demanding that the governor be sacked, if not put in jail. Not wanting to provoke a war with

Britain, the Dutch admitted that they hadn't meant to formally recognize the United States as a sovereign nation. It must have been some kind of misunderstanding—maybe the hot Caribbean sun had gotten to de Graaf.

But the Netherlands still kept doing its part for America, allowing the smuggling to continue (and only giving the governor a slap on the wrist). Consul General McNamara hit this point at the end of his speech. "Beyond the First Salute, the Golden Rock played a pivotal role in America's seven-year struggle for independence, with arms, ammunition, and diplomatic messages—all passed through this strategic location," he said. "They allowed our nascent nation to survive and eventually achieve our independence.

"In America, we honor General Washington—the motto we use about him is first in war, first in peace, first in the hearts of his countrymen," he concluded. "He and the Continental Army would not have survived without the great support of weapons and ammunition that came from Statia."

The First Salute ceremony.

With the speeches done, it was time to recreate the famed First Salute itself. A recording of a cannon shot boomed from the loudspeakers. Twelve more followed, then a pause. From far below Fort Oranje, a much louder sound came—the Dutch reply. Everyone rushed to the walls of the fort to peer over. We spied a small group on Lower Town, near the water, engulfed by a plume of smoke. "They're setting off fireworks," Liana said.

That night, we went to the town's main street, where the Statians were in full First Salute party mood. Stands sold chicken curry and fried fish and beer, and kids darted through the crowd. A string band kicked off the music. One older woman started the dancing off, and others in the crowd—Liana among them—had soon joined in. In 1776, too, the governor threw a party for Captain Robinson of the *Andrew Doria* and all the American traders on the island. I wondered if they might have been feted on this very spot.

A soca band, playing music somewhat like calypso, took the stage next, and soon everyone was dancing. Liana opened the palm of her hand and smiled at me. In it was a speck, flashing the color azure. A bit of a blue bead. "That means we will return one day," she said.

I felt privileged to have gotten a chance to visit this island, with its historic houses and friendly people—and its resonance for our revolutionary struggle. While the First Salute proved to be mostly a temporary morale boost, the Dutch and Statians had played a crucial role in the early years of the war in running guns and ammo to the Americans, at considerable risk to themselves.

The party was still going strong, but we had had a long day. After one last song, Liana and I walked down the steep path, back toward Lower Town and took in a final view of Gallows Bay in the moonlight. After it filled its hold with military stores from Statia, the *Andrew Doria* began cruising north. Fortune kept smiling on this ship of destiny: First it encountered a British sloop, the *Racehorse,* off Puerto Rico and defeated it in battle. Then it took a British snow, a two-masted vessel named the

Thomas, off Jamaica. Captain Robinson sent the two ships, now manned by Americans, north and sailed on to the Delaware River.

On Christmas Eve 1776, Congressman Robert Morris wrote to Washington to let him know that the *Andrew Doria* had arrived safely home and that the captured ships were on their way too. Captain Robinson had brought hundreds of blankets, flannels, woolen socks, and muskets back from Statia—might the general have any need for them?

General Washington dashed off a reply on Christmas Day. Oh yes, blankets might come in handy. He and his men were preparing to cross the icy Delaware River that very night. He wished Morris that the next Christmas might be a happier one. For that to occur, Washington had to succeed in his plan—or the Revolution itself might be headed toward an early end.

The scene Washington faced couldn't have looked more different than the one Captain Robinson saw at Statia. Instead of palm trees, there were oaks and pines; instead of steep, volcanic cliffs, there was a flat floodplain; and in place of warm, tropical waters, there was an icy, treacherous river. Yet both events did have this in common—they were signs of hope following months of terrible news, indications that maybe, just maybe, the Americans would pull through the crisis they found themselves in.

I had come to a reenactment of Washington's Crossing of the Delaware to try to get a sense of the stakes faced by the Continental Army, at the close of 1776 and to better understand just what happened during that night, one now shrouded in myth and legend. Did the moment live up to the historical hype that surrounds it? And what was the international impact of the Crossing?

The reenactment began with soldiers marching along the Delaware River, led by a square-jawed man in a deep-blue coat with red trim, wearing a hat with a plume and carrying a sword. Behind him filed a troupe of men in red bonnets, carrying oars. And then came the man everyone was waiting for: the general.

"A profound silence is to be observed," George Washington said, "under pain of death." He walked up and down the ranks, silently inspecting his men. Then he turned and asked the man who had led the march—Colonel John Glover, leader of a regiment from Marblehead, Massachusetts—if his mariners were ready to row the men across.

"My men will do it," the colonel replied gravely.

"This is our one chance only," Washington told the assembled men. "Without this, I think we're finished. Once across, we must move swiftly. The password is 'Victory or Death.'"

If I had been there in 1776—or most recent years, actually—I then would have gotten to see the men clamber into large, black Durham boats and begin to row their way across the river. But I was out of luck. Every year since the early 1950s, volunteers have recreated Washington's Crossing on Christmas Day. They also put on a dress rehearsal a couple of weeks prior—that's the one I had come up for. But this year, following a long drought, the water levels were too low to get the clunky boats across.

No one in the crowd seemed to mind too much. There was a festival atmosphere, with kids running around and eating kettle corn. In any case, we still got to see a lot of reenacting and pay our respects to the memory of those soldiers who rowed through shards of ice that Christmas.

Later, I got to speak with the man who had played the role of Col. Glover, a reenactor and historical consultant named Ken Gavin. Now in his forties, Ken had done the crossing about a dozen times. Even if I had missed the spectacle of reenactors rowing, Ken helped make the scene come alive for me.

"New York was lost," he told me, "and the British had pursued Washington's army throughout New Jersey. Washington knew he had to preserve the army as a national institution. He was looking for an opportunity to strike." After so many defeats, Loyalist strength was growing; in many places, the Revolution had turned into a civil war. The Patriots needed some kind of jolt to keep their cause from crumbling. To compound matters, most soldiers' enlistments were due to expire on New Year's Day 1777. Before the attack, Washington had written to his cousin that if more recruits didn't come in soon, "the game is up."

"Through his intelligence network, General Washington learned that most of the British had gone back up to New York," Ken continued. "The British had spread their forces in a string of eight encampments; Trenton was one of them. Washington saw it as an isolated outpost, right east across the Delaware River from where he had taken safety in Pennsylvania. His army was in tatters. He needed to score a victory at all costs." So Washington boldly struck when the British least expected it, on the most important holiday of the year.

"What's it like when you are able to get the boats out?" I asked.

"It's physically challenging," he said. "The Delaware River is tidal. Once you get thirty yards out, you hit the currents. Halfway across, there are eddies, it swirls around. If we're fully loaded, there's close to thirty people on board, and the boat weighs about six tons. We've got to watch out for boulders." I appreciated even more the risk that the Continentals had taken.

Washington was never more determined than when he led his men on the surprise attack on Trenton. "He was leading from the front at all times," Ken said. "At one point, his horse lost its footing and might have fallen down. Washington used his bare hands, grabbed his horse by the mane, and moved it upright as it was starting to fall. That's severe strength and horsemanship."

Although no allies were yet ready to take the field alongside the Americans, the Battle of Trenton still had an international aspect to it, since the New Jersey capital was occupied by fifteen hundred German troops known as Hessians. "German states were not unified; Germany was a conglomeration of small states," Ken explained. "There was a lot of poverty, mixed with great wealth. One way for states to raise public funds was to rent out armies to get money."

Many Americans at the time, though, didn't see the Hessians as professional soldiers just doing their job, as Ken did. They saw them as mercenaries, hired killers, foreigners trespassing on American soil. "You can see that right in the Declaration of Independence," he said. "There's a line in there about how King George was 'transporting large armies of foreign mercenaries to complete the works of death, desolation, and tyranny' that he had begun, in the Americans' view." The American propaganda machine cranked out stories of abuses by Hessian troops—some real, some exaggerated, others imagined. These "motley mercenaries," as Warren called them in *History*, became the perfect foil for the Patriots.

"At Trenton, almost nothing went right," Ken went on. Washington's plan began to disintegrate almost as soon as the crossing began, with some regiments falling behind schedule and others not able to cross at all. Yet fortune smiled on the Americans for a change. Because of the holiday and the winter storm, the Hessians hadn't posted outer sentries or patrols. "The surprise was complete; the resistance small," Warren wrote. Washington took close to a thousand men prisoner.

Just five weeks after the First Salute in Sint Eustatius, the Americans had found a homegrown way to boost morale. The victory was a huge lift to the nation's spirits, Warren wrote. The general soon returned to Pennsylvania but recrossed the Delaware two days later with his "fugitive army," she recounted, and marched toward the British outpost at Princeton. There, the Continentals captured hundreds of Redcoats, seized more supplies, and again returned to the safety of Pennsylvania. There may be some misconceptions about Washington's Crossing (the famous painting got many of the details wrong, it turns out, from the type of boat to the width of the river), but its fame is well-deserved, I concluded.

"My great-grandfather times eight fought at Trenton," Ken told me. "Part of why I do this is to preserve his memory. What he struggled for and what he did. I think of him every time I do the crossing."

These victories came not a moment too soon. In December 1776, Benjamin Franklin landed on France's Atlantic coast and made his way along the Loire River to Paris. News of the triumphs at Trenton and Princeton would arrive in March of the next year and would be very welcome indeed, for the American ambassador had his work cut out for him. Would he be able to persuade the French to join in the war, to support a cause that was not their own? Could he get them to salute the Grand Union Flag, just as Governor de Graaf had?

The very day after the Battle of Trenton occurred, Franklin sat down for the first time with the French foreign minister, the Comte de Vergennes. The American knew that much was riding on how this relationship got started. Of course, being Benjamin Franklin, what he did next took everyone by surprise.

Chapter Five

THE FRENCH CONNECTION

How France Secretly Helped America Thanks to the Comte de Vergennes, the Founder You've Never Heard Of

December 1776–July 1777

"Dad, why are we still here?" Miranda looked at me quizzically. After a long wait in line, we had finally passed through security at Versailles, the sumptuous home of French kings southwest of Paris. But instead of touring the palace, I had made a beeline for the information kiosk and was showing no interest in leaving. "Are you looking for the bathrooms? They're right over there," she offered, helpfully.

"No, this is the place I most wanted to see in Versailles," I replied.

"The information kiosk?" she asked.

"Yes, because it used to be something else. This was once where the French foreign minister worked and where Benjamin Franklin met with him. This is where they debated the future of America, right here," I said. "Probably, uh, where those brochures are today."

She looked skeptical. "Can we go to the Hall of Mirrors now?"

Tripadvisor lists 3,712 attractions to visit in and around Paris. For whatever reason, this information kiosk did not make the list. But if you're a history-loving American going to Versailles, take a moment and appreciate this room. It should rank high on any short list of places where the fate of the American Revolution was debated and decided, right up there with Boston's Freedom Trail or Independence Hall (and with nicer *toilettes*).

After arriving in Paris, I had learned from my research, Franklin came to this room in the South Ministers' Wing on December 27, 1776, to meet with the Comte de Vergennes for the first time. The two men sitting across from each other made quite a pair. The seventy-year-old Franklin wore above his flowing gray hair a fur cap that he had picked up in Montreal. He was an instant hit in Parisian society, feted at parties and saluted at operas, and not above having a dangerous liaison or two. The adoring French slapped his image on everything from teacups to snuffboxes to medallions. Today he would be called an influencer. Yet it was all for a good cause—the more popular he became, the more popular the American rebels became in Paris as well.

The foreign minister Vergennes, thirteen years Franklin's junior, was his polar opposite, a workhorse who shunned the spotlight. He had a high forehead and earnest expression. Gossips made fun of him for being a "machine," as one of them called him, logging eleven-hour days in the office. Even more baffling, he did something that practically no other husband at Versailles dared to do: He stayed faithful to his wife. What kind of self-respecting count did that? Vergennes's behavior just wasn't natural, his enemies at court whispered; it wasn't French.

Franklin had brought a copy of the Declaration of Independence with him, but he needn't have bothered—the text had already reached France from London. It had made a tremendous impression on Vergennes, although he didn't share his reaction with Franklin. Unbeknownst to Franklin, the French minister was already working in secret to get more French arms to *les insurgents*. And Vergennes wanted to go further still. After he had read the Declaration, the minister had dashed off a memo to King Louis XVI. France should consider allying with America and attacking Britain right away, he wrote, ideally with Spain's help. It was a golden chance to put Britain in its place once and for all.

But not all the other ministers—or, more critically, the king himself—shared Vergennes's hawkish views. France had lost the Seven Years' War with Britain in a humiliating fashion. It wouldn't be easy for the foreign minister to move his country into a rematch with its old foe. For one thing, the French still needed time to rebuild their military after that crushing defeat. And France couldn't recognize American independence without immediately joining in the fight, for Britain would consider such a recognition tantamount to a declaration of war.

And so, for now, Vergennes could only wait to see what the American would do. Surely, he would demand that the French enter the war right away. *Mais non!* All Franklin did was ask for a commercial alliance, nothing else. This confused Vergennes; here was someone just as enigmatic as himself. Clearly, there would be a long diplomatic dance between these two, a game of strategy that would go on for years. Vergennes thanked Franklin, said he could not commit to anything on the king's behalf, and politely showed him the door.

The Comte de Vergennes, an unsung hero of American independence.

Not surprisingly, Miranda insisted on seeing the non–information kiosk part of the palace too, so I eventually agreed to move on. We crossed the Royal Court and entered the Grand Apartments, traipsing over thick red velvet through rooms filled with paintings of unhappy-looking royals. We reached the glittering Hall of Mirrors, where I took picture after picture of my daughter posing in front of chandeliers and wall-to-wall mirrors for her Instagram account. For centuries, the hall was as packed with courtiers as it was with tourists today, serving as the location for masked balls and furtive encounters, of plots, trysts, and seductions.

"What did you think about the Hall of Mirrors?" I asked her when we reached the end.

"It's a good place for reflection," she said, without missing a beat. (I have no idea where she gets her humor from.)

Yet this fun house hall—where nothing was quite what it seemed—did seem like the perfect spot to conjure up the dilemma Franklin faced. Where did France really stand on supporting America? Was anyone in this palace built on intrigue telling the truth? Whom could he trust?

Popular opinion, at least, was on Franklin's side. The French loved anyone who was fighting their old foe; French officers had grown up swearing blood oaths against the smug, roast-beef-eating, empire-stealing Brits. Other gravitated to the cause of liberty espoused by the Americans, dreaming that this freedom might come someday to their kingdom.

Back home, my research had given me some insight on the choices faced by France. It might seem from the opulence of Versailles that France had the power and riches to come to America's rescue if it felt like it, yet the reality was more complicated. In 1776, France had only roughly twenty-five operable ships of the line (large warships that could join in a line of battle) to Britain's sixty; the French would need a costly buildup to compete. France was also swimming in debt as its nobles resisted paying taxes, which meant that the burden of paying for the government fell to the country's peasants. The king's finance minister had made out a good case that war against Britain would be a foolish mistake, a risky foreign adventure that France couldn't afford. Britain remained the most powerful country in the world, while the Americans were an unproven gang of rebels. Who's to say they wouldn't run back into King George's arms and cut some deal with the British if France joined the fight?

Even helping the rebels on a more limited scale was causing the French headaches. American privateers—private vessels with commissions to attack enemy shipping, almost a sort of legalized piracy—kept seizing British merchant vessels. Each time one slipped into a French port to sell its contraband, the British ambassador howled in outrage. If this kept up, he threatened, it might mean war. Vergennes had to swear to the ambassador that France wanted nothing more than to stay neutral—a lie that he repeated each week, with feeling. In Paris, spies tracked everyone's every move, spreading falsehoods that rang true. No one said what they really thought, unless they pretended to be joking. Franklin was a master chess player, but the variety of potential moves here in Versailles appeared staggering.

As we continued through the palace, Miranda and I wandered into the Oeil-de-Boeuf room, just outside the king's bedroom. There, ambassadors (but not Franklin, who was not yet recognized as one) could join the crowds that gathered each day to view the king's ceremonious rising each morning, where nobles vied for the opportunity to hand him his clothes or his sword. (Could you imagine waking up and having a dozen people hovering over you, ready to hand you a toothbrush and a roll of toilet paper?)

King Louis XVI, just twenty-two, had been on the throne (the royal one) for only two years and was still unsure of himself. The job of presiding over a kingdom of close to thirty million people and a string of overseas colonies weighed on him; it was a job he had never wanted or sought. "I feel like the universe is going to fall on me," he said when he learned of his accession.

The cautious youngster was nothing like his forebearer Louis XIV, the Sun King, who had started five wars and built this ostentatious palace to house his royal court. This latest Louis liked nothing better than to ride alone with his thoughts in the woods, retiring at night to tinker with locks and keys for fun (some called him the Locksmith King). He loved ships—model ones, that is—that he could add to his collection. He had less appetite, however, for sending his actual warships into battle with the British. Much would depend, then, on one of the few men who might be able to persuade him: his foreign minister.

Vergennes thought that Britain's overwhelming victory in the Seven Years' War had upset the delicate balance of power in Europe. In his view, the Brits had been sore winners, lording it up over weaker states and ignoring France's role as a rightful equal in the Old World. A war might put the British in their place. To persuade the king and cabinet, though, he needed to convince France's traditional ally, Spain (King Carlos III was the uncle of Louis XVI by marriage) to stand with France, just as they had during the Seven Years' War. A combined Franco-Spanish navy would be as large as Britain's, and having the two countries share the heavy costs of war would be far preferable to France bearing the burden alone.

Unfortunately, Spain rejected Vergennes's quiet overtures to directly enter the war in 1776. The Spanish didn't want to encourage rebellious colonies in the New World; they had plenty of their own that might follow the Americans' lead if given the chance. Of course, the Spanish enjoyed watching their rival Britain lose territory and power, but any help they gave the Americans would have to be behind the scenes for now. So, Vergennes bided his time. He would spend the next year building and repairing ships and trying to convince Spain—and his own king—to join in the effort. Naturally, he told Franklin none of this.

Nor did he drop a hint about the unusual arms smuggling operation happening under his watch. In 1776, months before Franklin had shown up, Vergennes had launched a covert operation to arm the Americans. France and Spain each contributed a million livres—equivalent to about two billion dollars today—to the plot. Vergennes would provide surplus arms from the French stores, sold for a song to a front company, thereby concealing the involvement of the French and Spanish governments.

The company's head, Pierre Caron de Beaumarchais, had a most unusual resume for a gunrunner. He had started his career as a watch-maker and inventor, then became one of France's most celebrated playwrights—all the while serving as a spy for the French government. The flamboyant jack-of-all-trades met with the American representative Silas Deane, who was overjoyed by the proposal to send arms across the Atlantic. All throughout the fall of 1776, Beaumarchais collected artillery and muskets. French workmen filed the king's coat of arms off cannons so no one would know that they had come from the French Royal Armory. Franklin learned of some of these activities but never understood the extent to which Vergennes was actually behind the operation.

After finishing up in the palace, Miranda and I strolled through the gardens. We ended by having a late lunch in an outdoor café overlooking the Grand Canal—pizza and Coke for her, grilled trout and Chardonnay for me. "I loved this day, Dad," she said, smiling.

I too loved spending the morning with her—for that, the trip was more than worth it. The non–information kiosk part of Versailles turned out to be not so bad after all. Yet I left puzzled that I hadn't come across any mention of Vergennes in the palace. I hadn't seen his chubby, smiling face in any painting, nor his bust in its pantheon of heroes.

Afterward, I went to the building that once housed the Foreign Affairs Ministry's archives, now a public library. It looked ordinary enough from the inside. There were some historic rooms in the back that were preserved, a librarian told me, but they weren't open for visits. I did find a statue of Vergennes outside—at last, some trace of the great man. We joined a local pigeon and spent a few minutes gazing at it and then silently left.

Vergennes had once been the man to be seen in Versailles, but the town now held only the faintest glimmer of his presence. For my money, he did as much for American independence as anyone not named

George Washington, for he would be the one, as we'll see, who ultimately brought America's indispensable ally, France, into the war. But he now seemed mostly lost to time.

That wasn't entirely surprising. Vergennes always worked in the shadows and let few in on his machinations. Jefferson praised Vergennes's "original mind" (perhaps recognizing a man as perplexing as he himself was), but most Americans found the count shifty and inscrutable. The always-blunt John Adams, who arrived in Paris in 1778, bad-mouthed the French diplomat, claiming he helped America only so as to subjugate it to France. Nor did Mercy Otis Warren know what to make of Vergennes, writing that although he helped America, he secretly "dreaded the rising glory of the United States."

Who was he really? Why did he bring France into the war and orchestrate an entire coalition of nations to come together on America's side? What should I, as an American, know about this forgotten founding father?

To find out, I decided to set off to see where Vergennes came from and what traces he left in his native land. Luckily for me, that happened to be one of the most delicious places in France: Burgundy, famous for its rich stews and cheeses, the spiritual homeland of pinot noir and Chardonnay, a region with more grapes than people.

Vergennes, the gift that keeps giving.

Matthieu craned out the window of the château, his gaze fixed intently on the town of Beaune, and his ears perked as he held an empty stem glass. He was a little shorter and squatter than me, built like a French bulldog, albeit one that loved to guzzle wine.

"What are you doing?" I asked.

"We must wait for the bong." He paused. Suddenly, a church bell began pealing. "There it is, bong, bong, bong!" he said, with as much enthusiasm as the bell itself. "It is noon and now we can drink, it is good." He promptly thrust out his wine glass to the pourer.

I had just finished a tour of Domaine Chanson, a winery in Burgundy, with Matthieu and his wife Rachel. I had met the French couple on my earlier travels when I was pursuing the trail of Thomas Jefferson in Europe; our families had booked separate floors of a house near Naples, Italy, and we had hit it off. They had later hosted me in France. Now, I had pressed them into duty to help me find some traces of Vergennes, while Miranda was off on her own separate adventure.

Domaine Chanson was housed in a castle built in the Renaissance. The guide, Victor, a tall young man with an angular nose, had brought us through a room filled with oak barrels. I searched them until I found the one I was looking for, labeled "Corton Vergennes." This winery is one of only a few in the world to make wine from the eight acres of grapes once owned by the count.

"Can you tell me about Corton Vergennes?" I asked Victor, gesturing to the barrel.

"Ah yes, it is a very exclusive Chardonnay. We don't make much of it. We leave it to age for fourteen weeks in the barrel. You must have it with something powerful, like poultry with a creamy and cheesy sauce. Or veal blanquette, our traditional French dish.

"We have so little, we don't serve it at our tasting," Victor went on. "But you can purchase a bottle at the end if you want," he concluded, winking.

"Get ready to pay through the nose," Matthieu whispered to me. "I won't bother. I can't tell the difference between a twenty-Euro wine or a two-hundred-Euro one; I like them all." I thought about this. Would it be worth it to purchase such a pricey bottle for such a fleeting connection to history?

I had spent a couple of days in Burgundy on Vergennes's trail, learning whatever I could about him. He was born as Charles Gravier (his counthood came later) not too far from here, in the mustardy town of

Dijon. His family was noble but not too noble—D-list celebrities, rather than the A-listers who lived at Versailles. This vineyard was quite small, just a sliver of a hill in Burgundy. Nor was the castle in the family; Domaine Chanson bought it much later.

Vergennes might have spent the rest of his life as a local wine-loving lawyer, like other men in his family (not that there's anything wrong with that), had it not been for a stroke of fortune. A distant relative was named the French ambassador to Portugal; he then invited the nineteen-year-old Charles to join him in Lisbon as his assistant. From this humble beginning, Vergennes would embark on a four-decade-long career in foreign service, rising higher and higher through the ranks.

We moved into the tasting room. First came buttery Montrachet, then smooth Montigny—with Matthieu so enthused that he soon started forgetting to spit out the samples into the silver spittoon on the table. Rachel just rolled her eyes.

"I take it back," he said to me, "you must buy that bottle!"

After tasting a few more Burgundies, I was happy enough that I could have put the entire vineyard on my credit card. I walked out with a bottle of the Corton Vergennes, cradling it like a relic. I had no idea when I'd have the occasion to uncork it, but I figured I'd know when the moment was right.

"And now we go to find the house of Vergennes!" Matthieu said cheerfully. "Maybe there will be some more wine there."

After a pleasant hour's drive through the rolling Burgundy countryside (pleasant for Mathieu and me, anyway, as we dozed off our wine), we arrived at the ruins of the Château d'Alone-Toulongeon. Three small stone towers rose above a mound encircled by a moat. It couldn't have been a further cry from places like Mount Vernon or Monticello. Here, there were no staff of guides and interpreters, no fancy museum shop, no crowds of visitors. The place wasn't even open to the public; I had poked around online until I had discovered who owned it—a man named Bernard Gueugnon—and asked him by email if I could come by.

"Welcome," said Bernard when we got out of the car. He was stocky, with silvery white hair and a beard. After introductions, he showed us around, delighted to have visitors. I asked him about the château and how he came to own it.

"My parents bought this place in 1976 when I was a young man," he began. "We lived in the château's mill, from the twelfth century. The land around it was totally overgrown and a lot of it was underwater. My parents just got it so they could go trout fishing in their backyard.

"I was a teacher and a middle school principal," he continued. "When I retired in 2008, I dedicated myself to recovering this château, and I've been working on it ever since."

"What inspired you to do that?" I asked.

"I read in a book that the château was lost," Bernard replied, "that there was nothing left but the ruins of a wall. I knew it was there; we just had to work to uncover it. I wanted to prove them wrong and show the history that was here."

"I had to drain some of the water and raise the towers," he explained. "Now much more is visible. Yet people still do not know what we have here," he continued. "If you look at Google Maps, they don't even mention it—there's only a blue mark, indicating the moat."

Talk about a retirement project. I had heard about fixing up old houses, but not excavating a château, even a smallish one, mostly by yourself. It was a labor of love, he told me. When he wasn't moving earth, he was scouring archives in search of old maps to look for clues.

Bernard brought us to a strip of land where a drawbridge once stood, as geese waddled out of our way. "Vergennes bought this château in 1764. It was his getaway. He needed this to assert his authority as a diplomat and later a minister," he told us. Vergennes set out to beautify the grounds, installing manicured gardens, fountains, canals, and a number of outbuildings, I learned.

At the time he purchased Château d'Alone-Toulongeon, Vergennes was serving as the French ambassador to the Ottoman Empire. His fourteen years in that post couldn't have been more different than the quiet, grapey life he led in Burgundy. Constantinople was a cosmopolitan port city, a crossroads between east and west. Mosques stood next to Byzantine churches and synagogues, feluccas and xebecs beat back and forth across the Bosphorus Strait, markets sold every spice under the sun, and dozens of languages could be heard in the streets.

The diplomat was charged with propping up the declining Ottoman Empire, an old friend of France that was now threatened by Russia and other allies of Britain. In the course of his work, Vergennes became dedicated to maintaining the delicate balance of power in Europe. He came to view the British as predators and disrupters of the old order, extending their influence into places that France had once controlled.

Vergennes also became intrigued by the thriving community of French traders based in Constantinople. For centuries, a group of merchants had made a good living brokering deals. Instead of conquering lands to establish colonies—which cost so much to administer and protect—perhaps France would be better off just trading, he mused. Vergennes would bring those insights with him when he considered the Americans' request for help a decade later.

The expat community interested him for another reason too.

"In Turkey, Vergennes fell in love with a woman," Bernard told us. "Her name was Anne Duvivier. She was half-French, half-Greek and was born in Turkey. She was a commoner and not wealthy. This caused a scandal because of her background." Anne gave birth to two sons. Their relationship itself wasn't strange—*naturellement*, French aristocrats were expected to have liaisons. The mystifying thing was that Vergennes stuck by Anne despite their glaring social differences, rather than discarding her and their kids later and marrying up.

"Back then, diplomats needed permission from the king to marry. King Louis XV never would have given it—so Vergennes didn't ask and got married in Turkey anyways," Bernard recounted. "He loved Anne and would remain faithful to her the rest of his days." Vergennes had been a cautious diplomat for decades—yet, when he had to, made a sudden, dramatic decision that changed his life.

"The foreign minister at the time was very angry at Vergennes's disobedience, and he recalled him back to France in 1768," Bernard continued. "Vergennes retired to this château. Here is where he gave a ball for his wedding after he came home," he said, gesturing to the mound behind him, where the château's great courtyard once stood.

After the scandal of his marriage, Vergennes's career ground to a halt. But politics never stands still. The displeased minister who had fired the ambassador himself fell from power, and, in 1772, Vergennes rejoined the diplomatic service. He was sent to Stockholm where he engineered a coup that restored a pro-French Swedish king to power. In 1774, when the teenage Louis XVI ascended the throne, he named the fifty-four-year-old Vergennes as his foreign minister.

A man and his DIY home project—Bernard Gueugnon and the Château d'Alone-Toulongeon, along with the author.

After an idyllic afternoon exploring the ruins, we took our leave of Bernard by the car while Matthieu lovingly eyed my bottle of Corton Vergennes lying in the back seat. Bernard pressed a book into my hand containing his research into the château that he had clawed out of the ground. "I wanted to show people what was here," he said. "It would be a shame if the story of this place were lost." He smiled. "Who knows what will happen in a few years, someday when I'm gone?"

"There's Ben Franklin again!" Miranda said. Looking for a late afternoon treat, we had walked into Café Procope on the Left Bank, a three-hundred-year-old-plus restaurant, one of the few places in Paris that maintains a glimpse of the eighteenth century. We were seated near a bust of him, which peered down beatifically at the diners. Earlier in the day, we had trekked out to Rue Benjamin Franklin, across the Seine from the Eiffel Tower, to view a bronze statue of him leaning forward in his chair, as if to pass on some wisdom to whoever drew closer. An inscription on it praised "the genius who freed America and spread torrents of light into Europe."

"They sure love him here," I said. When Franklin died in 1791, the whole city went into mourning—and this café was draped in black. We ordered a slice of apple pie, one of his favorite desserts.

Franklin seemed very far from having such a legacy, though, when the new year dawned in 1777. Parisians adored him, but he and his secret partner Vergennes were light-years from delivering on an alliance. France's finances were a wreck, the news from America had been of defeat after defeat, and Spain was still saying *¡no!* to Vergennes's overtures.

It was the hardest assignment of Franklin's life. There was no manual on how to act as a diplomat from a country in rebellion, nor on how to persuade a monarchy to support a republic. Franklin decided not to push too hard, which might backfire and turn the French government against him. Instead, he made America a cause célèbre in Paris simply by being himself, showing up to parties in his plain clothes and acting like the character of Poor Richard from his almanac come to life.

Franklin spoke little, but when he had good news to share—like that of the American victories at Trenton and Princeton—people hung on his every word. Parisians ate it up. Those who couldn't see him in person crowded to see his bust, which was prominently displayed in the Louvre. Franklin's popularity skyrocketed, as did that of the insurgents he represented. But popular opinion wasn't enough to sway an absolute monarch like Louis XVI. The only man who could get the king to enter the war, it seemed, was his foreign minister.

My travels to Burgundy had given me some glimpses into who Vergennes was. He had started out his career as an underdog, a man from a minor provincial family who rose through the ranks thanks to his hard, methodical work. While posted abroad, he had come to view Britain as a bully, an empire that bossed other countries around and undid his careful work of establishing French influence in Europe. To most people, he seemed like a conventional diplomat, yet he had shocked the court by marrying a commoner, and a foreigner at that, without permission. (And he made a stupendous Chardonnay.) Thanks to this trip, I felt like I was just starting to understand this complex figure. I only wished that more people knew about him—just like we know all about the other great figures who helped America win its independence.

"The Declaration of Independence I always considered as a theatrical show," John Adams groused once. "Jefferson ran away with all the stage effect of that, i.e., all the glory of it," obscuring the hard work Adams had done behind the scenes to make that document possible. The same sentiment might apply to Vergennes himself. He's often portrayed as a bit player at best in the drama of the War for Independence—if he is mentioned at all, that is. Yet, without France, the American war effort might have foundered. All along, Vergennes was the secret star of the show.

Recent scholarship has uncovered the largely hidden acts that Vergennes took in 1777 as he slowly steered France into the war and made sure it was ready to fight. French dockyards worked overtime building ships of the line. France still had fewer of these large warships than Britain, but under Vergennes's watch it had cut the gap considerably. In the spring, with Vergennes's secret blessing, the ships of Beaumarchais, the playwright-turned-gunrunner, departed for America with rifles, cannons, and uniforms for Washington's army, which would prove essential to the Americans that year. The foreign minister also permitted key officers to sail to America to join in the cause.

All this help was sorely needed. By the time the first anniversary of the Declaration of Independence arrived on July 4, 1777, it was clear that the year was shaping up to be one fraught with peril for the Continental Army. Rumors crossed the Atlantic of two separate massive British offensives against the Americans. Vergennes began to worry; if the Americans were trounced on the battlefield, they might cut a deal for peace with Britain—and his chance to restore the balance of power would be lost.

Providing secret aid was no longer enough; the time had come to act with conviction. Vergennes ordered the dockyards to step up their shipbuilding program. He called the French cod fishing fleet, which was in Newfoundland, back home so he could impress the fishermen into the navy. In late July, he sent a message to his counterpart in Madrid. Within the next six months, France and Spain had to choose whether "either to abandon America to herself, or to help her courageously and effectively" and enter the war. There would be no middle ground. Just as the cautious minister had once shocked people by the decisive step he had taken in his personal life in Turkey, Vergennes now prepared to take the most decisive step of his public life, bringing his country into a war of choice. And he believed he had the king ready to approve his plans—particularly if Spain was on board.

Vergennes had done all he could to prepare for that moment, even though hardly anyone on the outside knew it. Now all he could do was wait and see how the Americans would fare on the battlefield that year. He did not necessarily need the Americans to win a great victory, but he did need them to avoid a catastrophic defeat that ended the war before France could join in it. Would the rebels survive?

Fortunately for the Patriots, a new ally would come to America's aid in that fateful year of 1777. Unlike the French, the people of this nation didn't need to cross an ocean to do so, for the war had reached their own homeland. They had wanted to live in peace, but the time had come for the Oneida Indians to choose a side.

Chapter Six

FIRST ALLIES

How the Oneida Indians and French Arms Helped Win at Saratoga

June–October 1777

July 4, 1777, the first anniversary of American independence, started out auspiciously enough. In both Boston and Philadelphia, cannon salutes were fired, church bells rang out, and a "grand exhibition of fireworks" occurred, as one observer called it. "It was the most splendid illumination I ever saw," John Adams wrote. But an undercurrent of tension ran through the festivities. Two major British operations were taking shape that aimed to crush the Revolution once and for all, before France could enter the war. If the British had their way, there would never be a second Independence Day to celebrate.

The first campaign had two parts. General John "Gentlemanly Johnny" Burgoyne was moving a force of over eight thousand men south from Canada down the Hudson Valley into New York State. Meanwhile, a second force of sixteen hundred fighters was heading east from the Great Lakes, following the Mohawk River. They planned to link up in

Albany, where the two rivers converged. If they succeeded, the British would control a huge swath of territory stretching from Quebec to New York City, while their navy patrolled the coast. New England, the hotbed of the Revolution, would be cut off from the other American states.

The second campaign that would follow the first, however, was shrouded in mystery. Late in July, British general Howe embarked his force of over seventeen thousand into some 260 ships, his destination unknown. Would he join up with Burgoyne in the north? Or perhaps target Congress in Philadelphia? Washington marched his Main Army up and down the mid-Atlantic states, wondering where Howe would land. Fortunately for the Americans, the winds were not in Howe's favor, and his troops languished at sea for a month. So we'll start with Burgoyne's campaign, which was making much progress on land.

On July 2, Gentlemanly Johnny laid siege to Ticonderoga, the fort that the Americans had taken in a surprise attack two years earlier. Now the tables had turned. Matt Keagle, the curator at the fort's museum, told me about the British reconquest when I met with him over coffee. "In 1777, the Americans had a shadow of an army, only thirty-five hundred men," he said. Burgoyne's forces simply overwhelmed the defenders—and even managed to get a couple of cannons up onto nearby Sugar Loaf Hill, overlooking the fortifications.

"The Americans spent the Fourth of July actively surrounded in the thick of siege," Matt told me. "They could have surrendered with honor, but instead they chose to evacuate." In the eighteenth century, such a move was often seen as cowardly, but Matt thought it was both smart and necessary. "They preserved their army," he said. "It was important for the rest of the campaign that the New Hampshire and Massachusetts Continentals pulled out," he said. "They were the first who had enlisted under new terms set by Congress, which were for three years or the duration of the war instead of for just a year. This was an investment in the future of the war. They were the future of the Revolution," he said.

Burgoyne set off "to traverse a forlorn wilderness, pathless thickets, and swamps" to Albany, as Mercy Otis Warren had put it, supported by Native American warriors. "The British had many allies among the Haudenosaunee, or Iroquois," Matt said. "Burgoyne had many other Native fighters with him too—Canadian Iroquois, Abenaki, the Mohawk."

"Why do you think they supported the British?" I asked.

"I don't want to speak for these Native American communities," Matt replied, "but I think most of them were concerned about the American colonists' interest in expansion into land that was theirs. Some of them saw the British as an ally against a greater threat in some ways."

"What did the Native forces do?" I asked. "Were they scouts?"

"Europeans did use them as scouts, as an advance guard, and to gather intelligence," he replied. "But they were more than that. They were fully autonomous and had a different understanding of their role than the Europeans did." Native warriors participated in many battles, he told me, and made their own choices about what role they wanted to play in the campaign.

"The Haudenosaunee had established a confederacy which had lasted for centuries, but it was shattering," he continued. "Most of the nations supported the British, but the Oneida and some of the Tuscarora supported the Americans." The Oneida in particular, I learned, had allied with the Patriots and helped them throughout the war. (The Tuscarora were divided in their loyalties).

Their story fascinated me—I had certainly never heard of it growing up. Unlike most of their Iroquois brethren, the Oneida had chosen to throw in their lot with the Americans who were pressing up against their lands. Why did they choose to make sacrifices, I wondered, for a nation not their own? And how did they help the Patriots stop Burgoyne's advance in what would later be called the Saratoga campaign, one of the most pivotal periods of the war?

To understand more about the people who became America's first allies, I drove to the heartland of Oneida country, in the northwestern corner of New York State, just in time for their annual spring festival.

The activities began with a message of thanksgiving, delivered by a young woman in Oneida, a language that the nation has been seeking to keep alive. Theirs is a story of survival. The Oneida have faced many setbacks over the years, I learned, but have continued to forge a path ahead. This spring festival—with dancing, crafts, and fellowship—was yet another instance of the community coming together, as it has in different forms for centuries.

The participants assembled in the parking lot in front of the Shako:wi Cultural Center, a handsome log building with a steep roof, in the town of Oneida. A group of Haudenosaunee dancers began with what they called a welcome dance, moving in a circle. Many were not Oneida, I learned, but members of the other Six Nations; the Iroquois often come together to put on cultural events like this. The dancers wore turkey feathers in their hair and were dressed in purple, red, and white garments with beaded designs. They started with what they called a stand and quiver dance, then moved into a fish dance, with dancers undulating like salmon swimming upstream. The leader, who had been singing throughout, showed the crowd the instruments he was playing, including a water drum and a rattle made from deer hooves.

"Here's a shuffle dance, which the women will perform," he told us. "Women pretty much run the show here. They pick our leaders, they used to grow our food." The dancers ended with a round dance, moving in a circle, while community members joined in the celebration.

I learned more about the festival, and the Oneida Nation, from one of its organizers, Doris Wilkins-Wilt, who was happy to sit down with me to talk. She looked to be in her late thirties and was wearing Native jewelry. "We have about a thousand members," she told me, "but not all live here." She pointed out the housing behind the center, rows of single-family housing, duplexes, and apartments. "We house elders and youth together," she said, "in two different wings of a building. There's a daycare side and an elder side." What a wonderful way to pass the culture on, I thought.

Doris also told me more about the recitation at the beginning of the ceremony. "Some of us give a thanksgiving every day," she said, "for people and insects, wind and thunder, the sun and the moon. You might do that the first thing in the morning, when we see the sun."

"It's interesting to hear about the role of women here," I said.

"Yes, women pick men into councils. Women were planters, they harvested and cooked while men would go hunting. We'd smoke meat for storage. We're still nurturing moms today."

She was on her own journey of discovery, she told me. She had grown up in Syracuse, with a non-Native father and an Oneida mother who had unfortunately been estranged from her family. It was only when she came here as a young woman, she told me, that she had been able to reconnect with her roots. Now Doris was making up for lost time, spreading her nation's culture as far as she could. Working with the cultural center, she went into local public schools, teaching kids about the Oneida language and customs, and practicing the culture herself as well. "It's a good feeling," she said. "I'm beading, sewing, trying to carve, learning how to weave baskets. I'm doing stuff my mom couldn't do."

She brought me over to speak with the center's manager, Ron Patterson. He was a tall, soft-spoken man a little older than me, who had worked for years to share the story of his people. I started by asking about the building itself.

"We built this in the early '90s," Ron said, "out of white pine. That's something important to our culture. The tree of peace on our flag—did you see that? It's a white pine. It's at the origins of our Confederacy. We were five nations at first, the Mohawk, Oneida, Onondaga, Cayuga, and Seneca," he said. (The Tuscarora joined later, I learned.) "They had been fighting each other. Peacemaker and Hiawatha brought all the nations together. They met where the Onondaga lived, which was a central location in the territory, which stretched from Montreal to Virginia and as far west as the Ohio Valley. The Onondaga had the capital of the Haudenosaunee, where the Grand Council meets.

"All fifty chiefs uprooted a white pine," Ron continued. "In the pit where it was, they threw in war clubs, bows and arrows, hatchets, and tomahawks. They buried them and replanted the tree over it. It became the tree of peace, signifying peace within the Confederation." He showed me a belt depicting the tree, now on display in the cultural center. The Haudenosaunee remained unified for most of the 1700s, helping the British fight the French colonists when wars broke out. But the peace within the Confederation would be severely tested—and ultimately broken—during the Revolutionary War.

I noticed dioramas of longhouses in the center. "Is that what the Oneida lived in?" I asked.

"We did back in the 1600s," Ron replied. "Five to ten families would live in each one. Then colonists began to come into the area." The Oneida was one of the easternmost of the Haudenosaunee nations and had more contact with the American settlers than nations to the west. Slowly, some Oneida began practicing more European-style agriculture and living in cabins and houses, I learned, rather than longhouses.

"We had good relations with Samuel Kirkland, a Presbyterian missionary who lived with them," Ron continued. I had seen a portrait of Kirkland in the center—he was a round-faced man from Connecticut who had learned Iroquois languages from Joseph Brant, a Mohawk student close to his own age. Kirkland would spend his career among the Oneida and other Native Americans.

"Kirkland had a rift with William Johnson, who was an Anglican." As British superintendent for Indian affairs in the region, Johnson managed relations with the Haudenosaunee in the area for the Crown, which included promoting Anglicanism, England's state religion. (Johnson would also become the common-law husband of Joseph Brant's sister Molly.) "Kirkland wanted to convert people to his faith. He convinced Skenandoah, an Oneida leader, to follow Presbyterianism, and he had the Bible translated into Oneida. He lived in the village and had a good rapport with people." The present-day town where we were now was, I learned, only a few miles west of the village of Kanowalohale, where Kirkland lived. Hundreds of Oneida attended his services.

While the Confederation officially remained neutral during the early years of the war, more and more Haudenosaunee were drawn to the British, who promised to protect their land from encroachments from American settlers. By early 1777, some Iroquois warriors—led by Joseph Brant—had joined with the British in western New York. The prospect terrified Americans, who had grown up on stories of Indian raids and scalping expeditions. Even Warren, sensitive on some other subjects, followed the spirit of the times in calling the Haudenosaunee "savages."

Unlike most other Iroquois, however, the Oneida were more sympathetic to the Patriots. "Samuel Kirkland was siding with George Washington," Ron told me, "and he helped convince the Oneida to side with the Americans." Inspired by the American talk of freedom and seeing in the conflict a chance to chart their own course, the Oneida quietly fed the Patriots information and served as scouts. A delegation of Oneida leaders even visited Washington's camp in New Jersey in early 1777 and were pleased to hear the general tell them not only that the French were assisting the Continental Army, but that he also thought they were about to join in the war. The American cause looked more and more promising to the Oneida. They still hoped, however, to remain officially neutral—and that the other Haudenosaunee nations would do the same.

When Burgoyne sent forces through New York in the summer of 1777, though, the Oneida couldn't remain neutral any longer, for the army was moving right through Oneida territory. The invading fighters included the British, Canadians, and Loyalists, as well as Mohawk and Seneca warriors led by Joseph Brant. They were marching toward Fort Stanwix, manned by Patriots and a few Oneida volunteers, the last line of defense standing to the west of Albany. The war had reached their homeland, and the Oneida would soon have to pick a side.

"On August 2, 1777, Fort Stanwix, it was called Fort Schuyler at the time, fell under siege," Ron told me. "Not far from here, Colonel Herkimer recruited Patriot militia to come help. They stopped near the outskirts of Fort Stanwix, at the village of Oriska; it's called Oriskany today. Chief Han Yerry and his wife, Two Kettles Together, and other Oneidas were with them, anywhere from around fifty to one hundred Oneida. They camped there overnight.

"Joseph Brant's sister, Molly Brant, lived nearby," he continued. "She alerted the Senecas and the Mohawks that the militia was coming through. They didn't know that the Oneida were going to be with them. They planned on attacking them, setting a trap, a few miles outside what is now Rome, New York. When they got into a ravine, they attacked.

"The battle ensued," Ron continued. "For the first hour, they fought with muskets, in the cover of brush. Han Yerry was wounded in the hand; he couldn't load his weapon. So, Two Kettles began to load muskets. He'd fire, she'd load it. Then she fired the musket too. She was very involved in that battle; she was looked at as a hero after that.

"After a while," he continued, "it began to pour. Flintlock weapons are no good in the rain. There was hand-to-hand combat in the rain for hours. The stream there was then known as Blood Creek, it ran red for three days." The ambush turned into the bloodiest battle of the Revolution, per capita, fought on American soil. The Patriots and Oneida lost well over half their combatants.

One of the worst parts of the fighting, Ron told me, was that it was between people who had been neighbors. "The militia were people that lived in the Mohawk Valley, and many of the soldiers with the British were colonists too. Everybody knew each other. The Seneca and Mohawks who attacked the Oneida knew them; they looked at them as brothers.

"That was the point that the Oneida officially sided with the American Revolution," Ron said. But the attack on them had its cost, he told me with a certain sadness. "The ripple is still seen today," he said. "The Council fire never burned as bright as before that last battle." The

Confederation had broken apart; the Haudenosaunee were now at war with each other. The Native warriors on the side of the British had lost many casualties at Oriskany too, and after the battle they took revenge by burning down the nearby Oneida village of Oriska.

The defeat at Oriskany left the American and Oneida forces in Fort Stanwix in a desperate situation. They came out of it thanks to a masterful ruse, one in which the Oneida played a prominent role. Two Oneida came separately to the British camp, breathlessly announcing that a huge American force was on its way. A third man, a German American Loyalist married to an Oneida (who had been pressured into participating in the scheme after the Patriots had captured him) also came into camp, his clothes shot full of bullet holes, swearing that the relief expedition would soon arrive. The Seneca and Mohawk warriors, having heard enough, decided to leave. Now undermanned, the British had to call off the siege. The Oneida had helped save the garrison through guile. Burgoyne would not receive the help he had planned on getting from the west; one prong of his two-pronged campaign was now broken.

The Oneida warriors had become America's first allies, the first to help the Patriots in their quest for independence, not just by sending arms but also by joining the rebels in the field. The Oneida would go on to serve with the Americans in future battles and campaigns, some of which Ron told me about—including the story, passed down through generations, of Polly Cooper, a woman who accompanied Oneida warriors to Valley Forge to cook shelled corn for the troops (which we'll return to later). In fact, Ron said, Oneida have served in every foreign war the United States has fought since. Despite their alliance with the Americans during the Revolution, though, the Oneida would ultimately suffer the same fate as the other Haudenosaunee nations and lose the vast majority of their territory.

Ron told me about the Oneida's fight to reclaim their land in the late twentieth century. "We always maintained the same alliance. We weren't there to evict people, just to buy back our own land, to be partners and neighbors," he told me. A 1985 New York State law authorizing gaming changed everything, he said. "When we opened a casino in 1993, some saw it as what you might call a cash cow. Yet with it, we went from an impoverished nation to one of wealthiest governments in New York State, one of the leading employers in New York State in a thirty-year span."

"What does the fact that the Oneida were America's first allies mean to you?" I asked.

"It an honor to be recognized in the development of this country," he said, and then paused. His story was complicated since, as it turned out, only his mother was Oneida. "My father was Seneca, and I grew up in the Seneca nation. They reminded me that I was Oneida; they looked at us as traitors." Some Haudenosaunee had wished that the Oneida had fought with them alongside the British, in what they saw as their last best chance to defend their lands.

"I grew up with people telling me we were traitors. I grew up with that shame," he continued. "When I was eighteen, I moved out here. The nation let me stay with the Native language teacher. Here, it was the total opposite. People were proud that they were recognized as allies of the greatest country. They no longer had to be shameful. I'm proud to be Oneida today, proud of all our ancestors that fell defending our country."

Doris Wilkins-Wilt and Ron Patterson, champions of Oneida culture.

Before I took leave of Doris, I asked her about how she had been able to reconnect with her community after not growing up in the nation. "I feel at home," she told me. "It's just amazing to see the different things our ancestors have done and how we're trying to make those things."

I left impressed by the role the Oneida had played in the war, as well as the resilience of a culture that has had to deal with unthinkable adversity over the centuries, from war to broken promises to the loss of much of their way of life. I had also found it fascinating to learn about the role women have played in the nation's survival—even contributing on the battlefield.

"I had a shirt made," Doris told me proudly before I left. "Be powerful like Two Kettles, and courageous like Polly Cooper."

In August, Burgoyne sent an expedition of some fourteen hundred British, Hessian, Canadian, and Iroquois fighters to the Vermont territory to obtain more military supplies. It turned into a disaster for the British when New England militiamen surprised them near the town of Bennington, killing about two hundred enemy soldiers and capturing nine hundred others. And that wasn't all. "After Bennington, the Haudenosaunee who had allied with the British split," Matt Keagle told me. "They didn't want to be taken prisoner."

Burgoyne hadn't counted on such a strong response from the militia, which, for once, was well-armed. They had France to thank for that. "The French were surreptitiously sending supplies," Matt said, "and arms, which came in from the playwright Beaumarchais." In the spring of 1777, Beaumarchais's five ships, sent with the support of the Comte de Vergennes, had arrived. By the time all the ships had landed, the Americans had received some thirty thousand rifles, four hundred tons of gunpowder, five thousand tents, and even fifteen thousand pocket handkerchiefs (the French thought of everything).

"New Hampshire took two thousand muskets from Beaumarchais," Matt said, "and put their state markings on them. Some were issued to the New Hampshire militia at Bennington."

Another European import had arrived too: the Polish nobleman and military engineer Thaddeus Kosciuszko. Inspired by the ideals of the Revolution, Kosciuszko sailed for America in June 1776 to join the cause. After surviving a shipwreck, he made his way to Philadelphia where he joined the Continental forces. He wound up giving Horatio Gates, who had taken command of the Northern army in August 1777, some of the most important advice of the entire war.

The Continentals had at first camped on flat ground. The Polish engineer persuaded Gates to instead move his men to the top of Bemis Heights, a hill that commanded the Hudson River below, nine miles from the small town of Saratoga (which later gave its name to the fighting that followed). Once Kosciuszko had fortified the heights, the British could not advance on to Albany without passing under American cannons.

"Saratoga was two separate battles," Matt recounted, "following weeks of protracted stalemate. It was a static front, almost like World War I in a way. Both armies were behind fortifications, eyeing each other across terrain. The Americans aimed to stop the British forces, so they wouldn't advance."

The first of the two battles came in September 1777, when Burgoyne moved away from the Hudson River and tried to flank the fortifications on Bemis Heights, leading to a clash with the Patriots on a stretch of farmland. Burgoyne took the ground he wanted, but his maneuvers came at a high cost: He lost seven hundred men, as casualties or prisoners, who could not be replaced.

All the while, reinforcements poured into the Patriots' camp, as thousands of militiamen and Continentals joined the encampment. Some 150 Native American warriors, mostly Oneida, showed up too, including Han Yerry and Two Kettles Together. The Oneida and other Native Americans would kill half a dozen British troops and capture many others, effectively preventing the British from sending out foraging parties unless they had a strong escort. The grateful General Gates later ordered three gallons of rum to be sent to Two Kettles as a gesture of goodwill for her service. "Sooner should a fond mother forget her only son than we shall forget you," General Philip Schuyler later wrote to the Oneida.

On October 7, 1777, the British and Hessians clashed with the Americans again, this time beneath the bluffs of Bemis Heights. The second battle was a bloody affair, marked by the courageous charge of Benedict Arnold into enemy forces. The defeated British fell back, abandoning the ground they had won earlier. Gates was effusive in crediting Kosciuszko for placing his army in the right spot, claiming that "the great tacticians of the campaign were hills and forests, which a young Polish engineer was skillful enough to select for my encampment."

Following the second battle—and with no help coming from General Howe, who by now was deep into his own campaign to take Philadelphia—Burgoyne surrendered his entire army of around six thousand soldiers. "So many thousands of brave men and distinguished officers led captive through the wilderness, the plains, and the cities of the United States was a spectacle never before beheld by the inhabitants," Warren wrote gleefully.

What Burgoyne didn't know was the other secret weapon (literally) that made victory at Saratoga possible—those French arms. Saratoga had been the "first opportunity of testing the qualities of the new French muskets," staff officer Caleb Stark wrote. "I firmly believe that unless these arms had been thus timely furnished to the Americans, Burgoyne would have made an easy march to Albany." One historian estimated that 90 percent of the military supplies that helped the Americans win came from French or French-connected merchants.

"Thus, to the consternation of Britain [and] to the universal joy of America," Warren wrote, "was the northern expedition finished. A reverse of fortune was now beheld that had not fallen under the calculation of either party." The Patriots hoped the spectacular victory would inspire France to enter the war on the Americans' side.

News of the victory at Saratoga would indeed prove useful for Vergennes. Not that he himself needed persuading—he was more than ready to bring France into the war, now that his preparations were complete and his navy rebuilt. But word that the perfidious English had lost once again would go over well, smoothing the way to getting the king's approval of his war plans.

My discoveries—on both the American efforts to stop Burgoyne and my earlier journey to learn more about Vergennes—changed my view of what had happened at Saratoga. I had always understood that the Americans won, thanks to their own bravery and Burgoyne's blunders, and that it was this victory alone, which proved the rebels knew how to fight, that persuaded France to enter the war.

Now I knew that the reality was more nuanced. Saratoga didn't convince Vergennes to enter the war; he had been convinced for over a year prior to the battle. He had mostly been biding his time to prepare his military for the war to come and to try to bring Spain along with him. Saratoga did make the American cause even more popular in France and made it easier for Vergennes to get final approval for his plans. But, barring a catastrophe in America, France was already on track to join in.

Capturing Burgoyne's army, of course, was a great triumph. But I had also learned that credit for the victory belonged to many—certainly to the Patriot forces, but also to the Oneida warriors, the Polish engineer Kosciuszko, Beaumarchais, and Vergennes himself, who had sent the needed arms to the Americans.

Nor was Saratoga the end of the story. Vergennes didn't necessarily need a great American victory for his plans to come to fruition, but what he absolutely needed was to avoid a complete American collapse that might end the war. The Americans had avoided that in New York State, but the fighting wasn't done yet. That same fall of 1777, the second, much larger British army under Howe was taking on Washington's men in Pennsylvania. If the Continental Main Army surrendered, or was annihilated by Howe's forces, the rebel cause might disintegrate. Vergennes needed Washington and his army to survive.

For that to happen, the American general would rely in part on a group of foreign fighters who provided him with expertise in everything from artillery to drilling the troops, as well as on a charismatic Frenchman who brought the Americans hope. To see how this unexpected assistance came, let's rewind to the scene of the first Independence Day, when Burgoyne was taking Fort Ticonderoga and Howe was preparing to launch his campaign to the south.

On that same day of July 4, 1777, a carriage clattered north on a long journey from South Carolina to Philadelphia. In it was a teenaged French officer who planned to offer to serve in the Continental Army as a general, even though he had never seen combat before. He would become one of the most fervent admirers of American liberty—and of the Oneida Indians too, who would help save him in battle. The Oneida called him Kayewla, "great warrior." You might know him as the Hero of Two Worlds, America's favorite fighting Frenchman. It's time to meet the one and only Marquis de Lafayette.

Chapter Seven

THE EUROPEAN AVENGERS

How Volunteer Officers Helped Washington's Army Survive

June 1777–May 1778

If you mention "foreigners and the Revolutionary War," one name instantly comes to mind: the man with thirty-six towns and cities in the United States named after him (as well as rivers, a glacier, a college, and even a brand of urinal). He was beloved during the war and still is today. I knew that at some point on my quest, Lafayette and I would inevitably cross paths.

That finally occurred in a bar outside Philadelphia, where my son Nico and I came face-to-face with two Lafayettes. One was a middle-aged professional reenactor, resplendent in his great coat with gold lacing and a tri-corner hat sporting blue, white, and red plumes. The other was a beer.

"What a pleasure, what an honor to have this delightful *repas* among friends," Lafayette said, speaking with a thick French accent. I was excited to meet him—as were the rest of the patrons in the bar, who were some of the seven-hundred-plus members of a most impressive group called the American Friends of Lafayette. With input from the Friends, this brewpub had recently crafted a beer in tribute to the Marquis, a spicy, fruity French-inspired golden ale.

When he arrived in America, the nineteen-year-old Marie-Joseph Paul Yves Roch Gilbert du Motier de La Fayette had more names (seven) than combat experience (none). Yet he was the right man to join the fight. The American cause seemed to him to be just—and also the perfect opportunity for both making his name and avenging his father, killed by the British in the Seven Years' War. The orphan had an outrageous fortune, the title to match, and endless energy.

The Lafayette in front of us told the tale of how, in the spring of 1777, he had left France in secret. The American agent in Paris, Silas Deane, was deluged with applications from officers, from both France and neighboring countries, who all wanted to join Washington's army. Since Europe was at peace, officers who wanted to make a name for themselves had to go where the war was. The enthusiastic Deane spent his days "promising offices of rank to fifty gentlemen at a time," Mercy Otis Warren wrote, and sending them on "with the most flattering expectations of promotion."

The Marquis was not supposed to be among them, however. Although the Comte de Vergennes willingly turned a blind eye to most of the volunteers, letting Lafayette go would be too risky. The young man was so close to the court that his participation might seem as if it had a royal blessing. In response, a furious Britain might even declare war on France before the French were ready to fight. To keep this from happening, the king signed an order prohibiting Lafayette from leaving.

If the Marquis had obeyed, the American Revolution would have unfolded differently and *Hamilton* would have been minus one rapping Frenchman. But naturally, he did what any teenager with unlimited funds and unbounded confidence would do: what he wanted to. Defying the order, he bought his own ship to leave on, a small frigate with two cannons that he rechristened the *Victoire.* Vergennes chose not to send the French navy out to detain him; maybe the boy would accomplish something useful in the New World after all. Lafayette sailed to South Carolina and in June 1777 began making his way up to the American capital, dreaming that he would be received by Congress with open arms.

The reception that the faux Lafayette was receiving here at the brewery was far better than the one the OG Lafayette got in Philadelphia in late July. The American capital was lousy with European officers demanding high ranks in the Continental Army, waving around the commissions Deane had handed out like candy. Weary of these has-beens and never-weres, Congress was refusing to honor any of Deane's promises, even with respect to officers who "were men of real merit, military experience, and distinguished rank," as Warren put it.

In the bar, Lafayette continued with his story. "I was told 'thank you for coming, but we don't need your help.'" The Friends of Lafayette booed. "But I was not ready to return. 'Perhaps I can serve as an aide-de-camp?' I asked.

"'We haven't money to pay you,' they said.

"'Then I shall serve at my own expense.' With those immortal words, your Congress made me a major general." Everyone laughed.

"I recently celebrated a birthday," he went on, "I'm 266 years old."

"You look great!" someone called out to laughter.

And so began Lafayette's story in America, one that went straight into the history books and legends. As a kid, he had been one of my favorites, the gallant Frenchman who had come to fight for liberty. But he wasn't the only European who helped the American cause in the critical year of 1777.

Before my trip to Philadelphia, I had started to read up on them. A pity that some of these officers aren't well-known, for they have quite a story. Some were charlatans; others tried to challenge Washington's authority. Still others were among the best that Europe could offer. Vergennes had made sure of that, insisting that the Americans take some men he knew would rise to the occasion. Each of these handpicked stars brought with them a unique skill set. A screenwriter for a Marvel movie might even describe them as a team of assembled superheroes.

They were led by Louis Duportail, the Brains of the Operation. A wise strategist, he would advise Washington on where to camp and when to attack. He paired up in Washington's Main Army with Francois de Fleury, the Tech Man, a military engineer who could design defenses that could withstand British bombarding for weeks.

Two Polish aristocrats joined the team, one of whom we've already met. Thaddeus Kosciuszko, whom I'll call the Artiste, had studied drawing at the Louvre. As we've seen, his fortifications at Saratoga proved to be one of the keys to the American victory. His compatriot, Casimir Pulaski, the Horseman, also made his home in France. He possessed unparalleled skill as a cavalryman, thinking nothing of dashing through bullets to ride up to the enemy's lines while brandishing a pistol. The last to arrive was the Baron von Steuben, the Muscle, a Prussian who would relentlessly drill his men.

All of these European Avengers would win Washington's confidence—as would the officer in the role of the Leading Man, our beloved Marquis. I was curious to learn more about them. Did Lafayette live up to the hype he's received over the years? Whose names should we remember alongside his? And how did these volunteers help Washington's army survive through what Warren called "the darkest times"?

The Lafayette in front of me seemed like a good place to start my investigation. I spoke with him later. The actor, Mark Schneider, had played the role of the Marquis at Colonial Williamsburg, as well as at events across the United States and abroad, for nearly a quarter century. He was the perfect man for the job: Mark not only knew his character's history backward and forward, but he also spoke French (his mother was from France), could ride horses, and had once served in the U.S. Army, giving him a keen appreciation of Lafayette's service.

"Why do you connect with this character?" I asked him.

"I see him as a twenty-first-century person who lived in the eighteenth century," Mark responded. "He was very forward-thinking. He was against slavery; he fought against it to his dying days. And he was friends with the Oneida Indians. He fought alongside them and was even adopted by them.

"I love that about him," Mark went on. "You know, I wasn't a trained actor when I started. I went to an acting coach. He told me, if you believe in what you're saying, the audience will believe it more. I believe in Lafayette. The things he said, I believe in them too."

"What's it like working with the American Friends of Lafayette?" I asked. Not every reenactor has his own built-in fan club that regularly shows up to cheer him on.

"They're fun, history-loving people from all walks of life," Mark replied. "The group was founded back in 1932. They all appreciate who Lafayette was. You'd like people to be like how he was today," he said, "a person who loves Americans, all Americans, no matter what their race or religion might be."

Lafayette, man (Mark Schneider) and beer (a French-inspired golden ale).

The Americans of Lafayette's day would need his help quicker than they had expected. Not long after he received his commission, the Marquis was pressed into service. As we have seen, Saratoga was only one of two major campaigns mounted by the British in 1777. While Burgoyne was marching down from Canada through New York State, the Howe brothers were sailing south from New York City with some sixteen thousand troops. After nearly five weeks at sea, they disembarked in Maryland in the upper reaches of the Chesapeake Bay, headed for Philadelphia. Washington moved to stop the Redcoats in the Brandywine Valley, about thirty miles east of the American capital.

The morning after my encounter with the Lafayettes (the man and the beer), Nico and I and some of the other members drove south to explore the lead-up to the Battle of Brandywine, where the young Frenchman first found glory. We headed for the Hale-Byrnes House in Delaware, a handsome brick building on the banks of the Cristiana River, south of Brandywine Creek. On September 6, 1777, the Marquis celebrated his twentieth birthday here with Washington and his other officers. Local Friends of Lafayette were waiting for us with a spread of food and a birthday cake laid out on a table behind the house, with a view of ducks paddling in the reeds.

"The eyes of all America and of Europe are turned upon us," Washington wrote in his general orders. A victory would be most welcome, but more importantly, he needed to avoid a crushing defeat as he defended the capital. The Main Army had to survive. At the Hale-Byrnes House, Washington held a counsel of war with Lafayette and his other officers, planning their stand.

Unfortunately, when the battle came, Washington once again was out-generaled. While he concentrated on repelling a British assault on the center of his lines, the main body of Redcoats stealthily forded the creek upstream and surprised his right flank. Although Washington's men fought bravely, "the fortune of the day declared against the Americans," Warren wrote.

One bright spot was the heroism of Casimir Pulaski, the Horseman, who charged the British lines with "bravery and enterprising spirit," keeping an American wing from breaking. The Tech Man, de Fleury, also got into the action; his horse was shot out from under him.

Observing this chaos from the command station, Lafayette wanted nothing more than to join his brothers in arms, both American and European. Even though the Continental Congress had granted Lafayette a major generalship, the title was meant to be for show. No one (except for Lafayette himself) had dreamed that he would actually fight in combat. He was far too valuable for that; he needed to survive the war and then return home to Versailles to talk up the American cause.

The Marquis begged Washington for permission to ride to support the Continentals' crumbling flank, the most dangerous place to be in the United States that day. The general, perhaps distracted by the battle in front of him, assented. Washington would be forever grateful that he had. Lafayette rallied the American line and exhorted the Patriots to hold their ground. His "distinguished gallantry," as Warren put it, continued until the Patriots, overwhelmed by a superior force, finally had to fall back. Only then did he realize that one of his boots had filled with blood. Filled with adrenaline, he hadn't even noticed that a musket ball had slammed into his left calf.

Even after he was led off the battlefield, the boy general wasn't done, inspiring the retreating troops to form an orderly column as they crossed a stone bridge over Chester Creek to the north. His "zeal and heroism," Warren wrote, "procured him the love, respect, and best wishes of the people throughout America." After the battle, with General Nathanael Greene wryly noting that "the Marquis is determined to be in the way of danger," Congress agreed to give the young man his own active command.

"Brandywine was important," Mark Schneider had told me, "because you never know how someone will do on the battlefield until they get there. Lafayette showed to George Washington—and himself—that he was ready to die for the cause."

At the Hale-Byrnes House that day, we Friends of Lafayette sang a happy birthday for the brave Frenchman. One singer stood out from the rest, a guy in the corner dressed in the uniform of a Continental artilleryman, a dark coat with red-and-gold trim. He was in his thirties, with a mustache and a calm expression on his face.

I sidled up to him afterward. His name was Joshua Peter Loper, he told me, and his family had deep ties to the Revolution, with some ancestors fighting at Brandywine. He led Nico and me to the front of the house, before an ancient sycamore tree with flaking bark, a drooping canopy of leaves, and a hollowed-out trunk. "This tree was already old in 1777," he said. "The council of war met right under it."

The tree was now mostly rotten, he told us. While just about everyone else had given up on it, though, Joshua couldn't bear to see it succumb to time. He had been making cuttings of the tree and trying to get them to grow in his apartment. After much trial and error, some of the cuttings survived. He's been donating the new trees to parks and other public spaces. "This way, the tree can survive for another three hundred years," he said.

"That's amazing," I replied. I wonder what Lafayette and Washington would have thought of the efforts a stranger would make in the future to preserve the memory of that day they spent under the tree's canopy. It surely had been a birthday for Lafayette to remember, the one right before the battle that would change his life—and help the cause. For Lafayette's heroism at Brandywine not only sparked his rise to fame but also gave Americans hope, a commodity that had been in short supply.

The Continental Army would soon need all the hope they could get. Two weeks after Brandywine, the British marched into Philadelphia. Washington, frustrated, attacked the British army camped outside the capital, aiming to surprise them. While the Battle of Germantown started promisingly, the Americans made strategic blunders in the heavy fog and wound up losing again. At least Washington had shown he was willing to fight. And his army remained intact. For now.

Not long after, word came south of the great triumph at Saratoga. While Washington had not been able to pair it with his own victory on the battlefield, he had managed to keep his army alive, thanks in part to the European additions to his forces. This was of the utmost diplomatic importance; even with the American success at Saratoga, the French likely would have turned down the overtures to form an alliance had the Main Army been destroyed.

Now, the Continentals were about to face one of their greatest ordeals, one in which survival itself would be tantamount to victory. In December, the tired general brought his troops to overwinter in Valley Creek, northwest of Pennsylvania, to camp alongside an iron forge in the shadows of Mount Joy and Mount Misery.

"I'm freezing to death," Nico said, and I couldn't blame him. My own hands had started shaking from the cold.

"Welcome to Valley Forge!" a jovial reenactor replied. "That's part of the experience. If you freeze, we'll chip you out in the morning."

I had wanted to visit Valley Forge with my son in the rawness of December to feel a glimmer of what the Continental soldiers were going through there. Now, with our cheeks turning blue, this decision seemed dubious. At least I had timed our trip to the park's annual celebration of Washington's march-in to his winter quarters, so there'd be plenty of reenactors to commiserate about the weather with. Nico left the freezing log huts and made a beeline for a campfire.

"Where ya from?" asked a young drummer, who was also warming up.

"Virginia," Nico responded.

"Well, you're in the right place then. This is where the Fourth Virginia Regiment was stationed in 1777." This news brought cold comfort to Nico, who had practically climbed into the fire in an effort to stay warm.

"So, do you want to join the army?" the drummer asked, pointing down at his feet. We saw they were covered in rags, not shoes. "Hope you don't mind weevils in your hardtack. They do provide protein."

Valley Forge was the great crucible for the American army. Washington's army was "nearly destitute of tents, poorly supplied with provisions, almost without shoes, stockings, blankets, or other clothing," Warren wrote. Their "marches over the snowy path had been marked by their bleeding feet." Meanwhile, the British, "in high health and spirits, lay in Philadelphia," she continued, only twenty-five miles away from the American camp.

Having lost the two battles he had fought in the fall of 1777, Washington faced a whisper campaign against him, with some officers disparaging him and even angling for his job. Yet his army remained intact. Americans sent a report of the triumph at Saratoga—and of the survival of Washington's army farther south—on a speedy brig, which left for France on October 30. American leaders prayed that the news would be enough to bring the French into the war.

At Valley Forge, I struck up a conversation with a park ranger who also was drawn to the fire, a bearded man named Dave Lawrence, wearing a colonial-style wool coat over a blue-and-buff Continental uniform. "Wool was wonderful," he told us. "It has great wick and keeps you warm. The problem was that there was not nearly enough wool in America to clothe the army. We got most of our wool from England and—surprise! They didn't want to sell it to us anymore. We got thousands of yards of wool smuggled in from France, but that still wasn't enough."

"Why were things so bad here at Valley Forge?" Nico asked.

"Most of the time here, it was cold," Lawrence replied. "They had freezing rain. That's worse than snow; it soaked in. If the ground were frozen, wagons could move, sleighs could go over snow. But they couldn't get through mud.

"There were lot of shortages," he continued. "The army had supplies, but it didn't have the logistical means to get them here. A true fighter looks to logistics; that's been said many times. That's been true throughout history, from ancient Alexandria to Ukraine today."

This breakdown—driven also by the worthless Continental paper money, which some local farmers refused to accept—left Washington with a "hungry and half-naked soldiery," as Warren put it. We thanked the reenactors (who were all mercifully clothed) and wandered among the recreated huts. "This is the best day to visit Valley Forge," Nico said. "You really feel for how they lived." The sweet smell of burning wood drifted over, and the sun shone bravely in the sky. I thought about how lucky I was to spend this moment with my son.

"Dad, this trip has really inspired me," he said, looking up at me with wide eyes. My heart warmed a few more watts.

"Inspired to do what, buddy?"

"I'm going to add some log huts to my Minecraft world."

A couple of hours later, the Continental soldiers marched to a clearing behind the huts of Valley Forge to the sound of fifes and drums. "That was great," one of the reenactors called out when the musicians stopped. "Know any Van Halen?"

The company's commander, a major wearing a blue greatcoat, ignored the comment and turned to the crowd. "We'll now show you some light maneuvers and a firing demonstration." His men cut out the joking and sprang into action. They executed a wheeling maneuver ("we're not here for anarchy," the major barked at his troops) and then presented arms. "We'll show you the steps set out by Baron von Steuben for firing," he told the crowd. "It shows the training the soldiers received." The major shouted the commands, retorts reverberated in the valley, and plumes of blue smoke rose into the air.

The commander was none other than Ken Gavin, the historian and versatile reenactor. At Washington's Crossing of the Delaware, he played the role of Colonel John Glover, in charge of getting the boats across the river. Here at Valley Forge, he was doing his more regular gig as a major in Spencer's Additional Regiment.

"My own ancestor was here at Valley Forge," he told me later. "After Trenton, he was at Brandywine and Germantown and then came here. He got crippled from exposure. I do this to keep his memory alive.

"When you're out here, doing it physically yourself, you appreciate it a lot more," he added. "You can read about it, but to really understand it, you have to come out here."

Nico and Ken Gavin.

I asked Ken about Baron von Steuben—I had pointed out a remembrance to the Prussian earlier that day when we visited the nearby Washington Memorial Chapel, an Episcopal church built in the early twentieth century to honor those who contributed to the American victory. Inside, it was dark, filled with flickering candles, with a faint scent of incense hanging in the air. Near the altar was a small statue of Washington, framed by a pair of old French flags.

Thirteen stained-glass windows glowed softly. On closer inspection, I could see that each featured scenes from the Revolutionary War and other moments in American history. Lafayette, like Washington and Jefferson, got his own window. Von Steuben wasn't stained glass–worthy, but he was featured in the Porch of Allies, a corridor that led from the chapel to the bell tower. On the ground was a plaque with the Prussian's coat of arms; other plaques featured those of other allied officers, including the Polish cavalryman Pulaski.

"Von Steuben was a really unique character, a seasoned military officer, and a member of the minor nobility too," Ken replied. "He wasn't a desk job kind of guy. He came as a volunteer, with no promise of rank or pay. George Washington saw value in his background and abilities. He told him, if you can help me professionalize this army, you can get a commission here.

"Baron von Steuben started here in February 1778 by observing. He wrote to a friend that European soldiers always obey orders without question. These Americans, they first want to understand why an order was issued. That's something unique about the American psyche."

"So, what kind of work did he do here at Valley Forge?" I asked.

"He started by forming a model company to drill," Ken responded. "He was very hands-on. And by doing that, he sent a message to the other officers—if you're going to lead, you've got to be intimately involved. He drilled the men for months. It was a culture shock, in a way. But he made the army at Valley Forge more unified."

"How about Louis Duportail?" I asked, about the man I had dubbed the Brains of the Operation.

"Yes, he was here too," Ken replied. "He had been a cartographer. He designed the defenses at Valley Forge. I know that Washington relied on him a lot."

De Fleury, the Tech Man, also assisted von Steuben with the training. Prior to that, the French lieutenant colonel had improved the defenses of Fort Mifflin, on the Delaware River, so well that the fort withstood an all-out assault from the British navy, only falling after three weeks of bombardment. De Fleury's genius had come close to preventing General

Howe from supplying his troops in Philadelphia and provided a major morale boost for the Americans.

And, of course, they were joined at Valley Forge by the irrepressible Marquis, who bought clothes and firearms for his regiment. He even made an unthinkable sacrifice for a French aristocrat, drinking water when the camp ran out of wine. *Quelle horreur!* Yet the European Avengers weren't the only foreigners in camp—plenty of rank-and-file soldiers joined their ranks. By some estimates, around 30 percent of Washington's army was born abroad. Many soldiers spoke German as their native language, while others came originally from Ireland.

By spring, things were looking up in camp—and not just thanks to the European transplants. The new quartermaster general, Nathanael Greene, had improved the flow of food and other supplies into camp. The whisper campaign against Washington finally died down as Americans rallied around the leader who had managed to keep his army together during that difficult winter.

The Patriots also continued to receive help from the Oneida, their first allies. "The Oneidas have manifested the strongest attachment to us throughout this dispute," General Washington wrote in March 1778, requesting a detachment to join him at Valley Forge. As scouts, the Oneida could help protect the camp and alert the Continentals to any roaming British reconnaissance parties. Lafayette seconded the request, and the Oneida answered the call.

In April, a leading Oneida sachem, Grasshopper, sent forty-seven warriors off with a speech extolling them to be courageous—if they were, it would "resound through the American army, be noticed by General Washington the Chief warrior and finally reach the ears of our father the French King." According to stories passed down through generations, as Ron Patterson told me when I visited with him, an Oneida woman on the expedition, Polly Cooper, would even demonstrate to camp cooks how to make the tribe's famous hulled corn soup.

Despite these bright spots, in the spring of 1778, realistic observers still saw a difficult future ahead for the Continentals. Even after Saratoga, the British army in America remained far more powerful than what the Patriots had to counter it with, while His Majesty's Navy was unparalleled on the seas. When the roads thawed, many expected that the British would march out of Philadelphia to mop up the rebels once and for all. Even the optimistic Lafayette had to admit that "the American situation was never more critical."

The United States clearly needed the help of a "powerful friend among the princes of the earth to establish our liberty and independence upon lasting foundations," as Washington wrote later. Otherwise, the Revolution might come crashing to a halt. And there was still only one obvious candidate for the job of powerful friend: a certain British-hating, cheese-munching, wine-drinking monarchy that also possessed the largest army in the world. The debate among Patriot leaders as to the need for a formal military alliance with France had long since been resolved: We would like one very much, *s'il vous plaît*. Now the question was whether Vergennes would deliver.

And here's where Lafayette truly stepped up. Following his madcap dash from Spain, the young Marquis had become a symbol, the Hero of Two Worlds. For the rest of 1777, all people wanted to talk about in the cafés of Paris and the ballrooms of Versailles were Lafayette and the Continental Army. Trading on his fame, he began a letter-writing campaign to French leaders, encouraging France to join in. Soon, even Queen Marie-Antoinette wanted to know why her husband wasn't doing more to help the brave insurgents.

Helping popularize the ultimate French decision to enter the war, I concluded, was one of Lafayette's greatest accomplishments. For that alone, he deserves to be remembered, on stained-glass windows, by reenactors, in the names of towns, all of it. Even the tree that he and Washington stood under has been rightfully preserved and reborn.

Now that I had come to appreciate the work of some of his fellow European volunteers, though, I only wish they too were remembered a little better. They had helped keep Washington's army alive; if it had crumbled, France would almost certainly have sat out the war. Kosciuszko, who designed the defenses at Saratoga; Pulaski and de Fleury, who helped save the crumbling American line at Brandywine; Duportail, who kept the men safe at Valley Forge; and that boisterous Prussian, von Steuben, who made the Continentals into a truly professional army—they all helped to keep the cause afloat that dark year. If not a full-fledged tree, they each deserve, at the least, a fine shrub.

Thanks to these contributions, the Americans were able to present themselves as a viable partner to the French. The Continentals had more defeats than victories, but they remained in the field and were not about to leave it. That was exactly what Vergennes wanted to hear.

On May 2, a rider arrived at Valley Forge with some of the most stunning news of the war: America and France had signed two treaties—a Treaty of Amity and Commerce, in which France recognized the United States as a sovereign nation, and a Treaty of Alliance, which would allow France to enter the war. After nearly two years of insider work, Vergennes had gotten Louis XVI to approve the decision that the foreign minister had wanted all along. And Benjamin Franklin finally got farther than the future information kiosk in Versailles; he was received with pomp and solemnity in the King's Great Chamber.

When the camp received news of the alliance, "no event was ever received with a more heartfelt joy," Washington wrote. Lafayette was so excited that he burst into headquarters and kissed the stoic commander in chief on both cheeks. Washington, recovering his composure, issued orders to his troops, setting "a day apart...for celebrating the Important Event."

"What were the celebrations of the French alliance like at Valley Forge?" I asked Ken Gavin, the reenactor. "I read there were firing demonstrations. Would that have been anything like what you all did?"

He chuckled. "A little, but those demonstrations were much, much bigger. The entire army came out. They put on something called the *feu de joie*, the fire of joy. They lined up and shot in turns. The fire started at one end, then people fired in succession, so the fire was rolling all through the line. Imagine that, ten thousand men firing—it must have been something to see."

The men fired and huzzahed the King of France, fired again and huzzahed the Friendly European Powers, and fired one last time for the American States. The rum flowed freely. Officers ate barbeque and played ball games, with even Washington taking a turn at bat. It was the "greatest day ever yet experienced in our independent world of liberty," one contented colonel wrote.

"By some accounts, George Washington was ripping drunk by end of the day," Ken went on. "It's a human reaction. With France in the war, they could threaten the British West Indies, the west coast of Africa, India—they could possibly even invade Britain itself. That changed the complexity of the war. Britain was stretched globally. Britain's ability to focus on North America was now reduced.

"So the celebration of the French alliance was more than just 'yay, we've got a partner.' Americans understood what the French were able to do at the time. And the Americans wouldn't have won it without them."

After hearing all that, I didn't blame Washington for having one too many at the party honoring the French alliance. He had survived the debacle at New York in 1776. He had endured with smuggled arms and gunpowder, with raw recruits and farm boys. Against all odds, he had outlasted the greatest military force in the world. And now he had survived a winter that had sought to kill him and his men.

Many hardships and setbacks surely awaited. But for Washington's men that glorious spring day, why not celebrate? America's future shone bright. Washington would never again bear the full brunt of the British Empire's wrath. The Revolution was no longer a provincial conflict: It was now a world war and we had allies to help us fight it.

Part Two

THE WORLD WAR

1778–1780

Chapter Eight

LOST IN TRANSLATION

Why the French Alliance Got Off to a Rocky Start

June–December 1778

"Follow me," said a man dressed in a black coat and black tri-corner hat, "and I'll try to keep the prostitutes away."

I've attended my share of historical reenactments, but that's a line I've never heard in, say, Colonial Williamsburg. Just another reminder that I was in France (and just as well that I hadn't brought the kids along on this trip).

The man in black—playing the role of the steward of the estate—led our group of about ten visitors to a pasture, where we watched farmers chattering as they raked hay, talking about the military camp that had just been installed in the region. The steward then brought us up a hill toward the château looming at the top. Along the way, we fell in with three soldiers wearing blue greatcoats, marching with their muskets on their shoulders.

"I can't lie, I must tell you that these training exercises were more than necessary," said one of the men, with a closely cropped goatee. "We've become flabby from such a long peace."

"The insurgents are keeping the English busy over in the New World," said one of his companions.

"Those cursed English won't be laughing when we get done with them!" said the third.

"Ooh, *mon cheri!*" cooed a woman in a low-cut dress, who came running toward the soldiers. "This one's mine!"

"No, I saw him first," said another gleefully.

One of the Reenacting Prostitutes sidled up to the group and pulled a tourist out of it, to the incredulity of the man's wife. "Your cologne smells so good," she purred. "Won't you give me a coin? Or a kiss?" He turned as bright red as her dress.

"Begone!" a priest yelled, rushing into the scene and scattering the ladies of the night.

The priest then returned to his meal; he was dining on a wooden table under a tent. Finally, a little sense, I thought. Maybe this reenactment will get back on the rails and begin to resemble the serious ones that I'm used to.

"*Vin rouge*," the priest called out to a servant, who poured some actual red wine into his cup, which he slurped down. No, we're still in France.

If nothing else, the episode reminded me that, while the French and Americans have much in common, we're not the same. I had embarked on a journey to understand one of the stranger years of the war, 1778, the first one with France in it. The French and the Americans began with the greatest of hopes; some thought that they'd finish off the British in a matter of months. Yet the year ended with more defeats for the allies than victories. Why did the alliance get off to such a bad start?

Un Nouveau Monde, A New World, as the event was called, was a good place to start my exploration. It was indeed a reenactment unlike any other I had been to, and not just because of the booze and hookers. The French have so much history to choose from—the Gauls, the Middle

Ages, the Belle Epoque—that it's hard for them to make room for this chapter of their past, although it's one they should be proud of. Yet here at least, at a small château called Vaussieux in Normandy, not too far from the English Channel, a nonprofit group was staging an elaborate theatrical event involving some 140 local volunteers in period costume. They were gamely reenacting that time in September 1778 when these Norman fields and pastures turned into a training ground for the entire French army.

Thanks to my earlier research on Vergennes, I knew that before agreeing to the treaty with the Americans, he had taken one last run at persuading Spain to join as an ally too. "Nothing can justify," he had written to the Spanish foreign minister, the Count of Floridablanca, "letting slip through our fingers the only opportunity in many centuries to put England in its place."

But Spain demurred. It didn't have the same interest that France had in restoring the balance of power. No, if they entered the war, it would be on their own terms, with a demand that the allies work together to regain Spanish territory taken by the British. Spain especially longed to recover Gibraltar, the stronghold on the Mediterranean that Britain had seized in 1704. Also, its great treasure fleets had not yet returned from the New World; the Spanish worried that a declaration of war would cause Britain to intercept them. Let us get our treasure first, then we'll talk. By entering the war prematurely, Floridablanca grumbled, the Comte de Vergennes was acting like Don Quixote, rushing into risk.

Vergennes didn't like these demands, not even *un petit peu*. In particular, taking Gibraltar seemed like a fool's errand. Had Floridablanca actually seen Gibraltar? It was a fourteen-hundred-foot-tall mountain, crowned by guns. He was also cool to Spain's other genius idea, invading England. The Spanish thought that the specter of French and Spanish armies landing at Plymouth and marching toward London would panic King George so much that he would sue for peace then and there. For the skeptical French foreign minister, the plan just sounded like a disaster waiting to happen.

No matter. Vergennes was determined to bring France into the conflict, even if he had to do so without Spain. True, the British navy was more powerful than the French, with sixty-six ships of the line to France's fifty-two. But if the French suddenly entered the war, they would have the element of surprise. Britain's ships and soldiers were spread out across the world; France could choose when and where to make a strike. Vergennes hoped then to win the war with one quick campaign in 1778, before Britain could build up its navy in turn. If that didn't work, though, he'd have to come groveling back to Spain and accept whatever demands they made in order to coax them into the war.

And so, following the treaties it signed with America, France began preparing in earnest for the expected onslaught against their sworn enemies. Since its thirty-five-thousand-man army hadn't seen action since the Seven Years' War, French generals split their forces into two and sent them into a two-week-long training exercise in Normandy, near where the reenactment was taking place today, where they would conduct pretend battles.

The French encampment was three times larger than the American one at Valley Forge had been. The French troops were far better clothed (in gleaming white uniforms) and fed (with considerably fewer weevils in their bread and a whole lot more red wine in their cups). Yet the French generals faced a challenge similar to the one Washington had confronted: How could they turn their men into a fighting force ready to take on the British?

To that end, the troops were doing more than camping out—they were drilling in the field and testing out different styles of battle. The soldiers were divided into two armies. One, employing the style of fighting in columns that emphasized heavy, powerful charges, was led by the Maréchal de Broglie, the army's overall commander. The other, their pretend opponents in the exercise, was led by an up-and-coming general named the Comte de Rochambeau, who was trying out a style of attack emphasizing quicker firing instead.

The steward escorted us into the château. The premise of the event was that we tourists were locals who had to lodge a soldier in our home during the war games, and we were looking for de Broglie (who was staying here) to make the proper arrangements.

A duel at Vaussieux.

It was a clever pretext to show how the war affected everyday French people. For it wasn't just French soldiers and sailors who helped out the Americans—the entire country mobilized to support their men at war. Sending an army overseas took a village, and here we were seeing that village in action. Older women spoke on how they'd survive as their sons and husbands went off to war, young ladies danced with officers at a ball, and farmers upped their grain production to feed the army, hoping that the military wouldn't simply confiscate it. Even the scene with prostitutes was grounded in reality, it turned out; entire battalions finished the training exercise laid low with syphilis. (The French were practicing all sorts of things in Normandy.)

"We want this history to be remembered," the group's organizer, Bertrand Bailleul, had told me. I had met him only minutes before the event started; he was tall and resplendently dressed in white furls of lace and a black tri-corner hat with gold trim. "And we would love for

American tourists to come to see it." I seemed to have been the only one they had ever had.

Yet many Americans came to visit the region, he told me, for Vaussieux is only ten miles from Juno Beach. Driving here from Bayeux, the closest city, I had passed cemetery after cemetery, wedged between the cornfields, where the allied dead were laid to rest. Who knew that when American GIs landed on D-Day in 1944, they were retracing the steps of the French army and navy that once assembled in Normandy to liberate the New World?

As I was speaking with Bertrand, a couple came up to join us, and the organizer introduced them to me—the Count and Countess de Bonvouloir. I was struck almost speechless.

"*The* Count de Bonvouloir? Like the one who went to America?" I had already visited Carpenters' Hall to see the spot where the French emissary had met in secret with Benjamin Franklin at the very beginning of the war. And I had learned how he had gone with Franklin on the diplomatic mission to Montreal as well.

"Yes, he was my ancestor." The Count smiled. I was as stunned as if I had been walking along Boston's Freedom Trail, thinking of the Revolution, and someone suddenly emerged from an alley telling me his name was Revere. Didier de Bonvouloir did what he could to preserve the memory of his ancestor, who came from this region. I couldn't talk long—my group had just left to start the pageant, and it was the last tour of the day. But he slipped me his card, which, fittingly enough, had a drawing of a unicorn on it. Nor would this be the last time I would find myself on Bonvouloir's trail on my travels. Like an eighteenth-century version of Forrest Gump, he seemed to pop up in this revolutionary world war when I least expected it.

Inside the château, our group finally found the elusive de Broglie, who was sitting at the head of a banquet table that groaned with food. Waving a wine goblet in one hand (no doubt filled with the real deal), he proposed a series of toasts.

"To the *Belle Poule!*" he began. The tourists shared confused looks. To the Beautiful Chicken? Thanks to Mercy Otis Warren, though, I knew exactly what he meant. Earlier in 1778, a few months before these war games began in the Norman countryside, the actual Franco-British war started on the seas.

In June 1778, France sent the *Belle Poule*, the finest frigate ever named after poultry, into the English Channel looking for a fight. (The French sense of humor has always been different.) France's military alliance with the rebels would only kick in *if* fighting broke out between France and its hereditary foes; France didn't want to seem as if it were instigating the war. Being the victim of another country's aggression might also trigger certain treaties of defense.

To the delight of the French, the British warship *Arethusa* intercepted the *Belle Poule* off Cornwall and ordered it to report to the main British squadron, which planned to quiz the French captain of this bantam ship about his intentions. When the French said *non*, the *Arethusa* fired a warning shot across the *Belle Poule*'s bow to emphasize the order.

Voila! The British had shot first, just what the French in their sacrificial chicken ship were waiting for. The *Belle Poule* responded, Warren wrote, with "the discharge of a whole broadside" into the *Arethusa*'s hull. A "severe action ensured," she went on, with both sides suffering heavy casualties. The French frigate "escaped only by running into a small bay on the coast of France." All of France was taken by the *Belle Poule*'s pluck. Society ladies at Versailles even began wearing their hair in a new fashion, with a replica of the *Belle Poule* perched on top of their head. And as planned, following the battle, King Louis XVI solemnly declared that his nation was now at war. The Beautiful Chicken would be avenged.

In the pageant feast, de Broglie's next toast was to Ushant, a much larger naval battle that occurred a month after the warm-up act (and which, you may be relieved to find out, provides no opportunity for poultry-based humor) some one hundred miles west of an island at the mouth of the English Channel. The French sent thirty-two ships of the line with plans "to strike at the trade of [the British] by interrupting their convoys and giving a wound to the honor of the English navy, which would redound much to their own advantage in the outset of a war," Warren wrote. His Majesty's Navy responded by sending its own squadron, of about the same size, to counter the French.

The result of the battle was a tactical draw, although at the cost of some seventeen hundred casualties—far more than would occur in any battle in the United States in 1778. Even though they didn't win, the French had proven that they could hold their own against a navy that, for years, had been "controlling the nations and defying the universe to attack their fleets," as Warren put it. (And with all these distractions, was anyone noticing the Spanish treasure ships slowly making their way home, far to the south?)

The ceremony at Vaussieux wound up with a few last toasts. "*Vive la France!*" de Broglie cried, holding up his glass.

"*Vive la France!*" we all responded.

"*Vive l'Amérique!*" he cried out.

"*Vive l'Amérique!*" we replied, with my voice the loudest of all.

Vergennes would have wanted a "*Vive Espagne!*" added to that list, but in the late summer of 1778, Spain still hadn't chosen to join the alliance. The fighting in the English Channel had been inconclusive; the French hadn't won any quick victories there. Instead, France's hopes were pinned on a naval campaign that was unfolding on the other side of the Atlantic. While the British focused on the threat in the north, a separate fleet of seventeen warships commanded by the Comte d'Estaing was sailing from the Mediterranean to America. D'Estaing's ships would outnumber the British navy's in the United States and hopefully catch them by surprise.

Could d'Estaing possibly end the war with one well-timed campaign? Vergennes certainly hoped so. If not, the French minister would have to crawl back to Spain and agree to its exorbitant demands. And he would no doubt have to deploy the enormous army training in Normandy against the British Empire somewhere—at a place of Spain's choosing.

As I was leaving the château, I ran into the event's organizer, Bertrand, again at the entrance. He gifted me a copy of a book written about the French at Vaussieux, which included a chapter written by Didier de Bonvouloir. When I read it later, I discovered that the original Bonvouloir's service in the Revolution didn't end at Carpenters' Hall or in Quebec. He had more adventures to come in the war, even journeying to the site of what would prove to be the final battle of the war, thousands of miles from here, where I'd encounter his traces once more. Didier de Bonvouloir's choice of a unicorn on his business card was a fitting one, for his ancestor truly was one.

Bertrand pressed a glass of Norman cider into my hand. I sipped it and took my leave of Vaussieux, the place where thousands mobilized—soldiers and generals, farmers and prostitutes alike—to prepare the French army for the difficult journey to come.

"Don't forget us!" Bertrand called out as I left. "We helped you get your independence!"

Indeed, they would. But the war would not end in 1778 as Vergennes had hoped. Far from it. That year was about to take a turn for the worse—and the allies would have no one to blame but themselves.

In the spring of 1778, the British prepared to evacuate Philadelphia. If there was any poetic justice in the world, this would have occurred because Washington's men, having survived their ordeal at Valley Forge, had come back stronger and better trained and forced the enemy out of the capital once and for good. A redemption arc—that would make a good screenplay, wouldn't it?

But the reality was nothing like that. The British departure had little to do with the threat posed by the Continentals. What the British were now focused on was the French. "The object of the war being now changed" the British Admiralty advised Admiral Howe in Philadelphia, "and the contest in America being a secondary consideration, our principal objects must be distressing France and defending...his Majesty's possessions." London ordered the Redcoats to abandon the American capital and make their way to New York, where five thousand of them would then be convoyed to the Caribbean. There they would protect Jamaica and perhaps seize a French colony or two as well. "Our islands must be defended," King George III sputtered. "[I]f we lose our sugar islands, it will be impossible to raise money to continue the war and then no peace can be obtained."

On May 20, 1778, Washington sent Lafayette out with his regiment and some Oneida warriors to see if, as rumor had it, the British really were planning to leave. Instead, after crossing the Schuylkill River, the Marquis blundered his way into a trap. The British sent a larger force after him, pinning him across the river. During my time at the Shako:wi Cultural Center, Ron Patterson told me about the battle that ensued.

"There were about fifteen to twenty Oneida warriors with Lafayette," he said. "But ten Oneida warriors could make themselves seem as if they were a hundred, because of their guerilla style of warfare. They ran back and forth through the woods, giving out war cries. Their voices kept moving." The ruse convinced the British that Lafayette's entire brigade planned to dig in and fight. "Oneida warriors stayed to fight the British off, while Lafayette got across the river to safety," Ron recounted. A courageous Oneida sachem died in the fighting at Barren Hill, but the young Marquis survived.

Finally, a month later, the British army slowly began making its way overland to New York. Washington attacked the rear of the British columns at Monmouth Courthouse in New Jersey, fighting to a draw. He would not engage his full army in battle again for over three years.

The Americans couldn't believe the good fortune that the French alliance had brought them. The British were on the run, and surely their new French friends would finish them off. "Houra, my good friend, now the affair is over," Lafayette wrote to the president of Congress. The Marquis wondered if he should return to France *tout de suite,* since America might no longer be the best place for him to make his name in battle.

Similarly, Nathanael Greene asked if he should stop gathering food for the army. Washington reminded him that the war was not yet over. "There may still be business enough to call for our most strenuous efforts," he replied. Even so, privately, the commander in chief wrote to his friend Richard Henry Lee that he now expected a "plain and easy road to independence." He wondered if Britain would even choose to stay in New York or instead evacuate it too, so as to fight France elsewhere. But then the problems began.

Admiral d'Estaing arrived with his fleet in Delaware Bay on July 8. Yet the star-crossed French admiral would meet "with a series of disappointments" that year, Warren wrote. The first came when he failed to arrive in time to attack the British, who were highly vulnerable as they ferried across a river in their retreat from Philadelphia, thanks to the nearly three-month-long, escargot-like pace he took across the Atlantic.

Disappointment Number Two came when he then failed to attack the British after they had reached New York, cautiously concluding that he wouldn't be able to get his large ships across the sandbar in front of New York Harbor. Whether this was a wise decision or not (did he get the right information from local pilots?), Americans were already were grumbling at d'Estaing's lack of action.

The admiral promised to make it up to them, sailing to Newport, Rhode Island, to seize the British naval base there. The plan was for him to land his four thousand French soldiers to the west of Newport while American forces under General John Sullivan would attack the port from the east.

Yet the operation immediately ran into trouble. D'Estaing and Sullivan squabbled over whose troops had the honor of moving on Newport first and whose men would get to occupy the high ground. And then a British fleet showed up offshore. D'Estaing immediately sailed out to meet it—but ran straight into a fierce storm, which mauled his ships.

The Americans on land, now without French naval support, were suddenly in grave danger.

The battle that ensued might have turned into a catastrophe had it not been for the bravery of the American defenders—including the Patriots' first largely Black regiment, the First Rhode Island. To learn more about those soldiers, I met up with the president of the current First Rhode Island Regiment reenactors' group, Antoine Randolph Watts, after he finished a reenacting event.

Antoine was about my age (that is to say, middle-aged, sigh), with a fife in one hand. A trained flautist, he sometimes added eighteenth-century music to his reenactments. He showed me a striking black hat with blue-and-white plumes, with an anchor and the word *Hope* on it.

"This is a reproduction of the leather helmets that the First Rhode Island wore," he said. "The anchor is because Rhode Island was a seafaring colony. They couldn't get enough White manpower in the regiment because most men were going to sea—they made more money in privateering. So, Rhode Island turned to recruiting Blacks and Native Americans." The African American recruits included both free Blacks and enslaved men who would win their freedom through service (including some men who had been born in Africa). "The motto of the regiment was 'I've come to fight for my freedom,'" Antoine told me.

The political leaders of Rhode Island, facing criticism from slave owners, did an about-face and stopped recruiting additional enslaved soldiers after only four months. Many of the Black soldiers would face discrimination and mistreatment by their White counterparts. Yet they would serve honorably throughout the war, including at Newport. Thousands of Blacks would serve on the Patriot side; even more joined the Crown forces, hoping that would secure their freedom.

Antoine recounted the story of the August 1778 Battle of Rhode Island. "The Americans under Sullivan were to the north of Newport. They were *supposed* to be getting naval support from the French. But due to miscommunication and a bad storm, the French withdrew and went down to Boston to refit. The British, after seeing the French leave, attacked."

"How did the fighting go?" I asked.

"The British sent the Hessians towards the left flank of the Americans. There they met with a company of the First Rhode Island, which fell back. These were green troops, who hadn't been able to train. But when they reached Butt's Hill, they reformed and poured a devastating fire on the Hessians. Along with the Second Rhode Island, they were able to repel three advances of the Hessians," coming in for praise after the battle from General Sullivan, Antoine told me.

"Newport was a holding action," he continued. "The Americans pushed back the British and Hessians but then had to retreat." The lack of French naval support doomed any further allied operations in Rhode Island. Sullivan was furious, claiming that the French had abandoned the Americans "in a most rascally manner," leaving them to face a British onslaught alone. "This disappointment occasioned some temporary murmurings against the conduct of D'Estaing," Warren wrote, "and even the connection with France." It was the French admiral's third failure in only two months' time in the States.

Antoine Randolph Watts portraying a sergeant in the First Rhode Island.

Meanwhile, tensions rose in the city of Boston, now swelled by thousands of French soldiers and sailors. Bostonians had long resented the French, their foes in the Seven Years' War; nor was the French troops' Catholicism popular in this Puritan town. D'Estaing's abrupt departure from Newport only infuriated them more. Some angry American shipwrights refused to repair the French vessels. French and American men fought outside a Boston bakery, probably because Americans resented that the city's bread was now going to French sailors who could pay with hard currency. Worst of all, a mob even attacked a group of French officers walking down a street, clubbing a naval lieutenant, the Chevalier de Saint Sauveur, to death.

Horrified, Washington tried to calm tensions down and ordered Sullivan to apologize. Washington worried that "first impressions are long remembered," and an American mob murdering a French officer wasn't exactly how the general had hoped to begin the alliance. The chagrined Bostonians agreed to erect a memorial to Saint Sauveur. (If you're ever walking on Boston's Freedom Trail, stop by King's Chapel, where you can still see an obelisk honoring the slain officer.) One well-meaning American merchant even hosted a dinner for French officers. Hearing that frogs were a great delicacy in France, he served each officer, to their astonishment, a soup consisting of a whole bullfrog in a bowl of liquid. Or so the story goes.

D'Estaing left for the Caribbean where, incredibly enough, even more setbacks were waiting for him. (What's with this guy, anyways?) He arrived in December 1778, a little too late to prevent the British from taking the major French sugar-producing island of St. Lucia. D'Estaing tried to take it right back, launching twenty-five hundred men against the island's fortress. The assault failed: Disappointment Number Four, in the span of just six months.

The embarrassed d'Estaing agreed to return the following year to try to retake the port city. To do so, he would rely on the services of a new regiment that had just been formed in the Caribbean, the Chasseurs-Volontaires de

Saint-Domingue. Like the First Rhode Island, this was a regiment composed of free Blacks and enslaved men serving to obtain their freedom; it also included some African-born men in uniform.

"They were an important unit," Antoine told me. "And I love their uniforms—they had a dark-blue coat with green facings, yellow shoulder strappings, and white turnbacks." Spoken like a true reenactor, I thought. The Chasseurs would even come to the United States and play a heroic role when d'Estaing tried to retake Savannah, acting just as bravely as the First Rhode Island had at Newport, even though they would be "cut up in pieces" by British fire, as Antoine put it. As had happened at Newport, the failure to coordinate well between the French and Americans meant that infantrymen would pay the price—with Black soldiers, alongside their White comrades in arms, making sacrifices in both battles.

Following the Battle of Rhode Island, things would be quiet for the First Rhode Island for a spell. Most of the war was shifting to the south, or overseas. But the regiment (later combined with another one) would continue to serve during the war, eventually showing up at Yorktown to perform more heroics. Yet, when it was all over, the state of Rhode Island failed to give them the bounties they had been promised, while some masters even attempted to re-enslave the soldiers after the war. "We still wanted to prove that we were men, just like you are," Antoine explained. "We aspired to principles of liberty and freedom. And that promise of freedom at the end was not always kept."

I asked him about what led him to portray Black soldiers in the Revolutionary War. "I always loved history as a kid," he replied. "And after I visited Yorktown, I knew I wanted to do this. Our history is *American* history. Some of us came to America because we were immigrants, some because we were forced here. That story should be told," he said in his soft voice. "If we don't tell our story, who will?"

My explorations—in both France and America—of that first year of the alliance gave me a sense of the disappointment each partner felt by the time the year ended. Both the French and Americans had assumed that the British evacuation of Philadelphia was just a prelude to greater victories to come. Yet, as 1778 drew to a close, the new partners were instead doing a postmortem on where things went wrong.

To be sure, some of the blame went to Admiral d'Estaing, who was "seldom a favorite of fortune," as Warren put it drily. But, to me anyway, it seemed that neither the French nor the Americans had figured out how to listen to each other and plan an effective joint campaign. The Patriots had sky-high expectations for what their allies could do; when the French didn't immediately deliver on them, some were quick to turn on them. If it hadn't been for the bravery of the First Rhode Island and other regiments, the Americans might have suffered a devastating defeat.

For their part, the French hadn't always valued the local knowledge—or interests—of their allies. D'Estaing hadn't worked well with his American counterparts at New York or Newport; by sailing to the Caribbean in late 1778, it seemed as if he had abandoned them. The allies needed to work on their communication and trust.

Vergennes had his own conclusions to draw from that rough year of 1778. His plan to win with a lightning campaign had failed; now the element of surprise was gone. British dockyards had spent the year building new ships of the line, and their navy would far outnumber France's in the year to come. We "cannot struggle long on equal terms with the English," Vergennes admitted to his king at the end of the year. The time had come for "combined operations" with Spain, he wrote, even if the Spanish demands were "gigantic." The French foreign minister reluctantly wrote to his Spanish counterpart, restarting the conversation about Spanish entry into the war.

At least the cagey Vergennes had prepared for this contingency. An ulterior motive for sending d'Estaing to America was to prompt the British to send their own navy after him, thereby clearing the way for the

Spanish treasure fleets, laden with silver, to return home from Mexico. Once again, Vergennes had been playing three-dimensional chess. In the fall of 1778, the fleets arrived safely in port. Now Spain would have more than enough pesos for an upcoming campaign.

If all went well, then, soon enough all those celebratory drinkers—in Valley Forge, Vaussieux, and elsewhere—would have to add another toast to the growing list. It would no longer just be "Long Live America" and "*Vive la France!*"—how about raising a glass to "*¡que viva España!*" too?

From a global perspective, 1776 had been a cry for help. 1777 was the year of the American collaboration with the Oneida and the European volunteers. 1778 belonged to the French alliance and the great hopes that it had raised. 1779, though, would be the year of Spain.

Chapter Nine

NOBODY EXPECTS THE SPANISH INTERVENTION

Gibraltar's Surprising Connection to American Independence

April 1779–January 1780

"It looks like a little Versailles," Miranda said, "except it's a lot hotter here." Aranjuez, once one of King Carlos III's four palaces, did resemble a mini version of the massive French château. It was good to be the king, I thought. Not only did he control an empire that covered a lot of what is now Latin America, much of what is now the American Southeast and West, and the Philippines to boot, he got to pick up and move to a different sumptuous residence each season. Aranjuez, his spring palace thirty miles south of Madrid, was perfect for hunting parties and leisurely cruises down the Tagus River.

We passed armed guards at the entrance. This was still an active royal palace, although neither the king nor the queen were there today, we learned. We walked through giant wooden doors and entered—something that American emissaries would have loved to do in early 1779. France had not delivered the quick victory that the Patriots had hoped for. Now American hopes were squarely placed on the potential combination of France plus Spain. If the two great powers joined, Washington wrote to Congress, that would probably compel the British "to abandon America."

Yet Spain was not prepared to receive American diplomats, not yet anyway. Doing so would mean it had recognized the United States as a sovereign nation, which would surely provoke a British attack. Sure, Spain had been heavily arming the rebels for years, but always in secret. So, for now, the Spanish officially remained neutral as the king weighed his options and figured out what course to chart.

I had come here to Aranjuez to try to answer some questions. Who was Carlos III, this ruler who held American independence in his hand? And what was at stake for Spain if it chose to enter the war?

Inside, we met Antonio, our young tour guide, who led us into the Room of Mirrors, with its shimmering glass walls, gold fringe, and beaming cherubs on the wall. "I didn't know the king had a charger port," Miranda whispered to me, noticing an electrical socket. (She was in fine form this trip.) Antonio led us through rooms filled with fantastical porcelain sculptures of dragons and saints, arabesque rugs, and a chandelier that weighed a quarter of a ton. Through the windows, we caught glimpses of gardens and fountains and a lazy river snaking its way past in the distance.

"This wasn't like in France," Antonio said, "the king didn't bring his entire court with him when he traveled from palace to palace. He only brought certain advisers."

"So there weren't as many parties here," said Liana, to some chuckles. Even if he didn't bring the entire court, Carlos III would travel with his cabinet, which included his reformist foreign minister, the Comte de Floridablanca, and the dynamic minister of the Indies, José de Gálvez. In turn, the cabinet brought with them their assistants, known as *covachuelistas,* or cave dwellers (bureaucrats have been called worse). But this collection of government workers surely wasn't throwing ragers here like the aristocrats of Versailles were.

Antonio brought us to the throne room, where two golden chairs stood on a dais of velvet. Carlos III, we learned, was the first Spanish king to start the tradition of having his own personalized throne, different from his predecessors.' "He was a great statesman, a true man of the Enlightenment," our guide said. Although he wasn't ready to grant political rights to his subjects, the monarch did help modernize his country's economy, liberalize its trade, and promote its sciences.

After all this buildup, the portrait of Carlos hanging in the king's antechamber was underwhelming. He had a goofy smile framed by a bulbous nose and a missing chin. He was clad in armor but still resembled someone cosplaying as a warrior rather than the real deal. "He looks a little like a dog," said my bemused daughter.

The king was a creature of habit, I discovered. "He didn't like parties or music," Antonio said. "He woke up every day at the same time and kept to the same routine." Carlos liked to take his chocolate in the morning, play with his egg at the table in the same way each day, eat the same meal at lunch (three kinds of soup), hunt in the afternoon no matter the weather, and take his tea each afternoon from the same teacup (until it broke after thirty years, a catastrophe).

"And now I will take you to the private rooms of the king," Antonio said. Very private indeed—here was the monarch's bathroom, featuring a plush red toilet, from which the king could contemplate scenes of gardens and woods painted on the walls. "It's his other throne room!" Miranda whispered gleefully. (Palaces seem to bring out her inner court jester.)

In 1779, the king had one of the most important decisions of his life to make. I imagined him thinking it over while he played with his breakfast egg and rode on his hunts, maybe even mulling it over when he sat on his throne (no, not that throne). Should he bring Spain into the war?

The cost might be high. Britain had demolished the Spanish in the Seven Years' War and might do so again. And even an American victory could come with a hidden downside. The Spanish worried that "the spirit of freedom might be contagious," Warren wrote. If Carlos's colonies caught this communicable disease from *los yanquis*, he'd have a whole lot less empire to govern. So much of the wealth in this palace came from the gold mines of Peru and silver mines of Mexico. What if the example of the American Revolution roused those people to independence too?

On the other hand, the war might prove to be just what Spain needed. Carlos III and Floridablanca were less concerned than the French were about restoring the balance of power in Europe. What they really wanted was their old land back. Earlier in the century, the British had seized Minorca, an island in the Mediterranean with a deepwater naval base, from the Spanish. The British had also taken over Spanish territories in Florida and Jamaica. Now British loggers were expanding operations in present-day Belize, threatening Spain's control of Central America. Yet as frustrating as all these losses were, one failure rankled Spain above all else: the British heist of Gibraltar.

In the Middle Ages, the Moors had built a towering fortress on the top of a mountain, the Rock of Gibraltar, at the southern tip of the Iberian Peninsula, which helped them control the passage into the Mediterranean. Spain took Gibraltar in the fifteenth century and held it for nearly 250 years, but the British seized it in 1704. Spanish kings had longed to regain their lost Rock ever since, as obsessively as Gollum trying to recover his ring. In 1778, Spain even negotiated with Britain over its grievances. If only the British returned their precious Gibraltar, Spain would stay neutral, they promised.

Yet King George III refused the deal—a decision that mystified Floridablanca. Why Britain insisted on hanging on to "this pile of rocks called Gibraltar," the Spanish minister wrote, "which gives them nothing except worries and expenses, troubles us, and prevents our permanent friendship," was beyond him. George Washington was flabbergasted as well. King George's insistence on holding on to a rocky promontory only two and a half square miles in area might lead Spain to enter the war—which could wind up costing Britain its control of America. Britain's obstinance on this point, Washington wrote, was "more strongly tinctured with insanity than anything she has done in the course of the contest."

But the talks at least bought Spain the time it needed to rebuild its navy—and for its treasure ships to come back. Each year or two, an armada brought gold from Peru and silver from Mexico to Spain, some of it destined for palaces like Aranjuez. Declaring war on Britain while the bling was still at sea was too risky. By the fall of 1778, thanks in part to the distractions provided by the French navy, the fleet had reached Spain safely. Spain had its ships and the money it needed, and Carlos III now had options.

With the advice of Floridablanca, the king finally reached his decision. This creature of habit, this man of inflexible routines, chose to make a move filled with risk, one that would wind up pushing the course of world history in a different direction. He said yes to war.

Yet it would be on his terms. The Spanish would go all in, but they wanted a quick campaign. As we have seen, Floridablanca had been preparing an aggressive plan of attack: immediately lay siege to Gibraltar while simultaneously invading England itself alongside their French allies. Doing so would surely panic the British and cause them to sue for peace, allowing Spain to recoup its lost territory, especially the Rock. Vergennes thought these twin plans of attack were foolhardy, yet he had no choice but to agree to them. Admiral d'Estaing had not gotten the job done the year before, and the British Empire, which had been rebuilding its own fleet, looked stronger than ever with its ninety ships of the line. France, with only sixty-three ships of the line, needed Spain to add its own fifty-eight to the equation.

And so, on April 12, 1779, right here in this palace, Spain signed a treaty with France. The French would be the only formal allies of the Spanish, who considered it too dicey to formally recognize the rebels in America yet, given the effect this might have on its own colonies. But Spain nonetheless pledged to fight for American independence and to stay in the war for as long as the French wanted to. In exchange for this,

Spain wrote its own war goals—retaking Gibraltar, Minorca, and Florida, and kicking the British out of Central America—right into the treaty, so France clearly understood what it had gotten into.

With Spain involved, Britain had a lot more to fear. Now new theaters would open up across the globe: the Mediterranean, Central America, the Gulf of Mexico, and even England itself. Wasting no time, the minister José de Gálvez wrote secret letters to his brother Mathías, the captain-general of Guatemala, and nephew Bernardo, the acting governor of Louisiana, sharing the news. They were to commence hostilities against the British two months after receiving their letter. The world war was on.

At the end of our tour, Antonio brought us to the banquet room, which was decked out in a rococo style, with chandeliers blazing. I imagined Carlos sitting down to celebrate his great decision, perhaps sipping an extra glass of wine with his habitual three bowls of soup. I bet even the cave dwellers were popping Champagne, amazed at the surprisingly bold move their king had taken.

In the Caribbean, the much-maligned Comte d'Estaing threw a grand party when he heard the news; now his fleet wouldn't have to go it alone. Americans were also thrilled. "The declaration of Spain in favor of France has given universal joy" to the Patriots, Washington wrote to Lafayette, "while the poor Tory [Loyalist] droops like a withering flower under a declining sun."

After thanking Antonio, we left, walking through orchards of fig trees and past an old canal to a restaurant for our own small celebration. There, we feasted on octopus and on beef *solomillo*, washed down by Tempranillo (and Cokes for some). "That palace was really something," Liana said. "Now I know where the gold from the Americas went to."

We ordered a round of flan to end on. "This story of Spain joining the war is still new to me," Liana continued, a moment in the history of her ancestors that was not taught to her when she grew up in Cuba. "I had never heard of it before. I'm just now learning about everything

Carlos III did." For years, she said, she had crossed an avenue in Havana once named for the king but had no idea what he had done.

To understand Spain's next move in the war, we would need to travel some four hundred miles to the Mediterranean coast. It was time to see about a Rock.

"You're American? Brilliant," the young guard at the border said, stamping our passports. We had left our car in a parking lot in the Spanish town of La Linea de Concepción and walked up to an immigration checkpoint. The sunlight was blinding, the palm trees were swaying—and, strangely enough, it was time to enter Britain.

We had spent a few days rambling south from Aranjuez until we reached the narrow stretch of land connecting Gibraltar with the Spanish mainland. Today, much of it is an airstrip, but it once was known as the Neutral Ground, a shared space where British officers could exercise their horses and Gibraltarians could tend to small gardens. All that changed when Spain declared war on Britain in June 1779. The Spanish abruptly cut off all entry to Gibraltar and reinforced their fortifications at the end of the isthmus. The Neutral Ground turned into a no-man's-land.

After clearing customs, we hopped on a city bus that would carry us into town. I might as well give you the spoiler now: Although the Great Siege of Gibraltar would last for years, the Spanish never did take the Rock back. Today, it remains a British overseas territory. Not without some controversy, mind you—Spain still officially takes the position that it is Gibraltar's rightful owner. I was hoping to get a sense of the terrain of this place that was so bitterly fought over for so long.

Back in 1779, Gibraltar was a melting pot of Brits, Genoans, and Jews. It's still diverse, with many townspeople speaking Llanito, a local mash-up of Andalucian Spanish and English. They included our bus driver, who called Liana *guapa* as she got in, then immediately began careening around corners at a breakneck speed. He called out to friends he saw on the side of the road and other fine-looking *guapas* as we ascended the slopes of the town. "He reminds me of that crazy bus driver in the Harry Potter movies," Liana whispered to me. We passed by pubs named the Pig and Whistle and the Hackney Carriage Tavern, and English banks. It looked like a sliver of London had been transported to the Mediterranean and nestled along the slopes of a mountain.

I wondered why Spain and Britain both obsessed over Gibraltar so much. The fight for the Rock captured the imagination of the English public in a way that the battles against their American cousins never did. Even though it's largely missing from American histories of the Revolutionary War today, the Gibraltar campaign was seen as one of the centerpieces of the war when it occurred.

After exiting the bus we got onboard a cable car, ascending above the town of white houses and slopes covered in wild olive trees, until we reached the top of the Rock, fourteen hundred feet above sea level. We wandered into a café with a panoramic view. Below us was the bay on one side, the Mediterranean on the other. Tankers that looked from here like toy boats moved slowly across the water.

"I can't believe we're eating British food," said Miranda, as her curry sandwich arrived. "After all this Spanish food we've had. I'm having a little culture shock."

Liana picked at her own soggy sandwich. "Yeah, we've left all this wonderful Spanish food behind and walked into the disappointment of British food." Liana's family left Spain for Cuba only two generations ago, and her latent Spanish nationalism was coming to the fore. I know which side she would have been on during the siege.

Looking at a map, I found a place where we could learn more about the bombardments. The only catch is that we'd have to walk several miles down the Rock to get to it instead of taking the cable car back to town. With varying degrees of enthusiasm, the rest of my party agreed. As it turned out, we wouldn't be the only ones on this path.

"Look, an ape!" Miranda cried out.

"It's a Barbary macaque," said Nico, who had read about them. A second monkey bounded onto a nearby rock. A third jumped on the roof of a taxi that had just parked, startling its passengers. Supposedly, so long as these tailless beasts remain on the Rock, the British will too. "They're living the good life," Miranda said. "They sit around, get fed, and harass tourists all day."

We outdistanced the monkeys but not the sun, which beat down on us in the early afternoon. "Lord, it's hot," said Liana.

"Imagine if you were a British soldier, hiking in your wool uniform," I added as we kept descending in the heat, "or hauling cannons up here." We had passed a few iron rings on stone walls; pulleys ran through them, helping the Redcoats hoist their great guns to the summit.

"I just want some water," Miranda said in a small voice.

The author (wearing the white shirt) with a Barbary macaque on the trek down the Rock.

Finally, we reached a plateau where an ice cream truck had parked, as welcome as a rogue privateer sailing into the bay with a cargo of roast beef and claret would have been during the siege. Next to it was a sign for the Great Siege Tunnels. We entered and found immediate relief in the dark, cool passageways. "I want to stay here forever," Liana said.

I had hoped to come across a knowledgeable guide or reenactor in Gibraltar, as I had in most places, but my luck finally ran out. Although the people we met were friendly, I didn't stumble across a good source this time. No matter, I thought. When all else fails, turn to the guide who'll never let me down: Mercy Otis Warren. The Siege of Gibraltar might be barely mentioned in histories of the Revolutionary War today—if it is at all—but Warren devoted pages to it in her *History*. I called an online version up on my phone. What if an 1805 book could tell me enough about the siege to give me my bearings, even if recent histories ignore the event?

The "impregnable strength" of the Rock, as Warren wrote, had defied hostile forces for generations. Knowing that a head-on assault of the Rock would be a fool's mission, the Spanish instead decided to starve the inhabitants out, putting siege lines in place and then beginning a bombing campaign. For three years, she continued, the garrison of Gibraltar survived "against the most tremendous attack and bombardment that perhaps ever took place." The siege was a sort of duel between military engineers. The British cleverly blasted these tunnels near the top of the Rock in order to place a battery high on the north face of the mountain.

We walked through the passageways and looked at the displays of mannequins of miners digging through the rock and artillerymen firing a cannon. The kids, who had gone ahead around a bend, suddenly came running back to Liana and me.

"Guys, come with me," said Miranda, unable to hide her grin.

I turned the corner and came face-to-face with a sentry holding a lantern, who barked "Halt, who goes there!" when I drew closer. Even though I should have known something was coming, I still gave a start. The kids both collapsed in laughter. They decided to camp out nearby on a bench to watch tourist after tourist involuntarily jump when they passed by and triggered the recording. I was more interested in what the mannequin was guarding—what was called a depressing carriage, invented by the British during the siege. British engineers placed a cannon on a carriage consisting of two planks with a hinge, which allowed the gun to be lowered and swiveled to fire almost directly down at the Spanish fortifications across the isthmus below.

The Spanish artillery more than matched the British firepower. "A prodigious number of cannon of the heaviest size, and a vast apparatus of mortars," Warren wrote, "spouted their torrents of fire and brimstone on that barren rock. With equal horror and sublimity, the blaze was poured back by the besieged, with little intermission." Well, there was a slight intermission in the bombing—the Spanish, being Spanish, insisted on taking a two-hour long siesta each day.

Signs inside the tunnel told of the other episodes in the Great Siege—the Moonlight Battle, fought between the British and Spanish navies off Portugal, and the Grand Assault that came at the end of it all. I paused and looked out a portal. I could make out the Gibraltar cemetery with the blue bay beyond it. "The awful play of the artillery of death," as Warren put it, sent some British defenders to their graves. Far more died from famine and disease, as we'd learn on our next stop.

After exiting the tunnels and dodging a couple of frisky apes, I led us to the ruins of an arms magazine, where you can still see bullet holes in the wall and graffiti left by bored Redcoats on guard duty. Displays had been set up in the open air to give a sense of the suffering of the Gibraltarians as the siege wore on. Videos piped in the sound of babies crying, the thudding of bombs in the distance, and people coughing, for a smallpox episode broke out during the siege. A sad display showed a sick boy holding onto a cross and two corpses covered in sheets.

Gibraltar is arid, with no rivers or streams and little land suitable for farming. Before the siege, traders had regularly brought food by sea—particularly from North Africa, across the Straits. We stopped before a mannequin depicting a trader from the Barbary States sitting on the ground. Spanish diplomats had been working on the Sultan of Morocco before the war started, emphasizing the differences he had with Britain, until he agreed to stay neutral in the war and stop his merchants' trade with the Rock. "Such a defection had taken place," Warren wrote, "that no relief could be expected from that quarter, or any supplies of provisions obtained from them for the garrison." Food supplies ran dangerously low. "The garrison...was reduced to such distress that they were several weeks without bread, except a few worm-eaten biscuits, sold at an enormous price," she continued. "A guinea [worth just over a pound] was refused for a calf's head, a chicken sold for nine shillings sterling, and everything else proportionately scarce and dear."

We left in a quiet mood and continued our hike. "After seeing this, the trip down doesn't seem so bad after all," Miranda said. Finally, we reached the town. I called up *History* again to see what else Warren might have in store for us. "Let us now rest a little from the roar of cannon," she wrote at the end of her chapter, "and the dread sound of bombardment, thunder, and death, those horrid interpreters of the hostile dispositions of man," I read.

She didn't have to ask twice. We staggered into a tavern called the Lord Nelson and collapsed into our seats. The place was decked out with portraits of the long-ago admiral and Union Jack pennants. It felt like we had stumbled into a pub on Trafalgar Square in London, albeit one in which the waiter and bartender were both speaking Spanish. We all ordered fish and chips, which Liana and I washed down with pints of ale.

As for the starving defenders of Gibraltar, their hopes rested on the prospect of the British navy smashing through the blockade. In late December, a British fleet left England escorting a relief convoy, aiming to do just that. They wound up encountering their Spanish foes long before they reached Gibraltar. The fate of the garrison and civilians depended on who won this titanic naval battle, which, unusually for the eighteenth century, would be fought at night.

For us, that meant only one thing, which I announced when we finished our meal.

"Guess where we're off to next, kids?"

"Back to Spain?" Nico offered.

"Yes. And then where, can you guess? When we were in the Great Siege Tunnels, did anyone see the sign about the Moonlight Battle?"

Quizzical glances met me. Clearly, the kids had been too obsessed with the scary mannequin to read all the signs.

"Road trip to Portugal!" I said, triumphantly.

"It's so special to be on this point of land," Liana said as we walked in the dark. "I feel like we're between worlds, between the Atlantic and the Mediterranean." We had driven three hundred miles to Cape St. Vincent, across plains and past old churches perched on hills to the very southwestern tip of Portugal, once thought to be the edge of the known world. In ancient times, people thought the sun sank each night into the waters below us.

We were walking to a fort on the coast. The moon was shining, just as it had been at the time of the battle. We wanted to get a sense of the setting of what was considered one of the most famous battles of the Revolutionary War when it happened. For my money, the Moonlight Battle should rank up there with Paul Revere's ride on the short list of thrilling nighttime episodes of the war.

On the British side, the battle involved one of their greatest characters of the time, Sir George Rodney. A chronic gambler, he had run up so many debts that he spent the early years of the Revolutionary War hiding out from his creditors—in Paris, of all places. Rodney was an irascible, domineering man. He was also the toughest fighter in His Majesty's Navy, famed for his coolness in battle. He was escorting a huge convoy of some two hundred ships. Once at sea, some would peel away for the Caribbean, while Rodney was to continue on with the rest to Gibraltar and Minorca. To protect them—and fight his way past the Spanish blockade—he commanded a fleet of some thirty-two warships.

We arrived at the Fortress of Sagres and scrambled down the rocky slopes on the side of the fortress, through juniper and saltbush, toward the water. We had toured the fort during the day after fueling up at a food truck that billed itself as offering the "Last Hot Dog Before America." Innumerable naval battles had been fought through history off the coast of the Cape, a watery crossroads where the Mediterranean joins the Atlantic. A long row of cannons was still trained at the sea.

If things had gone according to plan, the Portuguese soldiers in the Fortress of Sagres would have been on the British side during the war. Portugal had long been a British ally and had fought alongside them in the Seven Years' War. Over the years, the Brits had served as a useful counter to the Spanish, Portugal's powerful neighbors. The emboldened Portuguese had recently even been encroaching on Spanish settlements in what is now Uruguay and welcoming British traders, who set up shop under their protection.

No more. In late 1776, Spain decided to show Portugal who was the boss. The Spanish sent a fleet to Uruguay and forced the Portuguese and British traders out. Simultaneously, Spain sent another squadron to Lisbon, where they anchored in the harbor with their great guns trained on the Portuguese capital. Britain dared not intervene, not wishing to provoke Spain to join the war at this early date. The Portuguese got the message; they wanted no part in this developing world war. The next year, Floridablanca got them to sign a treaty with Spain that established their neutrality.

Similarly, another one of Britain's closest allies, Prussia, also decided to sit the conflict out, upset that the British hadn't kept some of the promises they had made in the Seven Years' War. In 1780, Russia, another state that had been sympathetic to Britain in the past, even formed what it called the League of Armed Neutrality. The League sent out warships to protect its merchant fleet from the British navy, which had been raiding ships in search of contraband destined for the allies. The League started small, with just Russia and the Scandinavian states, but other countries would eventually join, including Portugal. While a multinational coalition fought against him, then, King George III had no European powers on his side, with help only coming from some Haudenosaunee, American Loyalists, and hired Hessians. At times, it must have felt like Britain against the world.

During the battle off Cape St. Vincent, however, the British didn't need anyone else. A lookout spied sails on the horizon, a fleet commanded by Juan de Langara. The Spanish admiral immediately struck out for the safety of Cadiz, with Rodney in pursuit.

We settled down on a rocky ledge and watched the pulsations of light coming from a nearby lighthouse. Below us, smoke drifted up on a warm breeze from the beach; someone was making a fire out of driftwood. "Look at the color of the sea," Liana said, "it's like silver-plated sepia. And the sky is the same color."

"It's just like in the battle!" Nico cried out, pointing to fishing boats that were bobbing in the water. "The boats are fighting a war against the fish!"

Road trip to Portugal!

We laughed and then fell quiet, listening to the surf crash at land's end. I wondered if on that long-ago night, villagers from Sagres could make out the firing of British cannon at the Spanish ships racing for safety. "Admiral Rodney, determined to pursue his success, gave chase until the enemy were nearly involved among the shoals," Warren wrote. The old gambler was taking a big risk; in the darkness, the lee shore of Cape St. Vincent could wreck his ships just as easily as it could destroy the Spanish vessels.

Yet Rodney's bet paid off, and he caught up with the Spanish. (One reason for his speed: unlike the Spanish, the British sheathed their hulls in copper, which kept seaweed and barnacles from clinging on and slowing ships down.) The fight did not go well for Langara. "The Spanish ship San Domingo, of seventy guns and six hundred men, blew up and all on board perished," she recounted. "[T]he Spanish admiral was dangerously wounded and most of his ships had surrendered." Rodney had won one of the greatest victories of the war, capturing six ships of the line and destroying two others.

Gibraltarians were overjoyed when Rodney arrived safely and began unloading the cargo he had brought. English food had never tasted so good. As for the Spanish, they blamed the French for not passing on intelligence about Rodney's movements. The Franco-Spanish alliance was off to a rocky start. Washington too received the unhappy news of the defeat, along with a prediction that it would mean "the end of the siege," from a correspondent. But this forecast underestimated the Spanish obsession with Gibraltar. The Great Siege would carry on and on.

"What did you think about the time we spent back in Gibraltar?" I asked my family as we wound up the night.

"It's so crazy that Britain still controls that place," said Miranda. "It was strange being there. Almost like being in a fever dream."

"They tried to British-ize things, but the Spanish culture was very much present," Liana said. "There are so many Spanish people working there. I think it's rubbish that the Brits still have Gibraltar," she went on, warming to her subject. "They should give it back." She looked ready to join in a siege herself.

"I really liked the apes," Nico said.

I did too. And I liked being in a tiny spot of Britain, transplanted to a mountain on the Mediterranean. But I wondered if the Great Siege was greater than it needed to be. Spain utterly obsessed over Gibraltar, while Britain was equally obstinate in its enormous efforts to hang on to it. Some of the largest battles of the whole war occurred at the small isthmus. Our road trip to Portugal made the scale of the Gibraltar campaign come into focus even better.

It struck me as odd that the Great Siege was such a big deal at the time—so much that Warren's book covered the action blow-by-blow—yet today is mostly ignored, at least in America. How many of us even know it happened today, I wondered?

Even though it ultimately failed, the campaign against Gibraltar was not the only trick the allies had up their sleeve when Spain entered the war in 1779. If the British thought an attack on the faraway Rock was terrifying, imagine how they would feel when an allied armada reached the shores of Old England itself.

Chapter Ten

THE BRITISH INVASION

France and Spain Try to Invade Britain; Chaos Ensues

May–September 1779

The ferry sounded its horn and slid out from the dock, churning up waves that slopped against the town's ramparts, the smell of diesel fuel and seaweed mixing in the air. Truth be told, I didn't want to leave. Saint-Malo had a magical feel, with winding, medieval streets and turrets and spires spiking into the sky, all enclosed by honey-colored walls. Every street seemed to offer a hole-in-the-wall that sold Breton buckwheat crepes and cider served in porcelain cups. I had read every historical marker I could find; I had visited the museums, prowled the bookstores, and chatted with the guides. I even began to more or less tolerate the drone of the Breton bagpipes played by students on the docks.

But each night I returned alone to my favorite crêperie and drowned the day's failings with another cider. For my inquiries about the 1779 invasion of England invariably brought back a polite "*non, monsieur, je n'en sais rien*" if I was lucky, a dumbfounded stare if I wasn't.

Yet, to me anyway, this episode of the war was unforgettable. In the summer of 1779, the French and Spanish assembled a fleet of some 186 warships, larger than the notorious Spanish Armada of 1588, to support an invasionary army of thirty-one thousand troops. The armada reboot struck just as much fear in the English as the original one had: People fled coastal towns, panicked investors sold off stocks, worried lords formed servants into makeshift militias. No matter that the invasion attempt ultimately failed—it still changed the course of the war. So why isn't anyone talking about it today?

If any place would help me learn more about the invasion, I had reasoned, it would be Fort National. Half of the invasionary force had been based here in Saint-Malo, in Brittany (the other troops camped in Le Havre in Normandy), and this stronghold protected them. The previous day, I had walked across the tidal flats and clambered up the rocks to the fort's entrance.

There, I had taken a tour and listened as an enthusiastic young guide, his hair in a ponytail, took us into the fort's dungeons and leaped onto its walls, spinning tales of fantastic battles all the way. There was the time the Dutch, invading Saint-Malo in the seventeenth century, sent a boat full of explosives to try to detonate the fort. The boat drifted to the wrong place, and the exploding bombs resulted in only one casualty: a cat that went flying high into the air. "Even today, we have a place which we call the Street of the Cat Which Dances," the guide said, to the uncomfortable chuckles of the group.

The guide also told the much more somber tales of the occupation of Saint-Malo during World War II, when the Nazis housed prisoners in the fort, and of the seemingly eternal battles with the English. The French and English fought over two dozen times over the centuries, crossing and recrossing the Channel to lay claim to each other's land. The Hundred Years' War, the Nine Years' War, the Seven Years' War—there were so many conflicts that historians gave up on inventing creative names for them. My armada seemed to have gotten lost in this bellicose shuffle, I thought. The next morning, I boarded the ferry to leave town.

The hulking white ship moved into the Gulf of Saint-Malo, gliding past the fort, which, at high tide, had again become an island. The town's parapets and towers grew smaller until they seemed to belong to a toy castle. Why was I leaving Saint-Malo with more knowledge of the martyred cat of 1693 than of the armada of 1779? Not to disparage the cat's accomplishments, but they do not include participating in one of the greatest French invasionary forces of all time.

When I stumbled across the story of the armada in my readings, I was stunned. As a kid, I had understood the Redcoats to be a faceless, menacing force chasing Washington and the Patriots, mindless Stormtroopers seeking to snuff out our dreams of liberty. That England itself was in danger—that Englishmen and women might also have known what it felt like to have a marauding foe threatening them at their door—had never entered my consciousness.

And so I read whatever I could on the episode before embarking on this trip to find out more in person. For too long, Mercy Otis Warren wrote, Britain had been the "mistress of the seas," able to "interrupt the commerce, lay waste the cities, [and] destroy the towns" of its enemies. After Spain entered the war in April 1779, the allies adopted a plan (pushed by Spain) to counter this British dominance, based on the theory that the best defense is a good offense. By joining the navies of the two kingdoms together, they could outnumber the British Home Fleet and strike King George where he least expected it—the English homeland.

The French fleet would leave on May 1 to rendezvous with the Spanish at a cluster of islands off the northern coast of Spain in the Bay of Biscay and practice maneuvers together. When they felt ready, they would sail up the English Channel, overwhelm the Home Fleet with the force of their numbers, and "humble the pride and power of Britain," as Warren put it.

Once the way was clear, troops would cross the Channel in some four hundred transport boats, seizing the Isle of Wight and burning the dockyards at Portsmouth. (The foot soldiers would all be French, since Spain was simultaneously sending its own troops to assault Gibraltar.) The French military commanders made detailed plans for occupying England, even specifying what their soldiers would imbibe in a land sadly lacking in vineyards: They would order the English to "brew or provide small beer for the troops, which is much healthier than any other drink; but every effort should be made to prevent our men from having opportunities of getting drunk on strong beer."

Thus, in relative sobriety, the French Royal Army would breezily march through England—which was lightly defended, with most of its troops in America or protecting other colonies. In the most ambitious version of the plan, the French would seize the arms contained in the Tower of London and drive the British home forces north to Scotland. Perhaps the Irish would take advantage of the unrest to launch their own independence uprising. In any case, Britain would surely sue for peace. France and Spain would magnanimously return England to the English once their price was met (which included restoring Gibraltar to Spain). America would be free, and the balance of power would be restored. What could go wrong?

Obviously, something did go wrong, for I doubt you've heard tales of French soldiers cavorting through the Tower of London during the time of the American Revolution, drinking up King George's wine and roasting the Tower's ravens in a demi-glace sauce. As things would have it, just about everything went wrong. The armada never even made landfall on the English mainland. Yet for all its failings, the French and Spanish expedition wound up having an unexpected effect on the war. Sometimes, even defeats can lead to victory.

It wasn't going to be easy to retrace an invasion that didn't invade anything, but I had found an angle, thanks to *History*. Before the massive armada reached the Channel, a smaller French vanguard set off to capture the British island of Jersey, and Warren wrote all about the battles that ensued. Although it was only fourteen miles from Saint-Malo (and some eighty-five miles from England), the island had nonetheless passed to British rule centuries earlier, bestowed by the Norman William the Conqueror.

Taking Jersey would allow France to deprive British frigates of a port they could use to monitor the progress of the armada. And of course the French, with their Gallic pride, assumed they would be eagerly welcomed by the inhabitants, who were of Norman descent and most of whom still spoke a Norman dialect, Jèrriais. Even an ex-Frenchman would want to swap out his ale for *vin* and spotted dick for *soufflés* if given a chance, wouldn't he?

Not to say that the entire allied invasion strategy depended on taking Jersey—this was just a small part of the plan. But visiting an island where actual fighting took place seemed much more interesting than endlessly cruising around the English Channel, so on to Jersey it was. Hopefully, I would find someone there who actually remembered this long-forgotten invasion.

After a couple of hours on the Channel, our ship slid into the working port of St. Helier, a marina with sailboats, low-slung houses in the distance, and, off to the left, a shambling castle on an island looming out of the fog. Welcome to the Jersey Shore, Old World edition. Above Elizabeth Castle's keep flew the flag of Jersey, a diagonal red cross on a white background with three grinning lions with their right paws raised in the air, eternally waiting for a high five. A memorable symbol for this small, quirky country. My British invasion had begun.

A musket shot rang out in Elizabeth Castle as our duck boat exited the bay and began driving up a concrete rampway to the castle's entrance—like Fort National, the castle was surrounded by water at high tide. "Don't worry, we're not under fire," the driver of the amphibious transport assured the passengers, "that's just Gunner Gilly starting his demonstration. If you hurry you can catch him."

I broke into a brisk trot, hustling past guardhouses and bastions and hurrying over a drawbridge, until I nearly crashed into Gilly, who was busy barking orders at an army of tourists he had cowed into submission.

"Why aren't you over here marching? You should be over here marching if you're on the parade area," he shouted as I entered the parade ground. "Or I'll see you later on at punishment detail," he added.

Gilly, who looked to be about sixty, was dressed in full eighteenth-century military regalia—a blue coat with scarlet trim, cream-colored breeches, and a particularly jaunty tri-corner hat with a plume waggling on top. He was recreating the role of a master gunner in the Royal Artillery at the time of the invasion of Jersey, but his demeanor was more like that of an American marine sergeant having a bad day. I took my place at the back rank of tourists. It was only as I started executing his commands that I realized I had crossed a Rubicon of sorts—for the first time in my life, I was role-playing a Redcoat. I was one of the bad guys.

"When I shout the order, you'll put your right foot to the left, you'll pin your arms to the side, you'll pull your shoulders back, you'll put your chin up as so. Is that UNDERSTOOD?" he shouted.

"Yes, sergeant!" we replied.

"I can't hear you!"

"YES, SERGEANT!"

"Very good. New recruits, atten-SHUN! Chins out, shoulders back, bellies in!" Gilly marched his motley troops back toward the drawbridge, where we executed a semi-credible left wheel and then made our way to the Green, where Gilly fired his musket some more and showed us practical bayonet-stabbing techniques.

"The British believed in the rate of fire; we fired quicker than the enemy did. Then we got in with cold steel before the enemy could reload. This bayonet," he growled, holding it high in the air, "was covered in bacteria. A piercing wound with a bayonet caused infection four out of five times. That was your biggest cause of death on the battlefield—bacteria." Gilly lunged forward, stabbing the air with his bayonet and shrieking "Die, demon! Die!" to the impressed silence of his fake troops, including the one who until very recently had been on the side of the demons.

When Gilly brought his army over to a cannon overlooking a bay and asked for volunteers to help fire it off, I couldn't help myself. The setting looked so perfect—the cannon gleaming black, the bay below reflecting the clouds like an Impressionist painting—and the gunner sounded so persuasive that I felt my right hand rising as if by its own accord. There was no denying it: I had become a Benedict Arnold, my turn to the dark side now complete.

Gilly named me and the other five volunteers cadet gunners and asked us to help him as he went through the steps of firing the cannon. He scraped the bore with a worm, a long pole with a corkscrew at the end of it, then swabbed it. He then ordered his cadets to heave on ropes, pulling the cannon forward until it was pointing menacingly over the bay. "I haven't got cannonballs, they won't let me use them," he said, sheepishly. "It upsets the locals on their paddleboards when we put cannonballs out there." He finished by lighting a match; there was a hiss, a boom, and a huge cloud of white smoke, followed by applause from the crowd.

Gunner Gilly, sworn foe of the allies, with his trainee.

After he wrapped up his presentation, I began asking him about the invasion, and, to my surprise, he knew all about it, inviting me over to the parade ground café to talk more.

The café smelled like a funnel cake stand at a county fair, thanks to something called a Jersey Wonder, a sort of hole-less local doughnut. Gilly ordered me coffee and a plate of Wonders ("employee discount, mate") and we found a couple of seats outside, along with one for his bayonet. He slowly transformed into his milder alter ego; Christopher Dankler was his actual name, he told me, and he seemed much calmer when he wasn't showing how to stab people. But whether as Gilly or Dankler, the man was a fountain of stories, delivered in a baritone voice made for radio. He began in that fateful year of 1779, when the allies attacked Jersey in a prelude to the great invasion that was planned.

"The battle happened because the Jerseymen were robbing the French blind," he told me. "Privateers—that was where the money was at. You were commissioned by the king, you were allowed to arm your merchant ship, and you could attack any vessel bearing the flag of the king's enemies, including Dutch, Spanish, American, and French. Of course," he paused, "the French were doing the same over at Saint-Malo with the corsairs."

To rid the island of these privateers, in the spring of 1779 a French prince put together a fleet of half a dozen ships and well over a thousand soldiers, with the Baron de Rullecourt playing a prominent role. "Phillip de Rullecourt—he called himself a baron, but he wasn't really one," Christopher continued. "He was a bit of a chancer and he was good at swordplay, so if anyone dared question his legitimacy, he'd challenge him to a duel and be happy to kill him."

The French launched their expedition hoping that the populace would support them. "Most of the Jerseymen were from Normandy, nearly all had French names. But they were loyal to the *King of England*," Christopher said, his voice dropping to a low rumble, rapping the table for emphasis. "The king had favored islanders with privileges, like lower taxes. And they did *not* switch sides."

Christopher described how the guns of the castle blazed when the French entered this bay; the Baron regrouped his forces to the north, out of the range of the guns. But they soon ran into more trouble. "The French didn't understand the tides here," he continued. "It's a long, shallow beach, and the tide moves quickly, and it's a riptide. And they had trouble landing the troops; by the time they were ready to land, the British were on the beach." A few good duck boats were what the French needed, but those were still centuries in the future. While the French struggled, British soldiers dragged cannon onto the beach to fire at the invaders, who finally turned and left without even disembarking their troops. "Jersey persevered," Christopher concluded, triumphantly.

Listening to the gunner bring this forgotten battle to life as we sat in the shadow of the castle walls, with seagulls trying to swipe my Jersey Wonders, was an experience I would not soon forget. "How did you find all this out?" I asked. "Are you from here?"

"No, mate, I came to Jersey seventeen years ago from England," Christopher responded. The island, I learned, is a self-governing Crown Dependency that does not legally form part of the United Kingdom, and he even had to get a visa to work there.

"One day I saw an advert," he continued. "A weird advert. They were looking for someone to play the role of a gunner here at Elizabeth Castle. My wife said, why not you? I had always loved history. I *looked up* to history. And I had always been interested in firearms and the longbow.

"So I interviewed, and they gave me the job. The rest is history, so to speak. I learned how to fire a musket—I have to do that straightaway when I'm working here, to get a crowd around me and keep them there." To play his role, Christopher also had had to hit the books to uncover the mostly hidden story of the island's military past. "You have to dig deep to find out about the Battle of Jersey," he told me. "British people come here from the mainland, they know nothing about all this."

"Why not?" I asked.

"Hard to say," he said thoughtfully. "It's just not taught."

I thanked Christopher as he left to go wreak havoc on more imaginary enemies.

George Washington tracked the action at Jersey too, receiving intelligence about the attack. Even though it had failed, everyone understood that the attack there was really just a warm-up act to the main event, the great invasion—which the British were "greatly apprehensive" of, Washington's correspondent informed him. This intelligence "bears a most agreeable aspect," the general responded. The Jersey expedition, after all, was just a prelude to what the mighty armada might do.

Among those who couldn't wait to set sail was the Comte de Rochambeau, who had been tapped to lead the invasionary forces after his impressive showing at the military exercises in Vaussieux the year before (the site of the reenactment I had visited with the hard-drinking priest and friendly prostitutes). One of the chief commanders under him was none other than America's favorite fighting Frenchman. After France entered the war, Lafayette returned home in January 1779 to seek glory in his homeland.

Yet, unfortunately for those in it, the armada was encountering just as many problems as the unlucky Baron's squadron had.

The French fleet was supposed to leave for their rendezvous with their Spanish counterparts in the Bay of Biscay on May 1, 1779, the same day as the attack on Jersey. Yet they fell weeks behind schedule as they struggled to ready their ships. Finally, the impatient French prime minister ordered the fleet out of port, and the commanding admiral, the much-decorated Comte d'Orvilliers, complied, even though his ships did not yet carry enough water or enough doctors on board. That wouldn't be a problem, would it?

They rushed to the secret meeting point, a chain of islands north of Spain, where they found *nada*. None of the Spanish ships had yet arrived. The French sailors spent six weeks stuck on board, broiling in the sun, falling sick, and cursing their AWOL allies. The first Spanish ships only began to arrive in early July from Galicia; the second Spanish fleet, out of Cadiz, remained stuck in becalmed seas and would take three additional weeks to show up, after the winds changed.

When all had assembled, the French were shocked at what they found: decrepit vessels, poor-quality gunpowder, untrained officers, and crews filled out with released convicts. And yet, ready or not, once the Cadiz fleet arrived, the armada had to depart if they wanted to enter the English Channel in August, before autumn's wicked storms would put an end to any invasion. They would have to work things out as they went.

Not everyone was happy about that prospect. "Never before have two squadrons at sea had to improvise their signals," d'Orvilliers complained to the minister of the navy, "but that is what I have been forced to do." The Spanish had their own set of orders and signal flags and hadn't read or translated the French book of naval signals that had been sent to them. "I foresee a fatal outcome," wrote one French officer, whose name is not given in the history books but whom I will call Monsieur Foreshadowing. "France and Spain, having neither affection nor esteem for each other, are going to ruin this business by mutual suspicion and recriminations."

Of course, outsiders didn't know about all this; all they knew was that the largest fleet in the world was sailing somewhere to cause trouble. On both sides of the Atlantic, the suspense mounted as people guessed where the armada planned to bring their destruction. "At present, the imagination is left in the wide field of conjecture," Washington wrote to Lafayette. "Our eyes one moment are turned to an invasion of England, then of Ireland...In a word we hope everything, but know not what to expect. Or where."

On August 16, Britain's worst fears came true: The great armada sailed within sight of the shore of Plymouth, with the British Home Fleet nowhere in sight. Together, France and Spain had sixty-six ships of the line; the Home Fleet (wherever it was) only had thirty-nine. The British reaction to this murderous fleet at their shores was less Keep Calm and Carry On and more Panic and Completely Lose Your Mind. Plymothians ran from the expected destruction; investors rushed to Exchange Alley to sell off stocks. Farmers dusted off muskets and drilled in militia companies, while Cornish miners rushed to hastily dig fortifications along the coast, some of which can still be seen today. King George III ordered all cattle and sheep to be driven far inland, to deprive the invaders of a tasty meal after they landed. Some argued that it would be smarter to preemptively burn the great Portsmouth dockyard before it fell into the allies' hands.

Wasn't the British Empire supposed to be the invader, not the invadee? Yet the British were woefully unprepared to defend England, with their military forces strung out across the globe. "Since the time of the Invincible Armada" of 1588, one English observer worried, "Great Britain and Ireland were never in such danger from foreign enemies as they are at this day."

Yet even as the fear mounted, so did the allies' own difficulties. The commanders could not agree on tactics, with the Spanish all for landing straightaway while the French insisted on first finding and defeating the Home Fleet. Meanwhile, allied sailors fell sick by the thousands as dysentery raged on board. Admiral d'Orvilliers lost his only son to scurvy, leaving the commander distraught. The lack of water and food added to the suffering, with one French official describing the vessels as "more hospitals than ships of the line." The French and Spanish threw so many of their dead overboard that the people of Devon reportedly stopped eating fish. After nearly four weeks of patrolling the Channel, the allies reluctantly returned to a French port for their own good, putting an end to the armada, at least for 1779.

What a sad tale, I thought, as I climbed up Elizabeth Castle's watchtower, gazing out toward the Channel and thinking about this invasion that wasn't. Like the precursor Jersey expedition, it conquered nothing. But I thought back to some of the words Christopher had left me with after our discussion of the failures of 1779. "That wasn't the end of the story, mate," he told me. There was much more to it. "To understand what happened next," he said, "you have to go to the Peirson Pub. Have a pint and look at the marks of the musket balls in the walls."

Yes, sergeant—that sounded like the best order of the day.

The Peirson was in the heart of St. Helier, Jersey's capital. It was an old stone building, painted white with red trim, on a quiet, tree-lined Royal Square. The interior was pleasingly dark, with a bar worn smooth by age and a warren of small rooms where customers drank below portraits of long-dead sea captains. The pub's resident bulldog tottered from room to room, eating food from the floor. I ordered a Liberation Ale and sat on the patio, trying to imagine Royal Square in the eighteenth century, when inhabitants worried that the allies would return.

Even after the failure of both the small Jersey expedition and the huge armada, the anxiety didn't dissipate for islanders, or anyone else who lived in a British coastal port. The allied threat remained; it just kept taking different forms. One of those forms was that of a maniacal, Scottish-born near-pirate with a commission in the fledgling American navy, John Paul Jones.

Jones had spent the summer of 1778 terrorizing the Irish and English coasts, basing himself out of French ports. In August 1779, just as the armada was making its way into the Channel, the French sent Jones out in a squadron of six ships, including a forty-two-gun ship the French named the *Bonhomme Richard* (in homage to Benjamin Franklin's *Poor Richard's Almanack*), to cause a diversion. He brought with him an international crew of Americans, French, Malays, and Portuguese, as well as

137 Irish marines from the ferocious Wild Geese regiment of mercenaries stationed in France. The terrified Brits didn't know where he would strike next.

Off the coast of Yorkshire, Jones ran into a convoy of British merchantmen escorted by the *Serapis*—"an English ship of superior force," Warren wrote, along with another British warship. Jones immediately engaged in battle. Jones lashed his ship to the *Serapis*, fighting in closer quarters, "valorous and desperate," until a grenade tossed by one of his men blew up the enemy ship.

"The *Bonhomme Richard* was reduced to a wreck, and sunk soon after the action," Warren continued. Jones was admired by all, except the British, who considered him no better than a buccaneer. London became even more incensed when the supposedly neutral Dutch allowed him to stay on their island of Texel to repair the damaged *Serapis*. It was a great story, even though Warren had to admit that it was of "less magnitude than many others" in terms of its actual importance to the war.

Nonetheless, Jones's fame spread far and wide in his day and has only grown over time. Today, if histories of the Revolutionary War discuss naval engagements outside of American waters, they normally focus on Jones's dashing battle. What was intended to be a sideshow to the invasion wound up entirely eclipsing the main event in the history books.

For the rest of the war, British coastal communities lived in fear of all future naval incursions. Would the dreaded Jones pay their town a visit? Would the Franco-Spanish armada return? Rumors that the allies might relaunch their invasion fleets "causes a universal depression and a more than usual abuse of our wise rulers," a friend in London wrote to Franklin.

John Paul Jones never did attack Jersey, but his swashbuckling French counterpart, the Baron de Rullecourt, returned in 1781 with fourteen hundred soldiers and a better plan. This time, the French landed to the east of St. Helier in a sheltered cove at night, while the islanders were preparing to celebrate the Feast of the Epiphany on January 6. (This story takes us forward in our narrative a couple of years, but, face it, I wasn't coming back to Jersey anytime soon, so let's just jump ahead.)

"The design was so secret and the attack so sudden," Warren wrote in *History*, "that the out-guards were surprised and the avenues to the town of St. Helier seized." Yet Major Francis Peirson countered by assembling the militia of the island and launching a "desperate enterprise" of bloody street fighting in this very square. Rullecourt was mortally wounded, and the French troops fell back—even as Peirson, too, took a bullet right in front of a doctor's house in the square, the same house the dying Baron was brought to. It later became this pub, named after the glorious young major, with musket ball holes in the ceiling left as proof of the violent defense of Jersey.

The islanders repelled the attack, even getting a good backstory for their future pub out of it, but the assault only heightened apprehensions. Where would the French strike next? The British government ordered new watchtowers to be built at Jersey and more ships to patrol the Channel.

All this played into the plans of Vergennes. He had discovered a silver lining in the failed armada of 1779: He did not actually have to invade Britain to cause panic in that country. Merely keeping troops at the ready and ships in port, and occasionally sallying forth against places like Jersey, would do the trick. "If we succeed only in interrupting Britain's trade" through these maneuvers, he wrote, "you may depend on it that the resultant alarm and despondency will be as great as if we had landed in some part of that island."

And so, in the years to come, the French and Spanish would periodically get the band back together, sending their fleets to make brief cameos in the Channel, where they stayed just long enough to create a sense of dread in England. For the British, it felt as if the French were "watching over us as a leopard over his prey, just ready to spring upon us," one observer wrote—like in a horror movie today, the suspense worsened as they waited for the inevitable shock to arrive.

It never did; France and Spain never again attempted a full-scale invasion of England. But the invasion threat "exhausted England and detained at home forces which would have done much mischief in other parts of the world," Lafayette wrote to Congress. Britain, chagrined by the "checks to their pride and power which they had not before experienced," as Warren put it, doubled the size of their home militia. They sent additional troops to Ireland, which was experiencing internal "discontent and dissatisfaction," Warren wrote, and which could be the focus of the next invasion attempt. They built coastal fortifications and deployed soldiers to guard their ports.

And, for the rest of the war, the worried British kept a huge Home Fleet close to their shores, waiting for the invasion that never came, rather than being deployed to America. (We'll see what effect that had when we get to the Yorktown campaign.)

These events seemed important to the outcome of the Revolution, I thought as I ordered another Liberation Ale at the pub. How odd that Gunner Gilly was the only person I could find who could tell me about them—along with Warren, of course. Yet even Warren wrote far more about John Paul Jones and Major Peirson than about the doomed armada itself. Why was that?

Part of the reason the story remained under told, I reasoned, had to be the shame the failed invasion triggered—for all sides. The French and Spanish saw the expedition as nothing more than a costly failure at the time. D'Orvilliers, the commanding admiral, returned to port to face a torrent of criticism. He resigned and went off to live the rest of his days with a group of monks.

Britain also wanted to put the whole affair behind it. The British had escaped defeat only thanks to the failures of their adversaries. If the allies had managed to land at Portsmouth, they would have found a terrified population, an untrained militia, and a clear road to London. The embarrassed Brits were happy to move on as well.

By contrast, the stories that everyone did remember—of Jones and

Peirson—were of heroic individual fights. So what if they didn't have all that much strategic impact; these were rip-roaring tales to be told in a tavern by the fireside. They were far more exciting than a narrative of two gigantic fleets slowly maneuvering around each other in the English Channel, even if that's what helped win the war for the allies. Even though Warren admitted that Jones's fight was not particularly significant, she, like other authors since, spilled much ink on it, keeping her readers interested with stories of pirates and martyred majors. These stories reminded me of the musket shot that Christopher fired off to catch everyone's attention—he wasn't shooting at anything in particular, but everyone was drawn in by the sound and smoke.

But I at least would remember the doomed armada and the people who lost their lives on it. As night fell at the Peirson Pub, I raised my glass to those unfortunate French and Spanish sailors who left wives and mothers back home in Breton fishing ports and on Galician farms never to return, not even to be buried. Forgotten souls in a forgotten campaign, who nonetheless helped turn the tide of the war toward American victory. After this trip, I would remember them as men who did not die in vain. And now you can too.

Chapter Eleven

A DAY IN THE LIFE OF A WORLD WAR

A Snapshot of the War Around the Globe on July 4, 1779

July 4, 1779

If you ever get tired of the crowds in old Philadelphia, of the lines and summer heat and vendors of *Rocky* merch, walk just a few blocks south of the Liberty Bell. Old St. Mary's Church, built in 1763, looks like it would fit right into Independence National Historical Park, with its handsome brick front and a green field dotted with old gravestones. It's the perfect spot for a moment of respite. And it has a most curious plaque on its facade.

This site was holy ground, it read, for here was the first public religious commemoration of the Declaration of Independence. On July 4, 1779, the third anniversary of the approval of the document, congressmen filed into St. Mary's for a special mass. Liana and I had come here to bear witness to the place.

Philly is rightfully obsessed with the year 1776, but I was trying to get my head around the overlooked period that came after, the so-called "middle years" of the war. The books I had read growing up raced through them. For the most part, the story that's told about the war starts with a bang (Boston! Saratoga! Valley Forge!) and ends with fireworks (Victory at Yorktown!), but yada yada yadas the middle parts. Many histories would leave you with the impression that the year 1779, for example, featured a failed American attempt to retake Savannah from the British, some small battles between Patriots and Loyalists, and not much else.

And yet, an active war was being fought—just not, for the most part, in the United States. If you looked at the Caribbean, or Europe, or India, though, you'd find plenty of battlefield heroics, of armadas clashing at sea and armies launching assaults. The year 1779 alone saw fighting in a Louisiana bayou, across the Bay of Gibraltar, in a Central American tropical forest, off the Azores islands, and under the shadow of a castle in Yorkshire, as well as a heroic stand by free Blacks from the Caribbean against the Redcoats. Actually, all that occurred in the span of just *one week* in 1779 (in the middle of September). Imagine what happened the rest of the year.

I had been trying to find out what I could about these supposedly quiet years that were actually anything but, of the time when the French, Spanish, and Americans were learning how to work as partners. After discovering all I could about this forgotten time in the historical record, I decided to pay a visit to the church that played at least a small role in cementing these new alliances.

It was remarkable that St. Mary's existed at all at the time of the Revolution. Anti-Catholic prejudice ran rampant in the Thirteen Colonies. The church—its construction paid for by Irish, German, and French immigrants—was purposefully built far back from the street to provide a buffer should a mob attack it. American newspapers of the time railed against "popery," while some chaplains pronounced that Catholic lands were the "dwelling of Satan." In October 1774, the First Continental Congress even went on record that Catholicism "dispersed impiety, bigotry, persecution, murder, and rebellion through every part of the world."

Once a year, St. Mary's gives a nod to its Revolutionary War past. It doesn't recreate that mass of July 4, 1779, but it does hold a special mass each year to honor one of the earliest American naval commanders, the Irish-born John Barry, who was a member and is buried in the church graveyard, and to mark the date of his death. We slipped in just before it started.

As the congregation stood and began singing "Amazing Grace," two men wearing green vests hoisted an American and an Irish flag and walked slowly to the front of the church. A priest, a wiry man with a goatee clad in white robes and a green sash, followed them. Above the church's stained-glass windows, with their scenes from scripture, was a ceiling of blue, spangled with stars. On a back wall hung a poster of the Founding Fathers.

"Have you ever seen flags at a mass?" I whispered to Liana, a practicing Catholic. She rolled her eyes and hushed me. After more singing and prayers, the congregation—many of whom were wearing green vests like the flag bearers were—fell hushed as the priest, Monsignor Paul DiGirolamo, started to talk.

"For those of you new to here, we always have a word in our homily that serves as the theme," he began. "Today the word is 'signs.'" The priest told a story about a clueless driver who blew past stop signs, followed by one about a jaywalker who ignored traffic signals. And then, turning more serious, he spoke of signs of God's presence, drawn from the Bible, and then turned to the subject of the American Revolution.

"John Barry and his men, his associates, were signs," the monsignor said, "signs of strength, of courage, of freedom, of these United States. And many people read the signs and understood them, and sacrificed, as the saying goes, their faith, their lives, and their fortune for these United States and for where we are today.

"It's important to pay attention to the signs," he concluded, "because if we don't, we really miss out on a lot."

After the mass, I followed the congregation as it filed out into the graveyard. A bagpiper played the pipes, navy seamen presented arms, and a lieutenant laid a green wreath at Barry's grave. Speakers extolled him as a military hero and son of the Emerald Isle. The Continental Navy, as small as it was, wouldn't have been the same without immigrants like Barry; many of its sailors were foreign-born.

We walked up to Monsignor DiGirolamo and found him happy to share more. "This church is kind of like a historical record. John Adams described the stars on the ceiling of it. We still have those stars there.

"Before the internet and radio, we had bars and churches for getting the news," he continued. "It was a smaller world; everyone knew each other." That's why the July Fourth Te Deum, that service of blessing, at St. Mary's was so important—it sent a message to all of Philadelphia that the French and Spanish visitors in town, as well as Catholic immigrants like John Barry, were to be respected.

We went back inside the church. Liana took pictures of the stained-glass windows, while I sat on a pew and reflected on what had happened here. Such an event—Protestant American leaders attending mass at a Catholic church—would have been hard to imagine before 1779, given the prejudice against Catholics. The mass had been sponsored by the French ambassador to the United States, Conrad-Alexandre Gerard, who had set up shop not far from what is now called Independence Hall. So had Spain's emissary, Juan de Miralles, a merchant normally based in Cuba who served in that role. (Since it hadn't officially recognized the United States yet, Spain didn't send a formal ambassador.)

Catholic France and Spain were a source of salvation, a lifeline for the battered American cause. At St. Mary's on that long-ago Fourth, a French chaplain asked God "to inspire the rulers of both nations with the wisdom and force to perfect what He hath begun." If you were to read the signs from that mass, what you would take away was that the Americans desperately needed help from their partners and allies—and were willing to look past their differences to get it.

The mass was the highlight of the city's Independence Day

celebration that year. While earlier ones had involved parades, fireworks, and a "great expenditure of liquor and [gun]powder," as one congressman put it, the 1779 version was much more low-key. Philadelphia was in rough shape after its recent occupation by the British. Inflation was rampant, Continental currency was increasingly worthless, and goods were scarce. Three states even voted in Congress against having any kind of celebration at all, while others thought Americans should just engage in fasting and quiet reflection.

As important as that mass at St. Mary's must have been, the real place to see and be seen that Independence Day, I had discovered from my research, was Paris. Fasting was Benjamin Franklin's least favorite activity; instead, he threw a party to end all parties, inviting Lafayette and other French VIPs. They and American expats dined in Franklin's garden on duck, turkey, lamb, and pigeons, accompanied by strawberries and figs under the lantern light. Guests admired a portrait of George Washington holding a copy of the Declaration and the treaty with France, and called for more wine to help them get through a long poetry reading.

Then came the toasts, with glasses drained after each one. "To the King of France and his Queen! To the King of Spain and the success of Spanish arms! To Lafayette and Washington! To Congress, may they always govern with the same Wisdom that has hitherto distinguished them." (That one didn't take.) "To the brave Foreigners who have hazarded their Lives in our Cause and the valiant Americans who have fought in Defense of their Country. To the combined Fleets of France & Spain, and may Fame swell their Sails, and Victory crown all their Enterprises." Bottoms up!

Would Victory indeed crown their Enterprises? The Americans, of course, had barely withstood the British when they were on their own in the first years of the war. The French had not done much better in 1778. And, as we've seen, the Spanish made a bold push to end the war quickly in 1779, through the twin campaigns of besieging Gibraltar and, with their French allies, attempting to invade England. Yet both of these operations ultimately failed.

Instead, the war would turn into a grind, as Spain and France fought Britain in a number of new, far-flung theaters. The plan, as Vergennes saw it, was to wear Britain down in a war of attrition, putting so many British colonies in jeopardy that King George III would eventually sue for peace. New fronts opened up, in Central America, India, Africa, and the Caribbean. I had counted up the battles and overlaid them on a current-day map—they were fought on, or off the coast of, thirty-three modern nations.

Keeping track of all these battles—most of which I had never heard of—practically made my head spin. When did one campaign start and the other stop? How did they all relate to each other? What else was happening around the world on, say, the day that the Independence Day mass took place here at St. Mary's? There were so many clashes, it was easy to lose the bigger picture as to what was going on. To make sense of it all, I felt like I needed to make some kind of chart, or map, or spreadsheet even.

Or maybe a church?

As Liana came back to the pew, enthused with her pictures of the stained-glass windows, an idea was taking shape in my mind. I thought back to the Washington Memorial Chapel, which Nico and I had visited at Valley Forge. That church had thirteen stained-glass windows illustrating scenes from American history. If only someone had done the same, but showing scenes from war around the world. What a way that would be to honor the allies, I thought.

By the time we had driven back home, I had dreamed up a tableau of thirteen different scenes, illustrating what our partners and allies were doing on that day of July 4, 1779, on that supposedly quiet moment in a forgotten year of the war. (Don't worry, Monsignor, I also looked out for the traffic signs.) And then I set it down.

So, welcome into my imaginary chapel and get ready for a whole lot of history coming your way. But don't worry, there won't be a test—and you can revisit this list whenever you like. I hope it gives you your bearings for the journeys we'll be taking after it.

The first stained-glass window would show Washington in camp, watching and waiting. He spent Independence Day 1779 with his troops outside New York City—the exact same way he would spend the Fourth of July the following year. This was a frustrating time for the general. Even though thousands of Redcoats had been shipped off to the Caribbean after France entered the war, General Clinton still had a formidable force in New York City, more than Washington was able to attack by himself without the help of the French navy. Yet the French were off fighting in the Caribbean. Once again, the Americans were on their own.

And so, the naturally aggressive general was forced to wait. He slung his troops in a circle ringing the city, biding his time in case the French navy ever came back. Just keeping his army together was challenge enough. Recruitment was down, he had no hard money to pay his men, and the American public was growing weary of the war. Washington spent the Fourth of July writing a letter to Lafayette, who was still back in France. "When, my dear Marquis, shall I ever embrace you again?" he wrote to the young man whom he loved like a son. "Shall I ever do it?" At least hosting the French and Spanish representatives at his camp a few weeks earlier had provided a break from the tedium. Miralles was a particularly welcome guest, showering the general with a barrel of sherry, guava desserts, twenty chocolate cakes, and "one small box full of cigars" from Havana.

Without French or Spanish help, Washington didn't dare launch a grand assault against the British. Instead, the Continentals directed their forces at a weaker enemy—which brings us to our second window, the saddest one in this chapel. It shows fields of corn and villages blazing with fire and the Haudenosaunee grieving their losses, for Washington had launched a campaign against Britain's Iroquois Nation allies, in retaliation for raids they had been conducting against Patriot communities. In the same letter he wrote to Lafayette on Independence Day, Washington told the Marquis how he had sent General John Sullivan and four thousand men with orders to "destroy their settlements and extirpate them from the country."

Sullivan only engaged in sporadic combat during his expedition, but his men burned some of the villages of the Seneca, Cayuga, Onondaga, and Mohawk to the ground. The Oneida, America's first allies, were horrified by the scorched-earth campaign; they had not wanted to turn against fellow Haudenosaunee. But they could not stop the onslaught.

After the expedition concluded, the Oneida warrior Peter Agwalongdongwas (known as Good Peter) set out on a mission to try to persuade other Haudenosaunee nations to agree to peace. Instead, his fellow Iroquois, angry about the losses they had suffered, took him prisoner.

The third window would show a regiment of Canadians and Americans hacking their way through the woods of what is now northern Vermont to support a possible invasion of—wait for it—Quebec. Oh no, they were at it again! Congress never did learn its lesson after the Canadian debacle of 1775–76 and kept proposing that the United States take another try at conquering the land to its north. A regiment of Canadian volunteers even served in the Continental Army throughout the war. In this case, though, the march north wound up being just a feint to scare the British. Just to make sure, Britain left a great force in the province to guard against further American shenanigans.

The next window would show freshly dug Patriot graves near a rice field in the Carolinas. After France entered the war, the British began what became known as their Southern Strategy, hoping that if they took key Patriot strongholds in the American South, Loyalists would rise up to support them. Holding ports such as Savannah, Georgia, and

Charleston, South Carolina, would also let the British more easily transport Redcoats and food supplies down to the Caribbean as needed.

The British had already taken Savannah in late 1778. A couple of weeks before Independence Day, they sent a probing expedition toward Charleston. At Stono Ferry, the Americans attacked the British but were driven back, suffering around 150 casualties. Washington would eventually send some of his best officers and troops to the region to counter the growing British menace there. In the end, the campaign in the south would wind up providing Washington with the great opportunity at Yorktown that he was waiting for—but that seemed very distant in 1779, when prospects looked dark indeed.

The hottest theater of the entire war—in terms of action, not just temperature—was the Caribbean, where the British and the allies took turns attacking each other's islands. On the morning of July 4, 1779, a pitched battle was being fought on the island of Grenada, Britain's richest sugar island in the Lesser Antilles. The Comte d'Estaing had landed two thousand soldiers, who rushed toward the British lines and captured the cannon before the British could spike them. The French then turned Britain's own guns on the British defenders in Fort George, who had to surrender. The fifth window, then, would show the French celebrating their victory under the palm trees.

But the struggle wasn't over. On July 6, a British relief expedition arrived and the French soldiers quickly reembarked on their ships. The naval battle that followed was titanic, involving twenty-six ships of the line and resulting in over fifteen hundred casualties. Both sides fought "with laudable spirit and bravery," Warren wrote, until the British finally gave up and sailed away. D'Estaing, who had faced disappointment after disappointment when he had tried to work alongside the Americans, finally had a great victory operating on his own. His victory was the talk of Paris; a new play that reenacted the battle was a great hit.

Not long after that, d'Estaing would receive Washington's plea to free Savannah from the British. He would rely in part on the

Chasseurs-Volontaires, the regiment of free and enslaved Blacks that Antoine Randolph Watts, the reenactor from the First Rhode Island, had told me about. D'Estaing would bring some 750 of these soldiers with him to America when he launched an assault on Savannah in September 1779. After a siege failed to dislodge the British, d'Estaing's men "attempted to storm the town, but were defeated with great slaughter," Warren wrote.

The losses included the gallant Count Pulaski, the Polish volunteer whom I had dubbed the Horseman, slain in a desperate cavalry charge. The Chasseurs took on casualties as well as they covered the French and American retreat. The window in my chapel would take inspiration from the memorial that honors the regiment today in downtown Savannah, which features four proud Afro-Caribbean men firing rifles, a drummer boy playing throughout the danger, and a wounded Chasseur fallen to the ground.

The monument to the Chasseurs-Volontaires de Saint Domingue in Savannah.

Before we leave the Caribbean, we can't forget Sint Eustatius, the small Dutch island that was the site of the First Salute back in 1776. By 1779, Statia had become more important to the American cause than ever. Now that France and Spain were officially in the war, their ships were subject to attack by the British and the ports of their own

Caribbean islands were subject to blockade. As a result, the Dutch—who claimed to still be neutral—stepped up their smuggling to Sint Eustatius. In 1779, some seven to ten American ships visited its port every day. This stained-glass window, then, would show men loading ships with guns and ammo on the waterfront below Fort Oranje. And—in a tiny corner of the window—there would have to be a blue bead.

With that, we're a little over halfway done with our visit to the chapel. Get ready, for we're about to get to some of the most dashing campaigns of the war.

In New Orleans, Bernardo de Gálvez, the man who I had first come across at the Fourth of July pageant in Andalucia, was preparing to lead his men on a march. Window Eight would show the young governor of Louisiana hunched over a map, plotting with his officers. Bernardo spent July 1779 building a multiethnic coalition of Spanish settlers, Cajuns, free Blacks, and Americans. In the fall, he would launch a lightning campaign against British forts in the bayous of Louisiana and then move on to the Gulf Coast. His surprise attacks would win him victory after victory.

Bernardo wasn't the only Gálvez preparing for battle in the summer of 1779—so was his father, Mathías, the head of the Spanish province of Guatemala, which stretched from the Yucatán to Central America. The ninth window would show Mathías in a Mexican fort overlooking the Lagoon of Seven Colors. Like Bernardo, Mathías had also gotten early word from his brother José that war was coming. A couple of months later, his troops would attack the British in what is now Belize. Fighting would rage throughout the region for the next year.

The next two windows will hopefully be familiar. One would show the sun rising over the Rock of Gibraltar, which bristled with cannon. As we have seen, Spain began a blockade of the Rock in late June. The day after Independence Day, the guns of Gibraltar erupted against the Spanish blockaders. Britain would send countless ships and war material to prop up its defense of Gibraltar, to the neglect of its operations in America and elsewhere.

The next one would be of Elizabeth Castle on the island of Jersey, rising out of the mist. (I'm going to try to sneak Gunner Gilly into a corner of the window too.) On July 4, the French and Spanish fleet was still gathering north of Spain as it prepared to sail to the English Channel, a bold stroke that might have ended the war at once. It didn't succeed, of course. Or did it? The recurring threat of invasion would scare Britain into ordering a huge part of its army and fleet to remain in home water.

And then we have a window that I bet you didn't see coming (unless you read the Table of Contents, that is). It would show a palace in India, with a rocket on one side of the window and an elephant on the other. In 1779, India was a patchwork of independent kingdoms and principalities. Many were increasingly controlled by the British East India Company, a corporation that was a quasi-state, with its own army and navy. The French had their own trading companies on the subcontinent too.

The British made a mistake by attacking the French in India, though, for this angered the sultan of the powerful Mysore Kingdom, Hyder Ali, who was aligned with the French. He and his son Tipu Sultan would become two of the most formidable opponents the British would face in the entire war. They pioneered the use of rockets in warfare and would strike fear into the British by sending a most unusual cavalry against them—with some men riding horses, others on elephants. The India theater would become a worrisome distraction for the British.

The final window might be the most surprising of all: a British opposition leader giving a thundering speech in Parliament denouncing the war. "The American war had become very unpopular in England and discontents prevailed in all parts of the Empire," Warren wrote. Some politicians denounced the "absurd and fruitless war," she continued, with its "waste of human life and the treasures of the nation." (One reason that the conflict was proving so absurdly expensive for the British was the challenges they faced with their supply chains; food, horses, uniforms, and arms all had to be sent on convoys of ships across the Atlantic.)

Unrest was increasing in Ireland too, with some Irish inspired by the example of the American revolutionaries.

To win, the coalition of nations did not have to decisively defeat the British in all (or even most) of these theaters—they just had to grind down the British public's willingness to keep supporting the war. The speeches against the war by opposition lawmakers in 1779 were an early sign that British patience was beginning to wear thin.

Whew! Have you got all that? Here's the summary: By the midpoint of the war, things were relatively quiet for Washington's Main Army, save for the tragic expedition against some of the Iroquois. In the American South, tensions simmered as the British poured more troops into the region. The fighting was hotter in Central America, the Gulf of Mexico, and the Caribbean, where the British and allies tried to grab each other's colonial possessions. In both Europe and India, titanic armies maneuvered for battle. And the British public was beginning to tire of this war that threatened to dismember their empire.

What should be clear is that these middle years, given only a faint nod in some history books, were the setting of a raging world war. No wonder the Continental leaders in Philadelphia were praying for the success of their allies and partners, while Franklin was busy raising glass after glass to their well-being. (Not that he needed much of an excuse to raise a glass.)

As for me, it was time to get back out on the road and step into a few of the scenes I had described. We'll start with the campaign that was the farthest away from Old St. Mary's. It all began in a busy port city on the sweltering southern coast of India.

Chapter Twelve

THE FAR SIDE OF THE WORLD

The British Opened a New Front in India—and Got More than They Bargained For

August 1778–March 1780

The auto-rickshaw driver sped through traffic, first in the left lane, then in the right lane, now down the stripe in the middle of the road. He was far from alone—everyone else was weaving around as well, all to the nonstop soundtrack of beeping horns. I had never been in one of these vehicles before; it was an orange, open-framed contraption on three wheels. I looked away from the chaos of the traffic. To my left was a row of roadside stalls selling everything from flower petals to jackfruit to roosters in cages. A cow ambled contentedly in the shadow of high-rises. To my right, a group of boys played cricket under a banyan tree, with the sea glittering under the sun.

I couldn't be farther away from those Revolutionary War battlefields I visited with my parents as kid, I thought. I only wished they could have been here with me to see it. My mother had passed away from cancer not too long after my family had visited Andalucia on the

Fourth of July. My father was in declining health himself, struggling with Alzheimer's and heart problems. If only we were able to talk together about this trip, the most far-flung of my journeys yet, I thought. For I never would have made it here if it hadn't been for the love of history and travel they had instilled in me. How surprised Mom and Dad would have been to find out where I was headed now—and that it formed yet another link in the chain of Revolutionary War travels we had started together when I was a kid.

If I could only find it, that was.

"Here is the beach," the driver said in his heavily Tamil-accented English. "Will you get out here?" he implored.

"No, we're looking for the Fort St. George Museum," I reminded him, trying hard to remain polite. I had caught on that the driver had no idea where the place was. He had already tried to deposit me at other non-fort locations, claiming that I'd like them just as much—a cathedral, a temple, a palace. The fact that he had never heard of this historic landmark didn't surprise me in a way; Chennai struck me as a city looking forward, a megapolis focused on its industry and commerce, not its somewhat murky past. But I had come here with a one-track mind. I was in search of the spot where British dominance in India truly began—the ancient fortifications of their strange, commercial-political-military entity, an organization that helped spark the American Revolution itself, the East India Company.

After pulling over for consultations with a passerby, my driver at last found it, and I tumbled out into the sticky air. All around me was lush greenery: palm trees and banana tree fronds, bougainvillea and sweet-smelling jasmine. The fortifications today enclose some forty-two acres, with many of the old buildings standing, albeit repurposed. The Tuscan-columned British military barracks are now controlled by the Indian army, while the fort's white tower now houses the legislative assembly of the state of Tamil Nadu. I wandered up to the museum, a three-story building with columns, passing by Indian cannons with intricate carvings and a flowery script that I couldn't read on their shaft. The museum was housed in a squat eighteenth-century building that once served as the residence of a wealthy merchant and later was a bank and tavern.

Inside, I wandered among the collections and learned about the history of the place. The East India Company was such a strange organization, neither fish nor fowl. It started as a small trading company in the early seventeenth century. By two centuries later, it had grown into the de facto ruler of India, a multinational corporation with its own army and navy, a fact that seemed crazy to me. Could you imagine if, say, Starbucks had its own fleet of fighter jets today?

I looked at prints on the wall with scenes of the Company's rise. Here were traders landing at Madras, as Chennai was originally known, in the heavy surf. There were elephants parading by in Black Town (what the Company called the neighborhoods where the natives lived) and snake charmers working before a crowd. Here were the walls of Fort St. George going up, protecting White Town and the Company's investments.

Other rooms displayed collections of East India Company muskets and mortars, as well as the coins it minted and the uniforms its soldiers wore. And, to my surprise, a nine-foot-tall marble sculpture of Lord Cornwallis, one of the most important British generals in the Revolutionary War, stood by the winding staircase. Cornwallis didn't just serve in the Thirteen Colonies, I learned, but also here in India. Company merchants loved him for the battles he won to protect their commerce, particularly against the powerful Mysore Kingdom to the west.

After a happy hour of wandering, I walked out and hailed another auto-rickshaw. I still had a lot to learn about this weird corporation that transmogrified into a state. How did the East India Company go about doing that—and why? What role did it play in the Revolutionary War? Fortunately, I had a meeting set up with an expert who could tell me all about that, and more. Appropriately enough, we met up over tea (for me, anyway), the drink that got the East India Company in trouble to begin with.

Sriram Venkatakrishnan was in his mid-fifties, wearing glasses that framed an inquisitive face. We sat in garden café filled with tropical plants with raindrops dripping from their fronds, for a torrential storm had just blown through, a forerunner of the monsoons that would soon come. Sriram was many things—a columnist, leader of historic walks, commentator on Indian classical music, and tireless researcher, a man who spent part of each day trying to unearth the past of his city and share it with others. All of this activity was on top of his actual job as an engineer who headed his family's firm.

He began by recounting some of his city's remarkable history. Located on India's southeastern Coromandel Coast on the Bay of Bengal, Chennai had a tradition of trade that dated back to the ancient Greeks and Romans, who came to do business with the local Tamil population. "One of the reasons why I believe that this region is the last surviving outpost of secularism and communal amity is because it's been exposed to people from outside since God knows when," he told me. "And they didn't come here due to war. They came here to trade. So, what happens then is that your relationships develop on a different wicket altogether. We have never had interracial or intercommunal riots in this city. It's a remarkable record in a country that is as volatile as India."

"When did the British arrive here?" I asked.

"In 1639," Sriram replied. "The British began further north, near Calcutta, but came down here to the south." They weren't the only ones. "The Dutch were the big bosses here," he went on. "They had nineteen trading stations on this coast. Can you believe it? And today, they are not even a memory. People don't know about them. The Portuguese were here too," he added. Soon they were joined by French traders as well. The French outpost in Pondicherry, one hundred miles south down the coast from Madras, would prove to be the East India Company's biggest rival.

"What were they all trading?" I asked.

"The Europeans came to trade in cloth," he said. "Our region has been known for its cotton cloth for centuries. It's not just yesterday or today, this goes back to Greek and Roman times. And we had cotton of multiple grades; here were superthin varieties which were probably liked in the summer season in Europe, and heavier ones too. They used our cloth for bedspreads, tablecloths, and handkerchiefs." Words such as *calico, dungarees, khaki,* and *pajamas* all came into the English language from India thanks to the trade in fabrics. India also exported saltpeter, an essential ingredient in gunpowder.

At first, Sriram told me, the British in Madras were dealing with local Hindu or Muslim rulers. At the end of the seventeenth century, however, the ancient Mughal Empire in Delhi, whose rulers were descended from Genghis Khan and the Mongols, became interested in the small states of south India. "Gradually, the Mughals swallowed them, one after the other, one after the other, one after the other. In 1687, the Mughals became the overlords of this entire region."

Sriram sketched out an overview of the changing face of India in the eighteenth century, even grabbing a pen and paper to draw a rough map illustrating how the influence of the different powers waxed and waned. The gist of the complicated story was that the overstretched Mughal Empire—which ran from Afghanistan to the south of India—began to crumble and other states competed to take its place.

"India went through anarchy during that period," he told me. "There was no powerful central administration. So, revenue collection was rapacious. Everybody was a law unto himself."

The largest and most powerful of the new kingdoms to emerge from the chaos of the mid-eighteenth century was the Maratha Empire, a loose confederacy that took over much of central India. Yet the one most important to our story was the Mysore Kingdom in southwest India. "Mysore was an independent Hindu kingdom," Sriram said. "But they were dependent on their generals to wage war for them. And Hyder Ali was one such person who came up through sheer merit and hard work." The general, who was Muslim, "made it big in the army," Sriram continued. "He finally became the de facto ruler of Mysore. And he believed that the French were a far better people to deal with than the British."

The fastest growing of the new powers to emerge wound up being none other than the East India Company itself, which began to take over competitor states. The Company would make them an offer they couldn't refuse: agree to become a puppet ruler or watch their kingdom become obliterated. ("What honor is left to us," one Mughal official complained, "when we have to take orders from a handful of traders who have not yet learned to wash their bottoms?") "The Company transitioned from just trading," Sriram told me, "to becoming an empire. We went from the age of trade to the age of conquest. The Company became a plunderer and conqueror thereafter. And it had its own army in a very big way." By the 1770s, the Company had thousands of men under arms in its bases in Calcutta, Bombay, Madras, and elsewhere, as well as a fleet of warships. Many of those who fought for it were sepoys, Indian-born soldiers, Sriram told me.

"Why was that?" I asked.

"It was the pay. That was the most important thing. See, in a time of anarchy, when wages to many armies were often in arrears, if they were being received at all, the East India Company was a proper paymaster. They kept their troops happy. Why else do you think people were loyal to them?"

The East India Company at Fort St. George, shown in a nineteenth-century print at the end of its rule.

Even if it took care to pay its soldiers on time, the Company was fundamentally corrupt, Sriram said, with every member of it trying to make money on the side. "They looted, on a very organized, kingdom level," he said. (*Loot*—another word from India that passed into the English language during this time.) All the while, the British kept strengthening Fort St. George in Madras. They were still worried about their main commercial rivals, the French Compagnie des Indes in Pondicherry, which threatened British dominance of the region.

The waiter came and I ordered a guava pie. All this was a lot to take in—and we had just covered the basics. Sriram had to leave soon for another appointment, but before he did, I asked him how he came to have such a passion for history. It all started with his grandfather, he told me.

"He was the first chief engineer under the British who was an Indian," he told me proudly. "But above all he was a Renaissance man. He bought some four thousand books in his life, many of them in Sanskrit. And he loved history—that's not common for an engineer. After working for twenty-one years," Sriram continued, "he took his retirement, much earlier than people expected, so he could have time to read and write. Towards the very end of his life, he decided he would learn French."

Following his grandfather's example, Sriram went to Delhi for his own study of engineering but found himself staring out windows, looking at the domes and minarets of the ancient city, and tramping through the streets in search of long-forgotten buildings. "You can never escape history there," he told me. He carried this passion with him to Chennai, with the aim of showing that even this frenetic megapolis has a hidden past to uncover.

After Sriram left, I finished my dessert and thought about what he had shared with me. By the 1770s, the East India Company had become a massive multinational company, "a strange absurdity," as the economist Adam Smith called it, that was able to control a number of states in India. Its trade connections kept expanding, as it imported tea from China and began to export opium grown in India to Canton. But then came a plot twist. The Company had been mismanaged for years, with corrupt officials siphoning off money. In 1772, with the business hopelessly overstretched and deeply in debt, the Company's stock value crashed.

And that's how the East India Company entered the story of American independence. The Company was simply too big to fail, British policymakers decided—its unpaid taxes added up to a tenth of the country's revenues. To help it out, the Crown gave it a monopoly on selling tea directly to the Thirteen Colonies (before the Company had shipped its tea to middlemen in England), with an export tax to be paid by the colonists. The outraged Americans, of course, responded by dumping ninety thousand pounds of the Company's tea into Boston Harbor—helping to spark the conflict with Britain.

For many in America, the East India Company had become a symbol of all that was wrong with the British. Not only were the British in effect forcing consumers to buy the Company's tea—and pay taxes for the privilege of doing so—but the Company's rule in India was increasingly criticized for its "catalogue of cruelties," as Mercy Otis Warren put it. The people of India "have been reduced to slavery," she wrote, "and the innocent inhabitants of the eastern world involved in famine, poverty, and every species of misery" thanks to the Company's depredations. In Congress, delegates thundered against the Company's "barbarities" in India and warned that they had given Britain a blueprint for how to act tyrannically in America too.

The next chapter of the East India Company's story became even stranger, for this militarized business joined in the Revolutionary War as a combatant. The Company had learned of France's 1778 entry into the war long before its rivals did, since British merchants were able to pass news on through Egypt, whose rulers favored them, while the French had to sail around South Africa's Cape of Good Hope. The British would make the most of this head start. Here was a golden opportunity to drive the French out of the subcontinent altogether before they even realized that their country was at war. Little did they realize that their campaign would put the very survival of the British in south India in jeopardy.

To find out more about what happened next, I took to the road to the one city in India where French culture still survives, Pondicherry.

After forty-five minutes of driving in a hired car with a driver (Chennai had not inspired me to try to take the wheel myself), we left the city and the landscape opened up. We beep-beeped our way south, the Bay of Bengal shining to our left, through a countryside of palm trees and rice paddies, roadside shrines and murky canals, and mango orchards surrounded by barbed wire. Cows calmly strayed into the road, parting the sea of drivers that swerved around them. We drove by a lotus pond that was next to a trash heap, passing from serenity to grunginess in seconds.

The outskirts of Pondicherry (today officially called Puducherry) appeared at first glance much like the other towns we had driven through, with the familiar hum of auto-rickshaws and the cries of vendors. But when we reached the French Quarter, a neighborhood of colonial houses with balconies, with a bakery every block or two—I had found the telltale signs that this had once been the land of frogs. Huge Francophile that I am, I loved seeing the blue-and-white street signs, just like the ones you'd find in Paris, and policemen wearing kepis, those flat-topped French hats. Flaky croissants at breakfast, glasses of sauvignon blanc with dinner? *Pourquoi pas?*

Pondicherry was filled with Indian tourists: young, well-dressed people taking turns snapping pictures of each other in front of the old French buildings. The historic district seemed a little like that other French Quarter, the one in New Orleans, which also had a Gallic-inspired backdrop that tourists could use as a playground, but sans debauchery. Here, instead of beads, there were floral garlands; instead of liquor-spiked Hurricanes, mango lassis.

I made my way to the town's museum, hidden behind palms and banana plants near Rock Beach. One room displayed the weapons of the Compagnie des Indes: muskets, sabers, and cannons. The French, I learned, were more accommodating to local beliefs than their British counterparts were, even minting coins with Hindu gods on them, ignoring the protests of the Catholic church. The enclave of Pondicherry wound up remaining part of France until 1954, when the French reluctantly turned its administration over to the Republic of India.

I left the museum with a musty old book that the ticket-taker found in the back room and sold to me for just a few hundred rupees, after carefully wrapping it in a newspaper and tying it with string. I unwrapped it back in my hotel room, located in what was once an eighteenth-century French building. Sitting on a bed perched on intricately carved wooden posts, with the ceiling fan whirring, I read about what happened here during the Siege of Pondicherry.

In August 1778, nearly twenty-five hundred British soldiers—both East India Company troops and Redcoats—marched up to the city's gates. The invaders outnumbered Pondicherry's Franco-Indian defenders by perhaps twenty to one but saw no need to rush things. The British dug siege trenches and battered the town with artillery barrages. After nearly two months of this, and with the city's defenses having crumbled, the French commander finally waved a white flag in October.

News of the fall of Pondicherry reached Europe during the spring of 1779 and arrived in America a few months later. Washington, Franklin, and Adams all received letters informing them of the unhappy news, while Loyalist newspapers gleefully publicized France's latest defeat. Over on the far side of the world, the French were slowly losing what overseas empire they had.

If only the East India Company and the British military had stopped at Pondicherry, they could have congratulated themselves with a tidy victory. But greed, I discovered, compelled them to keep going. And in

March 1779 they attacked the wrong town, a miscue that would change the course of the war.

Today, Mahé is a small fishing town on the Arabian Sea, on the other side of south India from Pondicherry. In 1779 it was France's main trading outpost on India's southwestern coast. The British surrounded the port in March of that year, and the French quickly surrendered. Yet the triumph would prove to be a Pyrrhic victory, for it turned out that I wasn't the only lover of French things in the subcontinent. Two centuries earlier, a man named Hyder Ali was as pro-French as they came, and it wasn't because he liked baguettes or mimes. *Mais non*, Hyder was in it for the guns.

Hyder, as Sriram had told me, was the sultan of the Mysore Kingdom. For years, France had shipped arms and gunpowder to Mahé and sold much of it to the Mysoreans. With the loss of that port to the British, Hyder's shipments were cut off; now he would be at the mercy of the ever-expanding East India Company. He wouldn't stand for that. Later that same year, Hyder would launch a preemptive attack against his foes. Thanks to the Mysoreans, the British would wind up suffering one of their worst defeats of the war. (We'll come back to Hyder's campaign—but let's leave it there for now, for there's plenty of other action across the globe from that fateful year of 1779 to catch up on first.)

This first leg of my trip on the trail of the Revolutionary War in India had already brought me a world of different experiences. Here, the scenery was so different from back home, the food so much hotter, the roads so much more crowded. It still astonished me that the places I had visited formed part of the same world war that Lexington and Concord or Valley Forge did. I also now had a better understanding of the East India Company than I did before. From here on out, whenever I thought of the Boston Tea Party, I'd keep in mind the multinational company that had sent the tea to America in the first place—the one with its own forts and army and navy.

Hyder Ali wasn't the only leader spending the summer of 1779 preparing a surprise assault on the unsuspecting British. Thousands of miles away, one of the few men who could match the sultan of Mysore for sheer boldness was also assembling his own surprising army. He was a long way from home—for this was the young governor I had first discovered at the beginning of my journey in Andalucia. In the bayous of Louisiana, Bernardo de Gálvez was preparing to shock the British.

Chapter Thirteen

BATTLE OF THE BAYOU

How the Spanish Surprised the British in Louisiana

July 1779–March 1780

I had never seen a wild pig before—yet here were a pair of them, snuffling and snorting along the banks of the river. I couldn't take my eyes off them as our boat glided past. Maybe I should have, for at first, I didn't even see the log floating toward us.

"Those hogs are vicious," the captain said in his musical Cajun voice. "They tear up the brush pretty good. I got a couple on my own land," he went on, "they're my lawnmowers. But watch out, they'll charge you." As he talked and the boars grunted away, the object in the water kept drawing closer and closer. It finally raised its head, abandoning all pretense of being a log to reveal beady yellow eyes and dinosaur-like scales. The passengers went wild, brandishing their phones.

"That gator's about thirty years old," the guide said. "Eight feet long. He's a big boy. And you know we're gonna see some even bigger ones."

I had joined this swamp tour to discover—from the safety of a flat-bottomed boat—the hazards that Bernardo de Gálvez, the young governor of the Spanish province of Louisiana, led his troops through. In August 1779 he embarked on an epic march through the bayous to surprise the British, who, sleeping in their forts along the Mississippi, were blissfully unaware that Spain had just entered the war. His Gulf Coast campaign would wind up making a key contribution to the allied victory at Yorktown later on.

Until I embarked on this quest, I had no idea that the war was fought in the swamps of the lower Mississippi Delta. And wasn't Louisiana supposed to be French, anyway? Why were the Spanish leading the charge?

Here in the bayou, I hoped to find out more about Gálvez, who had fascinated me ever since I had visited his hometown in the hills of Andalucia. He was a leader who inspired people from all walks of life to join in his madcap adventure. Best of all, the coalition that he assembled actually won battles. The French and Americans had failed in 1778 at Newport; the French and Spanish had done the same in the English Channel and at Gibraltar the following year. How was Gálvez able to break the mold?

The boat drifted through a maze of bald cypress trees dripping with Spanish moss. I glimpsed a snake as thick as my arm slide from a branch and submerge into the silence. As they waded through the waters of the bayous, their rifles hoisted high, Gálvez and his troops were not just at risk of being gored, bitten, chomped, or ambushed. They could also suffer lacerations from the saw grass—"that grass will cut your skin like a razor," the guide cheerfully told us. Others were exhausted by "the great heats of the weather," as Gálvez put it in his action report. Soldiers could sink into the mud itself, weighed down by their packs, to reemerge covered with leeches—if they emerged at all. A third turned back.

Yet the biggest problem Gálvez faced wasn't the hazards of the swamp. The British in nearby West Florida (which they had taken during the Seven Years' War) were far more powerful than his Spanish were, with nearly twice as many troops, a much larger navy, and forts all along the Gulf Coast and the eastern bank of the Mississippi River. Gálvez's men had recently intercepted secret British dispatches revealing that if war broke out, British forces were to simultaneously sail down the Mississippi from Detroit and west from Florida to seize New Orleans in a pincer movement.

Gálvez's officers counseled caution. Faced with such a superior force, the Spanish should hunker down and defend the colonial capital the best they could. Spain had only taken possession of Louisiana in 1762, when the province was given to them by France, and the local French population had not warmly embraced their new rulers. The independent-minded Creole elite had driven the first Spanish governor out of the province after he had tried to curb their authority. Whispers circulated that some Creole merchants might prefer to let the British take New Orleans so long as they didn't bomb or burn it. Did it matter who was in charge of the port city, the capital of smuggling and guilty pleasures, so long as the money kept flowing and the good times kept rolling?

Gálvez had other ideas, for he had his own advantages over the British. The first was knowledge. Bernardo's uncle, José de Gálvez, the minister of the Indies, had sent his nephew advance notice of Spain's declaration of war before it happened. Bernardo and his men had thus "prepared themselves for a rupture a considerable time" before it came, Mercy Otis Warren wrote. He would have a brief window of time to act before the British in Florida learned that the war was on and attacked.

The second advantage was himself. He was Bernardo de Gálvez, a man able to "overcome storms, dangers, disappointments, difficulties almost innumerable," as Warren put it. Not only a fighter but a man of the Enlightenment, he had calculated that there was only one path possible toward victory: He would "go and find our enemies in their own fortresses and posts," he wrote. "If not taken one by one, I know full well they are going to come find me." No matter that he held the weaker hand; Gálvez was all in.

To carry out his scheme, he assembled a most unexpected force of

Spanish soldiers from the Canary Islands and Cuba, French Creoles, free Blacks, Indians, German settlers, and Americans, each with their own reasons for joining the combat. With luck and leadership, the plan might just work. But would all these troops follow him?

He was about to find out.

It's hard to find a better place for people watching than New Orleans's Jackson Square, I thought as I settled onto a park bench. Sure, the slate gray sky looked ready to dump sheets of rain at any moment. Yet even that prospect didn't darken my mood, for in my lap I held a piece of heaven: a bag of steaming beignets, sticky with powder sugar and fried deliciousness, procured from Café du Monde across the street. The sound of a jazz quartet floated out from a nearby window. Street artists sketched tourists, fortune tellers shared omens, partiers wearing last night's beads stumbled home, and an entire congregation spilled out of St. Louis Cathedral in front of me, blending in with the sinners. Every size, shape, and race imaginable mingled in the square's steamy heat.

It was the perfect start to the morning after my bayou tour. And it wasn't only the beignets that brought a smile to my face. I must have been the only one in the crowd who knew that this plaza once was one of the magical spots in the world where the course of the American Revolution began to turn from defeat to victory.

But before I went any further exploring Gálvez's 1779 campaign, I needed to back up a bit. What were the Spanish doing here in this quintessentially French city, anyway? To find out, I attended a talk given by two New Orleans residents dedicated to uncovering the city's hidden Spanish heritage.

"Is Louisiana different because of France?" one of the presenters, a guide at the Louisiana State Museum, asked rhetorically. "Yes, but also because of Spain." A Brazilian American, Robert Freeland sometimes even dressed as Bernardo de Gálvez, in full colonial regalia, to help make New Orleans's Latino past come alive.

In 1763, he said, France gifted its Louisiana province—which included parts of fifteen current U.S. states—to Spain as recompense for coming to France's aid in the Seven Years' War, a war that had cost Spain several of its own territories. France wasn't all that sorry to see the province go. Countless Frenchmen had died in its unhealthy climate and countless French funds had left the treasury to develop the colony. For Spain, this unusual present would serve as a buffer zone for its viceroyalty of New Spain, which included Mexico and much of what is now the American West, from the English-speaking settlers to its east.

Spanish cultural influences still lurk under the surface in Louisiana today, I discovered. "Jambalaya, that's the poor man's paella, without the saffron," Freeland said. "It's a Spanish contribution." His fellow presenter, Maria Isabel Page, an honorary consul of Spain, echoed this. "The French Quarter should be called the Spanish Quarter," she said, explaining that the Spanish had built many of the neighborhood's iconic buildings. In the late eighteenth century, devastating fires destroyed most of what the French had constructed in the city, which Gálvez—who became the acting governor of the province on January 1, 1777—and his successors rebuilt. With recent Hispanic migration to the city, Page said, New Orleans was having a second Spanish renaissance.

All this amazed me. I had just come looking for military history, but it turned out some of my basic premises about New Orleans were wrong. The Spanish Quarter! Now that I thought of it, the arches and doorways and graceful interior courtyards reminded me of places I had seen on my travels in Spain and Latin America. The Spanish even thoughtfully left New Orleans all those wrought iron balconies, giving future generations of partiers a convenient place to fling beads from.

What the Spanish didn't have in centuries past, however, was a good PR agent. "Ever since the time of the Spanish Armada in 1588, Anglos have looked down on Spain and made up all sorts of stories about the

Spanish," Freeland said. "The Armada was the first step in Spain's long decline," he said. "The prejudice is even carried on today, when some look down on Hispanics in the U.S."

"We're not rewriting history," he concluded, "we're recovering lost memories." He hoped to restore the place of Gálvez in the pantheon of heroes who helped bring about American independence.

The young governor didn't have much room to maneuver. "In New Orleans, Gálvez was at ground zero—the borders with Britain were nearby," Freeland explained. "The British had a fort at Baton Rouge, on the east side of the Mississippi." Given this heavy British presence near him, whatever help Gálvez gave to the Americans at the beginning had to be in secret. He sent his private secretary to meet with the American agent, the Irish-born Oliver Pollock, in the dark of night, to give the rebels arms and munitions on credit. Pollock shipped the guns up the Mississippi to George Rogers Clark, the Virginian officer fighting in the west. Clark used these arms to take British outposts in the Illinois Country. Some Spanish supplies reached Washington's Continentals in the east and the Virginia militias as well; Governor Jefferson confided to his Spanish counterpart that he had a "grateful sense of the favors we have received at your hands."

In August 1779, with Spain having joined the war, Gálvez would soon be able to put an end to the skullduggery and work with the Americans in the open. With his secret advance knowledge of Spain's declaration of war—and also of Britain's planned invasion—he prepared to "proceed immediately to surprise and conquer wherever he could," as Warren put it.

Yet five days before his departure, a hurricane swept through New Orleans, sinking his ships, flattening houses, and ravaging farms. "Children [were] wandering through the deserted fields abandoned to the elements," he wrote, "the land flooded, and everything drowned in the river, along with my resources, supplies, and hopes."

But Gálvez was not the kind of man whose hopes could stay submerged for long. Didn't each setback contain within it an opportunity?

Surely, the enemy would never expect an attack by an army that had barely survived a hurricane. He would continue on. To do so, he needed his people to rally around him more than ever before, and not just the Spanish residents either. To inspire them, he came up with a strategy—even if it was a gamble.

On August 19, 1779, he walked out to the Plaza de Armas, today's Jackson Square, to play the hand of his life. Before throngs of people, Warren wrote, "Don Bernardo de Gálvez, Governor of Louisiana, proclaimed the independence of America at New Orleans at the head of all the forces he could collect." It was a bold move—and not a sanctioned one either. As we have seen, when it entered the war, Spain hadn't yet recognized American independence, worried about the message that would send to its Latin American colonies. Gálvez's message was by no means authorized by Madrid. Yet he was the type of man who asked for forgiveness, not permission. He knew that Spain was helping the United States in practice, even if they weren't formal allies, and that his message of solidarity would appeal to the Americans and many American sympathizers in the port city.

Equally important was what he said afterward. Rather than ordering people to follow him, he did something more radical—he asked them what *he* should do. Gálvez revealed that he had just been named the permanent governor (he had only been the acting governor until then) but didn't know whether he should accept the honor and take the oath of office. "I shall defend the province," he pledged, "but, although I am disposed to shed the last drop of my blood for Louisiana and for my king, I cannot take an oath which I may be exposed to violate, because I do not know whether you will help me in resisting the ambitious designs of the English."

He paused, the fate of the war in the southeast hanging in the balance. "What do you say? Shall I take the oath of governor? Shall I swear to defend Louisiana?"

Oui, yes, *sí*, cried the crowd. The people were with him, inspired by both his courage and his openness with them. They would swear to defend their homeland as well. They carried Gálvez on their shoulders to his house, pledging loyalty to this man and his mission. They raised sunken ships from the waters, fastened the cannons to their caissons, and prepared the provisions. They would march where he led.

With all the preparations done, there was nothing left for Gálvez to do but to take to the road. He wrote in his diary, in language that Bilbo Baggins would have admired, that he "set off in search of adventure." And, following his trail, so did I.

Today, only about 5 percent of the residents of New Iberia, a small city some 130 miles west of New Orleans, are Hispanic, but during their annual Spanish Festival their culture once again reigns supreme. Reggaeton played in the background while men stirred jambalaya in an iron pot, its smell mingling with that of funnel cake frying, crawfish boiling, and *paella valenciana* simmering. A troupe of flamenco dancers loosened up by the banana trees, getting ready to take the stage on the town bandstand.

And then came the parade, with people marching and holding yellow-and-red banners emblazoned with the name of New Iberia's seven founding families: Romero, Viator, Segura, Lopez, Prado, Migues, and, incongruously enough, Gary (who knew that Garys were so international?). Cars and jeeps and tractors cruised down the street, each ferrying a tiara-bedecked girl wearing a black-and-red sash that proclaimed the title she had won. There were the Queen, the Teen Queen, the Petite Queen, the Cattle Festival Queen, and a dizzying variety of lesser nobility, some throwing candy to the crowd, others flinging beads. They were followed by one of the few male royals on the scene: the Baby King, a beaming toddler whom several queens were fawning over.

I spied an older man proudly marching in a tri-corner hat and a greatcoat. Could that be? Yes! Another Bernardo de Gálvez. Immigrants from the region of Málaga—Gálvez's home turf—founded this town in the spring of 1779, only a few months before Bernardo's lightning campaign, and the memory of that long-ago event still remained. Some of the marchers were likely the descendents of Gálvez's militia army.

Bernardo de Gálvez was not only a governor but also a general. Yet, under the structure of the Spanish Empire, the province of Louisiana reported to the Captaincy General of Cuba on military matters. And Havana wanted no part of Gálvez's ambitious plan of attack. The officers in Cuba were perfectly happy to stay right where they were, thank you very much, sipping proto-mojitos and taking bets on just how spectacularly the young upstart would fail. They eventually would send a battalion, but it came too late to help.

Instead, Gálvez had to construct a DIY army through the militia companies that were under his direct command. He had been working on this for some time, arranging for settlers to come from Málaga and from the Canary Islands, where his father Mathías had served as governor. When unmarried young men arrived, Gálvez quickly assigned them to his new army and began training them up. Yet the Spanish population never made up more than 15 percent of Louisiana's population. For his militia to turn into a formidable force, he'd have to bring in other peoples too.

He started with the French. The French residents were an unruly bunch, having chased a prior Spanish governor out of town after he had reduced them to eating tortillas rather than baguettes. (True story, although the lack of French bread was only one of several grievances.) But Gálvez had spent a couple of years on a charm campaign, restoring rights to the French elite and buttering them up *en français* as much as he could. His popularity soared, especially after he married the most eligible French Creole in New Orleans, Marie Félicité de Saint-Maxent d'Estrehan, a woman "of surpassing loveliness," as one swooning admirer called her. Soon the Creole elite was clamoring to join the militia, especially the

Distinguished Company of New Orleans Carabineros, the cavalry group personally led by the young governor.

Nearly two hundred free Blacks elected to join the New Orleans Colored Militia. Unlike some American commanders, Gálvez welcomed Blacks serving alongside Whites in combat. He was no abolitionist, to be sure, yet he did soften somewhat the harsh slave laws that the French had established. The population of free Blacks in New Orleans grew under his rule, even as generations of enslaved people continued to live in bondage in the region.

"One hundred and sixty Indians undertook the march" too, Gálvez wrote in his campaign journal; he had established relations with the Biloxi, Atakapa, and Choctaw. After leaving some troops behind to protect New Orleans the best they could, Gálvez set off in August 1779 at the head of "600 [men] of all kinds and colors," as he wrote in his journal. He marched with Spaniards, Mexicans, Irish, German settlers, free Blacks, French Creoles, Indians, and nine Americans. Gálvez was "in total command of the troops," his treasurer wrote, for "he not only treats his troops with the cordiality that is natural for him and that wins his soldiers' hearts, but he also transforms himself into an Indian, a creole, a soldier, to flatter each in his own way, without losing the decorum he owes to his own person.

"He, the first to sleep out in the open, because of the haste of the march and the lack of tents, was imitated by everyone," the treasurer went on, "if the lack of bread makes him eat rice, everyone does the same as if they were feasting."

Their objective was to conquer the three forts held by the British upstream along the Mississippi, which threatened New Orleans and blocked American trade along the river. Gálvez recorded that his men covered 105 miles northwest through the bayous in six days, marching up to the gates of the first of the strongholds, Fort Bute. And, not far from the site of his first battle in Louisiana, I had found one of the few people in the world who could tell me about it.

⸙

Stephen Estopinal asked me to meet him at a Vietnamese café on the outskirts of Baton Rouge, a few miles away from where Fort Bute once stood. He had gray hair, a broad smile, and a lilting New Orleans accent. Today he hadn't dressed in his full colonial era military regalia, which he only put on when engaging in living history. But he still had quite a story to tell, both about Gálvez's battles and how he had come to learn about them.

Gálvez and his men marching through the bayous.

"I grew up in St. Bernard Parish, east of New Orleans, which was named for Bernardo de Gálvez," he started. "My dad was almost pure Isleño—all his ancestors came from the Canary Islands, except for one Acadian mixed in. My grandfather spoke Spanish and French. He was a trapper and a 'market hunter,' which means that he sold what he hunted at the market in New Orleans. At the age of twenty-one, he got a job in a tannery, and that's when he had to learn English.

"My grandfather later worked at a funeral home," he continued. "He lived in an apartment above it. I'd visit him sometimes as a kid, and he'd take me out hunting for rabbits at night. But he didn't have room in the apartment, so I slept below with the caskets. He told me, don't worry, that *monsieur* over there won't bother you."

After an experience like that, nothing fazed Stephen. He began working as a land surveyor and, as he researched the history of land grants in his region, became fascinated by the number of Spanish surnames he encountered. He began to realize that the history of Louisiana owed much to the Spanish, but that group—his group—was often written out of the history books.

He became just as upset by this bias as Robert Freeland was. "The British put down the Spanish; they portrayed them as criminals, as horrible people. This was their political propaganda, to downplay the importance of the Spanish in the world. It was very effective, particularly because most of the early writers here were Anglophiles. It played into their prejudices very well." Mercy Otis Warren, I realized, was one of the few early historians able to overcome this narrative and give the Spanish their due place in the story of the Revolution.

Stephen began to portray a Spanish soldier at historical reenactments—and then took things a step further, writing a series of novels exploring forgotten periods in Louisiana's early history. Of all the stories he encountered in his research, none captivated him more than that of Bernardo de Gálvez.

"His original plan was to bring his troops up here by barge," he said, but the hurricane struck and destroyed most of his transport boats. "Instead, he had to march them up. The swamp was pretty rough. He sent the big guns up on what barges they had. Trying to get through cypress swamps with any equipment is very hard. You can't slide them across because of the cypress knees. And there are plagues of mosquitoes. I know, I grew up in it."

The British had reinforced Fort Bute with four hundred German mercenaries before the war broke out. Yet they were no match for the army that suddenly emerged from the swamps. "When General Gálvez moved in with his army, the British mostly abandoned the fort," Stephen said. "A few men stayed behind, while everyone else boogied up north to Baton Rouge."

Gálvez likely could have waited out the few soldiers who remained in the fort and eventually received their surrender, but he saw an opportunity for his novice army to practice combat operations. So he attacked at dawn, ordering his father-in-law to be the first to scale the enemy walls, assuring him that this was a great honor. (Do not try this with your own father-in-law.) Gálvez's men won the battle handily, providing a morale boost for his army and achieving Spain's first victory of the war.

The fort at Baton Rouge would present a much tougher challenge: It had nine hundred defenders with thirteen cannon, and was protected by a moat and sharpened wooden stakes. Gálvez paused before attacking. "He was waiting for intelligence to come," Stephen explained. "No general of the time used intelligence as much as General Gálvez. He knew more about British forces at a fort than the British did. He learned that no relief had come yet for the British from Pensacola, so he went on to attack them," despite the odds.

"General Gálvez came up with a pretty neat trick," Stephen continued. "He had the militia demonstrate in an area east of the fort to distract the defenders. The British began to fire at them. Meanwhile, south of the fort, he hid his siege cannon behind trees. Then at night he had his engineers cut down the trees so he'd have a clear shot at the British." When dawn broke the next morning, the British realized their mistake. All night long, they had been firing at the wrong place.

Gálvez opened his artillery on the fort. After three hours of this, the British waved the white flag—but, in a brilliant tactical stroke, Gálvez said that he would only accept their surrender if they also agreed to give up an additional fort upriver at Natchez. The third and final post thus fell without a shot being fired. Never again would those British strongholds "infest and ruin our trade on the Mississippi," as Patrick Henry had put it.

While this was going on, Spanish and American ships battled the British on the lakes of Louisiana. The American naval commander, the fearsomely named Captain William Pickles, took a British naval brigantine without casualties. With the British neutralized on the lakes and the Spanish occupying their forts, Gálvez's victory was total. He took a thousand prisoners and now controlled a thousand miles' worth of terrain. "[I] had to return back for lack of anything else to conquer," he explained.

The people of New Orleans greeted him with a hero's welcome, with church bells pealing and people crying out in joy. Gálvez deflected the praise, instead showering it on his soldiers, those men of all nations, noting their "bravery, intrepidity, and constancy" in his report of the battle, "and of the love, zeal, and extraordinary goodwill with which they have behaved."

"He was the one who drove the British out of the Mississippi. If there's anyone great in the history of Louisiana, it's General Gálvez," Stephen concluded. "He was never defeated."

The following month, George Washington's aide-de-camp, an officer named Alexander Hamilton, must have been surprised when he saw the mysterious care package that arrived at Continental Army headquarters in West Point, New York. It contained a "Sea Tortoise weighing more than 100 pounds (in a very good condition) and a Quantity of Lemons." Along with the gifts, the shipment included a letter from Juan de Miralles, the Spanish merchant who had moved to Philadelphia to serve as the liaison between the rebels and the Spanish Crown, recounting how Gálvez was moving against the British in Louisiana.

Washington found the tortoise to be of a very good condition indeed, but the news that came with it to be even "more agreeable," the general replied. "I promise myself the most happy events from the known spirit of your nation. United with the arms of France," he continued, "we have everything to hope over the arms of our common enemy, the English."

The next spring, Washington got even better news from the Spanish (along with some chocolate cakes and almonds from Havana—what is it with the Spanish and their gifts?). Gálvez had launched an attack on the British-held Fort Charlotte in Mobile. The Spanish authorities in Cuba had once again refused to help him, yet once again the young governor set out anyway, alongside his trusty sidekick, the American naval officer Captain Pickles (whose name I really, really love). Together, they assembled a DIY fleet of their own of fourteen sloops and brigs they had captured from the British and commandeered from Louisiana fishermen.

And once again, tragedy struck. A severe storm hit the fleet just outside of Mobile; some of the ships foundered on the sandbars and four hundred men drowned. Yet Gálvez and the valiant Pickles continued on. After all, Bernardo's uncle José, the minister of the Indies, considered the British forts at Mobile and Pensacola, in the territory of West Florida, to be the "keys to the Gulf of Mexico"; taking them was a necessity, not to mention a point of honor.

Following a brief siege (during which Bernardo gallantly sent the British commander of the fort a package of wine, cigars, and oranges to help tide him over), Gálvez and Pickles took Fort Charlotte. The Spanish now held Mobile and the British forts along the Mississippi. If he could take Fort George in Pensacola as well, Gálvez would be master of the Gulf, while Pickles would be the lord of the briny sea. After Washington got the news of the victory, the thrilled general set the day's passwords and countersigns for his sentries in camp as "Mobile, Pensacola, Gálvez, and Spain." (The good captain did not make the list, for it would never do for a Continental sentry to call out "Pickles!")

I ended my journey as impressed with Bernardo de Gálvez as Washington had been. Gálvez's story had opened a window into the rich history of when the French Quarter was Spanish, a side of Louisiana's past that I had never known existed—and that some intentionally downplayed over the years.

And Gálvez's leadership—in taking control of situations in which he was the underdog, bringing disparate forces together, and respecting his soldiers as men—was one for the ages. I thought back to my visit to Macharaviaya, the village where he was born. Perhaps because his own father had started out as a shepherd, Bernardo had been able to connect with soldiers of humble backgrounds. He walked the walk, sleeping on the ground next to his comrades in arms, sharing their rice, and putting himself (and his long-suffering father-in-law) in harm's way. Thanks to these qualities, Gálvez had brought people together into a cohesive fighting force, one that could overcome hurricanes and storms to achieve great victories. Here was a lesson for the rest of the coalition, should they wish to follow it.

Incredibly, to the great chagrin of the British, he wasn't the only Gálvez who would surprise them in battle in 1779. Further south, on the other end of the Gulf, Bernardo's father Mathías was preparing a lightning strike of his own. It all began in Mexico's Yucatán Peninsula, on the shores of the Lagoon of Seven Colors.

Chapter Fourteen

WHEN THE AMERICAN REVOLUTION WAS MEXICAN

How the Spanish in Mexico Aided the American Cause

July 1779–July 1780

The morning sun was already climbing high, bathing the town of Bacalar in light. Reggae music drifted over from a house painted in pastel blues and yellows down by the water. We watched an itinerant coconut salesman pedaling his bicycle while I parked our rental, and Liana happily waved him over to us.

We had spent a few idyllic coconut-fueled days in the area, much like a normal family on vacation in Mexico's Yucatán Peninsula would—swimming in freshwater *cenotes*, exploring ruins, and trying different versions of *pibil*, a dish of slow-cooked pork wrapped in banana leaves. We had persevered through sunburn, upset stomachs, and a disturbing lack of sites related to the American Revolution to visit (an affliction that seemed to be bothering only one member of our group). The kids tumbled out of the car, looking forward to perhaps another swim in the lagoon below us, followed by Mexican Cokes made with real sugar.

But—as always—we were on the clock. I had to gently turn the family away from the inviting lagoon, directing them instead to the fort looming at the top of the hill, its gray limestone walls visible through the palm fronds. I alone in our traveling party knew that this peaceful-looking scene masked centuries of bloodshed and violence. The San Felipe fort played a role in countless wars—including, of course, my favorite one. You didn't think I came all the way down here just for the coconuts, did you?

In the fall of 1779, word reached the sixty-three-year-old captain-general of Guatemala, Mathías de Gálvez, that the British were planning to make a move in the region. Mathías had only recently been posted to this job, one of the seven captaincy generals that Spain had established in the New World. He governed a sprawling territory that stretched from the Yucatán to Costa Rica. Mathías's brother José, the foreign minister, had sent him here knowing that Central America was likely to be a flash point in the fight against the British, just as he had named Mathías's son Bernardo as governor of the territory of Louisiana, another hot spot. Both Mathías and José reported to the viceroy of New Spain in Mexico City, who governed from California to Central America and the Caribbean.

In Bacalar, we—at least I—had come to get a sense of Gálvez's campaign, for it was here at this fort that he assembled his troops to respond to the growing British threat. I wanted to explore the campaign that ensued through the challenging terrain of the jungles of Central America and also discover, more generally, how the Spanish in Mexico helped the American cause.

Outside the fort, a short, smiling man wearing sandals emblazoned with the words *Dos Equis* walked up to us and introduced himself. His name was Carlos Cruz Hernández; he was a guide whose services I had arranged the day before. Originally from the nearby state of Tabasco, he had come to the Yucatán years ago and fallen in love with Bacalar and Mayan history, enrolling in state-run classes to become a guide to his adopted town. I quickly learned that the fort's Revolutionary War history was just one moment in the centuries of conflict it had seen.

'"The Mayans called this place Sian Ka'an Bakhalal," Carlos told us. "The word *Bakhalal* means 'reeds' and *Sian Ka'an* 'the place where the sky is born.' The Spanish came in 1544, and this place saw many years of violence. Pirates were constantly attacking." For well over two centuries, Spain had occupied much of what is now Mexico. However, the Mayans had put up a fierce resistance in the Yucatán and the Spanish had a relatively light presence in the peninsula as a result.

"Starting in the eighteenth century, the British and Spanish began fighting," Carlos went on. "That's why the fort of San Felipe was built, to protect the community of people from the Canary Islands from the British." Liana perked up—her family in Cuba descended from Canary Islanders. She might even have had (very) distant relatives still living in this town.

"Come, I'll show you our artifacts." Carlos led us over a stone bridge into the fort. An iguana in the thick grass growing in the moat below looked up at us bemusedly and flicked its tongue out. Carlos pointed out a rusty cannon in the yard of the fort, then brought us inside the main building of the fort to view glass cases stuffed with cutlasses, blunderbusses, and pistols, the detritus of centuries of bloodshed.

"The worst fighting was between the Spanish, and then the Mexicans in the nineteenth century, against the Mayan peoples," he said. "When priests asked the Mayans to stop the killings, the Mayans responded, 'You showed us the way. We are only doing what you taught us.'"

He paused and looked sad. "These stories aren't taught in Mexico today. People don't know the story. Schools don't tell how it is, they don't discuss the massacres." Here at San Felipe, though, the proof of these years of fighting is very much on display. The fort's museum preserves—a tad gruesomely for my taste—the skeleton of a Spanish soldier killed by a Mayan warrior in a case embedded in the floor. "There is some talk of giving him a proper burial," Carlos added, somewhat sheepishly.

This fort had seen a lot more action than I had expected; it had witnessed hundreds of years of warfare. "How did all this fighting start?" I asked.

"Follow me," Carlos replied. "I will show you what they were fighting over." He led us back across the bridge to a gnarled tree. "This was what brought the Spanish and the British here in the first place. We call it *palo de tinte*." The wood has a number of names in English—Campeche wood, logwood, bloodwood. "You cut it," he told us, "and put it in water, and it will produce a dye." And not just any dye—bloodwood produced a rich, royal purple, in fantastic demand in the seventeenth and eighteenth centuries. "It was worth its weight in gold," Carlos said.

British loggers set up settlements along the Bay of Honduras, ignoring Spanish claims, particularly in what would come to be called British Honduras (and which I'll call by its modern name, Belize), a land that begins just thirty miles to our south. The Spanish spent the greater part of a century trying to dislodge them; the loggers retaliated by joining pirates in attacks on Bacalar and other Spanish towns. "This is why the Spanish built Fort San Felipe in 1733," Carlos explained. "It was to protect against the British just on the other side of the river."

The resounding British victory in the Seven Years' War changed the equation. The Spanish, on the losing side, were forced to acknowledge British rights to log in Central America. The British, in turn, promised not to erect fortifications. And then the Revolutionary War broke out.

I knew something about this part of the story from the excellent works of Thomas Chávez, a scholar in New Mexico who specialized in Spain's role in the American War of Independence. According to Chávez, by the time of the Revolution, the Spanish had concluded they had gotten a raw deal. The British had broken their promise; they had built forts in Belize and looked prime to make a territorial grab.

In fact, things were worse than the Spanish even realized. The British didn't just want to control the bloodwood trade; they wanted Central America itself. London had developed secret plans to annex land around Lake Nicaragua in the event that Spain joined the war. If ships headed up the San Juan River to the lake, they would then only be eleven miles from the Pacific, making that ocean accessible if a canal were built. His

Majesty's Navy could cut weeks off the dangerous voyage around Cape Horn. The lightly defended west coast of Mexico itself might even fall to British forces. Where would the British Empire stop?

The Spanish resolved to evict their pasty foes from the region once and for all. His Catholic Majesty made the "expulsion of the British from the Bay of Honduras" a prominent military objective, writing it right into the Treaty of Aranjuez with the French.

Our tour of San Felipe ended with Carlos bringing us up to the fort's watchtower, where we thanked him and bid farewell. The water below us—known as the Lagoon of Seven Colors for its shifting hues of green, blue, and turquoise—stretched to the horizon, with lilies floating along its edges. Liana stared wistfully at a small fish restaurant nestled in a grove of palm trees, their fronds rustling in the soft breeze. The scene couldn't have looked more peaceful. And yet it was right here that the bloody war between the Spanish and British in the tropics began.

On a fine day in September 1779, the lagoon filled up with unexpected colors: the brown hulls of transport ships, the blindingly white uniforms of the eight hundred Spanish infantry troops aboard them, the somber black of their cannonade, and the splendid gold trim on the tri-corner hat of Lieutenant Colonel José Rosado, the expedition's commander. The Spanish—following orders issued by Gálvez, who had received an advance warning of Spain's declaration of war—had assembled this force in the fort and were now sailing south to launch a surprise attack on a British position in Belize. The fighting in the region would continue for three years.

I recounted some of this story to Liana and the kids. "How would you like to follow your Canary Island ancestors?" I asked. "Who's ready to invade Belize?"

"I am," said Liana, always a good sport. "But first some ceviche."

Later that afternoon, we were on a motorboat crashing through whitecaps on the Río Hondo, the broad river that divides Mexico and Belize. Its captain, a man named Pablo, normally takes fishing parties out on the river but was happy to oblige our request to travel along the river—following the route of the Spanish, of course. To do so, we'd backtrack from his town of Chetumal to a spot he knew where the canal that led south from Bacalar spilled into the river.

Pablo was in his thirties, built like a wrestler, short and stocky. He was trained as an agronomist but was a waterman at heart, he told us. As the boat crashed through the green, foamy water, he pointed out wildlife along the way—cormorants perched on posts, searching for fish, an albatross soaring above the red mangroves.

"There's Belize, right across the water. Look at all those pine trees growing—we don't have them on our side." A Black fisherman on the bank across from us smiled and waved. I thought about the unusual history of Belize, the only country in Central America that once was a British colony. With many descendents of enslaved people and of the Garifuna—freed slaves who intermarried with Indigenous peoples—it has the highest population of Afro-Caribbeans in the region.

I had always wanted to visit Belize, but it wasn't in the cards on this trip; the country required a visa and a three-day minimum stay at the time. I hadn't even brought our passports with us on the boat; they were back at our Airbnb. We'd just have to see it from afar.

Pablo reached an opening among the mangroves on the Mexican side of the river and dropped his engine from a roar to a putter. "This is what they call the Canal of Pirates," he explained. "It goes from Bacalar here to the Río Hondo." He turned his boat into the gap, more of a watery path through the jungle than a full-fledged canal.

"Those are white mangroves," Pablo said, gesturing to the swamp around us. "They clean the water." He pointed out old trunks submerged under the water. "Before, everything was infested with wood. They shipped so much wood down this canal, you could walk down it on top of the logs." He told us how his grandfather was from Belize, a logger and rubber plantation worker. His grandfather had met his Mexican wife, who came from a family of fishermen, and moved across the border to live.

After a while, Pablo killed the motor altogether. "This is a great spot for a swim if you want," he said. With the sun relentlessly beating down on us, we quickly agreed and splashed in. The water was as warm as a bath, the mud squishy around our toes. Palms swayed in the breeze.

"I never imagined this history was here," Liana replied. "People come to the Yucatán for tourism, and no one knows the role this place played."

I too had found this trip to be fascinating. Before my journeys, I had had no idea that people in Mexico—from Spanish soldiers, to mestizo craftsmen of mixed ancestry, to Indigenous peoples who provided food and maintained buildings—had all made contributions to the allied effort in the Revolutionary War. The fact that troops left on a historic expedition from a fort only a couple of hundred miles south from Cancún, that worldwide party destination, somehow made the whole story seem even more improbable.

Finally, Pablo revved up the engine and we moved back toward the river, passing blue herons and a tree weighed down with an enormous termite nest. The water again turned deeper.

"Can I take the wheel?" I asked Pablo. Under my direction, the boat veered a little wildly, scattering a heron as I overcorrected with the steering wheel, but I soon got the hang of it. We moved smoothly down the canal. The wind ruffled my hair as the Río Hondo came into sight. With the adrenaline pumping inside me, I felt like the captain of an expedition—which, momentarily, I was.

This campaign isn't well-known today, but I had read up on it in Thomas Chávez's works. Gálvez's fleet came down this canal out of Bacalar and surprised the British logwood men on the other side of the river, taking two sloops and schooner. After mounting guns on these ships and adding them to their small navy, the Spanish then sailed some one hundred miles south to the main British stronghold on the island of St. George's Caye.

The Spanish silently brought landing parties ashore in the dead of night. As dawn broke on September 15, 1779, the guns roared from the Spanish ships while the landing parties attacked the astonished British. Three British frigates arrived on the scene later, too late to help. The Spanish had already conquered Fort St. George, burning the settlers' houses and taking some four hundred settlers and enslaved workers prisoner.

In retaliation, a month later, the furious British sent their own force out of Jamaica to attack the Spanish stronghold of San Fernando de Omoa, in today's Honduras. Twelve British ships bombarded the fort from the water. When the Spanish still refused to surrender, the British landed an assault party in the middle of the night (the same tactic the Spanish had used at St. George's Caye earlier), which managed to open the gates. The British took both the fort and two Spanish ships moored in the harbor—and discovered, to their amazement, that the holds of the ships were bursting with silver.

During the fighting in Honduras, legend has it that an English soldier gallantly offered an extra sword to an unarmed Spanish defender.

Gálvez would never let this stand. He considered San Fernando de Omoa to be nothing less than the "key and outer wall of the kingdom." Two months later, after assembling a new, well-armed attack force, he laid siege to the fort, bombarding it with cannon. The British, suffering from tropical diseases, waved the white flag and the Spanish regained San Fernando. The "arms of Spain," Mercy Otis Warren wrote, had prevailed in the Bay of Honduras.

As for us, it had been a day of discoveries, a glimpse at how battles of the American Revolution were fought deep in the tropics. "If only we had had the chance to go to Belize," I said to Liana wistfully. "Then this day really would have been perfect."

Pablo overheard and just smiled. Suddenly he was gunning the engine, making a beeline for a cove on the other side of the river.

"Wait, are we leaving Mexico?" I asked, confused.

"Over there is the Lagoon of Belize," he told us, pointing to an opening in the forest. "It's on the other side of the frontier." He looked around, but there were no officials patrolling, no fishermen present. Not a soul in sight as we headed ever faster toward Belize.

And since declaring here that we might have crossed an international border without papers or permission might get all of us, including Pablo, in some sort of trouble, you'll just have to wonder whether he then roared his boat into the small lagoon, the wind whipping our hair wildly, some of us struck dumb with surprise, others laughing uproariously as he took us on the fastest lap of a lagoon you could ever dream of, our friendly invasion of Belize finally complete.

Sometime later, I noticed that Professor Chávez was giving a book talk in D.C., not far from where I live, so I reached out to him. We met up at a bistro and, over a dinner of steak and Malbec, he told me about his own decades-long journey learning about the Spanish contributions to the American Revolution.

"It all began when I was a young PhD student in history, working as a curator at the Palace of Governors in Santa Fe, New Mexico," he began. "One day, I was rummaging around in the museum's basement and found a box with a notation on it—'Three Flags from Spain.' I opened it up and found three hand-painted regimental flags just sitting there. I thought, what the hell is this? No one had any idea why we had them.

"So, I called the Spanish embassy. They answered and told me that we fought in your war for independence. During the Bicentennial in 1976, they told me that Spain sent regimental flags to all the U.S. states that had been part of the Spanish Empire.

"I had been through grad school, but no one had ever talked about this. So, one day when I was in Washington, D.C., I stopped in the National Archives and asked for documents about Spain's involvement in the American Revolution. They looked at me like, 'what are you talking about?'

"But as I kept asking for documents about Louisiana during the war, I found a lot of information. And then I realized that there was something there." After that, Tom—for the professor eschewed formality—began a journey that took him across Spain, where he poked into dusty archives and forgotten corners of libraries until he had constructed a full narrative of Spain's immense involvement in the conflict.

I told him about my adventures in the Yucatán with the family. "How else did the people of Mexico contribute to the Revolutionary War?" I asked between bites of steak.

"Lots of ways," Tom replied, "starting with cattle." I guess we ordered well, I thought. "The first cattle drives in what is now the United States happened because of the Spanish in Texas, which was part of New Spain. They sent around twelve to fifteen thousand head of cattle to Bernardo de Gálvez's army in Louisiana." The first cowboys might have been people from what was then Mexico—and the first cattle drive was undertaken to support Spanish troops during the Revolutionary War? Once again, I felt as if I had slipped into an alternative universe. But Tom had tracked down the proof. Today, I learned, a statue in San Antonio commemorates the event.

"That's not all," he continued. "Mexico was where Spanish *pesos fuertes* were minted—that's where the silver came from. It was the only place allowed to print money outside Spain. Have you heard of pieces of eight? That's what they called the Spanish dollar, it could be broken into eight. 'Two bits' meant a quarter. Spanish money was so valuable that some U.S. states used it as currency. Our first printed money said, 'worth one Spanish dollar.'"

"What about the dollar sign?" I asked. "I heard that has a Spanish origin?"

"Sure," said Tom. "Have you seen the flag of Spain? It has two columns with ribbons wrapped around them. They represent the Pillars of Hercules, what they called the Strait of Gibraltar in ancient times. When the American agent Oliver Pollock got money from Bernardo de Gálvez, he put a line through an S to represent Spanish pesos. He might have been drawing a Spanish symbol, or he might have been just writing 'Ps' for pesos," he said. "But it stuck."

In March 1780, Tom continued, King Carlos III instituted a special tax to support the war—each Indian in New Spain had to pay one peso; each Spaniard, two. The Spanish collected 300,000 pesos in Oaxaca, in Mexico, which Mathías used for his campaign in Central America. People across New Spain contributed their money, from California to Arizona and beyond. The tax would have been paid by his ancestors too, he said. "My heritage in part is Spanish. My ancestors came to New Mexico, then part of New Spain, in 1601. I'm thirteenth-generation New Mexican."

"What were they doing at the time of the American Revolution?" I asked.

"They were in Santa Fe," he replied. "They likely had corn and an orchard of fruit trees out of town. Some dealt with sheep." I imagined a distant Chávez, paying the tax to raise money that supported the American War of Independence. "That's amazing," I said.

Tom smiled and swirled his wine. "People get surprised sometimes when I tell them what my ancestors were doing thirteen generations ago. But, of course, everyone has thirteen generations of ancestors and more. You just have to know the geographic locale that they were in."

One attempt to support the war effort backfired, however. "Spain tried to tax pulque in Mexico, which is a drink made from the maguey plant," Tom said. "They threw a tax of half a real on each glass. Guess how well that went over!" he laughed. The liquor kept flowing, tax-free, in the *pulquerias*, the speakeasies of the day. Help with the war effort, sure, the people of Mexico said, but lay off our drinks.

I recounted our trip down the canal, which interested Tom greatly. "So, what happened after Mathías de Gálvez pushed the British out of Belize and Honduras?" I asked.

"After that came one of the most vicious campaigns of the war," Tom replied. He spun out the fantastic tale of how the British navy—led by the twenty-one-year-old Horatio Nelson in his first command—escorted a force of some three thousand soldiers to Nicaragua. The flotilla sailed up the San Juan River, headed toward Lake Nicaragua. The British planned nothing less than slicing Spanish-held Central America in two and building a canal to allow their ships to cross from the Caribbean to the Pacific. That way, they could establish a permanent foothold in the region, while their navy could terrorize the Mexican coast and strike against Spanish possessions in the Pacific, like the Philippines. Mathías de Gálvez would never let that stand.

"Mathías might have been the most successful general of the entire war," Tom said. "That's because he had to fight in the worst conditions, the jungles of Central America. It was humid, there were all sorts of snakes. It was slash and burn—imagine it kind of like Vietnam.

"The English took a fort in Nicaragua, the Fortress of the Immaculate

Conception. Mathías de Gálvez countered by building another fort upstream and laying siege. There was bloody fighting, with bayonets. Imagine the humidity, and being in those uniforms. It was a miserable place to be fighting."

We spent so much time talking about jungles and pesos and Spanish diplomats that when the waiter finally dropped off the check, we had closed the place down. Yet even though we had been chatting for hours, there was still so much ground left to cover. The fighting in Central America would go on for years to come (and we'll return to it later to see how it turned out). As we got ready to leave, I asked Tom what his lifelong quest to bring Spain's role in the Revolution to light meant to him.

"It means a lot to me for two reasons," he said. "When we remember Spain, it gives us a more complete history, which, as a historian, I advocate. We have to remember what really happened and say it."

But there might have been more to it for Tom, this thirteenth-generation New Mexican, whose ancestors had lived in New Spain for nearly 250 years before their land became part of the United States. "Knowing about the Spanish makes a beautiful story even more beautiful," he said.

On September 15, 1779—the very same day that Mathías de Gálvez's troops were attacking the British in Belize and Bernardo was laying siege to Baton Rouge—George Washington was bringing the new French ambassador, the Chevalier de la Luzerne, up the Hudson River to West Point for a meeting. The American general was worried; his troops' enlistments were about to run out, and he couldn't pay them even if they stayed on. The general had gone the extra mile to make his guest feel at home, ordering fine Bordeaux for the occasion and asking his military bands to play French songs. Washington needed the meeting to go well, for the Americans were desperate to receive more French help—particularly naval support (and more cash would be fine too). To make sure his guest arrived safely, the American general even took over the tiller of the boat himself when a storm hit. He was leaving nothing to chance.

The next day, after a fine dinner, the two men got down to business. They discussed Bernardo de Gálvez's planned campaign in Florida, with Washington pledging to send Continental troops to support it if he was able to. And then La Luzerne finally got to the question he had been waiting to pop: Would Washington agree to host French soldiers on American soil?

That would be something new. The French had sent arms, money, officers, and even fleets but had never sent troops to the United States. Many Americans shuddered at the very idea—what if these Catholic soldiers from a superpower never left? Would they be trading one monarchy for another? The Comte de Vergennes, though, wanted to win the war quickly, and he had begun to think that American troops needed some help to finish the job.

Given the precarious state of his own army, Washington felt that he had no choice but to let the French march in, as "humiliating" as he admitted that it was in private. Now it would be up to King Louis XVI to decide whether to approve this plan.

And so, it's time to turn our gaze back to France, for the success of the war in America would largely turn on a decision made there. (Yes, as if exploring the Yucatán wasn't enough, I had more travels to do in France. Please don't hate.) In March 1780, a frigate left a French port with the king's decision. The man carrying the message containing it was none other than the Marquis de Lafayette, on board a ship named the *Hermione*. In a rainy, windswept port in France, that was the very ship I was about to board.

Chapter Fifteen

WHOM CAN WE TRUST?

How the French and Americans Began to Work Together

May–October 1780

"Welcome on board," said a short, wiry young man wearing a beret, who introduced himself as Teva. I climbed into a frigate with a striking black-and-gold hull, a jaunty-looking gold lion on the bow, and pennants snapping in the wind. In better times, it looked like it could outrace British cruisers on the open sea. But today, the *Hermione* was in dry dock in the French port of Anglet, surrounded by scaffolding and sheets of heavy plastic.

"Our boat is sick!" Teva said sheepishly. "It's at the doctor's. We hope to get it back out to sea in another year or so." Each day, the crew brought interested landlubbers on board for a tour, which helped raise money for the ship's repairs.

"This ship is an exact replica of the one that Lafayette took to cross the Atlantic in 1780 to join George Washington and the American rebels," he went on. "We launched it in 2014 after seventeen years of work. But now there is a fungus that is attacking its hull. That is why we have it here." The fungal attack had destroyed more than 5 percent of the hull already. I hoped the restoration efforts worked and helped keep the memory of the ship's namesake alive, for the original *Hermione* would prove to be among the most important vessels in American history.

As 1780 dawned, Frenchmen in the great shipyard of Brest were working overtime to overhaul their country's fleet. The Comte de Vergennes's shipbuilding campaign, carried out over years, had borne fruit; France now had nearly as many ships of the line as the British did. But many of the French ships had come in for hard use and needed an overhaul before they could return to the seas. The question was where they would sail when they did.

Vergennes had heard reports from some returning French officers that the American army was in bad shape. Recruitment was down; some thought the American public's enthusiasm for the war had flagged. Vergennes had to choose: Should he press on to win the war in America? Or should he cut his losses in that theater and focus on other places where France had interests, like the Caribbean and India?

The stakes were high. Some in the French cabinet were urging the king to put an end to this costly war. One proposal that was starting to be discussed in back rooms would have Britain agreeing to recognize American independence, but only with respect to the lands that the Patriots firmly controlled. Under this scenario, New York City, key parts of the American South, and the western lands between the Appalachians and the Mississippi would remain British and not form part of the new nation. Should Vergennes agree to push for a deal like that?

In early 1780, Vergennes made up his mind—and got King Louis's blessing for his plan. France would send a force to America, which he called the *Expédition Particulière,* the Special Expedition, under the command of the Comte de Rochambeau. The minister was hedging his bets a little; the force would be smaller than Washington wanted. Still, Vergennes committed to sending thousands of French soldiers and a flotilla of ships to help the rebels, with more to follow after more ships had been rehabilitated. The *Hermione* would serve as the advance party, with Lafayette on board. His orders were to cross the Atlantic, share the happy news of this new expedition with Washington, and start making arrangements for the French army that would follow in his wake.

On the modern-day *Hermione,* Teva brought us to the main deck. "It took us two thousand oak trees to construct this ship," he said. "We followed the old methods of shipbuilding wherever we could." The frigate carried thirty-two guns, more than enough to overpower a brig or a sloop. Yet while it looked impressive to me, in the eighteenth century the *Hermione* would have been considered only a medium-sized ship.

The Hermione *in better days.*

Teva showed us one of the ship's cannons—brought onshore during the restoration—and the vessel's giant steering wheel. He then took us into a small cabin. "Shield your eyes if you want to remain in the eighteenth century," he said, laughing, and pointing out the modern equipment. "We have radar here, just in case."

He led us down an iron ladder below deck. "Here is the big bell," he said. "It's very important to this ship. It used to be to signal a call to battle. Now it's used to call us to dinner!" He went on to lovingly describe the menus on board. "It's very important to our morale that we eat well." (They are French, after all.) Teva then showed us where the sailors sleep. "On board we have six professional sailors and sixty volunteers. Some of us sleep in these hammocks, others in beds. You might get an elbow or two in the night from a sleep mate, you'll never know who did it.

"But this is nothing. In Lafayette's time, there would have been 306 men down here. Can you imagine the smells? When we sleep here today, we smell the toilets, the kitchen, the rest of the crew. Can you imagine with five times as many men?" He paused dramatically. "And guess what else they had with them?" he asked expectantly. "Thirty sheep!"

Teva then led us into the captain's cabin. Even though it was small, it was a refined, sheep-free zone. "This was where the captain took his meals. Today, of course, the captain eats with us." He pointed out the system of ropes that kept the table and chairs secure when the captain was eating; afterward, the furniture could be taken away and lashed securely. A portrait of Lieutenant de Latouche, the fifty-three-year-old aristocratic commander of the ship back in 1780, hung on the wall next to one of Lafayette. The two would set sail on the *Hermione* without an escort, relying on speed and skill to avoid the British and make it safely across the Atlantic.

What a heroic journey, I thought. The officers and crew easily could have been captured and imprisoned, or the ship could have gone down in a storm. Having seen this replica firsthand, I better appreciated the risks Lafayette and the sailors took, and the discomforts they endured, for the cause. When they bedded down to sleep, less than a foot of wooden hull (hopefully fungus-free) separated them from the depths of the sea.

After the tour concluded, I chatted with Teva some more. He had been in high school in Rochefort—France's historic shipyard on the Atlantic—when the replica was being constructed. "I visited the worksite one day as part of a school trip, and it really moved me to see all that work," he told me. "I knew I wanted to be part of it."

The French nonprofit that built the ship wanted to honor Lafayette as well as France's maritime heritage in general. The building of the ship was an odyssey of sorts; ship plans had to be discovered, funds raised, cannons obtained, artisans recruited, crews trained. Sadly, the frigate only got six years of good sailing in before the spores attacked.

Teva had accompanied the ship as a crew member on many trips in its happier days: to ports up and down France, Portugal, and Morocco. Best of all was a trip to Yorktown to commemorate the great siege there, in which the *Hermione* participated in 1781. With Teva aboard, the frigate arrived at Yorktown blasting its cannons while nearby ships set off fireworks in tribute. For days, American well-wishers climbed aboard the ship and gave the crew a hero's welcome.

Today, the *Hermione* stands as a symbol of Franco-American cooperation. But it took a lot to get to the point where there was something worth celebrating. The first two years of the alliance had not been a success, with the coalition against Britain racking up more defeats than victories. Unfortunately, the spring of 1780 brought with it yet another devastating defeat, this time at Charleston, South Carolina.

It was one of the allies' darkest hours. Doubling down on their Southern Strategy—their renewed focus on conquering the American South—the British laid siege to the port with six ships of the line and eighty-five hundred Redcoats in late March, not long after the *Hermione* had started its journey to Boston. The French provided three frigates for Charleston's defense, as well as sixty members of the Chasseurs-Volontaires, the Black soldiers from the Caribbean. But this would be nowhere near enough to withstand the forces surrounding them. The American commander, Benjamin Lincoln, sent a frigate to Havana with a desperate plea for help. Yet the Spanish declined to come to their rescue, preoccupied with protecting their island colonies (as the French were as well).

Alarmed, Washington sent Louis Duportail, the French engineer whom I called the Brains of the Operation, to assess the situation. Recognizing that the Americans had no hope of escaping the predicament,

Duportail pleaded with Lincoln to evacuate and save his army to fight another day. Lincoln ignored his advice. As a result, the British wound up capturing not only Charleston, but also the entire Southern Department of the Continental Army, over five thousand men in all. The allies had suffered a defeat similar to the British loss at Saratoga two and a half years earlier, due in large part to their failure to cooperate with each other.

The upcoming campaign, then, might be their last chance to get it right. Lafayette arrived in Massachusetts on the OG *Hermione* in late April 1780, after a speedy seven-week voyage. He was met with enthusiastic celebrations, just as Teva had more recently. "It was a day of universal joy," Abigail Adams wrote, with "the ringing of bells, firing of cannons, bonfires, etc." One of Lafayette's companions on board—who had also crossed with him the first time, in 1777—wryly noted how much happier the Americans were to see them this time.

The Americans' desperation had overcome the suspicions they once had of these foreigners who had once been their enemies. The Continental Army was in dire shape, having suffered through a brutal winter. Soldiers hadn't been paid in months; many had died of disease, some had deserted, others had even mutinied. "If we are saved," Alexander Hamilton had written to his friend John Laurens, "France and Spain must save us." Once again, Lafayette served as a much-needed symbol of hope, receiving cannon salutes in towns he passed through as he made his way to Washington.

On May 2, after many delays, the Special Expedition left Brest and slipped into the Atlantic, with the hopes of both the French and Americans resting on it.

For one summer weekend a year, the city of Newport, Rhode Island, goes French, keeping alive the memory of the remarkable year in which Newport played host to the French army. French colors were draped around Washington Square, the historic heart of the town. A band played under an elm tree while dignitaries laid a wreath on the graves of a French officer and two soldiers from the Special Expedition who were buried in a nearby church graveyard. The tri-corner hat set was well represented too: There was a Lafayette, a Rochambeau, and reenactors portraying common French soldiers. Throw in a mime and some stinky cheese and you might think you were in a port city on the other side of the Atlantic.

This was far better than the reception the real General Rochambeau received when he disembarked. The town was dark and the shops closed, with Rochambeau noticing only "a few sad and frightened faces in the windows." With nowhere to go, he found a local inn and asked for a room. Incredibly, a French lieutenant general had just crossed the ocean at the head of an army pledged to secure America's freedom, and he had to find a place and check in by himself.

As it turned out, the lack of a welcome was just yet another misunderstanding. The people of Newport hadn't known when their guests were coming. They quickly tried to make amends when they saw how miffed Rochambeau was. The next day, the town fathers gave speeches and the city lit up at night with illuminations.

The allies could ill afford to have more faux pas. Lack of communication and understanding of their partner's perspectives had contributed to the many disappointments of Admiral d'Estaing back in 1778—including here, when he had failed to take Newport from the British, which nearly turned into a disaster. (With the French now in the war, the worried British chose to evacuate the port in 1779.) Now that France had sent a small fleet and fifty-five hundred soldiers, the need to cooperate was even stronger. The allies couldn't afford to miss this chance. That's what I had come to Newport to explore—how the French and Americans began to put the mistakes of the past behind them and begin the slow process of building trust.

I wandered over to the center of the square. There, none other than Matt Keagle, the curator at Fort Ticonderoga, was holding court, explaining the role he had taken on to a group of festivalgoers. Clark Kent–like, he had transformed from a museum professional to a convincing French fighter, a hero of the Revolution. He was decked out in a white coat and vest with red trim and brass buttons, every detail based on his historic research.

"I'm representing a common French soldier from the expedition," Matt said. "The French were the leaders in style with their military uniforms in the eighteenth century," he explained. "They were the ones who had really brought military uniforms to the world." (The French were clotheshorses? I never would have guessed it!) What a contrast these fashionable French soldiers must have made with the motley American militia, I thought. Matt even made his knapsack himself out of calf leather. He carried with him a replica of a 1766 model French light musket—just like the tens of thousands shipped by France to the Americans during the war.

"This was the first and only time a foreign force has been active on American soil," he told the crowd. "It was a monumental event."

I was so glad I got a chance to see Matt in character. The crowd around him kept growing as people came to hear his stories. He spent hours that day chatting with anyone and everyone who passed by, answering whatever question they threw at him, from the great political questions of the Founding to how he cleaned his musket. Just as he had caught the spark of history when he visited Colonial Williamsburg as a kid, he was now passing it on to a new generation.

"There were no cheers when the French came," Matt continued. "Newport was a war-weary city by 1780. The British had evacuated it and left buildings destroyed. The inhabitants had suffered. And now, finding common ground with the French was a challenge. They were vastly different people, Catholic. The fathers and grandfathers of American soldiers had fought the French for a century and a half before, and now France had landed an army on this island. They were a bitter, existential enemy, and it's hard to overcome that. Imagine if, in a few weeks, we were suddenly allying with the Islamic Revolutionary Guard troops of Iran?"

Rochambeau set the tone, I learned, by immediately writing a letter to Washington in which he announced that "[w]e are now, sir, under your command." Versailles had instructed him to let the American general take the lead to demonstrate respect. Even better, the French went on a shopping spree. The mood in Newport immediately brightened, for the French had figured out a surefire way to our hearts: through hard cash. *Vive la France!*

"Newport was no Paris," Matt said. "The men were getting bored and antsy." But Rochambeau made his best efforts to keep his soldiers and sailors in good spirits and to win over their American hosts. Not only did the French pay for their food and supplies in silver, but they also paid to rebuild houses that the British destroyed, then paid rent to stay in them, Matt told us. "That brought them a lot of goodwill. Families in town learned French and gave English lessons in return. The French set up a printing press to give their men something to read. Rochambeau even started a gaming house to let officers blow off steam," he said.

By the end of August, the people of Newport were so taken with their generous guests that they even threw a birthday party for the king of France. The French came to appreciate their hosts as well. Some wrote in their journals about the astonishing religious liberty that Americans enjoyed; others commented on the Yankees' predilection for hot coffee at any hour and long toasts before dinner. Officers admired the beauty of the women of Newport—if only they could dress a little less in the English style and a little more French, they sighed.

A remarkable event for the French occurred when a delegation of nineteen Haudenosaunee, mostly Oneida, arrived in town to establish relations with their onetime enemies. The French presented them with medallions showing Louis XVI's coronation while the Iroquois performed dances late into the night. One Haudenosaunee asked a particularly pointed question of Rochambeau: Why was his master, the French king, supporting a group that had rebelled against their own monarch? The French general stammered something about the importance of natural rights and the need to lessen the burdens of the Americans. He later confessed in his journal that he had had to wriggle his way out from a "very embarrassing question."

Washington had his own embarrassments to deal with, too. He had been putting off meeting Rochambeau in person because he felt ill at ease about showing off the American troops, in their camps near New York City, to his French counterpart. The Continental Army was undermanned, without enough uniforms, weapons, tents, pay, or, at this point, even much enthusiasm for the war. Instead, Washington sent Lafayette as an intermediary to Newport to convey the American desire for an immediate attack on New York.

Rochambeau brushed off the request. Many of his troops were still sick from the ocean crossing, and he was waiting for promised reinforcements to come. After Lafayette kept insisting, Rochambeau asked to speak with the young Marquis's boss directly. For the transatlantic partnership to work, the two commanders needed to break bread together in person.

They finally did so in September 1780, in Hartford, Connecticut. Washington didn't have good news to share. Recruitment was down. He couldn't even tell Rochambeau how many people he would have under his command in 1781, for Congress hadn't informed him of that yet. And the Americans' battlefield results from the last few months were even more embarrassing.

After the fall of Charleston, Congress had sent Horatio Gates at the head of a new army to challenge the British in South Carolina. Gates found Lord Cornwallis near the town of Camden. Even though Gates had nearly a two-to-one advantage, "his troops were totally routed, and the general himself fled," Warren recounted. "Picture it as bad as you possibly can," a Virginia general wrote to Governor Jefferson, "and it will not be as bad as it really is." Gates rode an incredible 170 miles on horseback over three days to escape, fleeing so fast that he left the remnants of his own army in the dust. (At least there was something he was good at.)

But the other members of the coalition against Britain didn't have much better news to share. The Spanish had achieved only mixed results in 1780. Their greatest success came in May of that year, when Spanish defenders in St. Louis, alongside American frontiersman, had repelled an attack by a much larger force of British and their Native American allies. Thanks to their bravery, Fort San Carlos—in the shadow of today's Gateway Arch—held.

However, the twin campaigns of the Gálvezes, father and son, had seemed to stall somewhat. Bernardo de Gálvez and his trusty sidekick Captain Pickles had hoped to follow up their victory at Mobile with an attack on Pensacola. Yet, once again, the authorities in Cuba had refused to cooperate in the campaign, not wanting to weaken their own island's defenses. Havana was "worth more than 50 Mobiles and Pensacolas," the naval commander in charge sniffed, refusing to send a fleet in support of Bernardo. Meanwhile, Bernardo's father, Mathías, continued to fight the British in Nicaragua but had not yet been able to dislodge the enemy from the Fort of the Immaculate Conception.

As for Rochambeau, he had received some unwelcome news that summer too. A French frigate had arrived in Boston with thousands of muskets for the Americans (and with Mercy Otis Warren's oldest son serving on board as a lieutenant) but also with bad news. The British navy had blockaded the French in their port of Brest, so the extra ships and reinforcements that Vergennes had promised would not be sailing out this year. Rochambeau would have to make do with the troops he already had. France also had a fleet based in the Caribbean, but the admiral in charge there was showing no interest in bringing his ships north to help the Americans. On top of it all, the British navy was blockading the *Hermione* and the other French ships in Newport. For the time being, Rochambeau was stuck.

Despite all these setbacks, Rochambeau and Washington spent two days at Hartford planning a future campaign. The French general immediately set a positive tone. "He very much understood that he needed to defer to Washington," Matt said. "His orders were to be auxiliaries of the Americans. He didn't try to take command from Washington or usurp his authority. Contrast that with Admiral d'Estaing, who had more challenging relations with the American high command. Rochambeau was more levelheaded, and you needed to have that at that level."

Both generals agreed that to take action, they would need naval superiority, which they didn't have at present. Rochambeau reluctantly agreed to Washington's obsessive desire to attack New York in principle, but to put off any attack until his reinforcements arrived, presumably sometime in 1781. This decision frustrated Washington, who was desperate for a decisive action, and he pled with Rochambeau that "more ships, more men, and more money" be sent from France. The French general agreed to ask the king and Vergennes for all that—once the blockade was lifted and he could get a ship out to cross the Atlantic, that was.

For his part, Lafayette left the conference convinced that the two armies "will work together in complete harmony." His fellow French officers agreed, gushing with admiration for the godlike general. Their quotes almost read like blurbs for a movie: "illustrious, handsome, majestic!" wrote one. "The greatest and best of men!" said another. Washington "looks like a hero," and the French "cannot find strong enough words" to praise him, others wrote. Rochambeau too would later write that his heart would be united with Washington's, in life and death.

Washington wasn't nearly so happy with the conference; he had grown tired of waiting for a decisive campaign that never seemed to come. From Hartford, he was traveling on to what promised to be a much less stressful meeting, catching up with a man who was a friend and trusted officer. The general he was traveling to meet had shown incredible courage on his trek to Maine during the invasion of Canada, where he took a bullet in the leg. He had done the same at the Battle of Saratoga, where he received another ball in the same leg. As a reward, Washington had put his protégé in a sweetheart post, as commandant of West Point, the fort on the Hudson River. His friend's name was Benedict Arnold.

"Arnold has betrayed us! Whom can we trust now?" Washington thundered to Lafayette (even when furious, he still knew the difference between "who" and "whom"). The commander in chief normally did everything he could to keep his composure, but when he got mad, a titanic rage would burst forth. After arriving at West Point, Washington had learned that Arnold had betrayed the cause, making secret plans to turn over the fort to the British. If a spying British officer hadn't been arrested by the Patriots outside of New York City with incriminating documents stuffed in his boot, the traitor's plans just might have worked.

Arnold fled just before his boss arrived. On October 7, 1780, the turncoat even had the gall to write an "Address to America," in which he cited the French alliance as one of the reasons for his betrayal, warning his countrymen that he preferred to return to rule by Britain than to trust in the "insidious" French, who secretly wished to destroy America.

Would the answer to the (rhetorical) question that Washington had posed to Lafayette—whom should he trust now—wind up being none other than Rochambeau? Despite the evidence of treason, not to mention general discontent, in the American ranks, the French general still planned to send a ship back to France requesting troops, money, and naval support for the planned joint campaign once he was able to get past the blockade in Newport. He sent a tactful response to Washington, congratulating him on the fact that Arnold's plot was discovered before West Point was delivered to the British. This "proves to us that Providence is for us and for our cause," he told his American counterpart.

Rochambeau might have been right, for what Providence served up next—a pair of cataclysmic hurricanes—brought tragedy with them but also, strangely enough, wound up providing the allies with the opportunities they had been waiting for. In October 1780, what was later called the Great Hurricane swept through the Caribbean. It flattened islands, destroyed buildings, and even deposited a warship on the roof of St. Lucia's hospital. The death toll was at least twenty-two thousand, making it the deadliest hurricane in the history of the Atlantic.

The Great Hurricane also changed France's strategic thinking—for the better. Before, Vergennes had been reluctant to send the French fleet based in the Caribbean outside those waters, worried that Britain might seize islands if they were left unguarded. Now he began to reconsider this principle. After the Great Hurricane, it seemed safer for most of the French ships to sail away during hurricane season. If they had to leave, why not go to America to help Washington? This newfound willingness to remove the French fleet from the Caribbean during hurricane season would prove to be a game-changer in 1781.

Then, just weeks after the Great Hurricane, a second hurricane hit. Unfortunately, Bernardo de Gálvez had just taken to sea, having finally cajoled the authorities in Cuba into providing him with an army and fleet to attack Pensacola. Some of his ships sank, while others were scattered across the Gulf—yet another adversity he'd have to overcome.

The remnants of the hurricane made their way all the way up to Newport. "A very severe storm has yesternight been agitating our ships and our tents," Rochambeau wrote to Washington. Yet the storm also scattered the British ships maintaining the blockade. Suddenly, the French had the chance they had been waiting for. In the chaos, the *Hermione* slipped out to sea, along with the *Amazone*, another frigate. Once free, the *Hermione* turned south, where it would harass the British in Long Island, while the *Amazone* made a beeline for France.

On board was Rochambeau's son, a twenty-five-year-old aide-de-camp named Donatien, headed to Versailles to plea for help. It was a true act of faith on the French general's part, sending his son out after a storm in order to help the Americans. Rochambeau had made good on his promise to Washington. Now it would be up to Vergennes and the king to deliver.

My trip to Newport had helped me appreciate just how far the French and Americans had to go to transform themselves from squabbling frenemies to effective partners. It was here, I had discovered, where the French and Americans had begun to put their differences behind them and make common cause. The trust that they were slowly building together would be put to the test in the campaigns to come.

The middle years of the war were drawing to a close. The coalition of allies and partners hadn't gotten off to a good start in the world war, from d'Estaing's failures in 1778 to the unlucky Siege of Gibraltar and failed invasion of England the following year. The campaigns by the Gálvezes, father and son, had brought hope, but neither had yet achieved the ultimate victory he was seeking. The news from India so far was bad too, as France had lost its foothold in the subcontinent. In America, the British still held New York City and much of South Carolina and Georgia. Washington's army remained underpaid and undermanned.

The year to come, 1781, would be a crucial one then. The allies had to turn this string of setbacks around and find a way to work together. America's freedom depended on it.

Part Three

ALL FOR THE COMMON CAUSE

1780–1783

Chapter Sixteen

THE TIGER OF MYSORE

How a Kingdom in India Won the Bloodiest Battle of the War

March 1780–March 1781

The horse cantered through the village, the bells on its harness jangling wildly as it pulled the tanga behind it along. Inside the small cart were the driver, my guide Venkatesh, and me. An auto-rickshaw and a motorcycle buzzed past us; our horse, inspired by his colleagues, decided to go faster. Until, that is, all traffic ground to a stop: A herd of sheep had meandered onto the road. Rush hour in Srirangapatna. When we could move again, we could see a palace with towers shining in the sun, the long-ago home of Hyder Ali and his son Tipu, the sultans of Mysore and the most improbable of the allies during the Revolutionary War.

Earlier, I had discovered how India had fractured into smaller states in the eighteenth century as the great Mughal Empire declined. The British East India Company, that weird organization that was half-business, half-armed state, had been on the march, gobbling up smaller kingdoms and becoming the de facto ruler of much, but by no means all, of the subcontinent. When war broke out with France in 1778, a force of East India Company soldiers and British regulars had seized the southeastern French trading outpost of Pondicherry.

Yet continuing on to take the southwestern French outpost of Mahé the following spring would prove to be a colossal mistake, for the French used that port to supply the Mysoreans with arms and other trade goods. Angered by this disruption, Hyder Ali decided to go on the offensive. And so I had traveled here to the town of Srirangapatna, once the center of Hyder and Tipu's kingdom, to learn more about who they were and what happened when they entered the war.

"We can get out here," said Venkatesh. He was a few years older than me, wearing glasses and a white dress shirt and sporting a jet-black mustache. As would be expected, he spoke English with a Kannada accent, for that was his native tongue. The tanga ride was a fun gesture he had arranged, like taking a carriage ride in Colonial Williamsburg. For the rest of the day, we'd move around the town on foot or on the back of his motorcycle. Venkatesh led me to the palace gates.

"There has been a temple dedicated to Vishnu here since the ninth century," he began. "Today it's a very, very small town, but it was quite busy in the eighteenth century." That was the time that Hyder and Tipu made it the capital of a kingdom that eventually stretched across much of south India, about the size of the state of Kansas today.

Two yellow octagonal houses, with a dome that looked like a minaret, stood just inside the gates. "What were these used for?" I asked.

"These were the pigeon houses," Venkatesh replied. "They were the post office; they carried messages. This was the outbox, where they left from. And over there was the inbox, where they would drop the letters when they came back."

"Look, there's even some pigeons living there now," I said.

"Yes, but they're not working today," he said, laughing.

We walked a few hundred yards through formal French gardens and past mahogany trees toward the palace, a low building. "It was built in the fifteenth century by the kings who ruled here; it started as a mud fort," Venkatesh told me as we drew closer. "Later on, in 1784, it was rebuilt by Tipu Sultan with French engineers to commemorate his victories over the English. It looks very simple from outside, but it is very, very beautiful inside," he continued. "It was his summer palace, known as Daria Daulat Bagh. *Daria* means 'ocean,' *Daulat* is 'wealth,' *Bagh* is the 'garden.' So it was the 'wealthy garden from the sea.'"

"Why the ocean?" I asked. We were well over a hundred miles east of the Arabian Sea.

"It looks as if the palace is by the ocean because the river Kaveri runs around it. The town is basically an island in the river." I was liking this landscape crisscrossed by rivers much better than that of Chennai and Pondicherry, on the other side of south India. Here in the southwest, the temperature was much milder and rainier. We were now in the land of spices, of cinnamon and nutmeg, and of occasional drenchings from the monsoons.

In front of the palace, Indian tourists were taking selfies in front of a row of Mysorean cannons. Inside, the palace was striking, with an interior balcony made out of rosewood and teakwood and scalloped arches. One of the rooms continued the military theme, with a squat brass cannon and cases filled with muskets. Venkatesh pointed out a dagger with intricate carvings, which he then pantomimed how to use. "You don't stab someone in the chest, no. You go underneath—you stab and twist, into the stomach, to get at the intestines," he said, with an enthusiasm that I hadn't expected. I made a mental note to be extra nice to him and to tip well.

Venkatesh recounted Hyder and Tipu's backstory to me. The military theme made sense, since neither came from a hereditary line of rulers; they were soldiers who made good. "The Wodeyar dynasty had been ruling the Mysore Kingdom for nearly four centuries," he said. "Hyder was working as a soldier, he was a very clever soldier. Once, he was sent to Hyderabad in the north, where princes were fighting for power. Both princes were killed in battle. Hyder seized the treasure and suddenly became very rich.

"At the time, Mysore couldn't pay their soldiers, who were protesting," he continued. "Hyder Ali paid their salaries with some of the treasure and from then on, the soldiers favored him. In 1761, he deposed the ruler. He didn't become the king, but he became the de facto king." Rather than taking the throne in his own name, Venkatesh told me, he would rule as a sultan, the real power behind the Wodeyar dynasty, a Muslim leading a mostly Hindu kingdom. After his death in 1782, his son Tipu would do the same.

Tipu Sultan, one of Britain's most feared enemies.

Hyder reminded me a bit of José de Gálvez in Spain. For starters, they were both the same age (sixty years old in 1780). More importantly, both were self-made men who rose from relative obscurity to the heights of power (Gálvez had started as a shepherd and wound up as Spain's minister for the Indies), thanks to their own strong will and clever strategic moves. As for Tipu, he shared at least a few qualities with José's nephew, Bernardo de Gálvez—both young men were energetic, bold military leaders and each loved the latest scientific advancements. Tipu was a slight man with a cheerful-looking mustache, yet he became so known for his ferocity in battle that he was called the Tiger of Mysore. The British would come to fear and despise him.

Hyder's hatred for the British stemmed from a war he had fought years before the American Revolution. He had always favored the French, I learned, even though he had not yet formally allied with them. French engineers had strengthened his forts, mercenary French officers had drilled his troops, and French traders in Mahé had happily sold him arms. By 1767, the Mysorean sultan had even created his own small navy, led by a European officer. That same year, Hyder attacked the East India Company in a dispute over territory. The teenaged Tipu surprised the Company by raiding Madras. After two years of fighting, with Mysore victorious on the battlefield, the British negotiated an end to the war.

As part of the peace settlement, Britain agreed to come to Mysore's aid should the kingdom ever be attacked. Yet when the neighboring Maratha Confederacy launched an attack on Mysore not long afterward, the British never lifted a finger to help their supposed ally. Hyder had been had, and his hatred for the Brits rose tenfold. "The English are today all-powerful in India," he later bitterly told Tipu; they were not to be trusted and were to be combatted at all costs.

When the British seized Mahé in 1779, cutting off his supply of French arms, the sultan resolved to take revenge. In July 1780—just as the French Special Expedition was settling in in Newport—Hyder sent some ninety thousand troops through a mountain pass into the plains of the Carnatic to challenge the British. Mysore had entered the world war.

The British belatedly sent troops out to combat this new threat. Madras ordered Lieutenant Colonel William Baillie, who was leading his East India Company regiment on a march west of the city, to link up with the main British and East India Company army under Colonel Hector Munro in a small village. The move would turn out to be one of Britain's greatest blunders of the entire war. Venkatesh brought me to a different section of the palace to show me what happened next.

I almost gasped when I saw it: an entire interior wall of the palace was covered with a mural depicting the battle fought near the village of Pollilur in September 1780. Before me, in vivid color, were hundreds of soldiers engaged in fierce combat, with sabers slicing throats, muskets discharging plumes of smoke, and cannons roaring.

"This reminds me a little of the Bayeux Tapestry in France," I said after a few moments. My parents had been so taken by the tapestry, which illustrates the gore of the Battle of Hastings in 1066, after they saw it on a trip that they bought a replica of a section showing a sword going through an Englishman's neck. Naturally, they hung it prominently in our dining room, to the discomfort of their dinner guests. (Seconds, anyone?)

"Yes," Venkatesh replied. "Sometimes I show this mural to French tourists, and they clap. They hate the English people."

"Wow, the mentality hasn't changed. I love it." I could only imagine my boisterous friend Matthieu from Lyons here—he would have been giving out high fives if he saw this.

"Here, this is what happened before the battle," Venkatesh continued, leading me to the far left-hand side of the mural. "Here you can see Tipu Sultan on his horse, preparing to march to face the British at the head of his troops." Some soldiers even rode on elephants, I noticed. "And here, in the upper left, is the Nizam of Hyderabad, Ali Khan, coming with his armies to help the British; he had an alliance with them. But he didn't come on time, and the British were defeated. Afterwards, he was considered a traitor."

With tens of thousands of troops, Tipu vastly outnumbered Colonel Baillie's forces of a few thousand men, mostly sepoys (Indian soldiers in the service of the British) and Scottish Highlanders. Venkatesh pointed out the scenes of fighting and how to distinguish the nationalities of the soldiers in the melee. "The English have no mustaches, while the French soldiers all have mustaches," he said. "The Mysorean fighters are wearing blue. Here is a man named Lallée looking through a telescope; he was the head of the French fighters who were there." The French officer sported a plumed hat and a particularly jaunty mustache. "And this is Tipu Sultan in the middle on horseback." The young leader looked defiant and proud, even though the pink polka-dot robe he wore into battle made him look to me like a particularly fierce clown.

"The British army tried to protect themselves by forming a square," Venkatesh said, pointing. Right in the middle of the mural, I saw their formation, reminiscent of the phalanxes of ancient Rome. Tipu ordered his artillery to bombard it. And that wasn't all. The night before, he had sent an urgent message to his father asking for reinforcements. On the mural, I saw Hyder's cavalry answering the call, charging into the battle, wearing turbans and brandishing sabers. "Here's a British soldier being captured," Venkatesh said. "Here's another soldier—look at his head and arms chopped off. This soldier lost both the hands. The other one lost the right hand," he said cheerfully.

"What's that big explosion over there?" I asked, pointing to a huge cloud of smoke.

"That's when Tipu's men fired rockets and hit the British ammunition, which blew up," he replied. The Mysoreans pioneered the use of rockets encased in iron tubes, he told me, which could travel over a mile. The British were so taken by these weapons that their military engineers later reverse-engineered them. Britain used them with much success during the War of 1812—impressing their American adversaries too. When you sing the "The Star-Spangled Banner" and get to the line about the "rockets' red glare," you're unknowingly praising missiles that originally came from Tipu's army.

Following the explosion of the British ammunition stores, the Mysoreans launched a final charge, bringing their pachyderms with them—one Scottish Highlander later couldn't get the "hideous roaring of elephants as they trampled about" out of his mind. With this, the Battle of Pollilur was soon over. "Colonel Baillie was captured by Tipu Sultan soldiers—there he is in the palanquin, being carried off," Venkatesh said, gesturing to the mural. "He's surprised because he never expected he'd be caught. That is why he is biting his finger." Sure enough, the beleaguered colonel had placed his pinky at the side of his mouth, looking like a dispirited Dr. Evil.

In terms of survival rates, Pollilur was the most severe British defeat of the war. Out of the nearly four thousand men they started with, only 250 were alive and present at the end of the battle—and all of them were taken prisoner. The guilt-ridden Colonel Munro, who had never sent his main army to the aid of his comrades, called the loss "the severest blow that the English ever sustained in India." With the Mysorean army victorious, and still on the march, the very survival of the British in south India was now in jeopardy.

The victory cemented the reputation of Tipu, the man who swore he "would rather live a day as a tiger than a lifetime as a sheep." He even commissioned a wooden sculpture of a tiger ripping apart the flesh of a nearly life-size British soldier (now on display at London's Victoria and Albert Museum); when a crank was operated, the soldier shrieked and the tiger let out a satisfied grunt. The British were terrified of him, and not just because of his toys. Tipu and Hyder had sent tens of thousands of soldiers against them, some riding marauding elephants, others shooting sophisticated rockets. Most importantly, they had dispelled the myth that the British were invincible in India. The fear increased when rumors spread that Tipu's men treated the prisoners they took with cruelty.

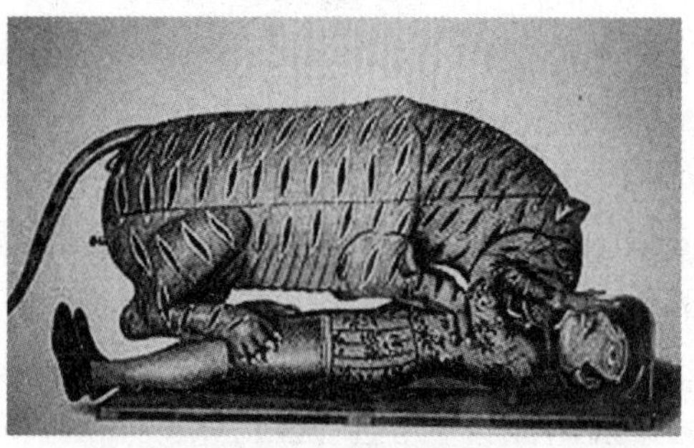

Tipu's automaton of a tiger feasting on a British soldier.

We left the palace and rode a few miles on Venkatesh's motorcycle to the site of one of Tipu's prisons. A troop of macaques cavorted on the old stone fortifications, which made me think of all the monkeys we had seen at Gibraltar earlier. We walked down a long staircase into a low, covered building with arches.

"This prison was built in 1782 by Tipu Sultan to house British prisoners. They were chained like this," Venkatesh said, spreading his arms out and resting them on two stones jutting from the wall. "Here, I'll take a picture of you like a British prisoner."

"No, I'm on the side of the allies," I protested. I had been talked into being a Redcoat once before, by Gunner Gilly in Jersey, and I didn't want to do that again. Venkatesh volunteered to pose instead, so I snapped a picture of him playing the part of a captive Brit, his arms splayed wide.

Despite our goofing around, visiting the prison did make me think of the hardships the British prisoners suffered. The British press in India railed against the harsh conditions, calling Tipu a barbarian (not dwelling on the fact that thousands of Indian captives suffered in British jails too). Even Mercy Otis Warren, who criticized the East India Company harshly—blaming them for famines suffered in India in 1779 and 1781—included in her *History* a (likely apocryphal) story of Tipu killing a greedy imprisoned British military officer by pouring molten gold down his throat.

An added charge that the British made against Tipu was that he forced Christian prisoners to convert to Islam. I asked Venkatesh about this allegation.

"All kings had prisoners," he said, shaking his head. "It's not true what some say, that he converted fifty thousand people to Islam against their will. I've read that he did convert five hundred personally, though." Venkatesh saw Tipu as a ruler with serious faults, but not the monster that his British enemies had portrayed him to be. There was another side to the story too. Tipu devoured Enlightenment philosophy, promoting science and the arts, and began the cultivation of silkworms in the region, an industry that lasts until today.

Tipu's Muslim faith—and how he acted on it—has become a point of contention in modern times as well. For years, the state of Mysore had promoted him as a sort of freedom fighter for, as it turned out, he was the last ruler of an Indian state to mount a serious challenge to the British in the subcontinent. More recently, though, Hindu nationalists have claimed that he was a religious fanatic who aimed to turn Mysore into an Islamic state. Or was the truth more nuanced, somewhere in between the two extremes?

We got back on Venkatesh's motorcycle, and he brought me to two different places of worship in Srirangapatna. First was the Masjid-i-Ala, a yellow mosque with arches and two minarets jutting high into the sky. We took our shoes off before entering; it was still used for prayers each Friday, he told me, and about 14 percent of the region was Muslim. "Tipu built the mosque in 1787, some say over a Hindu temple," he told me. "That led to controversy, some people don't like it. But Tipu allowed the statue of Hanuman, the monkey god, to be reestablished in other temples."

As we drove to the next site, Venkatesh told me about a recent push from some Hindu politicians to emphasize the darker side of Tipu's rule—how he allegedly destroyed some Hindu temples (as well as Christian churches). His name has been removed from some places; for example, a touristic train called the Tipu Express has been renamed the Wodeyar Express, after the Hindu kings who once ruled Mysore, Venkatesh said.

We stopped at Ranganathaswamy Temple. Dedicated to Ranganatha, a form of Vishnu, it had a huge tower and many smaller gateways and shrines, all featuring intricate carvings. Although an earlier temple had stood for centuries, much of the current version was built in the fourteenth century, I learned. "So this obviously survived when Tipu was in power?" I asked.

"Yes," Venkatesh replied. "He left it here and let it be. Tipu wasn't against Hindus; he had many Hindus working for him as soldiers." The sultan also sent money to support some Hindu temples, even as he wound up battling some Hindu kingdoms over land, complicating the story. "But Tipu was no freedom fighter either," Venkatesh said. "He wasn't fighting to get the British out of India, he was just fighting for his kingdom. There was no 'One India' movement then."

Who was Tipu Sultan really? It was a question that I couldn't resolve on this trip. Finding that out wasn't the true purpose of my journey; I came here to discover how the Tiger of Mysore helped the allied cause, not to evaluate his rule. Nor would I, a traveling foreigner, be the best-placed person to judge him in any case. "What has happened, happened," Venkatesh concluded, making a case that the sultan should be remembered despite the wrongs he committed. "You can't change the past."

What I did come away with from my trip here was an appreciation of Hyder and Tipu's military might and the innovations, like war rockets, that they developed. They delivered a shock to the British in a way that few of the allies would during the war. I'd also long remember the soft beauty of the Mysorean capital, now a sleepy village, just as it had been long before. And, of course, of the friendliness and deep learning of Venkatesh, who was really quite mild-mannered when he wasn't pretending to stab people.

We wound up by the Kaveri River with a view of lush rice fields in the distance. Hindu pilgrims were walking to the shrines of gods placed on the shore then wading out into the water, in a ritual that had been practiced here for millennia. Venkatesh was not an especially religious man, he told me, but every year he participated in similar ceremonies to honor his late parents, who were.

We sat under a banyan tree, taking a break to eat a bunch of small, finger-sized bananas, the smell of jasmine in the air. "In villages, even today, people meet under banyan trees and decide legal matters," he said. He also told me the heart-wrenching story of how he fell in love with a young woman when they both were in college but was prevented from marrying her since they were from different castes.

We both fell silent. "Where are you from originally?" I asked.

"A small city in the state of Mysore, far from here," he replied. He came from a family of millet farmers. "My city used to have many industries—iron factories, silk factories, paper factories. Now most have closed; the place feels like a graveyard when I go back home." He too left when he was a teenager, relocating to the state capital, whose quiet charm he loved. Although he had always been interested in history, he studied commerce, which seemed more practical. It proved not to be, for the business he started after school failed, leaving him with debts to pay off for years.

Venkatesh at Tipu Sultan's prison.

In his early thirties, Venkatesh switched careers and trained to become a historical guide, teaching himself French in the process, he told me. Covid had hit his tours hard—India was completely shut down during that time—but business was slowly picking up again. For him, sharing the complicated history of Mysore was a way to support his family and pay for his daughters' higher education. And it let him embark on a journey to understand the complicated past of his land, giving him an excuse to constantly read and study. "It's never-ending," he told me, smiling.

✦

The Battle of Pollilur was fought in September 1780, not long before Washington and Rochambeau sat down at the Hartford Conference in Connecticut to plan out the next year's campaign. The coalition against Britain had suffered a surprising number of defeats up to that point. The year to come would prove to be the climactic year of the war, one in which the partners and allies would have to make "common cause," as both Washington and a French admiral put it, and fight well together. American independence depended on it. The Franco-Mysorean victory at Pollilur was an important step in the right direction.

Even though ships sped across the seas with the news, it still took six months for Europeans to learn about the crushing British defeat in India. John Adams, serving as a diplomat in the Netherlands, was among the first Americans to learn about it in the spring of 1781, receiving a detailed report from a correspondent. When word finally reached America, the Patriots were thrilled. The young delegate James Madison crowed that British "possessions in the East Indies, which were so rich a source of their commerce and credit, have been severed from them, perhaps forever." In Philadelphia, Patriots toasted the Mysoreans, poets penned verses in their honor, and a sixteen-gun sloop was later bought into the Pennsylvania Navy and renamed the *Hyder Ally*—a wonderful play on words for Hyder Ali, for he and his son had acted like true allies.

The British, on the other hand, were stunned by the loss of an entire army. "India and America are alike escaping," one politician worried. The desperate East India Company pleaded for help. "The object that is at stake," its leaders wrote, "is the preservation of India to Great Britain." In April 1781, the British ordered a squadron of five ships of the line and four battalions of soldiers to India. Britain's fear of losing its hold on the subcontinent led it to send these ships and men thousands of miles away from the American theater, giving the Patriots and their French allies a weaker opponent to face in the United States—and ultimately defeat.

The year 1781 would prove to be the year the British overstretched their forces, while the coalition learned to put its differences aside and finally fight effectively as a team. The next step in this British overreach—one that would ultimately help spell their doom—would happen in early 1781, nearly ten thousand miles from Mysore. There, the British prepared to invade an island whose people they had long despised, a place that we've already visited: Sint Eustatius, the Golden Rock.

Chapter Seventeen

THE EMPIRE STRIKES BACK

How the British Assault on St. Eustatius Backfired Spectacularly

February 1781

The small jeep putt-putted its way up the road and pulled up alongside the town park. A regal-looking man emerged from it. He was tall, with strong, sinewy arms despite his age, and wearing a black beret. We shook hands, and he gestured toward a park bench under a shade tree.

"I'm Ishmael Berker," he greeted me. "I grew up in that house right over there. My father bought it in 1917." He spoke softly, with frequent pauses, in a lilting Statian accent. The house he was gesturing to was gray with a sloping orange roof and white gingerbread trim. It overlooked Fort Oranje, the fortification that guarded Sint Eustatius, the Dutch island affectionately known as Statia. I had arranged this meeting during my trip exploring the First Salute, which occurred here.

"I'm the youngest of eleven children," he told me. "And I'm the last one left." He told me about his childhood, a time of little money but of much joy, on an island where all of its inhabitants pulled together to survive. "We didn't have running water or gas stoves. But we had fresh cow's milk, fresh goat's milk. If we only had one slice of bread, we'd share it so everyone would have a bite."

He gestured to the water far below where we were sitting in Upper Town. "Fishermen would come each day with strings of fish, so cheap. Do you know swordfish?"

"Sure," I replied.

"We'd buy the swordfish from them. Each one of us kids would have a whole swordfish on our dinner plate. We'd swim in the sea after school, we'd play marbles with cashews. Life was fun." At Christmastime, he recounted, he and his siblings would stage a play based on a scene from the Bible and go house to house to perform it, receiving cakes in return. "We liked to perform David and Goliath, that was my father's favorite," he said.

For decades, Ishmael had poured his energy into the work of preserving the history of his small island, helping found its museum and spearheading countless restoration projects. To do so, he often had to seek support from the faraway Dutch government. "I sat right here once with the king and queen of the Netherlands," he told me, when they had come to Statia on an official visit. "The queen was sitting where you are now. The king was over there. I spoke to them about our heritage and about slavery. My ancestors came out of slavery," he added. "I am so thankful for them."

"What did the king say?" I asked.

"He didn't say much, he just listened. The queen gave me her direct number, though. She said to call if I ever needed anything." As I'd find out later, he'd eventually take her up on her offer and call in a favor, to help save signs of his island's past before it vanished for good.

The decline of Statia—once called the Golden Rock when it was the center of trade in the Caribbean, the richest place for its size in the world—was long and slow. But the beginning of the end might be dated to a single day in history: February 3, 1781, when the British invaded and plundered the island, spiriting off every good of value they could find.

Ishmael offered to take me to some spots related to this dark day. I agreed and thanked him, for that is what I had come here to do—to bear witness to the tragedy that Statia suffered, as well as to understand the surprising effect the fall of the island had on the course of the war.

Ishmael Berker, who has long worked to safeguard Sint Eustatius's heritage.

Our first stop was the stone walls and tower of the Dutch Reformed Church, which Ishmael had helped restore. Here in the church's cemetery, framed by an ancient mango tree, stood the weathered tombstone of a Dutch admiral slain by the British. There were hardly any casualties during the assault in 1781 and none at all on land. The British invasionary force was so overwhelming that it was pointless to resist. I looked down to the sea below and imagined it filled with an armada deployed on a mission of revenge. The Dutch Republic had spent the first six years of the war happily smuggling many of the guns and ammunition used by the American rebels through this island. Now they were paying the price.

By 1781, the Netherlands could no longer rival the British navy, as it had a century earlier during its golden age. Despite their smuggling, the Dutch didn't want to trigger a declaration of war from Britain, which could put their lightly defended islands in the Caribbean and the Indian

Ocean at risk. They needed to stay officially neutral—and the Russian Empire, of all places, came up with what looked to be the answer to their prayers.

As we have seen, Catherine the Great of Russia had refused to join in the American war on the side of the British, instead creating the League of Armed Neutrality to protect the shipping of the non-aligned countries. Her League began in 1780 with the Kingdom of Denmark and Norway (which was one country back then) and the Kingdom of Sweden as fellow members. Portugal and Prussia would join the following year. The members of the League agreed to send their merchant ships together in armed convoys and to defend the League against attacks from either side in the war. Somewhat like NATO today, an attack against the shipping of one of these neutral countries would be considered an attack against all. In late 1780, the Netherlands was preparing to join too. That way its merchants could keep trading, while the Dutch Republic would continue to stay out of the war, now with the backing of powerful friends.

For the British, who had learned about these plans through their spies, this would be nothing short of a calamity. They couldn't take on the allied coalition and the League at the same time. By joining the confederation, then, the Dutch could keep smuggling shipload after shipload of arms to the Patriots. And so, right before the League was set to let them in, the British preemptively declared war on the Netherlands.

Orders flew across the Atlantic to the new British commander in the Caribbean, Sir George Rodney, whom we last saw defeating the Spanish in the Moonlight Battle off Portugal. Rodney now commanded a British flotilla in the Caribbean. London directed him to prepare an expedition against Statia and the other Dutch islands, which didn't know yet that their countries were at war. The Admiralty didn't have to ask him twice. From an earlier stint in the Caribbean, Rodney had cultivated a hatred for Sint Eustatius, which, he fumed, "has done England more harm than all the arms of her most potent enemies...and alone supported the infamous American rebellion." He sailed immediately, salivating at the chance to "take care [of] this nest of thieves," he wrote. They "shall be levelled with the earth, as an example to perfidious states."

"The storm burst on the Dutch West India islands before they were apprehensive of the smallest danger from a state of war," Warren wrote. The Dutch had posted only fifty soldiers at Fort Oranje, manning five working cannons. In contrast, Rodney brought ten warships, including his own ninety-gun flagship, as well as smaller bomb vessels, ten thousand seamen, marines, and over six hundred guns. Not even David had a chance against this Goliath.

Governor Johannes de Graaf, who had ordered the First Salute some four years earlier, wrote later that he had "extreme" emotion that day; the invasionary force "appeared to me as a dream." And not one of those nice dreams Dutchmen might have of waffles and tulips. It was more like one of those nightmares you have where you suddenly lose your job and house and are shipped to a prison in London, which is what happened to de Graaf.

"Look down there," Ishmael said, pointing to Lower Town far below us, a strip of land against the water. "There used to be a breakwater wall all the way down. Admiral Rodney eventually broke it, and water flooded the warehouses."

"Can you see remains of the warehouses today?"

"Yes, you can. As a boy, myself and other boys, we'd go to the Lower Town and walk through the ruins. Today there's nothing in comparison to what was once there; there used to be so many more. Come, I will show you."

We got back in the jeep and drove down to Lower Town. Ishmael pointed out cisterns and ruined walls. "When I was a boy, I'd see people in tractors pushing the ruins down to build things. I'd say, 'Why are you doing that?'"

We pulled over to look at the foundations of a huge warehouse, built with volcanic Statian stone and lumber shipped from America long ago, the sea now lapping against them. "Sometimes I wish I could go back in time and see all these buildings when they were standing," he said softly, "that would have been quite a sight."

Not far from where we were standing, Rodney seized all 130 ships in the harbor, many of which were American vessels that had come to trade Virginia tobacco for ammunition. So many hogsheads of tobacco lay in Sint Eustatius's warehouses, one British official gloated, that "[t]he loss of one half of it is enough to ruin all the rebel merchants in America." Statia was lousy with American merchants too, who fled to hide in the hills and in the shadow of the dormant volcano, never dreaming that the island paradise they loved would be suddenly swarming with Redcoats. "Hunger will compel them to surrender," Rodney wrote coldly. He formed a military cordon around the Upper Town and then turned his attention to the mile-long stretch of warehouses in Lower Town.

Under the laws of war, the admiral had every right to seize military stores destined for America, but he should have stopped there; private property was to be left untouched. Instead, he confiscated everything of value that he could find on the island, whether it came from friend, foe, or neutral. It was a scene of "general pillage," Warren wrote, with the admiral behaving "in a manner that would have disgraced the petty merchant."

The British conquerors "acted like robbers, searching, digging, confiscating," a Dutch contemporary disgustedly wrote. All the while, the Brits kept the Dutch flag flying over the fort to keep luring merchantmen into port; once there, the ships were seized and the cargo stolen. Even Rodney's subordinate, Rear-Admiral Samuel Hood, had to admit that British conduct was "wickedly rapacious." English merchants from the rest of the Caribbean, horrified by the plunder (and worried that the British were setting an example the French might follow someday), petitioned Rodney to stop. In response, the admiral assured the merchants that he had filed their petitions away in "a special place"—the loo.

Unfortunately, Rodney singled one group out for particularly harsh treatment: the island's thriving Jewish community. At the time of the invasion, over 350 Sephardic and Ashkenazi Jews lived on Statia and worshipped in a handsome synagogue built in 1739—one of the oldest in the Western Hemisphere. They maintained close ties to synagogues in Newport, New York City, and Curaçao, helping facilitate trade between these places.

Ishmael drove me to the synagogue, named Honen Dalim, or Charitable to the Poor. The walls, made from yellow Dutch brick, still stand, although the roof is missing. We gazed upon the Mikveh, the women's bath, the only complete one found in the Americas. "A Jewish family came from the States once and held a bar mitzvah here," he told me. "It was a special moment."

Rodney fell on the community with a vengeance, fuming that Jews "will do anything for money...and had been deeply concerned in supplying the enemy with provisions." He ordered all Jewish men on the island to be lined up and strip-searched, with the British stealing anything of value they found. "The garments of the aged and respectable were rent open in search of a bit of gold that might possibly have been concealed for the purchase of a morsel of bread for their innocent and helpless families," Warren recounted. "One rascal of a Jew" hid his coins in a chest in the cane fields, Rodney wrote; the irate admiral had him arrested. All Jewish men were deported to British islands, giving them only a day's notice to take farewell of their wives and children. Statia's Jewish community would never be the same.

Ishmael drove me to the Jewish cemetery. Its restoration, under his watch, was one of his proudest accomplishments, he told me. In 1781, some Jews, desperate, supposedly buried their family wealth in caskets here during the British occupation. "I designed the walls for this cemetery," he said. "And this Star of David." I looked at it—a striking hexagram on a wrought iron gate leading to old stone steps and a distant row of palm trees. "You always know when a Jewish family has been here," he said, "they leave a stone on a tomb."

He took me deeper into the cemetery and pointed out the landscaping.

"I did some research and planted trees similar to what was found at the Jewish cemeteries in Curaçao," he said quietly. "I haven't been here for years," he added, shaking his head at the tall grass growing between the headstones.

The Jewish cemetery in Sint Eustatius.

The Jewish cemetery looked out over the Old Church Cemetery—the third grave site I had seen in this small town in a short time. I mentioned that to Ishmael.

"For me, this whole island is a cemetery," he replied. "If you dig where you want, you'll find something."

Just before we got back in his jeep, I looked out at the farthest tomb from us. On it was perched a stone—a silent witness to a community that, through the pain of the past, left its mark on history.

⁂

We ended our afternoon at a two-story house with a pink roof and a lime-green balcony overlooking the distant sea. In front of it stood a cannon and a palm tree.

"This was the house of a Dutch planter in the eighteenth century," Ishmael told me. "In the 1980s, I was the president of the Sint Eustatius Historical Foundation. The owner of the house left it suddenly, he had some personal problems, and the bank put it up for auction. I wanted to buy it for our foundation. I wanted this to be ours, not to belong to some stranger. But we didn't have the money.

"I contacted the Dutch government's development cooperation office, but they didn't take me seriously," he continued. "Then I recalled that I had the private telephone number of the queen. I called but she didn't answer, so I followed up with a telegram. The Dutch development representative called me back right away. The queen had told him to give us whatever we needed." Ishmael and the representative secured the house for the foundation at the auction. Today it serves as the island's museum.

In February 1781, Rodney seized this very same building and took it for his headquarters. He had orders to continue his conquest of Dutch islands in the Caribbean—Surinam, Tobago, and Curaçao were all there for the taking. But the admiral couldn't be bothered. He instead hunkered down here, poring over account books. He wanted a precise tally of the riches that would soon be his, for King George III had agreed that he could keep the spoils of the war, rather than having them revert to the Crown. And Rodney wanted to make sure that not a single guilder or gold coin escaped him.

All the while, ships kept coming into Statia's harbor, fooled by the Dutch flag that the wily admiral had left flying. "Not a night [goes by] but an American arrives loaded with tobacco," he gloated. Rodney had the goods he had seized—Virginia tobacco, indigo, sugar, rum, molasses, Delft pottery, fine linen, gunpowder, and much, much more—sold at auction in Jamaica. The first month of sales alone netted 100,000 pounds, over 2 billion dollars in today's currency.

Allied leaders would be crushed when they learned of the fall of Statia, that island that had served the Patriots for so well for so long. The loss came on the heels of other enemy offensives in America, which formed part of Britain's Southern Strategy. As it turned out, these campaigns also involved seizing Virginia tobacco and plundering allied property, just as Rodney's had.

A month before the assault on Sint Eustatius, in late December 1780, the turncoat Benedict Arnold had appeared on Virginia's southern coast at the head of a small army. He proceeded to seize the state capitol in Richmond, burning tobacco warehouses and capturing supplies. In February 1781, Washington sent Lafayette south from New York State with a regiment of Continentals to counter the invasion. Washington also encouraged a French flotilla to sail to Virginia from Newport to try to capture the traitor, but the attempt failed.

In February, a second army appeared in the state, quite out of breath. For months, Nathanael Greene, the commander of Continental troops in the south, had let Lord Cornwallis chase his men up through North Carolina, fighting quick battles, and always leading the British farther away from the safety of Charleston. "We fight, get beat, rise, and fight again," Greene explained. Even after the frustrated Cornwallis resorted to burning his supply wagons to make better time, he still couldn't catch up to Greene's men, who made a beeline for the relative safety of Virginia.

Later in the spring, Cornwallis too would cross into the Old Dominion and link up with the troops that Arnold had commanded. Virginia was now the epicenter of the war in America, even as its trade with Statia, one of its principal export markets, was over for good.

In a back room of the museum, I found copies of the account books from Rodney's plunder. The consequences of his looting were far-reaching. The admiral's behavior was denounced in Parliament; for the rest of his life, Rodney was tied up in court, defending himself against lawsuits brought by merchants whose property had been seized illegally.

As for the Statians, they faced "immediate poverty, desolation, and every species of misery," as Warren put it. Things were worst of all for the Jewish community, which never recovered its former strength, and for the thousands of enslaved workers, who invariably suffered the most during times of hardship. While Sint Eustatius persevered, it never regained its international importance as a trading hub. The days of the Golden Rock were over.

I took my leave of Ishmael, but not before asking him one last question. "Why do you do all this? What motivates you to try to save all this history?"

He answered slowly. "We are born for a reason. And this is mine."

I was sorry to say goodbye to Ishmael—and flabbergasted to learn that he was ninety-one years old; I had him pegged for at least a decade younger. The next day, I was equally sorry to leave this island, once the glory of the Caribbean, now so quiet and humble. It had an improbable rise and an even quicker fall. Goliath had seemingly won.

Or had it?

What no one realized in the spring of 1781 was that Rodney's conduct would have ripple effects that would change the course of the war. Obsessed with counting his riches, the best admiral in His Majesty's Navy—and the man in command of the British fleet in the Caribbean—had been wholly distracted from his regular duties. His greed blinded him to the threat posed by the new French armada under the command of the Comte de Grasse that was sailing for the Caribbean. In May of that year, Rodney made only a halfhearted attempt to prevent de Grasse's arrival, despite orders to do so.

The groundwork would be laid for the emblematic campaign of the Revolutionary War: Yorktown. Now there was a powerful French fleet in the Caribbean and a British fleet under Rodney that couldn't be bothered to combat it. Up north, the British army under Lord Cornwallis would ultimately be at risk in Virginia if (and that was a big "if") the allies managed to pull off a combined naval and land assault against him.

In the end, then, the sacrifices of the people of Statia could count for something. David—my new friend Ishmael's hero—might just have the last laugh after all.

But for this unlikely campaign to get started, though, Washington, Rochambeau, and de Grasse would have to make one of the most critical decisions of the entire war. America's deliverance depended on it.

Chapter Eighteen

OUR DELIVERANCE MUST COME

A French General and an African American Spy Help Launch a Campaign for the Ages

May–July 1781

"Two porters, gentlemen," said the bartender, placing the mugs on our table. I knew that the Mount Vernon Inn brewed this beer from a two-hundred-year-old recipe, and I looked at my guest expectantly.

"It's pretty good," he said after taking a sip. I relaxed a little. Matthieu Haroux (not to be confused with my drinking buddy in Burgundy also named Matthieu) might have been French, but he was also down-to-earth; he wasn't about to fling some obscure tasting notes at me that I wouldn't understand. He was a thirty-something grad student from near Paris, working on the first full-length study of Rochambeau in French in many years. With an earring in one ear and wearing a sweatshirt rather than a tweed jacket, he looked like the kind of professor I wished I had in school.

I couldn't have found a better setting to discuss the Washington–Rochambeau relationship than this tavern in the shadow of Mount

Vernon, I thought. It was critical that the two generals found a way to work well together that year, and I hoped that Matthieu could shine some light on how they did so. For, from my research, I knew that the spring of 1781 was a desperate time, a sort of crossroads in the war. If the allied coalition didn't seize their opportunities and deliver a defeat to the British that year, they may never have another chance to do so.

That spring, the Continental Army—unpaid and facing increasing mutinies—was in difficult shape—and the very future of the Revolution seemed in doubt. "Without a foreign loan, our present force (which is but the remnant of an army) cannot be kept together this campaign," Washington groused to one of his officers, John Laurens. "Now or never," he continued, our "deliverance must come."

On May 8, 1781, the French ship *Concorde* landed in Boston with the response to the plea carried by Rochambeau's son the previous October, when he left Newport during a storm. After carefully turning the request over, Vergennes had decided on a sort of compromise. Unfortunately, he wouldn't be sending the fleet with reinforcements for Rochambeau that once had been promised; the expense would "surely ruin France," he concluded. The war effort had already plunged France deeper and deeper into debt. But Vergennes would not abandon the Patriots altogether. He sent the *Concorde* back with orders to give the Americans six million livres in hard currency as a gift for the Continental Army. The ship also carried with it a new officer to take command of the small French fleet in Newport, the Comte de Barras.

The *Concorde* also brought news that a huge armada of twenty ships of the line, carrying thirty-two hundred troops, had set sail from France for the Caribbean under the command of the Comte de Grasse. As we've seen, Admiral Rodney, still obsessed with counting his loot on Sint Eustatius, didn't make a strong effort to stop de Grasse and his convoy from arriving safely in Martinique. Vergennes would authorize de Grasse to head north for a few months later in the year to help the Americans, escaping the Caribbean during hurricane season. Just what the fleet would do when it got there would be up to the commanders on the ground to decide. They had to choose wisely, for the war was at a critical juncture.

"The European nations considered the present period a crisis of expectation," Mercy Otis Warren wrote, "and that the exertions of this year would either extinguish American hopes or establish their claims as an independent nation." Rumor had it that if the United States failed to win its freedom on the battlefield in 1781, the great powers might strike a deal at the bargaining table, giving each side claim to whatever land it currently possessed. Under this scenario, some of the American states might become independent, but not all, for the British were firmly entrenched in parts of New York, Virginia, Georgia, and the Carolinas. With all this hanging over them, Rochambeau and Washington convened an emergency meeting in Wethersfield, Connecticut, to make plans.

"The Comte de Rochambeau was the right man for the job," Matthieu told me as we sipped our porter. "He was very humble. He had already had a great career, so he wasn't looking for more honor. He was disinterested. He perfectly understood why he was in America," Matthieu continued, "to win and end the war between Britain and the U.S. That was the goal that he was working for, not for personal glory."

Those seemed to be the right qualities, I thought. In too many allied operations beforehand—from d'Estaing's failures in 1778 to the misguided attempts to invade Gibraltar and England itself—commanders had ignored operational problems that their partners had identified. Rochambeau, like Bernardo de Gálvez, seemed to be both a problem-solver and a good listener.

"What did he do before the Revolutionary War?" I asked.

"He fought as a young man in an early war with Britain, where he nearly died twice," Matthieu said. "In the Seven Years' War, he became famous at the siege of Minorca and then became a general. He also prepared to lead one of the regiments invading England in 1779, the invasion that never happened.

"He was a military nerd!" Matthieu went on, smiling. "He would transform your table into a battlefield to show where troops went." I imagined the obsessive Rochambeau moving a saltshaker and a wine glass to illustrate a flanking movement while his guests just tried to eat their dinner.

Our first course arrived—Colonial-style peanut soup, which delighted the Frenchman. "I get it here a lot," he said. He was finishing up a fellowship at Mount Vernon, where he was combing the archives for material for his dissertation on Rochambeau, and was staying in a guesthouse nearby. The bartender had greeted him like an old friend when he walked in.

"So where did Rochambeau learn how to be so diplomatic?" I asked.

"I personally think it was at Vaussieux, where they did the training exercises in 1778. Do you know it?" Did I ever—that was the reenactment I had attended in Normandy where I had been welcomed by priests and prostitutes.

"It was there that the French were testing out two theories of battle," Matthieu continued, "whether a formation in lines or columns was better. Rochambeau was chosen as one of the two generals in the war games. Then he had to talk all about it to defend his point of view. At Versailles, it's a battle of words. Rochambeau helped show them that you didn't need to choose one or the other; they each could be useful at different times."

"So, what were things like for Rochambeau in Newport?" I asked.

"It was hard. He hadn't gotten any letters from Versailles for a long time," he responded. "His letters hadn't gotten through to them and vice versa. So, he was on his own as to what to do. And he was still waiting for those reinforcements he had been promised. It was a tough time.

"George Washington even wrote a letter critical of the French," Matthieu continued. One of Washington's private letters had been intercepted and published in a Loyalist newspaper. In it, the American general had criticized the French for not sending a naval squadron sooner to try to capture Arnold. "Rochambeau didn't overreact to that," Matthieu said. "He came from Versailles. He knew all about rumors that could be shared. He kept his mind focused on his mission. He thought maybe Washington made a mistake, but he will give you something positive next."

The Comte de Rochambeau, who found a way to partner with Washington.

Our main course—we both were having the fried chicken—arrived. I asked Matthieu about the conference in Connecticut in 1781. There, Washington and Rochambeau dined and drank together. (Was the meal similar to what we were having? I wondered.) More importantly, they discussed strategy. Where should they ask the Comte de Grasse to bring his fleet?

"There were several options on the table," Matthieu told me. "The first was to go to New York, which Washington wanted to do. The second was to go south to the Chesapeake, which was Rochambeau's will. The third was to attack Charleston.

"Rochambeau didn't order Washington around. He knew his place. He was suggesting, not telling him what to do. So, he didn't say no to New

York at first. He was very pragmatic, not impulsive. He said, let's go to New York, then we'll look at it and we'll see what de Grasse wants to do." At the same time, Rochambeau privately let de Grasse know that he thought the Chesapeake would be the best option. New York was well-defended, and, as d'Estaing had learned, it was hard to get the French ships, with their deep drafts, over the sandbar into the harbor. In addition, Matthieu added, "the British sent new forces to Virginia. They might be trapped there."

That Rochambeau was trying to make things work at all was a testament to his good faith. He had secret orders to evacuate his entire force to the West Indies if it looked like Washington's army was crumbling. If he had wanted to, Rochambeau could have deep-sixed the entire 1781 campaign altogether, and no one in France would have blamed him.

Rochambeau also had to practice diplomacy with the commander of the French fleet in Newport, the Comte de Barras, who, as a naval officer, was not under his direct command. The allied plans called for de Barras to sail south (no matter what the ultimate destination was), bringing the French artillery and siege equipment with him. But the testy admiral realized that this campaign would leave him subservient to the Comte de Grasse, who outranked him. That was no way to win glory. De Barras would try to get out of it, declaring that he was going north to Newfoundland on an expedition he had just come up with himself. "Rochambeau had to fight with his own navy to get them to participate with him," Matthieu told me. "Patience was the key to his success."

Another round of porter arrived. "How did you become so interested in Rochambeau?" I asked Matthieu.

"I am a history teacher at a high school in France," he said. He was pursuing his PhD in history on the side. "I went to Rochambeau's château because a descendent of Rochambeau, a count, lived in Paris. Every year, he proposed to one class to visit his château. We took a three-hour bus ride to get there. I didn't know what to expect. When you drive up, you see the château at the end of a two-kilometer road lined with linden trees. It was incredible, such a big moment for me.

"I didn't know anything about Rochambeau!" he said, laughing. "People in France don't. My friends didn't even know how to pronounce his name right." (Good, I thought, even the French can butcher their own language. I'm not the only one.)

"I became fascinated by him," Matthieu went on. "And I asked the count if there was a book written about him. He told me yes, but it was very old. The last one in French was from the 1970s. I thought, that's very interesting, could I look at your château? He showed me the library that Rochambeau once owned, an entire room with old books on shelves. Then I knew it was time for me to begin. I would write about someone who the French didn't know about."

"What would you say was his ultimate value to the mission?" I asked.

"He kept his force together and dealt well with others, from Washington to Lafayette to Versailles," Matthieu responded. "He was patient and had empathy, he was gentle but direct. He let people be themselves when they needed to be. Washington recognized in Rochambeau a man of duties, in whom he could trust."

I thanked him and we walked out into the night. Matthieu would return to his guesthouse to keep at his yearslong passion of poring over Rochambeau's letters and records, trying to take stock of the man.

"Sometimes," he said as we parted, "I think of Rochambeau looking down on me and listening, and he might say, 'You're wrong! It wasn't like that at all.'"

We both laughed. "Too late now, I already wrote down what you said," I replied.

In late June 1781, Rochambeau marched the Special Expedition south, where they would meet up with Washington's Continental Army outside of New York City, wait for de Grasse's response to their letter, and plan their next moves. No matter what their target would be—New York, the Chesapeake, or Charleston—it was critical to know what Cornwallis planned to do with his forces in Virginia, for that would impact the Franco-American plans. Would he ship his Redcoats back north to New

York? Return south to the Carolinas? Or, for some unfathomable reason, was he planning to dig in and stay in Virginia for the long haul?

Luckily for the allies, they were about to receive precise intelligence as to what the British were up to in Virginia. For no one at Lord Cornwallis's table ever dreamed that James Armistead, the enslaved man waiting behind him, was actually a Patriot spy.

"I'm originally from Hampton, about half an hour from here," Moses Delaney told me. He had a mustache and goatee and a friendly, earnest face. He had met me on a bench along the banks of the York River in southeastern Virginia—the perfect spot for the story he was about to tell me.

"My mother is from Charles City County, my father's from Williamsburg," he said. "They would always bring us here to Yorktown when we were kids. My mother always told me we were related to James Armistead, even though I had never heard of him in my schoolbooks.

"When I was about nineteen, I started doing research on James at the public library," Moses continued. "I've always loved history and genealogy. I was trying to find out where James's property was; he acquired some property after the war. It turns out he lived very close to Charles City, where my mother was born.

"I told her this, and she said, 'You're going to hear voices from the ancestors, baby.' I didn't believe it at first. But sometimes when I'm up at 4 or 5 a.m. doing research, I'll hear something that says, no, look over here instead. I'll search those things. That's how I make my finds."

"What did you find out about your ancestor?" I asked.

"James Armistead was an enslaved person. He was the same age as a White man named William Armistead. William's father had willed James to him. James worked in a store and knew how to read and write, which was very rare. He wanted to fight for the Revolution.

"He became a spy, actually a double spy. He worked for the British as a servant and told them he was spying on the Americans for them but was really sending information to the Americans. He was assigned to work for Lord Cornwallis, and he'd eavesdrop, gather their plans, and take the information and bring it to General Lafayette. He overheard plans that the British were going to come to Yorktown and passed that on to Lafayette, who passed it on to George Washington."

This news excited the commander in chief. Washington knew Yorktown well—and knew it could easily prove to be a trap for the British. The York River flowed into the Chesapeake Bay. If an allied fleet stationed itself there, it could bottle up any army at Yorktown, preventing an escape by sea. Lafayette later passed on more detailed information from Armistead about Cornwallis's fortifications in Yorktown and Gloucester, on the other side of the York River.

"James risked his life for this information," Moses continued. "He was right there at the kitchen table eavesdropping. A White American couldn't have done that. Lafayette wrote years later that James Armistead provided essential intelligence, he helped corner the British.

Moses Delaney by the York River.

"Yorktown was essential to the history of American freedom," Moses said. "And it was based in part on the intelligence James Armistead got as a double operator."

Armistead wasn't the only enslaved person performing a difficult task in and around Yorktown that summer. Thousands of African Americans had fled plantations to join Cornwallis's army, hoping that the British would honor their promise of freedom to deserting slaves. They found themselves pressed into service, building the British fortifications and scouring the countryside for provisions for the Redcoats. What their ultimate fate would be was yet to be determined.

Many thousands of Blacks—both freed and enslaved—served on the Patriot side as well. As I learned from Antoine Randolph Watts, some of the most experienced soldiers in the First Rhode Island Regiment—who, in 1781, began marching south with Washington—were African American. And, of course, the Chasseurs-Volontaires de Saint-Domingue, the regiment of Blacks from the Caribbean, had fought valiantly at Savannah and Charleston.

They were far from alone; the conflict affected enslaved peoples across the world. In Sint Eustatius, Black workers had spent years helping load American ships with supplies, only to see their island laid waste by the British. When the French attacked the British island of St. Vincent, some escaped slaves took advantage of the temporary power vacuum to rise up and rebel. When British forces tried to regain the island, these "maroons," as they were known, burned plantations in response. The British and French also fought over possession of the slaving station in Senegal (with France ultimately victorious—and French is Senegal's official language today). So many of these battles have now been forgotten, just as some of the promises of liberty for Black Patriots were after the war.

"Years later," Moses told me, "James Armistead petitioned for his freedom via the Virginia General Assembly, because slaves who served in the Revolution were supposed to get their freedom. He was denied because they didn't deem him to be a veteran. That was heartbreaking. It must have been a tough pill to swallow.

"Lafayette wrote a letter on his behalf, setting out everything that James had done for him," he continued. "So, they gave him his freedom. James took Lafayette's last name after that. When I came across that story, it left me sad. My ancestor got his freedom because a Frenchman, not a fellow American, stood up for him. It took someone from a different continent to have the vision to see how someone had risked his life at that moment. This is the story of America getting its freedom, but there's some pain in there."

We paused and watched a boat drift in the water. A chilly wind blew off the river, but Moses showed no signs of wanting to end this conversation, as difficult as it might have been. Despite the frustrations he felt sometimes when he discovered his family history, Moses had not turned away from a desire to keep helping build this American Experiment that his own ancestor had played a role in constructing. He was an Air Force veteran, as was his brother George, and he had come all the way up from Georgia to attend an event commemorating Lafayette at Yorktown, put on by the American Friends of Lafayette—the same group I had met at the brewpub in Philadelphia and on the trail of the Battle of Brandywine.

"How'd you learn about the American Friends of Lafayette?" I asked.

Moses smiled. "It's quite a story. I was traveling to Fort Belvoir in northern Virginia for a job fair. I had a little time to kill so I went to have lunch at Mount Vernon. I had never been there before.

"I took an African American tour of the estate. Afterwards, I split off and walked up to George Washington's tomb. There was a crowd there, maybe twenty or thirty people, but as I walked up, everyone just walked away, everyone except a group of four women. So, I was there looking at George Washington and thinking, wow, there is where our founding president lies.

"And then I overheard a woman say that she was so emotional to be there because she was a descendent of General Lafayette. I was ten feet away. I walked up and said, 'Ladies, I'm so sorry, I heard you say that.' I looked at her in the eyes and..." Moses suddenly stopped talking. "I get touched by this," he told me, "I need to pause for a moment."

"I said, 'Wow, it's because of your ancestor that my ancestor gained his freedom.'" The woman, he told me, was named Virginie Bureaux de Busy-Demoittier de Lafayette. She and her two daughters had come to America to participate in a commemoration of their forebearer, and one of the Friends of Lafayette had volunteered to take them to Mount Vernon. Of all of the thousands of people who visited the estate each day, they had arrived at the tomb only moments before Moses did—and then the crowd there abruptly melted away as if on cue.

"I told her about James Armistead Lafayette," Moses went on. "She said, 'I know about his contributions.' She reached out with her hands, and we stared at each other. You feel a pull, your ancestor pulling you to look here, look there. It was like James Armistead and General Lafayette were looking at each other once again, through us. She teared up and I teared up. What was going through my mind was, two hundred years later, they hug again."

"It sounds like a movie," I said.

"It felt like a movie," Moses responded. "That night, I called my mother and told her what happened. She said, 'Baby, I told you. The ancestors are speaking.'"

Thanks to James Armistead, the allies knew exactly what the British were planning in July 1781. This information couldn't have come at a better time. That same month, nearly two thousand miles to the south, the Comte de Grasse was about to make a decision that would determine the course of the war, one that Washington was desperate to find out about. Would de Grasse head north? And if so, where would he go?

De Grasse was perplexed. The allied leaders wanted him to sail north. Yet if he left the Caribbean, the British would have a clear shot at conquering the French islands he was supposed to be protecting. Was it worth taking that risk to help the Americans? To better understand the choice he had to make, Liana and I had another stop to make in the Caribbean. It's a hard job retracing this world war, let me tell you. Thank God we would face this latest challenge together, with plenty of sunscreen.

Chapter Nineteen

INDEPENDENCE IN THE BALANCE

When a French Admiral Had to Choose Between America and the Caribbean

May-August 1781

Liana and I sat on top of the ruins of Fort Louis on the island of Saint Martin, a jumble of old stone walls and rusted cannons with a French flag flying on top of a high hill. Below us, we could see Marigot Bay, where sailboats bobbed in the water. The sounds of reggae music from a festival drifted up past the palm trees to the fort. An orange and black striped iguana, apparently not a fan of Bob Marley covers, scuttled into the underbrush.

Saint Martin is unusual—the northern half of the island is French while the southern half is Dutch. We had first stopped over on the Dutch side then, Francophiles that we are, crossed the invisible border into the north, trading our *stroopwafels* for croissants and Heinekens for Burgundy. We were pleased with our decision.

"This is the best of two worlds," Liana said. "We have perfect Caribbean beaches and good French food." We had only been there for a few days but already were banking memories of small villages with fruit vendors and French bakeries and nocturnal donkeys who roamed the dunes under the moonlight. "And the people have been so warm and welcoming," she added happily.

Saint Martin was half-French in the eighteenth century as well, but the island would change hands several times during the war. In the early years of the conflict, the British complained loudly that the Dutch in Saint Martin were helping the Americans—just as they were in nearby Sint Eustatius—and British ships would sail into the harbor to capture rebel smugglers. Britain seized the French half of Saint Martin in January 1779, but France quickly took it back. Then the notorious Admiral Rodney conquered the whole island in February 1781, the day after he took Sint Eustatius.

This ceaseless fighting over Saint Martin surprised no one; some observers thought that the Caribbean was the most important theater of the entire conflict. King George III insisted that the region be defended at all costs. For their part, the French swore to take every last British island in the Caribbean until the king wouldn't have enough sugar "to sweeten his tea for breakfast." Since he had arrived in the Caribbean in May 1781 with his fleet, the Comte de Grasse had been hard at work trying to do just that, taking advantage of Rodney's preoccupation with his Statian loot to seize the British island of Tobago.

In 1781, so many of America's hopes rested on what de Grasse chose to do next. The French admiral should be better known today, I thought, given the critically important role he would wind up playing in the war. So here's his backstory. Born in his family castle in Provence (don't hate), he joined the navy as a teenager and fought the British off the coast of India in the Seven Years' War. He was a huge man with a huge personality, known for his ferocity toward his enemies. "The Comte de Grasse stands six foot four," his sailors boasted, "and six foot five on days of battle." Unfortunately, he could be just as hard on his junior officers.

His flagship, the *Ville de Paris*, was practically a floating city, the "world in miniature," one observer wrote, with 110 guns and crew of 1,300. At the age of fifty-nine in 1781, de Grasse was looking for a glorious way to cap off his naval career. (Fun fact: He's also the direct ancestor of astrophysicist Neil deGrasse Tyson. And now you're ready for your next cocktail party.)

In July 1781, de Grasse was anchored off Saint Domingue (now Haiti) when the frigate *Concorde* arrived from Boston with an urgent message. Rochambeau and Washington were pleading with the admiral to bring his entire fleet north. That might be the allies' only chance to deliver a decisive blow to the enemy and, perhaps, secure the independence of the United States. These were desperate times. "[T]he Americans are at the end of their resources," Rochambeau wrote. With Washington's army undermanned, de Grasse should also transport thousands of French soldiers, as many as he could find in the Caribbean, to add to the land forces. And—oh yes—bring lots of hard cash too; they needed that too. And come quickly!

When de Grasse received Rochambeau's request, he had a difficult choice to make. If he took all of his warships north, he would have to put a halt to conquering British-held islands (which now included Saint Martin). Even worse, the British might attack lightly defended French settlements, which had been hit hard by the Great Hurricane, and merchant ships in his absence. What would be left of the French West Indies when he returned from America?

Perhaps he could have it both ways, de Grasse mused, splitting his force to send some ships north and leaving others behind to protect the Caribbean. Or maybe he shouldn't leave at all, for the French admiral didn't have the money on hand for a long expedition. Up north, Rochambeau was also running out of cash—and, unlike Americans, European soldiers were not about to fight without pay.

Whatever de Grasse chose to do would have enormous consequences for America, as it would for the different islands of the Caribbean as well. Here on Saint Martin, I wanted to get a sense of what life was like for the inhabitants, who very easily might have wound up with a different colonial ruler as a result of what he did and what the British did in response. Liana and I had signed up for a historical walking tour of Marigot with a young amateur historian, Stephi Gumbs, who met us at the base of Fort Louis, near the reggae band and the reggae-hating iguana.

"Marigot used to be a lagoon, full of ponds and mangroves," she said in a melodious French accent as she led us toward the town center. "It developed because of sugarcane—sugar was grown in all the hills you see surrounding the town. And the island was also known for its salt, which was used to preserve cod, which enslaved people across the Caribbean ate.

"The French first built a fort here in the seventeenth century," she continued. "The English were on the island of Anguilla nearby. The English and French did not have the biggest love story in history," she said, which made us laugh. That's an understatement.

The view from Fort St. Louis in St. Martin.

Stephi brought us to an old French church and told us more about the island's colonial past. "The French and Dutch split Saint Martin in the seventeenth century. There's a legend that they figured out where the border should go by having a Dutch soldier walk from one end of the island and a French one from the other. The Dutch soldier drank beer and didn't walk far enough, while the Frenchman only had some wine and covered more ground. So, France got more of the island." (My take-away: Wine is good for you.)

She then led us to an ancient sandbox tree, its branches spread in a great canopy. "This is where people on Saint Martin would gather to get news," Stephi said. I imagined people sitting under it back in 1781, wondering if the French would return to reclaim the island. Although enslaved peoples would lead difficult lives no matter which great power took over, who the colonialists were would have a long-lasting effect on their island's culture. As it turned out, the French would find a way to reclaim Saint Martin during the Revolutionary War (I won't spoil the story yet of how they did so) and it remains a French overseas collectivity, and part of the European Union, today.

Stephi had immense pride not only in her roots on this island yet also in her connection to the wider Francophone world. Her mother came from Guadalupe, a French overseas department in the Caribbean, and she moved effortlessly between these islands and Paris, where she went to study law at the age of eighteen. If the British had held on to Saint Martin, as they might well have, many aspects of this native French-speaker's life might have been different.

We finished the tour in the heart of old Marigot, where Stephi pointed out the elegant balconies on the French colonial buildings. She had started these history tours on the side from her regular job with a company. "Doing these tours lets us connect tangibly with history," she told us. "We can see buildings that witnessed much more than just our own passage through time."

Saint Martin is a small island, often overlooked, she said. But it had its own past and culture worth remembering, one irrevocably shaped by the world war that was the American Revolution. So did many of the islands of the Caribbean—far more than I can recount here were occupied by the French, British, or Spanish in turn, which in turn affected the lives of thousands of inhabitants. The decisions made by the allied leaders not only determined the fate of American independence but also left ripple effects on many other peoples and cultures as well.

In the end, de Grasse did wind up sailing north. I had to return as well, even if I daydreamed about staying on Saint Martin forever. What if we sold our house and bought a little boat here? What would be wrong with spending our days searching for the best baguettes and wineshops on the island and our nights on the dunes, watching the moonlight donkeys?

But these were just idle fantasies. I never could have thrown it all in and stayed here on the beach. Then we'd never find out how this war ends, would we?

When I had dinner with Tom Chávez, the professor from New Mexico, he told me some of the hidden history behind de Grasse's decision to help the Americans. I'll share some of what he said, for few people can tell this tale like he can—which introduces a new character to our story too. It all began when a Spanish emissary named Francisco de Saavedra arrived at Saint Domingue in July 1781 to make de Grasse a surprising offer. If the French admiral left to help the *yanquis*, Saavedra proposed, Spain would protect the French islands in his absence.

"Saavedra, what a guy," Tom told me. "I like him. Everyone who knew him liked him. He was a robust figure, super intelligent, swashbuckling." Back in Spain, he had served alongside Bernardo de Gálvez, and the two young men—who were the same age and from the same region—became fast friends, Tom said. Attaching himself to the Gálvez family was a smart career move, for soon Saavedra found himself appointed as an advisor to Bernardo's uncle José, the minister of the Indies. In 1780, José Gálvez sent him to the Caribbean to help jump-start Spain's cooperation with France there.

Saavedra met with de Grasse for days on the *Ville de Paris*, dining on

French food (the ship had a special brick oven to bake fresh bread) and wine, Tom told me. On the ship, Saavedra told his French host about how Bernardo de Gálvez had won a resounding victory over the British at Fort George in Pensacola when a Spanish shell exploded the fort's powder magazine, allowing the Spanish to successfully charge the fort. (That was the stirring battle I saw reenacted in Andalucia.) Gálvez's men—reinforced by their French allies—had captured over a thousand Redcoats, ending the British threat in the region.

Spain now controlled the Gulf of Mexico. Saavedra had orders to mobilize forces to conquer Jamaica for Spain, and France had agreed that he could borrow thousands of French soldiers in the Caribbean for that campaign. Yet he was willing to put those orders to the side for the time. Saavedra was convinced that de Grasse should sail north, Tom said, in full force. When would a chance like this to put the British in their place ever come again?

Although grateful for the offer, de Grasse remained suspicious, which was his natural state of being. Perhaps he should still leave some French ships behind just to be sure. What if the Spanish went back on their word and Britain nabbed more French islands while he was gone? He would be a laughingstock at Versailles, "reproached by all in case of failure," he wrote privately. Could he trust this Spaniard, whom he had just met?

"De Grasse told Saavedra that he would take most of his ships of the line—twenty—but not all of them. And he'd only bring one thousand soldiers with him," Tom told me. "That would be a mistake, Saavedra said," he continued. "Saavedra told de Grasse that this expedition could change the entire course of the war. He said, take all your ships, man, all of them."

Finally, the French admiral relented. He would follow Saavedra's advice and take his entire fleet north to help Washington and Rochambeau. Spain would guard the French island by sea, while the French militia—including the regiment of Blacks, the Chasseurs-Volontaires—would man them by land. In return, de Grasse agreed to help Saavedra attack Jamaica after he returned.

Yet one problem still remained: De Grasse didn't have money for the trip to America. He had heard from Rochambeau that the French general wouldn't have enough cash to pay his soldiers past late August either. De Grasse tried to raise the money from French planters on Saint Domingue, but "he didn't get enough money to get a cheeseburger at McDonald's," as Tom put it. Without the needed funds, the admiral was stuck.

The Comte de Grasse.

Again, Saavedra came to the rescue. He emptied out the treasury of the colony of Santo Domingo, giving de Grasse 100,000 *pesos fuertes*. But that still wasn't enough. So, Saavedra dashed off to Cuba, one of the richest Spanish colonies, on the fastest frigate he could find. "Can you imagine him on that ship?" Tom told me. "I see him holding on to the edge of the ship, his hair back in the wind, headed to Cuba as fast as he possibly could. You could make a movie about that."

Saavedra had hoped that the latest treasure fleet from Mexico would have arrived in Havana, which would have made his job easy. It hadn't, but the young man still didn't give up. He sent collectors out into the streets of Havana, going door-to-door. In only six hours, he raised over 500,000 *pesos fuertes* for the trip, the equivalent of tens of millions of dollars today, which Spanish merchants on the island pledged in return for only 2 percent interest. Legend has it (unfortunately not verified) that the women in Havana even donated their jewelry and family silver to the cause. The money collected would wind up being used to help pay the Continental troops too.

After I heard the story from Tom, I shared it with Liana, who grew up in Cuba. "That's incredible," she said. "I had no idea that Cuba played such an important role in all this." She beamed with pride. "But I'm not surprised. We were so affluent back then, we were Spain's richest colony." Saavedra's proto GoFundMe campaign would make one of the greatest victories in American history possible. The United States and Cuba, which have been sworn enemies for nearly seven decades, started off as partners. I wondered if we ever would be so again.

On July 28, de Grasse wrote a letter to Rochambeau, telling him he would soon sail with his entire fleet of twenty-eight ships of the line. "I have thought myself authorized to take everything on myself for the common cause," he wrote. His destination would be the Chesapeake. De Grasse had been able to read between the lines of Rochambeau's letter and understand that the Bay was the French general's true preference. Not many knew it at the time, but de Grasse's choice would wind up playing a crucial role in America securing its independence.

On August 5, the French armada set out. To try to avoid Rodney (in case the British admiral ever stopped counting his money and gave pursuit), de Grasse would take a dangerous route between the Bahamas and Cuba filled with reefs and sandbars. The British would never dream of looking for him there.

Washington got the news of de Grasse's departure later in August.

Although he was miffed that the admiral was headed to the Chesapeake rather than New York, the American commander quickly got over it. De Grasse's arrival was necessary to the allied plan, but by no means sufficient. Washington had to get his and Rochambeau's armies to Virginia as soon as possible to join de Grasse's fleet, which would stay in the Chesapeake for only a few months at most. Rochambeau also had to persuade the Comte de Barras, head of the French squadron in Newport, to sail south with his eight ships of the line, ferrying the artillery and siege equipment that the allies would need. All the while, the Marquis de Lafayette needed to keep Cornwallis in check in Virginia so the British general didn't slip out of the trap that was being set.

In short, three armies and two navies all had to converge on the Chesapeake at the same time. There were many ways this plan could fail—the British could attack any of these forces, on land or sea, or a storm could scatter or sink the ships. If everything went right, though, the allies could lay siege to Cornwallis's army and send the name of Yorktown into the history books for all time.

Before that could occur, Admiral de Grasse would have to fight one of the most decisive battles of the Revolutionary War. One thing was certain: It would either bring him glory or ruin the allied cause for good.

Chapter Twenty

SEAS OF GLORY

How the French Navy Won One of the Most Important Battles in American History

July–October 1781

"The Siege of Yorktown would not have been won without naval support," a thin young Continental soldier told a small crowd. He was wearing a blue-and-red coat over a worn and dirty white frock, the typical dress of a common soldier at Yorktown.

Jamie Richardson had set up an open-air classroom outside the Museum of the American Revolution at Yorktown under the shade of oak trees, with an easel displaying maps of the Chesapeake Bay and a table covered with naval equipment. The sweet smell of smoke came from a nearby kettle, where other living history reenactors were cooking a stew. Jamie, an educator at the museum, was giving a talk about the Battle of the Chesapeake. I had come here hoping to get a better sense of this critically important, yet underappreciated, clash. This time I was traveling solo; for reasons I couldn't fathom, Liana hadn't jumped at going with me to southeastern Virginia quite as quickly as she had for the trip to Saint Martin.

"The allies needed a navy for their plan to work," Jamie said. "The Americans didn't have much of one, while the British had the greatest navy in the world. They had to, they were an island! They needed to defend themselves. So, everything depended on the French navy."

Lord Cornwallis and his seven thousand men were entrenched at Yorktown and Gloucester, the two towns on either side of the York River, which flowed into the Chesapeake Bay, which in turn emptied into the Atlantic. The allies aimed to blockade the British (and Hessians) by both land and sea, then bombard them until they surrendered. For the plan to work, the French needed to control the Bay. If the British could defeat the French navy, however, they could relieve Cornwallis and the complicated allied campaign would come to naught. "Without a decisive naval force, we can do nothing," Washington wrote to Lafayette, "and with it, everything honorable and glorious."

Jamie held up a picture. "Here's the most underrated commander of the entire American Revolution," he said. "Any takers on who it is?" The crowd fell silent; this guy was a complete mystery.

"That's why I say he's underrated," Jamie went on. "It's Admiral de Grasse. He left the Caribbean in early August with twenty-eight ships of the line. Then he seemed to disappear. The English didn't know where he had gotten to." The British would have all sorts of trouble in discovering where the French fleet was headed.

Some of the blame for the mishaps lay with Rodney (surprise, surprise). Preoccupied with his plunder from Sint Eustatius, and suffering from gout and prostate problems, he decided to sail home for England in lieu of attacking the Comte de Grasse. He delegated the task of stopping the French fleet to his subordinate, Samuel Hood—but inexplicably didn't send Hood the intelligence he had received indicating that de Grasse was heading to the Chesapeake with all his ships of the line. British admiral Thomas Graves, in New York, also should have received various dispatches from Rodney, but these were all either delayed or captured.

To make matters worse, Rodney took three ships of the line back home with him when he left, including the impressive *Gibraltar,* "the noblest ship in the world," made from Cuban mahogany and cedar, which he had captured from the Spanish in the Moonlight Battle off Portugal a year earlier. And so, Hood sailed to America with only a modest fleet, unclear where de Grasse was and unaware that the French planned to show up in full force.

"Hood was like, where did he go?" Jamie recounted. "He assumed that de Grasse must have gone to New York City, because that's where Clinton and most of the British were. Hood went to Long Island and met with Graves there. Hood gave a rundown: Sorry, I missed him. It was kind of like the 'who's on first' routine. Graves said, 'I thought de Grasse was with you. Where else could he be?'"

Jamie paused and let that sink in for the crowd—just as it must have for the two British admirals. "'Uh-oh...*he's at the Chesapeake!*'" Jamie said, slapping his forehead in disbelief.

The combined British fleet set sail south on September 1 to try to intercept de Grasse before he got there. At the same time, the French admiral de Barras, who had finally been wheedled into participating by Rochambeau, was heading south from Newport with the artillery and siege equipment. Perhaps the British fleet might be able to catch him as well? No such luck; the wily de Barras took a route far out to sea to avoid them.

When the British reached Cape Henry at the mouth of the Chesapeake on the morning of September 5, they saw an astounding sight. De Grasse had arrived there a week earlier. The entry of his twenty-eight grand ships of the line and five fast frigates into the Bay, their masts unfurled to the wind, was the "most noble and majestic spectacle I ever witnessed," one American observer wrote. De Grasse stationed twenty-four of his ships of the line near Cape Henry and sent the remaining four up the York River to begin disembarking men and equipment. The scene was one of organized chaos, as rowboats filled the river, carrying the French soldiers from de Grasse's ships to the shore, along with cannon and supplies. Some two thousand French soldiers and sailors were already on land.

"Suddenly, the French saw sails and a British flag in the distance," Jamie said. "The French weren't prepared. De Grasse said, 'I need to fight now, I need to get out of anchor into open water.' Their fleet rushed out to meet the British navy."

De Grasse's titanic flagship Ville de Paris, described as the "world in miniature."

Jamie moved toward the replicas of ammunition on the table near him. "This was called bar shot," he said, holding up a metal object that looked a little like a dumbbell. "The navy would shoot it out of a cannon, it would be spinning, flipping, tumbling. They aimed at the masts of ships and meant to disable them." The French were masters of that technique, trying to knock the British ships out of commission, while the British preferred to pummel French decks and hulls with cannon shot, which killed more enemy sailors. Jamie showed us chain shot and grape shot, fired by the marines on board.

The French ships hastily moved to clear Cape Henry to fight in the open waters of the Atlantic. "The battle was smoky, bloody," Jamie said. "Limbs were blown off." I had seen relics of some of the ships from the campaign in the museum's display cases: cannon, bar shot fired into enemy riggings, a halfpenny, a whistle in the shape of a monkey, and even rat skulls (never forget that there were rodent casualties too). "If not for de Grasse's support, Americans would have lost this siege and they might have lost the war," he summed up. "If we say we wouldn't have won without the French, that's what we mean."

Afterward, I asked Jamie about his background. He was from Williamsburg, he told me. "My grandfather was a waterman for forty-three years here on the York River," he said. "He just passed, God rest his soul. He'd go out on his rowboat, I'd help him throw the lead line out." Perhaps due in part to his family's past on this river, Jamie held the naval battle fought near here in a special reverence.

He had studied forensic science before working at the museum, he told me, and had been happy to discover that some of the skills he had learned in his prior studies applied to his new job too. "I like to solve puzzles," Jamie told me. "When I figure out how something happened in history, I get that same feeling of solving something as I did studying forensics."

Puzzle-solving skills certainly come in handy when trying to figure out how that naval clash unfolded, the most important battle in American history that hardly anyone knows about. Historians can't even settle on its name; some call it the Battle of the Chesapeake, others the Battle of the Capes. I wanted to find out more about it—and also crack the mystery as to why it doesn't get its proper due today. For the next step in my sleuthing, I hopped in my car to drive the fifty miles southeast to Cape Henry to see where some of the action took place myself. If the U.S. military would let me in, that is.

Even though the Cape Henry Memorial commemorates the Battle of the Chesapeake, there's a catch: It's located on an active military base. Fort Story security only allows a limited number of visitors each day. And you'd better watch your step once you're there. After arriving, I surrendered my driver's license at the guardhouse, signed some paperwork, and went through a metal detector.

A man in navy fatigues then brought me outside to give me a briefing. "If you trespass, it's going to be a bad day for you and a long day for me," he barked. "You can go to the gas station on the base and buy a snack, but don't get anything from the military commissary. Do not purchase alcohol under any circumstances. If you buy some, I'll have to confiscate it," he paused. "I like bourbon and whiskey," he added under his breath.

After walking around the dunes, I came across a statue of de Grasse, looking resolutely out at the water and appearing considerably trimmer than he did in real life (the sea air here must have done him good). For a view of the early stages of the battle, I climbed to the top of the Cape Henry lighthouse. Below me, a long red-and-black cruiser chugged through the water. The lighthouse was on the southern boundary of the entrance to the Chesapeake Bay, the largest estuary in the United States. In the far distance lay Cape Charles, the northern boundary to the entrance to the Bay.

I tried to imagine the scene below me filled with ships of the line, the most impressive war machines of their day. The French had twenty-four ready for battle, while the British could only counter with nineteen. Given the famed quality of British seamanship, though, they would still be formidable opponents. The Brits had brought the *Invincible,* the *Intrepid,* and the *Resolution,* fearsome warships all, as well as the *Terrible,* a ship apparently suffering from low self-esteem (were all the good names already taken?).

I looked down at the surf crashing. I was able to track the movements of the battle thanks to interpretive signs posted in the park, as well as my readings of Mercy Otis Warren and other historians who recognized its importance. The French ships would have to clear this cape while also passing by dangerous shoals to their north to come out to meet the British in battle. It was tricky work; a French frigate had already run aground earlier in the day. And it would be even trickier than usual, for de Grasse was in a hurry.

In the eighteenth century, fleets typically engaged in a methodical, highly choreographed process of forming a line of battle, with ships neatly arranged at a certain distance from each other. But de Grasse wanted to get out of the Bay, where he had trouble maneuvering, as quickly as possible to join the fight. So, rather unusually, he ordered what was called the "line of speed," which basically meant rushing to the front as fast you could sail. This would reward the boldest commanders—whoever won this race would have the greatest chance of glory in the battle to follow.

None was more impressive than the officer who raced to the front: Louis Antoine de Bougainville. If his name sounds vaguely familiar, you might be thinking of his favorite plant—the papery pink or purple bougainvillea, named after him following his expedition to the South Pacific. A scientist and explorer, Bougainville led one of the three French squadrons on the day of battle. (He loved plants so much that he named his first child, born not long after the battle, Hyacinthe.) De Grasse was not one of his fans, though. The French count looked down on Bougainville, a commoner by birth, and had disparaged his action during the Battle of Martinique earlier that year. Yet here the horticulturalist was in the front in his eighty-gun *Auguste*, leading what was normally supposed to be the rear guard. De Grasse's fate would now rest in Bougainville's hands.

Despite being outmanned, Graves had the wind behind his sails and could destroy the French ships as they came one by one out of the Bay if he so chose. Yet Graves did things by the book, and the book proclaimed: Slowly assemble all of your ships in a neat line and let your opponent do the same. The British were ready first and, gentlemen that they were, waited patiently for their French opponents to be all set to fight. (True to its name, the *Terrible* started leaking even before any shots were fired.)

Finally, Graves realized that if he wanted to attack while daylight remained, he needed to get on with it. And so the vanguard of the two navies clashed in "the most violent naval concussions," as Warren put it. The battle would turn on "those few testing moments for which an entire naval officer's life has been built," Bougainville wrote later.

If it was a test, Bougainville got an A-plus. Despite being undermanned (two hundred members of his crew had disembarked onshore before the action), the *Auguste* seemed to be everywhere at once, darting so close to his foes that it looked as if Bougainville planned to board them. All was "thunder, foam, and fire," he wrote—the latter generated by his gunners, who shot an astounding 684 cannon balls in just a few hours. The man of science was relentless, laughing in the face of death. No one would ever mistake him for a tropical flowering plant again.

While Bougainville and the French vanguard mauled their opponents' ships, the British were dealing with a colossal mistake by Graves. The British admiral had ordered a flag hoisted with the signal to charge ahead—but forgot to pull down another flag that flew a contradictory signal. As a result, some British ships followed him into the fray, while others held back. If that was his testing moment, I'd give Graves a D-minus.

The fight ended after night fell and the two fleets drifted farther out to sea. Each side wanted to resume hostilities in the morning, but both had received heavy damage, especially the British. *Terrible* did not fare well (predictably enough), taking on so much water that Graves finally put it out of its misery and ordered it burned. On the French side, the normally prickly de Grasse could not stop singing the praises of Bougainville, the man he had once disdained. "That's what I call fighting," he said with admiration.

Graves eventually realized that he'd have no choice but to return to New York to repair his shattered fleet. And so, de Grasse safely returned to the Bay. The Battle of the Chesapeake had been a resounding strategic victory for the allies, who had fulfilled their main objective, controlling the Bay to support the siege of Yorktown. And there was more welcome news as well: While the two fleets were drifting south, the Count de Barras had slipped into the Chesapeake with his own fleet and the needed siege equipment and artillery.

The French now had a staggering thirty-six ships of the line in the Bay—truly a "grand sight," one observer proclaimed. Some historians have called the Battle of the Chesapeake the single most important battle of the entire war. The reason France had come out on top—along with

Bougainville's bravery—was the fact that, for once, they had naval superiority over the British, with nine more ships of the line at the battle than their opponents had. "To this inferiority...and to this alone," complained the British general Clinton, "is our present misfortune to be imputed."

The author at Cape Henry.

The British weakness was thanks in large part to the pressure that the allies had put on them around the world. The nineteen ships of the line that Graves had brought represented only about 10 percent of all the ships of the line in His Majesty's Navy. The others were spread out around the empire, guarding against the next allied attack, which could occur virtually anywhere.

The day of the Battle of the Chesapeake, a huge fleet of twenty-nine British ships of the line was uselessly patrolling the choppy waters of the Channel, waiting for an invasion of the homeland that never came. Seven British ships of the line had also been sent off to engage a Dutch fleet in the North Sea the month before (in a battle that resulted in a thousand casualties). Rodney had brought three ships of the line with him as he went home to England, while the commander in Jamaica had refused to give Hood three other ships of the line, choosing to keep them for the island's defense instead.

In 1781, the British also sent a squadron to reinforce India against Hyder Ali, Tipu Sultan, and the French there. And Britain had to assign part of its fleet to the Mediterranean too. Just a month before the Battle of the Chesapeake, the French and Spanish had landed troops on the British-held island of Minorca, near Spain, which was now under siege and would have to be relieved—as would Gibraltar again.

By trying to defend their entire empire against a worldwide coalition dead set against them, the British hadn't been able to assemble the fleet they needed in the most critical hour of the war. In contrast, the French had prioritized bringing every last ship of the line they could to the Chesapeake, trusting their allies, the Spanish, to guard their interests in the Caribbean. Despite the risks, they had committed all for the common cause, as de Grasse had put it.

I went down the stairs of the lighthouse and made my way back to the guard station, carefully not buying any alcohol along the way. I had been happy to see the small commemoration of the Battle of the Chesapeake—the statue of de Grasse and the interpretive signs—on the grounds of the base. But how odd it was that you needed to make such a degree of effort to pay homage to one of the key battles in American history. Without it, Yorktown wouldn't have happened. Not a single American fought in the battle or even was there to witness it, I thought. Is that why some histories don't give this battle its due?

Now, having visited Cape Henry, I would remember this victory as a testament both to allied cooperation and to the valor of the French navy. I'll give thanks to de Grasse, whose victory made Yorktown possible, and to Saavedra and the Cubans, who played such key roles in getting the French fleet to sail. And now that I know how the battle was won, from here on out, whenever I pass by a bougainvillea I'll whisper *merci* to it.

But the game was far from over. With the victory at the Battle of the Chesapeake, the allies had closed the sea route of escape to Cornwallis. Now they had to do the same on the land. And the fighting would break out in a most unexpected place.

Chapter Twenty-One

THE WORLD TURNED UPSIDE DOWN

A Victory Years in the Making

October–December 1781

It was far from an ordinary day at Abingdon Elementary, since I'm fairly certain that normal school days don't involve a group of active French military officers, in their beige dress uniforms and kepi caps, walking through the grass. They had come to commemorate the sacrifice that young French soldiers made over two centuries earlier, when this soccer field was a field of battle.

Gloucester Point is a small town on the northern side of the York River, a half mile across the water from Yorktown. It's at the tip of what's known as the Middle Peninsula, a stretch of land wedged between the York and Rappahannock Rivers and bounded by the Chesapeake Bay to its east. In the fall of 1781, the British stationed troops at both Yorktown and Gloucester, fortifying both towns. Little did they realize the scale of the forces that would soon be assembled against them.

While de Grasse was sailing north to the Chesapeake, Washington and Rochambeau's army of seven thousand men was marching south, keeping their final destination a secret for as long as possible.

Washington had spread rumors that New York City, which they would pass by on their way, was the real target. He made a great show of assembling landing craft, as if preparing for an amphibious assault on the city. The French played their part in the ruse by buying flour in bulk and bricks to make brick ovens—obviously, no self-respecting French soldier would dream of laying siege to a city without having an ample supply of baguettes at hand. It all seemed to check out. "The deception was so complete," Warren wrote, that "Sir Henry Clinton, apprehensive only for New York, had not the smallest suspicion" of the allies' true destination. The British general hunkered down behind his fortifications, waiting for the assault that never came, and let the allied armies pass by him unmolested.

The two armies marched for weeks, covering four hundred miles of terrain, a tremendous logistical challenge. The armies needed food and camping sites, and they had to pay for everything. (Logistics had been an even greater problem for the British, who often depended on supply lines that stretched across the Atlantic.)

Most importantly, the leaders had to forge these two armies, with different command structures and languages, into one cohesive fighting force that looked out for each other. And as they marched south, that's exactly what they began to do. When there weren't enough boats to ferry both the Americans and French across the Delaware River, for example, Rochambeau gallantly agreed that his men would instead wade through the waters upriver.

In the first days of September, the armies marched through Philadelphia. Practically the whole city turned out to huzzah the French, their saviors, with nary a jeer to be heard. (Not that Philadelphians would ever dream of booing; I couldn't imagine that happening.) What a far cry from the angry mobs in Boston only three years earlier, which had killed a French officer.

For their part, the French got a taste of the American capital, marveling at the wide array of religions practiced by the people. The Continental troops were happy too—Rochambeau had generously loaned Washington nearly $25,000 out of some of his last funds, knowing that his coffers would be replenished when de Grasse arrived. Finally, the Patriots had hard silver dollars in their pockets.

Their destination had finally been revealed. Even before the campaign had begun, John Adams had observed that the "Chesapeake Bay is a fine trap," predicting that "[o]ur allies will help us catch a grand flock of vultures there." Now the armies were making his prophecy come true. In mid-September, following the victory at the Battle of the Chesapeake, the allied troops assembled in Williamsburg and joined up with Lafayette's small army. The Marquis had done his part to harass Cornwallis and keep the British in check. He was overjoyed to reunite with the American commander, hugging him and kissing him on the cheek.

The French officers wouldn't stop emoting. When Washington met de Grasse in person on board the *Ville de Paris*, the admiral wrapped him in a bear hug and called him "my dear little general." Although the impetuous de Grasse kept threatening to return to the Caribbean, he finally agreed to stay until the end of October, allowing the allies to mount a siege. By the end of September, the allied armies had moved into Yorktown and Gloucester, encircling the British.

On October 3, Cornwallis sent Colonel Banastre Tarleton—Bloody Tarleton, as the Americans called him for the atrocities he had committed—out on a foraging expedition in Gloucester, seeking out corn and other foodstuffs that the besieged British desperately needed. He would also test the strength of the allied forces assembled against him on this side of the river. Tarleton and his cavalry quickly ran into a fierce onslaught of French cavalry and American militiamen. The fight that ensued, called the Battle of the Hook, was being commemorated today here at the elementary school.

Robert Kelly, the director of the Gloucester Museum of History, kicked things off before a small crowd gathered under a row of tulip poplars and oaks. Behind him, fourth graders sat in plastic chairs, surprisingly attentive. "We are here on the site of a battle that was crucial to the French and American victory," he began. "It paved the way to Yorktown. Today we gather to remember French soldiers who gave their lives for the American Revolution."

He was followed by a French general, Vincent de Kytspotter, the head of the French defense mission to the United Nations and a military historian in his own right. "As a former French hussar, I'm very proud of this cavalry engagement, which was the largest of the American Revolution. And it was one of the earliest examples of a joint French–American expedition.

"We succeeded in defeating the outrageous Tarleton, the butcher of Virginia," the general continued. The audience let out some lusty boos at the mention of the colonel's name. "It was not only a tactical victory, but it stopped the foraging and looting of this beautiful Virginia countryside. And it had strategic importance, as it seized off any exit Cornwallis might have had.

"Dear friends, dear fourth graders, in this very place, remember: Peace has a price." General Kytspotter moved closer to the kids. "Young soldiers fought shoulder by shoulder. Here in Virginia, French soldiers came to defend the right of Americans to freedom."

Following his speech, a French officer laid flowers at a stone that commemorated five Frenchmen who died in the battle. A soprano sang "La Marseillaise," while the fourth graders responded with the "The Star-Spangled Banner." The crowd left with a new understanding of the war that once swept through this sleepy small town.

Later, I caught up with Robert at his museum. It was housed in an old tavern—one in which some of the French officers might have stayed before the battle, he told me. Tall and lanky and in his thirties, he looked like he could still play point guard somewhere. He had come to work here after a stint at Fort Monroe across the river, where he had uncovered the stories of some of the enslaved men who had helped build that base. "I consider myself a public historian," he told me, "And here we have such a good story—a French commander with quite a personality, and the story of the battle itself. What's cooler than a cavalry battle?"

He shared with me a surprising fact: The supposedly French cavalrymen that charged during the battle weren't all from France, not by a long shot. "I was shocked to learn that the command language was German," he said. "This legion had soldiers from all across Europe. They were highly skilled, well trained, kind of like the special ops forces of our day." Orders might have been given in German, but by tradition, swearing, it turns out, was always in Hungarian. Some fifteen nations were represented in this legion of light troops, I learned, which was designed to move fast and hit hard. During the Revolutionary War, they had already fought the British in West Africa and would have been in the vanguard of the 1779 invasion of England had the allies been able to land forces there. "They enjoyed the high of being in battle," Robert told me.

"Kind of like an early version of the French Foreign Legion," I offered, "on horseback."

"Kind of," he replied. "It was led by the Duc de Lauzun. He was a real character, flamboyant and arrogant, a real ladies' man. In his memoir, he wrote about conquests of women as much about the battles." He would tell American women that he was in fact married, but only *un petit peu*.

Yet, at the Battle of the Hook, Lauzun rose to the challenge. He personally rode off ahead of the rest of his legion, hoping to duel Tarleton as if they were two knights of old. Tarleton fell to the ground after a French legionnaire thrust a lance into another British cavalryman's horse (yes, this legion had lances), which then crashed into his own. The two cavalries traded charges and countercharges. Finally, the British were forced to retreat to their redoubts at the tip of Gloucester Point. The allies had carried the day.

"The sheer number of men on horseback—imagine what that would have looked like, how it would have sounded," Robert said. "It was a morale boost for the Americans and George Washington. They repelled Tarleton; he left in disgrace. And Cornwallis didn't have a means of escape."

"I thought the ceremony was really moving," I said. "Especially when they read out the names of the French soldiers who died here."

"That's important," he replied. "Washington, Lafayette, Rochambeau, they get all the love. The ceremony reminds us that there are other French folks here who aren't household names. It's important to know the names of people; it humanizes them. At least two were buried right where they fell, on the battlefield where the school is now."

"I loved seeing all the kids out there," I said. "This isn't a famous place like Valley Forge or Bunker Hill, but it was part of the war too."

"It's important to try to engage the next generation with history," Robert replied. "When you can tell students this battle happened in their own community, it's an engaging story, an adventure. We can be proud of it," he said. "Something that happened in this little community had an impact on the entire world."

Thanks to the Battle of the Chesapeake, the sea route was cut off from Cornwallis; thanks in part to the Battle of the Hook, Gloucester would not serve as an escape hatch to the north either. The allies had Cornwallis blocked on all sides. As Adams had predicted, the trap was set. Now it was vulture-catching time.

J. Michael Moore got out of his old pickup truck at our meetup spot on the Yorktown Battlefield. Green fields stretched around us, while crows cawed in the trees. He was in his fifties, wearing a baseball cap, with a gray goatee. A historian who worked as the curator of a nearby historic house and museum, he had the privilege of actually living in Yorktown itself (population 221). And he seems to have had a much better experience in the town than his fellow resident Cornwallis ever did. He had kindly agreed to show me around the battlefield.

"Cornwallis was expecting maybe six thousand militiamen to come against him; he wasn't expecting eighteen thousand troops with French heavy artillery," Michael said in his soft Virginia accent. "He never expected the French to seal him up in Yorktown.

"The French were paramount to this," he continued. "The Yorktown campaign was the first successful multinational, multilingual operation in American history. And the allies pulled it off flawlessly."

Michael led me past rolling fortifications, grassy hills that I had once run up and tumbled down when I visited Yorktown as a little kid. (Which you're not supposed to do now, and maybe weren't then either.) "The playbook for the siege came from Vauban, a French military strategist from the seventeenth century. The idea was that the army would dig a series of parallel trenches." That way, they would advance closer and closer to their target.

The siegeworks at Yorktown were planned by the engineer Louis Duportail, whom I had dubbed the Brains of the Operation. Yorktown was a sort of reunion of those volunteers I called the European Avengers—de Fleury, the Tech Man, was there, as was the Muscle, the indefatigable Baron von Steuben. And no one could miss the irrepressible Marquis de Lafayette, overjoyed that the allies' greatest moment of glory was about to arrive.

Three heroes of Yorktown: Rochambeau, Washington, and de Grasse.

They all played a complementary role to Washington and the French commanders, who were the right men at the right time. "Rochambeau and de Grasse, they were like the Nick Sabans of the French army and navy," Michael said, describing these masterminds. "They were well respected, men who had helped rebuild the French army and navy."

But that wasn't all. Among the allied forces was a small delegation of Oneida warriors, led by Grasshopper, an important sachem. They had come south from New York, first stopping to meet with Congress and the French ambassador in Philadelphia, and arriving in time for the siege. Other Oneida fighters were back in New York State, serving as scouts for the Continental troops who remained behind. The First Rhode Island Regiment, which the reenactor Antoine Randolph Watts had told me about, was there as well. By this point the regiment, which had been combined with another, no longer consisted only of men of color but was integrated.

So many of the characters I had come across on my journeys met up at Yorktown, I thought. The siege reminded me in a way of one of those huge benefit concerts when all the musicians come out onstage at the end for an encore. If only Bernardo de Gálvez had made it, the scene would have been perfect. He actually had intended to sail north from the Caribbean in his sloop to join in the siege but was talked out of it; since Spain still wasn't an official ally of the rebels, it would have raised questions with the Spanish court if he had come. But Gálvez and his friend Francisco de Saavedra had done their part beforehand, securing the Gulf, protecting the Caribbean, and of course, paying for much of the operation. Meanwhile, back in Versailles, the mastermind behind the alliance, the Comte de Vergennes, waited to hear the outcome of the most important campaign of the entire war.

Michael led me to the site of the French Grand Artillery, where he showed me the guns—original relics of the siege—still standing there today. "Do you see those fishes on this cannon?" he asked me. "Why do you think they're there?"

"Were these naval guns?" I offered.

"No, these were the symbol of the Dauphin, the French prince. If you look at that famous Gilbert Stuart painting of Washington at Yorktown, he's leaning on a cannon that was French—you can see the dauphins on them." (The French had made a play on words, for *dauphin* meant both prince and dolphin.) "There was more French artillery here at the siege than American," Michael continued. "And even a lot of the American guns came from France. We weren't picky."

Once the first parallel trenches were in place, the allies could begin bombing the town. Michael pointed out the differences in the guns before us. "The howitzer had an exploding shell, with an arc. They were both effective, the cannon and the howitzer, shot and shell. One pounds, one pulverizes." He also showed me the squat-looking mortar at the end, which sent projectiles high into the air. "We've been talking for maybe half an hour, right?" he said. "They would have already sent thirty rounds in there during that time."

The allies proceeded to dig the second parallel but could only get so far. The British redoubts—earthwork emplacements outside the fortified town—were an obstacle, particularly two large ones, Numbers Nine and Ten, that protected the eastern side of the town. From their perches in these redoubts, the defenders could bombard the allied troops digging the trenches. The French and Americans would have to take these enemy posts out. Michael drove me over to them.

"The allies attacked on October 14. It was a moonless night. They were shelling the other side of town to freak them out. This was a big boy attack. The allies unloaded their muskets and just went in with bayonets. If you made any noise, they'd shoot you."

We walked over toward a pleasant-looking green hill. "This is Redoubt Ten, which the Americans had to take," he said. Lafayette sent a company of troops to do so, under the command of Alexander Hamilton, Michael told me. The redoubt was protected by abatis, a tangle of logs with sharpened ends pointing out at the assailants. The normal protocol was for a special unit of the military to clear this obstacle first, but the impatient Hamilton couldn't be bothered, and he ordered his troops to go right through them. "Someone got hold of Hamilton by the suspenders and threw him over Redoubt Ten," Michael said. After some fierce fighting inside the fortification, the Americans were victorious.

"The French were charged with taking the larger one, Redoubt Nine," he told me, leading me to it. "They were under the command of the Duc de Deux-Ponts—the Duke of Two Bridges. Everything sounds better in French, doesn't it?"

Unlike Hamilton, the French commander ordered his men to clear the abatis before he led the charge. The enemy spotted the intruders as they approached. "A Hessian was on guard duty, and he called out, 'Halt, who goes there?' He didn't like the answer he got, so he fired.

"The French yelled back, "*Vive le Roi!*" And Michael did just that, shouting the words in French like the attackers had. "I love doing that," he said, chuckling.

"It was nasty, close-order fighting," he went on. The French suffered a number of casualties, but they too were victorious. Now that the allies held both redoubts, they dug through the night. By morning, the second parallel was complete and the allies were closing in on the town. They unleashed a barrage of bombs, pulverizing much of what was left of Yorktown. Finally, after a day of this, Cornwallis realized that he had no choice but to send an officer up to the parapets with the white flag of surrender. "Everything that could go wrong, went wrong for the British," Michael concluded. "Everything that could go right, did go right for the allies."

We got back in his pickup, and Michael drove through the woods, pointing out places where the French had camped and where artillery guns had been placed. Along the way, he shared with me where his passion for history came from.

"Someone asked me once why I became a historian," he told me, "and I replied, 'because I suck at math and I enjoy being poor.'" It turns out there was much more to the story, though. He grew up in the Tidewater region of Virginia and loved going to museums and battlefields with his father. “When I was a little kid, my dad took me to Yorktown,” he told me, “and I found it fascinating. I watched a film in the visitor’s center, and I came out of it thinking that Rochambeau was still alive. I had just seen him in the film! My father had to break it to me that Rochambeau was dead and that I had seen an actor.”

“History always spoke to me,” Michael went on, as we bumped along through the woods of Yorktown, passing streams and duck ponds. “Rochambeau, Washington, Lafayette, Cornwallis—they all had stories. And I wanted to learn more about those stories. American history happened right here,” he told me. “The beginning and end of the British in America happened right here—Jamestown and Yorktown are only about twenty miles apart.” Even though his father has now passed, Michael has never stopped the quest he began with him to find those stories.

“What’s it like living in Yorktown?” I asked him. “I’m jealous.” I tried to imagine living with a battlefield in your backyard. It sounded almost as good as my relocating-to-Saint Martin fantasy.

“Victory Day is crazy,” he said, referring to the annual commemoration of the British surrender each October. “I like the more quiet moments.”

Before we parted, Michael told me about an unusual incident during the siege. Sometime before the assault on Redoubt Nine, the Highlander army musicians inside the fortifications mounted the parapet and played a song on the bagpipes. Impressed, instead of firing at them, the French troops saluted them with a regimental tune from their own band.

“On October 14, the anniversary of the taking of the redoubt, I’ll go out there,” Michael told me. “I’ll just sit there and play a recording of bagpipes in honor of the troops.” I left with this image in my mind, of a man sitting still while the sound of pipes echoed in an empty field, thinking of fallen soldiers, each one with a lost story.

For most of the year, Yorktown might be quiet, but Victory Day, as Michael had told me, is another story. Every October 19, the town fills up with parades, reenactors galore, and the constant soundtrack of fife-and-drum music. Dignitaries speak from a podium in front of the marble Victory Monument, draped by bunting and surrounded by flags. The year I went, representatives of both France and Spain showed up.

The original surrender was, naturally enough, a very different affair. Once the terms were finally agreed to, the British marched out of their fortifications looking forlorn (and/or drunk). Cornwallis claimed to be ill, and his second-in-command tried to offer his sword to Rochambeau. The French general, recognizing the symbolism of the moment, properly pointed to Washington, who in turn allowed his own second-in-command to receive it. Legend has it that the British army musicians played the old ballad "The World Turned Upside Down." Not long afterward, the British troops at Gloucester also surrendered.

The British surrender at Yorktown. Rochambeau, de Grasse, and the Duc de Lauzun are all on the left-hand side of the painting, while Lafayette and Von Steuben stand with the Americans on the right.

As impressive as the modern Victory Day hoopla was, for me the most moving part of the day was the ceremony at the Yorktown French Memorial, located on the banks of the York River a little west of town. Veterans' groups had raised money to place the monument there years ago on the spot where French soldiers had been buried in unmarked graves. After years of research, the names of over three hundred Frenchmen fallen at Yorktown have been engraved on the stone, along with the place in France where they came from. Today, the stone was bookended with French and American flags.

The ceremony began in the early morning with a group of several dozen French officers standing upright, their blue-and-khaki uniforms immaculate, solemnly singing "La Marseillaise" a capella. After the last lines rang out, everyone stood in silence.

A French colonel spoke. "We pay tribute to these soldiers and sailors," he said. "Through their bravery they changed the course of history. May their memory endure. They were the builders of an alliance which has stood the test of time." He went on to invoke the many other battles in which France and America had fought side by side, ending by talking about the gravestones of the Americans at Omaha Beach on D-Day.

A chaplain from the U.S. Coast Guard then came up to the podium to lead a prayer. "Yorktown was a gift," she began. She too shared some history about the Franco-American alliance—"which began when the good people of France came to secure our freedom." Since then, she continued, the two militaries have sought to not only establish security, but also to be a force for good in a world that needs peace. "When we come together," she ended, "we can do amazing things."

The French officers laid wreaths before the stone, gave a sharp salute, and turned and moved back into the ranks. I gazed at the names on the stone before me, these young men who never returned home.

So much had gone into this victory, I thought, so many acts of heroism and sacrifice that occurred long before the allied troops began digging their siege trenches. The victory belonged to de Grasse, Bougainville, and all the other French naval officers and sailors who had won the spectacular victory in the Chesapeake. To Francisco de Saavedra, who had put his own interests aside and persuaded de Grasse to sail in full force to Yorktown while Spain protected the Caribbean. To the Cubans who sent their silver for the campaign. To Bernardo de Gálvez, whose taking of Pensacola had removed the British threat in the Gulf of Mexico. To the foreign ministers of France and Spain, Vergennes and Floridablanca, who had committed their forces to this theater of war and ordered them to cooperate with each other.

And, in the end, to all of those brave people who had stood against the British around the globe, forcing King George to send ships and troops away from America to protect other theaters of war, including the Dutch, the Mysoreans, and the Oneida. So many soldiers and sailors had lost their lives in the long lead-up to Yorktown, names that will never be engraved on any memorial. But their sacrifices still counted—and should be remembered.

"Let history huzzah for you," Washington told his troops as they applauded the surrender, according to legend. After the battle, the overjoyed townsfolk of Williamsburg erupted in cries of "*Vive le Roi!*" One of Washington's aides made his way to Philadelphia with the news. In the City of Brotherly Love, people spilled into the streets, laughing and hugging each other. Cannons saluted the victory, the city militia paraded with the American and French flags, and the Liberty Bell happily bonged away.

The three principal heroes of the victory—Washington, Rochambeau, and de Grasse—were celebrated by the people as "the instruments of their salvation, the deliverers from impending ruin," Warren wrote. Three years earlier, the French and Spanish emissaries had hosted members of Congress at that special Independence Day mass at Philadelphia's Old St. Mary's Catholic church. Following the victory, the Catholic church again opened its doors to Continental leaders, who attended a mass of thanksgiving. But this time, Congress returned the favor, inviting the

French ambassador to a service at the Dutch Lutheran church, where the preacher gave "thanks to almighty God for crowning the allied arms of the United States and France with success."

Afterward, the overjoyed Congress did what it did best: It passed a resolution. That was pretty much all it could do—the government was so broke, it didn't even have enough money to reimburse Washington's aide for his trip expenses. (The delegates took up a collection among themselves to give him some cash.) Victory couldn't have come at a better time.

Rochambeau gave the honor of sailing home to France with the news of the victory to two officers: the Duc de Deux-Ponts, who stormed Redoubt Nine with his regiment, and the Duc de Lauzun, who had led his cavalry to victory at the Battle of the Hook. The French were already celebrating the birth of the Dauphin, the heir to the throne. Now they had even more reason to party (as if Versailles needed a reason). Fireworks exploded for days, and a candymaker even recreated the Siege of Yorktown in sugar. The rager went on for three days and nights.

In Britain, Prime Minister Lord North responded to the news "as he would have taken a ball in the breast," an observer noted, "exclaiming wildly, 'Oh God! It is all over!'"

Oh no, Lord North, it wasn't. Yorktown was a great victory for America, but the rest of the world would keep on fighting. There would be plenty of war yet to come, battles most of us have never heard of: huge naval clashes in the Caribbean, fierce fighting in India, even an assault on a fort near the Arctic Circle. Don't you dare put this book down yet.

Chapter Twenty-Two

THE LAST BATTLE

The Forgotten Ending to the War

January 1782–June 1783

There may have been parties everywhere from Philadelphia to Paris, but George Washington was not in a celebratory mood. "My greatest fear," he wrote to Nathanael Greene after the surrender at Yorktown, "is that Congress, viewing this stroke in too important a point of light, may think our work too nearly closed and will fall into a state of languor." The worried general made his way to Philadelphia to remind anyone who would listen that the war wasn't done yet. He and his army still needed the support of the nation.

There was at least one person who shared Washington's view: King George III. Lord North might have claimed that "it was all over," but his boss thought the opposite. Only two days after receiving the news of the defeat, the king gave a rousing speech to Parliament, insisting that Britain would fight on. Yorktown had resulted in Britain losing a major army and then pausing any further major operations in the United States as a result. That battle was thus obviously very important—yet, paradoxically enough, not "*too* important," as Washington had put it. Cornwallis's forces represented only about 7 percent of all British effectives in uniform, and His Majesty's Navy remained the most powerful one in the world. Britain had lost a battle but not the war.

The year after Yorktown would feature dozens of clashes, most of them far from America's shores. Even though the British shifted their focus to other theaters of the conflict, they still controlled New York City, Charleston, and other American ports. As the war continued, Britain still had a chance to win victories elsewhere—and then, with a strong position at the bargaining table, it could push to hold on to land that it had conquered in America if it wanted to. The year following Yorktown, then, would be a crucial one for the future of the United States.

Today, 1782 is the true forgotten year of the Revolutionary War. Plenty of histories don't mention it all, jumping straight from the 1781 victory at Yorktown to the 1783 Treaty of Paris as if nothing happened in between. Yet it wasn't always like that. Warren, for example, broke her *History* into three volumes, with the final volume *opening* with the Yorktown campaign (rather than ending with it) and then chronicling the battles yet to occur.

After Yorktown, Washington could only guess at what Britain's intentions were. The British still had more troops in North America than he had in his Continental Army; his enemies could still regain the momentum if they chose to. And so, Washington marched his men back to New York State, to once again keep an eye on the Redcoats in New York City. He left Rochambeau and the French army in Williamsburg for the next seven months to guard that region. Meanwhile, Greene and the Southern army encircled the British in Charleston. As it turned out, none of these armies engaged in major combat in 1782, however, and the war ground largely to a stalemate in America.

After some months of guard duty, Rochambeau received orders to move north to join French ships that would be arriving in Boston.

From there, his men were to embark on transports to join in the planned Franco-Spanish campaign to conquer Jamaica. The French divisions departed Williamsburg one by one, with the last troops leaving on July 4, 1782. Meanwhile, Washington was doing whatever he could to discover what was happening elsewhere in the war that had seemed to pass him by. He longed for intelligence from Europe, he wrote to General Greene, yet found himself "as much in the dark as ever."

Hmm. It's the Fourth of July on a completely forgotten year of the Revolutionary War. Would you, like George Washington, like to know what else was going on around the world on that very specific date?

I thought you'd never ask. Step back into my imaginary chapel.

As you'll remember, I had dreamed up a church with thirteen stained-glass windows that illustrated the war around the world on July 4, 1779, providing a snapshot of what was going on during the often-overlooked middle period of the conflict. Don't worry, I checked, the chapel is still standing. Let's pay it another visit to check on the state of play three years later. Get ready for another whirlwind tour through history—a whole bunch of battles you've never heard of are about to come flying your way. Never fear, I'll be waiting for you there at the end, for we have one last journey to go on.

The first window last time showed Washington waiting in camp in upstate New York, hoping something would happen to shake the war out of its doldrums. Now things were far different, weren't they? His troops had won at Yorktown! Three years later, he probably spent the holiday at a Fourth of July celebration, receiving the thanks of a grateful nation, right?

Nope. Washington spent July 4, 1782, waiting in camp in upstate New York, hoping something would happen to shake the war out of its doldrums. Incredibly, he spent this Fourth *less than three miles away* from where his troops had camped in 1779. Forget about Independence Day; he seemed to have been trapped in an endless loop of Groundhog Days.

Once again, the direction of the war was out of his hands. It was being fought between the allies and Britain, with America on the sidelines. Washington was again reduced to stationing his troops around New York City, keeping an eye on the British but powerless to attack them. He spent our nation's birthday writing a cranky missive complaining that his soldiers weren't getting enough flour for bread.

Washington itched to take the field again. After Yorktown, he had begged de Grasse to provide naval support for an attack on Charleston. But the French admiral declined; he had to return to the Caribbean to join in the invasion of Jamaica, as he had promised the Spanish. Instead, 1782 proved to be a year of mostly small-scale skirmishes in America, as Washington bided his time to see what his coalition partners—and Britain—would do.

Meanwhile, thousands of Patriots languished in the prison ships off Brooklyn and Charleston, with a hundred dying each month. With the French navy gone, the British were able to blockade the American coast, ruining the new country's trade. And Congress still wasn't paying the Continental soldiers or providing the pensions it had promised to the officers. Some even started whispering that Washington should seize control of the government to make things right—suggestions that the commander in chief immediately rejected. For his part, George III couldn't believe reports that the Virginian was contemplating retirement when the war ended. If he willingly gave up power, the king mused, he would be "the greatest man in the world."

In 1779, the second stained-glass window was an unfortunate one, showing the campaign in New York State and Pennsylvania against many of the British-leaning Haudenosaunee tribes, in which Continental troops burned Iroquois villages to the ground. America's first allies, the Oneida, were deeply saddened by these attacks. Unlike most of the other Haudenosaunee, they supported American independence, but by no means did they want to see their brethren killed and moved off their lands.

The 1782 update would portray a different scene for the Oneida: Washington giving a belt to leaders of that nation in gratitude for their service. The Oneida had continued to act as scouts and warriors alongside American forces in upstate New York as they battled the British. Since he had time on his hands, Washington set out on a weeklong tour up the Hudson Valley, visiting towns and touring the battlefield at Saratoga. Just two days before Independence Day, he met with a hundred Oneida warriors and encouraged them to continue the fight.

The third window in 1779 had shown yet another misguided attempt to send American troops into Quebec. Surely, the allies had finally let that dream die, hadn't they? *Mais non!* Even as late as 1782, Washington was still proposing to Rochambeau that they try one last invasion of Canada, just for old time's sake. The French general wisely declined.

But I'm still getting a good window out of it. Even though France didn't want to do a full-scale invasion of Canada, they did authorize a lightning strike there—so far north that the British never would expect it. On Independence Day, after five weeks of sailing from the Caribbean, a French naval squadron was drawing closer to Hudson Bay, Canada's vast inland sea that extends into the Arctic Circle. Their sudden arrival surprised the hell out of the British Hudson Bay Trading Company, which occupied the Prince of Wales Fort on the shores of the bay. The French quickly seized the fortress, destroyed its cannons and walls, and took thousands of beaver furs and marten pelts as war booty.

The fort was just across a river from the present-day town of Churchill, Manitoba, known as the polar bear capital of the world, a popular spot today for spotting these beasts. The war had come a long way from the green fields of Yorktown. This scene, then, will show a spooked polar bear running over the ice away from the French invaders.

Meanwhile, further south, Nathanael Greene and his Continentals kept up a loose siege around Charleston. The British in the port city periodically sent armed raiding parties into the interior to seize rice, corn, and beef for their troops, sometimes fighting American forces who showed up to stop them. It was during one of these clashes in August that the dashing Colonel John Laurens, the former aide to Washington and a committed abolitionist, mounted a charge against a superior British force. The fourth window would show Laurens slumped on his horse, killed close to a year after Yorktown in a "paltry little skirmish," as Greene sadly recounted.

The last version of our imaginary chapel featured three scenes from the Caribbean, starting with d'Estaing's triumphant victory at Grenada. Three years later, the French still held that island and had taken several others from the British as well. One window would show the Chasseurs-Volontaires de Saint-Domingue, the regiment of free and enslaved Blacks, manning watch posts in Grenada. Close to two hundred of them were stationed there, while France mobilized other Black soldiers for its planned invasion of Jamaica alongside Spain as well.

The next window would be one that no one saw coming: Admiral de Grasse imprisoned on a British warship. Who could ever have imagined such a rapid fall from grace for the hero of the Battle of the Chesapeake? De Grasse had been preparing to support the allied invasion of Jamaica when none other than George Rodney came to counter him at the head of a new fleet. Rodney wanted nothing more than to defeat the French and rehabilitate his (justly) ruined reputation. And the old gambler was prepared to take whatever risks he needed to do so.

Rodney attacked de Grasse near a small group of islands called Les Saintes, near the island of Dominica, before the French could rendezvous with the Spanish and combine their fleets. He stunned the French by pioneering the new tactic of "breaking the line," which involved sending his own warships through de Grasse's line of battle and then surrounding the French fleet. It was a daring trick, one that would much later be copied by Admiral Nelson at Trafalgar during the Napoleonic Wars.

Rodney's gambit worked like a charm. He captured de Grasse's flagship, the magnificent *Ville de Paris,* and three other ships of the line, while destroying a fourth. After he "saved Jamaica from its impending fate," Warren wrote, the criticisms in Parliament of Rodney's treatment of Sint Eustatius and its people quieted down. "The suffering islanders were forgotten in the exultation of national glory," she wrote in disappointment.

The victory of the Battle of the Saintes was Britain's greatest of the entire war. It proved to be a game-changer, shifting the momentum back in Britain's favor. "England is so giddy," John Adams wrote, "with Rodney's late success in the West Indies, that I think she will renounce her ideas of peace for the present." Despite this loss, the allies still made plans to assemble a new fleet and resume their plans to invade Jamaica.

OK, we're just about halfway done with our whirlwind tour. Take a stretch break if you need to—and then come back to hear some good news for the allies for a change.

After all the hardships they had gone through, the Dutch on Statia finally had some cause for cheer. In November 1781, neither the French nor British main Caribbean fleets had returned to that region from the Yorktown campaign. Noticing how overstretched the British were in defending so many islands, a local French commander saw an opportunity to act. The Marquis de Bouillé left Martinique on the warship *Amazone* and retook Saint Martin and other nearby islands—including Sint Eustatius, which France restored to the Dutch.

This victory was a rare bright spot in the war for the Netherlands. It had fought the British in a number of battles but had lost land in the Caribbean, South America, and India to Britain. The Dutch continued to fund the Americans, though, making a big loan to the U.S. government in 1782 and recognizing the new nation that same year. This window, then, shows the Dutch flag once again flying over Fort Oranje with the volcano looming behind it in the distance. And Saint Martin would again become half-French, half-Dutch, as it remains so today.

The coalition achieved other victories in the Caribbean as well. In April 1782, a combined Spanish and American fleet took the Bahamas. The commodore of the South Carolina navy (yes, it had its own navy) had sailed south with a small fleet; in Havana, he learned of Bernardo de Gálvez's plans to take the archipelago and eagerly asked to join in. When the British in Nassau saw the nearly five dozen ships arrayed against them, they immediately surrendered the military stores and merchant ships assembled on the island.

While Gálvez had fought alongside some Americans, most notably with the indomitable Captain Pickles, the action in the Bahamas was the only time during the war that Spain and America joined forces in significant numbers. Sadly, the good captain didn't get to join in it as he had been captured by the British. He managed to escape, but he met a tragic end. A gang of Italian sailors with knives accosted him on the streets of Philadelphia, and the brave Pickles was sliced to death (true story).

Last time around in our imaginary chapel, we saw Bernardo de Gálvez gearing up for his Gulf Coast campaign. Now, three years later, the eighth window would show him again in planning mode, poring over maps and plotting the Jamaica Invasion 2.0, this time to be led by him alongside Lafayette.

Meanwhile, Mathías de Gálvez, Bernardo's father, continued his own fierce campaign to control Central America. After the British had abandoned Nicaragua, the Spanish turned on British outposts in what is now Honduras and Nicaragua with ferocity, taking British outposts there. The British counterattacked with a force of Redcoats, local British settlers, Miskito Indians, and even a company of Loyalist Americans from New York. This scene would show the Spanish soldiers suffering from malaria, for, ultimately, disease-carrying mosquitoes would prove to be their biggest enemy.

Still with me? Good, we're reaching the end, as well as one of the most iconic battles of the war. On our last trip to the chapel, we witnessed the early days of the Spanish campaign to take Gibraltar. While the Great Siege continued to be a Great Debacle, another allied operation in the Mediterranean had gone much better. In August 1781, the French and Spanish navies landed troops on the British-held island of Minorca and laid siege to St. Philip's Castle. The British garrison, stricken with scurvy due to a lack of vegetables (remember to eat those mushy peas), surrendered in February 1782.

Now the French and Spanish could turn their attention to Gibraltar and prepare for what was called the Grand Assault. "All the powers of invention were called forth to bring into action the most ingenious and fatal means of destruction," Warren wrote, which consisted of "battering ships of formidable size." A French engineer designed what effectively were floating artillery batteries, ships that were heavily reinforced to withstand enemy shelling (and even included a clever system of internal water pipes designed to douse flames that might break out).

The idea was to bring them close to the bastions at the base of Gibraltar and unleash a close-range barrage, clearing the way for an amphibious landing. The Grand Assault was to be one from the ages; princes came down from Versailles to watch, while spectators spread out over the hills of Andalucia with spyglasses trained on the action, as if at the theater.

The opera started as a tragedy yet quickly turned into a farce. Several of the floating batteries immediately ran aground on sandbanks and couldn't continue on. The others began bombarding the Rock as planned, but British batteries quickly returned fire, shooting heated cannon balls back at them. "Six thousand cannon shot, and upwards of 1,000 shells were discharged on one side every 24 hours," Warren recounted, "while an equal scale of vigor was kept up by the unceasing blaze of the other, until several of the best ships of the assailants were blown up, others enwrapped in a torrent of fire."

The French suffered some fourteen hundred casualties and lost all of the floating batteries—one of which exploded spectacularly after a British shot hit its ammunition stores. The stained-glass window, then, would show the results of the explosion, which looked more like something from modern times: a mushroom cloud.

One of the French "floating batteries" exploding.

Further north, once again, a large allied fleet sailed into the English Channel—and, as had happened before, the English panicked. The eleventh window would show conscript laborers feverishly constructing a new fort near Portsmouth. (Now mostly rebuilt, Fort Monckton still serves an active British army base today.) The allies never did touch down on British soil, save for on the island of Jersey, but the fear that they might do so kept Britain playing defense throughout the war.

Meanwhile, with the Thirteen Colonies seemingly lost, Britain began to instead pour more resources into India, which became one of the hottest theaters in the war's last year. Hyder Ali, the sultan of Mysore, and his son Tipu kept fighting the British on land, while the French navy—bolstered by a twenty-seven-ship fleet that arrived in early 1782—battled them on the sea. The French were led by the legendary admiral Pierre André de Suffren, the Marquis of Saint-Tropez. He was a messy man, obese and hot-tempered. Yet he was also a naval genius, "full of audacity and lust for action," as one officer put it, and so dreaded in battle that the British nicknamed him Admiral Satan.

Suffren spent July 4, 1782, maneuvering his ships for a huge naval battle that would occur two days later. Window Twelve would show the cannons from the French ships firing on their British enemies in the Bay of Bengal. More clashes would follow, including a mighty battle off the coast of the Dutch colony in Ceylon (today's Sri Lanka). Hyder loved Admiral Satan's penchant for fighting—and equally marveled at how the Frenchman would attack the banquet table, not slowed down in the least by the fiery heat of the food.

Okay, that was a lot. (And, believe me, there were plenty of other battles that we could have covered that I decided weren't window-worthy.) The essential point is, of course, that Lord North couldn't have been more wrong when he cried out that it was all over. The world war still had a long way to go; much more territory would change hands and thousands more lives would be sacrificed. And that brings us to our final window in our 1782 chapel.

Last time, that scene showed an angry member of Parliament denouncing the war. Opposition to the fighting in America had simmered throughout the conflict. After the loss of Cornwallis's army, it boiled over for good. Britain simply couldn't afford to send more troops and money to combat these rebels, opposition leaders claimed, especially when so many other pieces of the empire were at risk. Let them have their independence. On February 27, 1782, the House of Commons voted to put a halt to future offensive operations in the United States. Lord North resigned and a new government, committed to ending the war in America, took office.

The final stained-glass window would show diplomats in Paris drinking chocolate and huddling over maps. By Independence Day 1782, peace talks had been underway for a couple of months. Yet while the discussions went on, the British and the coalition against them kept fighting. Even if a deal were struck, just who got what territory was still very much up for grabs.

Britain entered into preliminary peace accords with the United States, France, and Spain (separately) in late 1782. The last battle of the war came some nineteen months after Yorktown, and it took place nearly nine thousand miles away in India. The fighting only stopped when a messenger came with news that peace had finally been concluded. The last shot—fired before the messenger arrived—was fired in a seaport called Cuddalore.

To see the spot where the Revolutionary War truly ended, that's exactly where I headed.

If you want to visit the site of the last battle of the American Revolution, here's what you do. First, hire a car or even an auto-rickshaw and set off from the nearest large city, Pondicherry, that onetime French colony with its elegant mansions along India's southeast coast. You'll pass a seemingly never-ending line of stalls selling flower petals and jackfruit, sandals and cell phones, and birds in cages. You'll pass by half-ruined buildings, roadside shrines, and milk parlors. You'll blend in and out of your lane, cars and motorcycles continually merging, yet never hitting each other as if they're all swirling in a downstream current.

As you travel on, you'll see cows in the road and goats on the sidewalk and colorfully painted buses blaring their horn. You'll see signs for the "Happy Hotel" and "Genius School of Excellency" and "Gee Pee Computers—Rooms—Toilet." Outside of town, you'll pass over rivers and by rice paddies and under towering rows of coconut trees. And then you'll again find houses and shrines and the hum of human activity, for you've reached the seaport of Cuddalore.

Take leave of your driver and wander around the beach, with its strong smell of the sea and of drying fish. Take a peek at the fishermen preparing their nets to catch sand lobsters. Don't expect to hear too much English—Tamil is spoken here, as it has been for over two millennia.

Try to imagine the British fleet anchored offshore here in 1783, with the French fleet on its way to attack them.

A young man might come up to you just to shake your hand, for they don't see many foreigners in these parts. You might think to yourself just how big the world is, how there are millions of towns like this, each with their own history and traditions and human dramas, which you'll never see and all of which keep going on just fine without you. And yet this one town, which looks like it could be any other fishing port on India's coast, has a connection to you that no other place in the world has in the same way. For here is where the war that brought us our independence finally came to an end.

Hike up a hill toward the last fort remaining from the last battle. You'll pass fishermen rigging out their boats, gentle cows emerging from the brush, the occasional scooter zipping past. Crest the hill and there'll you see Fort St. David, built in the seventeenth century. It still has a porch and graceful columns, even though you can tell from a distance that it's partially in ruins, with vines clinging to its sides.

Hand a small bill to the stonemason working to repair the gate—he'll appreciate it—and wander up to the building. It's mostly deserted inside, with rooms filled with rubble and brush. A couple of scrawny stray dogs wander around. A squatter has pitched a hammock. Below lies the mouth of the Gadilam River, where a few fishing boats, painted red and green and blue, bob up and down.

Think back on the battlefield parks you may have visited in the United States, for this couldn't be a further cry from them. Here, there are no weathered plank fences or friendly park service guides or reenactors, no statues or gift shops with souvenir T-shirts and cold drinks. No, here you're on your own, far, far away from where it all started. Eight years after the Shot Heard 'Round the World was fired, here was the place where the final shot was fired, heard by no Americans. Here, under a canopy of palms and banana trees, you've finally reached the end.

❦

Earlier in the Revolutionary War, the French and Mysoreans seized the town of Cuddalore and this fort that had protected it. In June 1783, the British came with some twelve thousand troops—many of them Scottish Highlanders—to take it back. They constructed siege lines and aimed to starve the defenders out. But they hadn't counted on one of France's most crafty naval commanders.

On June 15, Suffren arrived with his fleet. The British outnumbered him, but if you think that fact would slow him down in the least, you don't know Admiral Satan. The Frenchman launched a spirited attack, driving off the British and landing thousands of reinforcements to help the besieged defenders. Suffren planned to deliver the coup de grace: a bombardment of the British positions from his warships, which might drive the invaders away for good. Victory was theirs for the taking—until, on June 29, a curious frigate bearing a white flag made its way to Suffren's flagship, the *Héros*.

The British captain boarded and solemnly handed over a newspaper with breaking news (from many months earlier): The warring parties had agreed to preliminary articles to put an end to the conflict. The French reluctantly agreed to lay down their arms, although the more cynical-minded grumbled that the British only shared the news when they did because they were losing the battle.

Tipu Sultan was apoplectic, finding the way this ended to be truly "abject." He had not been consulted about any peace, nor had he yet achieved his war aims. Mysore and the French had been on the offensive. With France agreeing to peace, what in retrospect was the last, best chance for keeping Mysore independent from the British had just gone up in smoke. Tipu couldn't have known that at the time, but he did sense that the Treaty of Paris had cheated him out of a great victory.

I entered the old fort and looked out a ruined window. I tried to imagine troops here, keeping watch, their muskets at their side—some of the same French models that the Americans used at Yorktown. Nearly four thousand men fell during the fighting on land and sea. Among the dead at Cuddalore was, of all people, Julien Alexandre Achard de Bonvouloir, the French spy who had met with Franklin in 1775 in Philadelphia. He had since joined the French army as a lieutenant in the navy and died of an illness before the battle even began, as I had learned from his descendent at the festival at Vaussieux. What an improbable journey, I thought, from Normandy to Carpenters' Hall to Quebec, finally coming to an end here in Cuddalore.

After a while, I left and started to walk down the hill back into town when I heard shouting behind me. A group of five kids, who looked to be tweens or early teenagers, came running up.

"Can I take a picture of you?" said one of the girls. Her name was Adeline, she said. She wore a yellow flower-print dress and was the most outgoing of them all. "Where are you from?"

I told her and immediately began to be peppered with a chorus of questions.

"What is America like?" one said.

"Do you have kids?" asked another.

"Would you like a small cat?" Adeline asked. "We have an extra one."

New friends at Fort St. David, Cuddalore.

As I declined the cat offer, an adult came up, smiling. His name was Agustin, he said. He was the caretaker of the fort; two of the kids were his children, the others his nieces and nephews. "We live right over there," he said, pointing to a small house. "The Lutherans own this place, and we look after it." His grandfather had been the butler when people still lived in Fort St. David, which had turned into a private residence. His kids, he said proudly, were the fourth generation to live here. Agustin told me more about the place's history and explained that its current ruined state has much to do with the great tsunami of 2004, which wrecked it.

I showed the kids pictures of Liana, Miranda, and Nico, and we shared stories. "The place you live by is very special to me," I said, "it helped us win our independence."

"Now we have friends in America," Adeline replied, smiling. "Would you like to come by and have my mother's chicken biryani?"

"Thank you so much," I said, yet I knew my driver was waiting for me and we had to hit the road again soon. "But I have to leave for the next stop."

"Ah, you are roaming India," Adeline replied.

Yes, I suppose I had been, a little anyway. And so many other places as well. And now my roaming was coming to an end. I waved goodbye and began hiking back down the hill. The sun was high in the sky, the light fierce.

Dawn was breaking in Europe right now, I thought as I descended. This same sunlight will soon bathe France, our greatest ally in the war. It will rise over Vergennes's ruined château, it will soak his vineyard of luscious Chardonnay grapes. It will make its way to a port on the Atlantic and light up the sails of the *Hermione*, the ship of our greatest champion, Lafayette.

The sun will illuminate the white walls of Macharaviaya in Spain, the hometown of the Gálvezes, who rose from shepherds to fighters in America's cause. It will cast its light over sites that resisted the allies to the end: Gibraltar, Quebec, and the isle of Jersey in the English Channel, places Britain defended at a tremendous cost.

The sun will travel across to the Caribbean to Sint Eustatius, lighting up the old fort, glinting off blue beads buried in the sand. It will bathe the Lagoon of Seven Colors in the Yucatán, where the fierce fighting in Central America began.

It will dawn over upstate New York, where the Oneida, America's first allies, still fight to save their traditions. It will trickle through the vines of the Louisiana bayous where Bernardo de Gálvez assembled his army of French, Spanish, Indians, and Americans both Black and White. It will light up Valley Forge, where American Patriots suffered, when survival was all they could hope for. And it will settle on the French big guns still standing watch at Yorktown, the crowning victory of the war, that master class of cooperation.

I suddenly felt a sense of oneness with all these places where, during a moment in time, people from around the globe all fought on the same side of a great conflict. A time when allies conquered their differences, when people from all races and religions sacrificed their lives for a common cause. A time when, in America's hour of need, the world answered our cry for help. When we won our liberty and began our march toward freedom. That time when we were all in it together.

Epilogue

AN AMERICAN FOURTH

Recovering Lost Memories

"What a glorious day for the Fourth," I said. And we were in one of the best places to celebrate it. When the war was all over, Washington came home. To complete our own journey, we made the short drive from our house in Fairfax County to Mount Vernon, the Georgian-style house originally built by Washington's father.

We passed through the gates and walked up the hill toward his mansion. The heavens seemed to be smiling down on us, for it was clear and only about 80 degrees that morning—we were being spared the swampy muck that's normally Virginia in the summer. We walked alongside serpentine walls, past blackberry lilies and oleander in bloom.

Miranda smiled. "I can't believe I'm going to be living in a place like this soon," she said. She had been accepted into the College of William and Mary, a stone's throw from Colonial Williamsburg, and couldn't be more excited about it. Maybe all these historical travels rubbed off on her more than I realized.

"Are we going to see George Washington here?" Nico asked.

"I'm pretty sure we will," I replied. "They've got to have a reenactor playing him today." But when we crested the hill, we instead found ourselves in front of someone I never expected to see on these travels. Standing before Mount Vernon, about to speak on a dais, was none other than the Terminator himself.

"There's so much to celebrate," Arnold Schwarzenegger said smiling, when he reached the mic. The crowd couldn't have looked happier. Not only had people come to honor our nation's birthday, but a group of about hundred immigrants had also just taken the oath to become American citizens. Some had come from countries that had fought on our side during the Revolution, like Spain, India, and the Netherlands, or from places that had supported the war effort, like Mexico, Honduras, and Sri Lanka. Arnold, who famously immigrated from Austria himself decades earlier, had come to congratulate them.

He talked about his journey, of the warmth and generosity of Americans who welcomed him after he arrived with dreams of becoming a world-famous bodybuilder, of a country filled with kind souls who invited him to Thanksgiving dinners and gave him old couches and chairs for his empty apartment. He had chosen to throw his lot in with his new country and was proud that he did. Now, after navigating through bureaucratic paperwork for years, this group of new citizens was doing the same.

When he tried to break into the movies, Arnold told us, studio executives would reject him. "That accent, that ridiculous accent, no one has ever become a movie star or a leading man with an accent like that," he recalled. But he didn't give up. "I was in the land of opportunities. I knew that if I worked my butt off, that I could do it. I could make my vision become a reality." He took accent removal classes, he said, spending all day practicing how to talk American. "And this is why today I have absolutely no accent at all." Everyone laughed out loud.

"You're laughing, but I mean, it's not funny. I'm still looking for that coach to get my money back," he said, to more chuckles. "The bottom line is that an accent is nothing to be ashamed of," he went on. "It is a memory of your past. It tells a story, and it's part of what makes your voice distinct.

"America needs your story," Schwarzenegger continued. "What I'm saying is that to be an American, you do not have to fit into a box. Trust who you are. Trust your vision of your future. Trust your vision of yourself. That is what is important." When he finished, the new citizens applauded and waved their American flags. And we did too.

America needs your story. What a fitting way to sum up the tale of our foreign partners in the war, I thought. They need to be part of the history of how we won our independence, because that's how it happened. Arnold had spoken of trust. And that too seemed to me to be a large part of what made the ultimate victory possible. The partners came into the war with different backgrounds and different reasons why they wanted to defeat Britain. They needed to learn how to work together to do so.

Admiral d'Estaing's early campaign in 1778 had been a disaster, in part because he and the Patriots squabbled about where his navy should go and who should claim the honor of leading operations. After the Spanish entered the war in 1779, they made similar mistakes, forcing the French into war plans that the French didn't think would work and failing to coordinate well with them along the way. As a result, both the planned invasion of England and siege of Gibraltar turned into disasters.

Yet, in 1781, the allies pulled off a campaign for the ages—because they were acting selflessly, placing the "common cause," as both Washington and Admiral de Grasse put it, ahead of the more narrow gains that each country might have wanted to win for themselves separately. The Spanish nobly put off their own planned attack on Jamaica, volunteering to guard the French Caribbean island while de Grasse sailed north—and giving him the silver of Cuba to fund his journey. They trusted that the French would return and honor their promises.

Washington and Rochambeau worked well with each other on their march south, sharing campsites and troop transports and making sure both armies stayed focused on the same objective. While they did so, nations from across the world—from the Mysoreans to the Dutch to the Oneida—were harassing the British in places they least expected. The strain on their empire meant that the British, for one of the first times in their history, brought a weaker fleet to a critical battle than their foes did. Yorktown, and ultimately the war, was won because of the trust these different people had shown in each other.

"That was a beautiful ceremony," Liana said. Following it, we toured the mansion, then got some barbeque from a food truck and sat back to watch our fellow Americans celebrate this, our day. There were young couples exploring the grounds together and grandparents holding their grandchildren's tiny hands. We saw a couple of America's newest citizens, dressed in fine suits, and congratulated them. Many of our compatriots wore American flag shirts; others were more creative—a lady dressed as Wonder Woman, a man with a cat on his T-shirt, proclaiming 'Meowica. Yup, I thought, these are my people.

"It's getting hotter," Miranda said.

"Well, we can go inside," I offered. "Who wants to see the museum?"

I was met with silence. "Or they have some shops too," I said begrudgingly.

In the end, I entered the museum alone; my troops had deserted me. But I'll give them a break—not every kid is forced to think about the eighteenth century on every single family trip they take. I'd just have to do this one myself, like Bernardo de Gálvez: *Yo solo*.

The most striking object on display was Washington's smallsword, with its steel blade in a silver scabbard, which he used on ceremonial occasions. He had it on, I learned, when he resigned his commission before Congress, meeting in Annapolis, in December 1783.

The general had been slowly drawing down the Continental Army all that year. When the British finally evacuated New York City at the end of November, he knew that it was time for him to go too. Washington's decision to give up power—at a time when many whispered he could easily become a new king of America if he had wanted to—was one of his noblest acts.

He had bid farewell to his officers at Fraunces Tavern in New York before he rode to Annapolis. The place was packed, the officers thirsty. They called out thirteen toasts, each to a mighty huzzah and the draining of a glass of claret. "To the Memory of those Heroes who have fallen for our Freedom," the men proclaimed. To the French, to the Dutch, and even to the Swedish, who had just recognized the United States as a free nation—they drank to them all and the toasts kept coming. "May America be an Asylum to the Persecuted of the Earth," one went, "May justice support what courage has gained." The 120 guests went through over 100 bottles of wine. But never fear, they had plenty of beer and punch to turn to when that ran out.

Washington bidding farewell to Lafayette at Mount Vernon in 1784. With time, the Marquis would become one of the few foreigners remembered in American histories.

That was an impressive guest-to-bottle ratio, I thought. But how interesting that Washington's men drank to our allies and partners. As we've seen, Mercy Otis Warren included chapters about them in her *History* too. And yet, over time, these foreign fighters slipped out of the story. Why was that? And what happened to the allies after the war?

Tucked into a corner of the museum was a key to understanding that second question. And by key, I'm literally talking about a key. Here, under the glass, was a heavy wrought iron object sent by Lafayette to Washington from France: none other than the key to the Bastille.

In 1787, the Comte de Vergennes died of an illness at age seventy-seven. When he heard the news, tears streamed down Louis XVI's face; "I have lost the only friend on whom I could count," he cried. When he passed away, though, Vergennes had no idea of the convulsions his country was about to go through—and for which he would share some of the blame. And His Majesty the King would soon be missing not just a friend, but something even more useful. (I mean his own head.)

France had sacrificed an enormous amount during the Revolutionary War: It had committed some one hundred thousand soldiers and sailors to the action, around five thousand of whom had lost their life. And it had spent millions of livres, for orchestrating a world war turned out to be an incredibly expensive undertaking (*quelle surprise!*). Not only were France's own military operations costly, but the French and Spanish had given the equivalent of some thirty billion dollars (in today's money) to the Patriots in direct aid. By 1786, over half the national budget went to servicing the debt.

All that for relatively little in return. The Americans had done exceptionally well in their own peace treaty with the British, not only winning recognition of their independence, but also gaining control of the land beyond the Appalachian Mountains, all the way to the Mississippi. By contrast, France didn't get much back in its own deal. It swapped some Caribbean islands with the British, regained control of its port in Senegal, and took back Pondicherry and some other towns in India. That wasn't a huge haul for a nation that had just defeated the British Empire.

Yet conquering the world had never been why France entered the war. Vergennes had wanted to right the balance of power in Europe, to restore his country to what he saw as its rightful place as a co-leader of the Old World. He died contented, having achieved his aims. And then, two years later, his dream came crashing down. In 1789, on July 14—which would become France's national day—a crowd stormed the old Bastille prison in Paris. It held few prisoners; what the people wanted from the place was its stockpile of gunpowder and arms (the same reason the Americans had raided Fort Ticonderoga). Parisians had risen up against their cake-eating monarchy, and France would never be the same.

There were plenty of grievances to go around. France's finances were a mess, and taxes—primarily paid by peasants and the middle class—kept going up. Much of the national debt (although by no means all of it) came from the staggering cost of supporting both the French and American militaries during the war. The ideals of the American Revolution, brought back by French officers to their homeland, also inspired some French to rise up against the monarchy. "The American war seems first to have awakened...the nation," ambassador Thomas Jefferson wrote, from "the sleep of despotism in which they were sunk."

At first, American leaders applauded the French Revolution; didn't it look somewhat like an overseas version of our own? Lafayette led the new French National Guard, after all, and he called himself a "missionary of liberty." Yet it soon turned bloody. The king was executed in 1793, and, a few months later, the radical Maximilien Robespierre took power. Soon the guillotine was working in overdrive against the country's aristocracy. By helping to bankrupt his state and allow a republic to take hold overseas, Vergennes, a nobleman who had served the Crown faithfully for years, had unwittingly helped bring down the system he had supported.

Not even heroes of the Revolutionary War were safe from the Reign of Terror. The Comte d'Estaing, the admiral who had been "seldom a favorite fortune," as Warren had put it, ended his string of bad luck with a visit to the guillotine. So did the Duc de Lauzun, the gallant officer who led the cavalry charge before the Siege of Yorktown. (The ever-chivalrous duke offered the executioner a glass of wine before the blade came down.)

Even Lafayette's wife Adrienne had been slated for execution until Elizabeth Monroe (wife of new American ambassador James Monroe) intervened and helped save her. Rochambeau also had a close call, barely avoiding his own appointment with the National Razor, as they called the slicing machine. A few days before that was to happen, Robespierre himself fell from power in the summer of 1794, ending the Reign of Terror. Instead, the dictator wound up being the one to get the shave.

During all this, the paths of the French and the Americans diverged. It wasn't just a reaction to the excesses of the French Revolution. After all, the United States had made common cause with France even when it didn't share the same values before; France had helped the rebels form a republic even though it was an absolute monarchy. The real problem was the wars that the French Revolution triggered in Europe. It turned out that other kings and queens were none too fond of a nation that preferred its monarchs to be of the headless variety. In 1792, a coalition of European countries—that would eventually swell to over a dozen in number—assembled against France. And America did not come to its old partner's aid.

We simply couldn't have afforded to, even had we wanted to. The United States was on shaky ground, its economy wrecked by the war. The American Experiment—a republic governed by rules set by the brand-new Constitution—needed time to grow. The last thing America needed was to fight another war against powerful European forces. Instead, President Washington pledged a course of neutrality. In 1796, as he prepared to leave office, he warned against permanent alliances, particularly in the context of the seemingly endless wars of that decade, during which some countries (most notably Spain) switched sides more than once.

Washington's successor, John Adams, even entered into a "quasi-war" with America's old French allies, fought only on the seas. The new opposition party of Jeffersonian Republicans—including Warren—sharply criticized the Adams administration over this foreign policy, as well as its attack on civil liberties. For his part, the always-prickly Adams became incensed when Warren's *History* finally came out, upset at how she portrayed him. "History is not the province of the ladies," he fumed.

Instead of looking across the Atlantic, Americans were increasingly turning inward. During my tour of Mount Vernon, a young guide had pointed out a painting that Washington had hung in his drawing room, of the Potomac crashing over rocks in far western Virginia. "It's basically an ad for American expansion," the guide told me. "Washington hung it to encourage people to go out and conquer the west." Beyond the mountains lay the new land won by America during the war. That was America's new focus—spreading across the continent, extending what Jefferson called the "empire of liberty." And a new current of isolationism took hold.

Looking to the west—and staking our claim to it—meant we had to change the stories we were telling about our founding. The tale of a country that needed the help of a foreign superpower to win its independence suddenly seemed out of place. Our Manifest Destiny couldn't have been handed to us by the foppish French, could it have?

Larrie Ferreiro, the professor who had become a friend during the course of my travels, has tracked how American histories of the nineteenth century discussed the role of the allies. As the century went on, they increasingly minimized the role of France, he found out. Lafayette made a triumphant return to the nation from 1824 to 1825; the hero's welcome he received cemented his place in our national story. (It also led to countless places being named after him, including my own birthplace of Fayetteville, Arkansas.) Yet although Rochambeau and de Grasse might be name-checked in these new histories, the true importance of their roles was minimized. And tales of the French campaigns in the rest of the world began to disappear altogether.

Au revoir, les français, I'll miss having you in our story. *Merci mille fois* for all the support you gave us, from Beaumarchais' guns to the Special Expedition, from your crazy armada in the English Channel to your dashing victory at the Battle of the Chesapeake. Sorry we helped bring about the guillotine.

The fall from grace for the Spanish came even quicker. One of my other new professor buddies, Tom Chávez, had clued me in to a remarkable story from the war. I was delighted to find a reference to it here in Mount Vernon's museum as well. Hanging on the wall was an engraving of a cheerful-looking donkey, next to the words, in an eighteenth-century typeface: GENERAL WASHINGTON'S JACK ASS.

In 1784, the Basque merchant and diplomat Diego de Gardoquí (who had run guns to the rebels in the early days of the war) sent a most unusual present to Mount Vernon: a huge, powerful donkey named Royal Gift. Washington had coveted Spanish donkeys for years; they were reputed to be the strongest in the world. They also practically constituted a trade secret—export from Spain was strictly prohibited without the king's consent. Washington had almost gotten one during the war from Juan de Miralles, the Spanish diplomat in Philadelphia (who had already sent him the sea tortoise and Cuban cigars), but Miralles died before he was able to get a donkey on a boat.

Now that he was back at Mount Vernon full-time, Washington was thrilled with the new addition to his farm. Please "lay before the King my thanks for the Jackasses," he wrote to the Spanish foreign minister. The general immediately got to work, breeding Royal Gift with jennies on his farm to create a race of Spanish American super-burros. (The exhibit noted that he also advertised his Don Juan donkey's stud services to other plantation owners, bragging that "Royal Gift never fails.") Washington then crossed his new collection of donkeys with mares to produce the most powerful mules in the land. Known as American Mammoths, there would be millions of them by the nineteenth century, hauling goods for pioneers headed out west and troops marching in the Civil War alike.

Gardoquí had hoped that his present would make Washington willing to hear him out on Spanish claims to the Mississippi. Spain had done well in its own treaty with Britain—it had gotten to keep Florida and Minorca, both of which it had conquered, as well as Central America. But two things bothered King Carlos. Britain had refused to give Gibraltar back (declining to take Puerto Rico in a trade for it). Nothing could be done about that—and the Rock remains British to this day.

But the other problem was becoming increasingly irritating to the Spanish. Spain had wanted the land between the Appalachians and the Mississippi, which Britain ceded to the United States, for itself. Now, American settlers were flooding into the zone—and some were even crossing over into Spain's Louisiana Territory on the western side of the rivers. Others were pushing up against the once-again Spanish territory of Florida (whose boundaries were vague). Alarmed, Spain banned *yanqui* traders from navigating the Mississippi River, a blow to American commerce.

Tensions with the Spanish, then, were on the rise. Did you notice which country was missing from the farewell toasts Washington's officers had given him in New York? Already, Spain's role in the Revolution was slipping from memory as the two countries came into competition over land. It hadn't helped that much of the Spanish aid had been clandestine, or that the kingdom hadn't officially recognized the United States during the war. Washington declined to discuss the Mississippi question with Gardoquí, explaining that he was now just a private citizen.

Jackass diplomacy had failed. Relations with Spain remained difficult, although the Spanish did reluctantly sign a treaty in 1795 that allowed Americans to access the Mississippi. The gift America gave in return was one that the Spanish monarchy wasn't thrilled to receive: the spirit of liberty (no refunds or exchanges). Spain had long worried that their own colonies might rebel. Even as the Revolutionary War continued, insurrections had broken out in Colombia, Venezuela, and Peru. Although the Spanish put down these uprisings, a few decades later, independence movements sprang up in the Spanish colonies of Latin America. One of the most prominent leaders, Francisco de Miranda, had even fought alongside the Americans in the taking of the Bahamas during the Revolutionary War (and had also dined with Mercy Otis Warren). Many of the leaders explicitly drew from the Declaration of Independence when they drafted their own independence charters. By the time Americans were celebrating the jubilee anniversary of the Declaration in 1826, the equivalent of some seventeen countries (applying modern borders) had won their freedom from Spain.

Hardly any of the Spanish generation that had fought in America's War for Independence remained to see these changes. Mathías de Gálvez, the leader of the campaigns in Central America, died in 1784, and his son Bernardo was appointed to replace him as the new viceroy of Nueva España. From his new headquarters in Mexico City, Bernardo began construction of Chapultepec Castle, which later became the home of Mexican presidents. Galveston Island, Texas, was named for him by an admiring Spanish explorer in 1786. Bernardo would never get to see this place that bears his name, though; he died of typhus later that same year and is buried in Mexico City.

King Carlos III died in 1788, succeeded by his son, the conveniently named Carlos IV. The only constant in leadership from the Revolutionary War days was Francisco de Saavedra, the young official who had collected the silver from Cuba that had allowed de Grasse to sail north. And when Napoleon invaded Spain in 1808, it was Saavedra—that swashbuckling hero Tom Chávez had admired so much—who came out of retirement to help lead the resistance.

Even though Spain had been on the winning side of the Revolutionary War, the conflict hastened the country's decline. They not only wound up losing most of their Latin American empire, they also gave up their the province of Louisiana, which they ceded to France in 1800 (which in turn soon sold it to the Americans). With the Louisiana Purchase, the Spanish who lived in that territory instantly became *americanos*, and the hidden past of New Orleans would be forgotten by most. The United States never paid its debts from the war to Spain.

In Louisiana, I had heard about the "Black Legend," the tales spread by Brits and Americans of supposed Spanish cruelty in the New World. By the nineteenth century, as the United States saw Spain as a rival—fighting it in two separate wars—American historians were only too glad to write the Spanish out of the story of the Revolutionary War. Many later histories wouldn't refer to them at all.

Adios, los españoles. I give a heartfelt thanks to you and all the Latin Americans who helped us win our independence. Gracias for the cattle drives, for Bernardo de Gálvez's bravery, for all that silver from Cuba—and especially for the dollar sign, I use it every day. *Vayan con Dios.*

Even though the Dutch role in the war was not as big as that of the French or Spanish, it was important in its own right. Their main contribution had always come through commerce (mostly the shady kind). And so, how fitting that the Dutch were represented in Mount Vernon's museum by a trade item.

A gorgeous porcelain plate was displayed in a glass case. Martha Washington's initials were in the center of a sun, while the names of all thirteen states ringed the edges. It formed part of a set given to "Lady Washington," as he called her, by Andreas Everardus van Braam Houckgeest, the head of the Dutch East India Company in China. An impressive man, both for his love of American liberty and for the number of vowels he squeezed into his name, van Braam had become a naturalized citizen of the United States. He hoped to keep relations between the two nations strong.

The glory days of the Dutch Empire were long gone. Even though the Dutch entered the Revolutionary War toward the end of it, they nonetheless had suffered heavy losses fighting the British. Their peace treaty gave them formal control over Sint Eustatius and other Caribbean islands, and returned possession of their seaport in Ceylon (today's Sri Lanka), but gave a key Dutch Indian port to Britain. Their military had taken heavy losses during the war. Within a few decades, the Dutch would lose their colonial possessions in India, Ceylon, and the Cape of Good Hope. Some blamed this collapse on their losses in the American war—that was the source of "all the subsequent disasters, sufferings and losses that befell the Republic," one Dutchman ruefully wrote.

Not only had the Netherlands run tons of guns to the rebels, but it had also provided loans that helped keep the new U.S. government afloat in the decade after independence. In 1787, Jefferson left on an emergency mission to Amsterdam to get another needed loan; when he returned to Paris, he wrote a travel guide called *Hints to Americans Traveling in Europe* about some of his experiences. (Apparently there's a book out there that talks all about this.) Warren had mentioned the Dutch contributions to the war dozens of times in her *History*, treating Rodney's looting of Sint Eustatius as an important turning point in the conflict. Yet, as time went on, it didn't take long for the role of the small country to be forgotten in the stories we told about the war.

And so, *Vaarwell*, my Dutch friends. We'll always have the First Salute.

I would have been surprised to find an item from India on display in the museum—and sure enough, there wasn't one. After all, even though poets praised the contributions of the Mysore Kingdom, and Pennsylvania named a warship the *Hyder Ally* to honor them, the American public hadn't grasped the full scope of the war in south India at the time. Yet I was astonished to find out about one object that Mount Vernon had in its collection, even if it wasn't on view that day: a banyan, a long, flowing Indian gown. And this particular garment was worn by none other than Washington himself.

I looked at a picture of it on my phone; it looked almost like a proto-version of a Jedi robe. It was hard to imagine the Father of Our Country padding around in it. And yet banyans were all the rage in Virgina in the late eighteenth century, worn by plantation owners in the steamy heat of summer.

India remained a huge source of goods traded to America after the war, from calico cloth to silk pajamas. (And now its tea was OK to buy again rather than dump in the harbor.) I wondered if this banyan might have come from Madras, for Sriram had told me about how his region was famed for its textile exports.

Although commerce from India continued, for Tipu Sultan, the American Revolution turned into a disaster. After all, his troops had been winning when their ally France signed a peace treaty. Mysore fought on for nine more months on its own, finally laying down its arms after the French pressured it to do so.

Two more wars with Britain would follow. Mysore had sought French help before the next one, sending ambassadors all the way to Versailles. (Jefferson noted the "pomp and ceremony" that accompanied their arrival.) But Louis XVI declined. He was having second thoughts about all the money French had spent helping the Americans in their Revolution, he confided; by 1791, he had understood the problems this debt had caused. "This occasion greatly resembles the American affair, of which I never think without regret," he wrote to Tipu. "On that occasion, they [his ministers] took advantage of my youth, and today we are paying the price for it."

In 1790, the British attacked, and you'll never guess who led the charge: none other than Lord Cornwallis. Last we saw him, he was sulking at Yorktown, refusing to attend the surrender ceremony. But colonies are places where men go to get second chances. Cornwallis mounted a fierce campaign, which President Washington and Secretary of State Jefferson closely followed through reports. Without French help, the Mysoreans suffered a crushing defeat, losing half their kingdom to the East India Company and its Indian allies. Cornwallis became a hero back home.

The final Anglo-Mysore war broke out in 1798. By this time, Tipu had gotten his alliance with the French back on track. The French general Napoleon saw Mysore as a key part of his plans—while he seized Egypt, the Mysoreans were to tie the British down in south India, dealing a blow to British commerce and weakening their common enemy. Worried about the damage the Mysoreans could do with French help, the British preemptively attacked them before Napoleon's fleet could arrive. Tipu's forces were diminished, but he still had his rockets—and had even developed an elite force of fighters dressed in tiger-striped uniforms.

The British laid siege to Srirangapatna, the village I had visited. When I was there, Venkatesh had brought me to the city walls, to the spot where Tipu found his end. A general had betrayed the sultan, letting the British enter the town unopposed. Rather than begging for mercy, Tipu fought alongside his men, receiving a musket ball in his shoulder and slashes from a bayonet. He died the way he always said he would: as a tiger, not a sheep.

As it would turn out, the Mysoreans were the last kingdom to mount serious resistance to the expanding British in south India. Having lost the American colonies, the British poured attention and resources into the East. They would not let India slip away as the Thirteen Colonies had, for it was now the crown jewel of the empire. By 1858, Britain had conquered nearly all of the subcontinent and assumed control of the colony from the East India Company. And the colonial rulers had learned a lesson—they would not tolerate dissent.

In the twentieth century, though, the British were challenged by a new independence movement. In 1930, Mahatma Gandhi issued what was known as the Purna Swaraj, a declaration of independence for his people, with some phrases inspired by Jefferson's document. After freedom came in 1947, the original Indian constitution included drawings depicting religious and historical figures from the subcontinent's past—including Tipu Sultan, the Tiger of Mysore. Today, Bangalore, a town that had thrived under Tipu's patronage, is known as the "Silicon Valley of India" for its IT centers.

And so I say *Vidāya*, farewell, to Mysore, the land of tigers and tech. May the years that come bring you the well-being you deserve.

I left the museum and walked through the estate. Far from the bustle of the crowds, a small group had assembled at the Mount Vernon Slave Memorial, tucked in the woods not too far from Washington's Tomb. "This is the first memorial to be placed at an enslaved people's cemetery anywhere in the country," a Mount Vernon staff member said during a ceremony that they were holding. Washington freed his enslaved workers in his will, the only founder to do so.

The guide explained how students from Howard University had designed it. "The students chose in its center a stone column, strong granite for the strength of the people buried here, the strength they had to endure their hardships," he went on. "The column is cut diagonally to represent lives cut short, and dreams and hopes left unfulfilled. The column rests on three bases, which are labeled faith, hope, and love. It was thought that these were emotional sources of that strength." People in the crowd read brief stories out loud about some of the African Americans who worked here. The ceremony concluded with the laying of a wreath.

For many Blacks who had participated in the war, life during the peace remained difficult. As Antoine Randolph Watts had told me, the men of the First Rhode Island, for example, didn't receive the pensions or land bounties that their White counterparts did. The African Americans who had joined with the British in the hopes of gaining their freedom saw an uncertain future ahead as well. Some were recaptured by American slaveowners. Others left as the British evacuated after the war, with thousands winding up in Canada and some ultimately moving on to a new life in Sierra Leone in West Africa.

They weren't the only ones heading north—tens of thousands of White Loyalist refugees were doing so as well. Some of these settlers would later encourage their neighbors to remain loyal to the Crown, even in the face of Canadian independence movements. Few of the Blacks who arrived, however, received the land given to the White refugees.

Mount Vernon archaeologists had found Indian artifacts in the graveyard too, I learned. Native American tribes had occupied the land that became the estate for thousands of years before the arrival of the Washingtons. John Washington, George's great-grandfather, had even been dubbed the "Devourer of Villages" during his fierce campaign against the Susquehannock across the Potomac.

After the Revolutionary War, the old story of American settlers driving Indians off their land repeated itself once again. The Iroquois who had fought with the British were stunned when London had given the land over the Appalachians—much of which they occupied—to the Americans. Conflicts with settlers would continue, and many Haudenosaunee would relocate to new lands in Canada as well.

"The late war proved almost fatal to the nation," the chief Skenandoah said. Many Oneida villages had been destroyed during the war, and their people were desperately poor, often without food. They had been on the winning side, but some aggressive settlers didn't bother distinguishing between the different Iroquois nations, burning any Native American houses they found in a misguided attempt at revenge for attacks their own communities had suffered during the conflict.

When I was at the Shako:wi Cultural Center, Ron Patterson had showed me a six-foot-long belt made out of wampum, presented by President Washington to the Oneida to commemorate a 1794 treaty. The Canandaigua agreement between the Haudenosaunee confederacy and the federal government set out the boundaries of the different Iroquois nations, allowing the Oneida to retain six million acres of land. Han Yerry, the leader who had fought at Oriskany, died before the U.S. Senate ratified it. He would not be around, then, to see the promises in it be broken—but his wife, Two Kettles Together, who lived for several more decades, would.

Unfortunately, New York State leaders refused to accept the terms of the federal treaty, pushing the Oneida to sell land to settlers and speculators and hinting that they wouldn't protect them if they refused to do so. Good Peter, the warrior who had tried to bring peace to the Haudenosaunee, did everything he could to resist this land grab, but the forces against him were just too great. In 1825, as he toured New York State, the Marquis de Lafayette was shocked to find no Oneida present. They had helped save him at the Battle of Barren Hills, and he had spent time with them on their homelands by a campfire. Now, when he asked after them, his hosts became uncomfortable—for the role of the Oneida in helping the Patriots had already been obscured.

The pressure on the Oneida became more relentless each year. In 1838, some felt forced to accept an offer to relocate to Wisconsin, where they established a separate nation. By the early twentieth century, the Oneida homeland in New York State had shrunk to only thirty-two acres. And then came the long process of reconstituting and rebuilding that Ron had told me about. Today, the People of the Standing Stone in New York own eighteen thousand acres and are working to pass their culture on to a new generation.

And so to the Oneida I say *Yawʌ'kó,* a big thank you for what you've done and what you're doing. May the future of America's first allies always be bright.

My family—now laden with bags from the gift store—made their way back to the Mount Vernon lawn, where I was sitting in the grass. The day was drawing to a close. It had been an almost perfect Fourth. We had seen reenactors do their thing—of course, George Washington showed up after all—and watched Patriot troops practice a bayonet charge. We watched a cannon get fired and daytime fireworks light up the sky, with orange and green explosions sending tendrils that drifted down toward the Potomac below.

The Baxters at the end of the journey.

Independence Day "ought to be solemnized with Pomp and Parade," John Adams wrote to Abigail, "with Shows, Games, Sports, Guns, Bells, Bonfires and Illuminations from one End of this Continent to the other from this Time forward forever more." Here, we had seen nearly everything on Adams's wish list, with some bonus items (Cat T-Shirts, Speeches by Bodybuilders) thrown in for good measure.

As we walked through Mount Vernon's grounds, I thought of the first time I went there as a kid, as part of Mom and Dad's never-ending "history house" tour, as my sister called it. Just as Jefferson had filed Warren's book under "Memory" in his library, I had archived these childhood memories away somewhere in the core of my brain, returning to them often. Now I felt like I was completing a journey that my parents had started me on. Even if they weren't able to see me finish it themselves, I felt them here with me at the end.

The day was getting hotter, and soon it would be time to go. We sat down to cool off under an ancient tulip poplar not far from Washington's mansion. "What will you remember about all our trips?" I asked my family.

"They were all either very cold or very hot," said Nico. Apparently, our trip to Valley Forge in shivering December and to Gibraltar in the roasting month of July had made quite an impression on him.

"I was so surprised that that tiny town in Spain put on such a celebration," said Miranda.

"I've been following the press in Macharaviaya," Liana said. Of course, I had almost forgotten—the town was putting on its annual *Cuatro de Julio* pageant and postgame paella party too. My wife had kept up with some of the people we had met there. "Let's send a video of our day at Mount Vernon to José and all his friends," she said.

"We should really go back and visit them again sometime. Maybe I'll bring that bottle I've been saving," I said. "How cool would it be for the Gálvezes to be drinking Vergennes's wine?"

"Derek, you're going to leave that bottle in the basement for the next twenty years," Liana said, rolling her eyes. "You never get rid of anything."

She might be right; I see the crawl space as kind of my own personal museum. Whenever I do open that wine, though, I'm sure the memories of my idyllic weekend in search of Vergennes in Burgundy will come flooding back. "All right. OK, everybody, what else will you remember from our trips?"

"I learned about Latinos," Nico replied, turning serious. "We've always contributed to America. We've done some of the hardest work. And I learned about African Americans in the Revolution and how hard it was for them afterwards."

"Now I know the depths of the role the allies played," Liana said. "They gave money, arms, even moral support. It was a war against the biggest empire in the world. Who's going to be with you?" she asked. "It took a lot of bold people and people behind the scenes."

"All of it," said Miranda. "I've loved learning about all this history so much."

"Me too," I said, forcing a smile even as my eyes turned moist. This chapter in my life with her was closing. In another month, she'd be leaving us to make her own way in the world. I hoped she'd hold tight to the memories of our travels as a family as she did so. I knew I would.

We had done our best to retrace the arc of that long-ago global conflict, walking the lands where armies once marched, diplomats talked late into the night by candlelight, and men and women laid down their lives for a cause. We had traveled around the globe and back through time, to an era when Washington's men, toasting him one last time, would drink "to the Memory of those Heroes who have fallen for our Freedom" and would be thinking of some of our partners and allies when they did so.

By seeing these places in person, I got a sense of the war's true terrain, from a misty island in the English Channel to the imposing Rock of Gibraltar, from the jungles of the Yucatán to the plains of India, and beyond. I would take with me too the encounters with so many people I had met along the way who worked to preserve the memory of a forgotten battle or a people involved in the struggle.

Mercy Otis Warren died in 1814 at her home in Plymouth, Massachusetts, at age eighty-six after an illness. She had found peace at the end of her life. In his later years, John Adams reconciled with her, just as he had with his old foe Jefferson. And Adams agreed with Warren about how the coalition of nations that helped the United States should be remembered. Telling the "complete history of the American war," he once wrote, must involve "the history of France, Spain, Holland, England, and the Neutral Powers" as well, for the Revolutionary War comprised "nearly the history of mankind for the whole epoch of it." Neither Adams or Warren had any idea that so many of the key figures they saw as essential to the story of our victory would no longer appear in many histories to come.

It's time to bring them back into the story. For me, recognizing the role of our allies doesn't diminish the bravery of the Patriots in the war; it only adds to it. For there are so many more stories to tell.

A general fighting the British in the South, boldly winning battles while outsmarting the enemy? Sure, that describes Nathanael Greene—but now we know that Bernardo de Gálvez did the same in his lightning campaigns along the Gulf Coast.

A heroic naval battle? Don't stop with John Paul Jones—make sure you remember the Comte de Grasse, who won the Battle of the Chesapeake with the help of his flowery companion Bougainville.

A woman fighting bravely alongside her husband against the British, during summer heat so bad that some men couldn't go on? Alongside the legend of Molly Pitcher, you can add the story of Two Kettles Together, firing her pistols into glory at the Battle of Oriskany.

I could go on and on. The point is that the war was fought by all of these heroes, and many more, in far-flung spots around the globe. Alongside Lexington and Valley Forge, let's also pay homage to these other places where our independence was won, from Spain to India and back again. Who knows—you might even feel inspired to travel and see some of these sites for yourself. I hope you do. (If you need advice on where to go, don't be shy—drop me a line and I'll be happy to pass on what I know.)

Our allies didn't always share our ideals, but they found a way to work with us. We wouldn't have won without them. To channel John Adams, then, let us remember them when we reflect on our freedom, from this time forward forever more. We owe it to them to remember the sacrifices they made.

And we owe it to ourselves too. For how can we find our way into the future if we don't understand our past? The truth is, we never went it alone. We became the country that we are today thanks to a cast of thousands, from all lands. Together, we took down the mightiest empire of the day in a war that stretched around the world. May it never be forgotten again.

Author's Note

I modernized the grammar of a number of quotes from the eighteenth century. Occasionally, however, I left the quotes as originally written for effect.

In several cases, I decided to use the more colloquial term rather than a term in use at the time. For example, the highest rank in the French navy was "lieutenant general," a phrase we're more used to using in the context of an army; I instead used the more familiar "admiral." I also occasionally referred to diplomats whose official title was "minister" as "ambassador."

The question of just who was an "ally" of America turned out to be somewhat complicated. France signed a formal treaty of alliance with the United States in February 1778. The Netherlands didn't do so until April 1782, although Dutch traders had supplied the Americans with arms for years before that. Oneida warriors fought alongside the Americans without a formal treaty, while the Mysore Kingdom only allied with France.

Spain did not formally ally with the United States until after the war was over. But the Spanish did sign a treaty with the French in April 1779 in which they committed to fighting until American independence was achieved. Spain sent vast amounts of money and arms to the Americans, cooperated on strategy, and occasionally fought side by side with them.

Given all this, I chose to only call the French and Oneida "allies" of the Americans for most of the period of the war. Spain was not a formal ally of the United States during this time; it was more of a partner. However, I did occasionally use the term "ally" for the Spanish when referring to their relationship with France, or their membership in the coalition of nations led by France. The same goes for the Mysoreans and the Dutch.

Finally, I sometimes used the term "Americans" as a convenient shorthand for the Patriots—recognizing, of course, that Americans (Loyalists) fought on the British side as well.

Acknowledgments

First, thanks to everyone I met who shared stories with me. Some worked in museums: Matthew Keagle at Ticonderoga, Robert Kelly at Gloucester, Bruno Paul Stenson at Château Ramezay, and Elisabeth Perrault-Corbeil at Fort Chambly. And Teva Margat at that ship museum, the *Hermione*. (I hope the ship gets well soon.) All of those places are well worth a visit, and the staff's commentaries made them even more interesting.

Others acted as guides, carrying messages from the past down streets and through battlefields, while dodging passersby who insist on living in the present. Thank you, Misha Spanner and Ishmael Berker in Sint Eustatius, Seth Johnson in Brooklyn, Sophie Gumbs in St. Martin, Carlos Cruz Hernandez in Bacalar, Venkatesh in Mysore, and J. Michael Moore (who took me around but is actually a curator at nearby Lee Hall) at Yorktown.

Actors and reenactors made many of these long-ago scenes come to life for me. Thank you, Bernardo de Gálvez (José Gálvez), Gunner Gilly (Christopher Dankler), Colonel Glover (Ken Gavin), the Marquis de Lafayette (Mark Schneider), and the sergeant in the First Rhode Island (Antoine Randolph Watts). Curator Matthew Keagle doubles up in this category as well. I hope to catch some of your portrayals again—and also to return to Vaussieux in Normandy to see the latest pageant put on by Bertrand Bailleul and company.

Others had different connections to history, such as Bernard Gueugnon, who has restored Vergennes's château, and Moses Delaney, who has kept the story of his ancestor, James Armistead, alive. I'm grateful as well to Ron Patterson and Doris Wilkins-Wilt for talking with me at the Shako:wi Cultural Center. To Pablo, our fearless boat captain in Chetumal (whose name I changed for privacy). And to Augustin and family at Cuddalore—what a warm and surprising welcome I got there.

Where would I have been without the academics setting me straight? *Merci,* Matthieux Haroux—I can't wait to read your forthcoming book, and yes, I think Rochambeau would say that you got it right. Larrie Ferreiro and Tom Chávez were both very generous with their time. My copies of *Brothers at Arms* and *Spain and the Independence of the United States* are now as dog-eared as they can get. I highly recommend reading the works of these scholars, among others, if you'd like to learn more about some of the topics I mention here.

Matthieu and Rachel: Come back to Virginia some time; I'll get the *apéro* ready.

Many others helped me along the way—sometimes, they might not have even realized they were doing so. From old friends to readers of my last book who kept asking about the new one, Tammy Mayer Rosario (who also kindly drove me to Cape Henry), Matt Keough, Matt Ward, Glen "the Iron Tourist" Bolger, Jeff Gross, Erik Woodworth, Rick St. Peter, Bryan Person, Charles "Chucksrule" Wood, Laura Resau, Jim Hughes, and many others deserve my appreciation for their words of support.

Thanks to my fellow writers Tim Grove, Kathy Tone, and Matt Phillips, who provided incisive comments on my early drafts. My sister, Davida Baxter Macdonald, also gave the manuscript a good read. Parents, keep taking your kids to history houses! Now Davida loves them and has even worked to preserve antiquities herself. Liana, Miranda, and Nico also all gave me valuable input.

Thanks to my agent, Amanda Jain, who helped steer this book on its way. And Anna Michels, my editor, for her wonderful feedback and championing of this project.

My parents weren't able to accompany me in person along these journeys, although they were never far from my thoughts as I did them. My mother passed away from cancer at the end of 2022, while my father persevered but dealt with both Alzheimer's and heart problems. They each gifted me the love of travel and history. My dad liked to say that the world is full of two kinds of people, those who are curious and those who aren't. I'm so grateful that Mom and Dad taught me to be in that first group. Thank you.

Miranda and Nico, you've been the best traveling companions I could ask for. Thanks for sharing this time together, journeys to palaces and campfires, of macaque-spotting and tri-corner hat wearing. And here's to many more trips. The next one doesn't have to be history-related, I promise! (Or maybe it could be, just a little. Only if you want to.)

And Liana, my ally in love and life: I never could have done this without you. I appreciate your constant support—this book belongs to you as much as me. Thanks for sharing all those trips with me, as well as for holding things down in the twenty-first century while I roamed around the eighteenth by myself.

Finally, I wish I had known about Mercy Otis Warren and this galaxy of unknown heroes when I was younger. But there is a time for everything. I'm so grateful to have been able to do these travels and share them with you. It's my hope that this book inspires you to get out on the road and find out a little more about this forgotten world war yourself.

Reading Group Guide

1. Before reading this book, how much did you know about the Revolutionary War? Which events in the book did you learn about in school, and which were new to you?

2. Did it surprise you how much (and how many) foreign nations and peoples aided the Americans in their revolution? Why or why not?

3. How do you prefer to interact with history? Do you like to watch or join reenactments, go to a museum, read a book, or watch videos or documentaries?

4. Did this book inspire you to want to visit any of the places in it? If so, which ones?

5. Why do you think certain parts of history aren't discussed or taught in school? What reasons are given in the book? Do you believe any history should be forgotten?

6. Consider the Native perspective on the war. Why do you think some Native American nations were against helping the rebels, while the Oneida chose to lend their aid? How did the government of the new United States treat the Oneida after the end of the war?

7. How important do you believe it is to continue teaching history to future generations? Why or why not? What do you think are the best ways to preserve history for those who come after us?

8. Consider the influence of foreign cultures on the United States in the late 1700s. How did those cultures and immigrants enrich the lives of people at the time, and how do they continue to do so today?

9. How did the American Revolution inspire other nations in their own revolutions? Why might a fight like that be infectious?

10. Were you aware of the battles in India at the time of the Revolutionary War? What effect did a fight on the other side of the world have on the United States at the time? Thinking about modern society, how do global events affect us in our daily lives?

11. How is history different depending on the perspective it's told from? Is it important to you to learn all the different sides to a story?

12. Consider the effect of the slave trade on the American Revolution. How did enslaved African Americans assist in the war effort? How were enslaved soldiers treated after the war?

13. How do current mindsets and societal norms influence what people know (or think they know) about history? What do you think is the best way to determine the bias of a source of information, and how might you best combat that bias?

14. After the end of the war, the United States turned inward, deciding to focus on expansion west rather than on aiding their former allies. What do you think of this decision? What were the repercussions, positive or negative, to choosing this?

A Conversation with the Author

Was it difficult to weave together modern stories with historical facts? How did you decide on the amount of modern versus historical information to include?

I loved the challenge of blending my own travel observations with history. I've always enjoyed reading about history, but visiting sites yourself can be a great additional way of making the past come alive—particularly if there are reenactors portraying what people once did there or experts sharing stories with you. When I'm writing, I try to roughly balance the past and present. For me, the key is not to go too far in either direction. My goal is to have my narrative of travel move the chapter forward while grounding it in the history I want the reader to know.

Considering all the travel you did for research, did you find there was one place more than any others where you felt the historical significance of where you were?

There are so many candidates for this! I loved the Fourth of July fiesta in Andalusia. It was so cool to think of members of the Gálvez family sitting in that same plaza back when they were shepherds, long before they helped us win our independence. Sint Eustatius, the site of the first salute of the American flag by a foreign power, was another amazing experience. Seemingly the entire island mobilized for the celebrations.

And the island of Jersey, where I got a blow-by-blow description of the fighting from someone who looked like he had just returned from the battle (Christopher Dankler, dressed as a British gunner) was also unforgettable.

Yet the place that moved me the most had to have been Cuddalore, the site of the last battle of the war, on India's Coromandel Coast. No one knew I was coming, but the kids of the caretaker who lived next door were thrilled to see me. Fort St. David seemed somewhat familiar—I had seen similar examples of eighteenth-century forts in America and elsewhere. I watched a brightly painted fishing boat bob up and down by the mangroves below the fort, not a tourist in sight, and realized just how far I was from home. It was there that the global scope of the war truly sank in for me.

P.S. If you are inspired to travel to these—or any of the other places in the book—and would like advice on where to go, feel free to go to my author website at jeffersontravels.com for my contact info and drop me a line. I'm happy to share what I know!

As you did your research and travels, did anything surprise you?

I had no idea of the scale of the commitment that America's partners and allies made. The French and Spanish, for example, sent over US$30 billion in today's currency in aid to the Patriots—beyond the astronomical sums they spent on their own armies and navies. The sacrifices of the allies and partners of America were immense too. Thousands of soldiers and sailors lost their lives. The war affected civilians as well—the island of Sint Eustatius was pillaged, while the Oneida homeland was devastated.

Nor had I fully appreciated just how important a role the allies played in the United States itself. The French weren't just at Yorktown; they helped out at a number of battles on American soil. For example, at the Siege of Charleston, there were French ships attempting to protect the city, French officers giving advice, and a contingent of the Chasseurs

Volontaires, the free Blacks from the French Caribbean. The Americans in Charleston even sent a desperate mission to Havana to plead with the Spanish to save them. My own ancestor, a lieutenant in the North Carolina militia, was at the battle. I can only wonder what he thought of the foreigners who were helping out.

Were there any places you didn't make it to that you would have liked to have visited?

The Caribbean was one of the hottest theaters of the war. The principal Spanish military base in the region was in Cuba, while France's was on their half of the island then known as Saint Domingue (now Haiti). But both countries have faced many problems, and I couldn't, of course, travel to either one at this time. When conditions improve on these islands (and I hope, for the sake of their people, that they will), there's so much history to discover there.

The Bahamas was also the site of a couple of daring actions. An early American expedition in 1776 captured the powder held in Fort Montagu (a fortification that still stands today). Later, in 1782, the Spanish and Americans sent a large force to the islands—the only time that both nations' military forces cooperated together to such an extent—and captured them easily. I'm adding this country to my bucket list for sure. (Plus—duh—it's the Bahamas!)

I'm also looking forward to visiting Pensacola, Florida, someday. The Franco-Spanish taking of Fort George was a key moment in the lead-up to the allied victory at the Yorktown campaign. I can't wait to see the section of Fort George that has been reconstructed.

Finally, I would have loved to have gone up to Hudson's Bay, in the north of Canada. There, a French expedition sailed all the way up from the Caribbean and surprised the British in the remote Prince of Wales Fort, where they were protecting a trading operation. The fort still stands today in Churchill, Manitoba—a town known as the Polar Bear Capital of the World. Talk about adventure travel.

There are many other spots the global Revolutionary War traveler could hit as well (Sri Lanka! Menorca!). If any readers wind up visiting any battle sites I missed, feel free to share pictures.

Which characters do you wish would be remembered more in histories of the Revolutionary War?

I'll just mention three here. First, the Comte de Vergennes, the French foreign minister. He led his own country into the war and helped persuade Spain to join as well. Vergennes served as the unofficial leader of the allied coalition against Britain. If it hadn't been for him, America may not have achieved independence at the time it did.

And, of course, Bernardo de Gálvez, the Spanish general and governor of Louisiana. He was among the boldest generals of the war, launching a lightning campaign that surprised the British along the Gulf coast. Gálvez knew how to put a coalition together, building a multiethnic fighting force that included Spanish, French, American, free Black, and Indigenous soldiers. Today, you can find sites of his victories in Louisiana, Alabama, and Florida—and also visit Galveston, Texas, named for him.

Finally, Tipu Sultan, the leader of the Mysore Kingdom. He's almost completely unknown in America today but was one of Britain's most feared opponents during the war. If you've ever sung "The Star-Spangled Banner," you've unwittingly paid tribute to Tipu. He pioneered the use of rockets in battle, which so impressed the British that they copied the technology. The "rockets' red glare" that Francis Scott Key wrote about came from missiles first developed by the Mysoreans.

What would you like readers to take away from the book?

I hope readers will appreciate the broad sweep of the war and that so many battles occurred beyond our borders. As surprising as it sounds today, back then the United States was a struggling country in need of help. We wouldn't have won our independence at the time we did without our foreign partners and allies. The Patriots were only able to do so after they overcame their initial reluctance to seek help from France and Spain and other countries and invited these outsiders into their struggle.

I also would like people to appreciate how the worldwide nature of the war was widely known at the time. Mercy Otis Warren wrote matter-of-factly about nearly all of the battles that I covered in *The Forgotten World War,* and Washington, Franklin, and Adams all paid close attention to the action overseas. It's worth contemplating why the stories of many of these foreign actions dropped out of the history books. I'm hoping that Americans begin to talk about this forgotten world war again—and even visit some of the far-flung places where our independence was won.

Illustration Credits

Page xxiii. José Gálvez and the author, courtesy of Liana Miranda.

Page xxviii. *Mrs. James Warren (Mercy Otis)*, John Singleton Copley, courtesy of Museum of Fine Arts, Boston.

Page 5. Matt Keagle and reenactors, courtesy of Fort Ticonderoga.

Page 13. British reenactors, Gabe Dickens, courtesy of Fort Ticonderoga.

Page 21. *The Death of General Montgomery in the Attack on Quebec, December 31, 1775*, John Trumbull, courtesy of Yale University Art Gallery.

Page 28. Carpenters' Hall, Carol M. Highsmith, courtesy of Library of Congress, Division of Prints and Photography.

Page 45. Misha Spanner, courtesy of Liana Miranda.

Page 50. The First Salute ceremony, courtesy of Liana Miranda.

Page 59. The Comte de Vergennes, Antoine-François Callet, courtesy of Library of Congress Division of Prints and Photography.

Page 69. Bernard Gueugnon and the author, courtesy of Rachel Didelot.

Page 83. Doris Wilkins-Wilt and Ron Patterson, author photo.

Page 93. Mark Schneider as Lafayette, courtesy of Nico Baxter.

Page 100. Ken Gavin and Nico, author photo.

Page 113. A duel at Vaussieux, author photo.

Page 121. Antoine Randolph Watts, author photo.

Page 134. The author and a Barbary macaque, courtesy of Liana Miranda.

Page 140. Road trip to Portugal!, author photo.

Page 149. Gunner Gilly and the author, author photo.

Page 169. The monument to the Chasseurs-Volontaires de Saint Domingue in Savannah, Carol M. Highsmith, courtesy of Library of Congress, Division of Prints and Photography.

Page 178. The East India Company at Fort St. George, Robert Montgomery Martin and Emma Roberts, *The Indian Empire* (New York, 1858), courtesy of Wikimedia Commons.

Page 195. *La Marcha de Gálvez* by Augusto Ferrer-Dalmau, Wikimedia, CC BY 4.0 https://creativecommons.org/licenses/by-sa/4.0

Page 208. *Gallant Behavior of an English Sailor,* in George Frederick Raymond's *History of England,* 1784, courtesy of Library of Congress, Division of Prints and Photography.

Page 217. The *Hermione*, courtesy of Jp.sembely, https://creativecommons.org/licenses/by-sa/4.0, Wikimedia Commons.

Page 236. Tipu Sultan, Edward Orme, courtesy of University of Edinburgh.

Page 240. Tiger feasting on a British soldier, *A Review of the Origin, Progress and Result, of the Late Decisive War in Mysore with Notes,* James Salmond, courtesy of PICRYL.

Page 244. Venkatesh V., author photo.

Page 249. Ishmael Berker, author photo.

Page 254. The Jewish cemetery in Sint Eustatius, author photo.

Page 263. *Comte de Rochambeau,* Charles Willson Peale, courtesy Independence National Historical Park.

Page 267. Moses Delaney, author photo.

Page 275. The view from Fort St. Louis, courtesy of Liana Miranda.

Page 279. The Comte de Grasse, Joseph-Rose Lemercier engraving, courtesy of National Archives Catalog.

Page 285. *Vaisseau le Ville de Paris en 1764 à Rochefort,* courtesy of Bibliothèque Nationale de la France.

Page 290. The author at Cape Henry, courtesy of Tammy Mayer Rosario.

Page 298. Three heroes on a stamp, Bureau of Engraving and Printing, courtesy of Wikipedia.

Page 303. The British surrender at Yorktown, courtesy of Wikimedia Commons.

Page 316. *A View of the North Part of Gibraltar, with the Attack by Land & Sea, on the 13th of Septr. 1783*, George Frederick Koehler, Courtesy Prints, Drawings and Watercolors from the Anne S.K. Brown Military Collection, Brown University Library.

Page 321. The author and friends at Fort St. David, author photo.

Page 328. *General Lafayette's Departure from Mount Vernon, 1784*, E. Farrell, courtesy Library of Congress, Division of Prints and Photography.

Page 343. The author and family, author photo.

Abbreviations

BAA: Larrie Ferreiro, *Brothers at Arms: American Independence and the Men of France and Spain Who Saved it* (Knopf, 2016).

FO: Founders Online, a project of the National Archives that makes documents of the American Founders publicly available, in cooperation with UVA Press; https://founders.archives.gov.

GW: George Washington.

HFSA: Tom Shachtman, *How the French Saved America: Soldiers, Sailors, Diplomats, Louis XVI, and the Success of a Revolution* (St. Martin's Press, 2017).

RPT: Mercy Otis Warren, *History of the Rise, Progress, and Termination of the American Revolution* (Boston: Manning and Loring, 1805).

SIUS: Thomas E. Chávez, *Spain and the Independence of the United States: An Intrinsic Gift* (University of New Mexico Press, 2002).

SSP: Sam Willis, *The Struggle for Sea Power: A Naval History of the American Revolution* (W. W. Norton, 2015).

WFA: Piers Mackesy, *The War for America: 1775–1783* (University of Nebraska Press, 1992).

Websites were accessed July 2025.

Notes

INTRODUCTION: EL CUATRO DE JULIO

I had heard that story: *SIUS*, 215. It turns out that the lapse of funding resulted from other sources. But it's true that the second tower was never completed after the war, and Spaniards have been using the tale to illustrate their commitment to the American War of Independence ever since.

hosted George Washington, the Marquis de Lafayette, and a Spanish officer: Nancy Rubin Stuart, *The Muse of the Revolution: The Secret Pen of Mercy Otis Warren and the Founding of a Nation* (Beacon Press, 2008), 94; Jeffrey H. Richards, *Mercy Otis Warren* (Twayne Publishers, 1995), xv, 14, 17. The officer in question was Francisco de Miranda, who reappears in the last chapter of my book.

portraits in writing: Mercy Otis Warren to John Adams, March 10, 1776, FO.

Warren even toured: Mercy Otis Warren to Abigail Adams, April 17, 1776, FO; Stuart, *Muse of the Revolution*, 110.

"high station": Jefferson to James Warren, March 21, 1801, FO.

recommended to his cabinet: Jefferson to Mercy Otis Warren, February 8, 1805, FO.

"clandestine assistance": *RPT*, 2: 273.

"negotiations with foreign powers": *RPT*, 2: 310.

their "hereditary enemy": *RPT*, 2: 86, 97.

"a different religion, language, habits, and manners": *RPT*, 2: 107.

"in conjunction with the armies of their brave allies": *RPT*, 3: 201.

PART ONE: A CRY FOR HELP

CHAPTER ONE: THE SHOT HEARD 'ROUND THE WORLD

First came Lexington and Concord: *RPT*, 1: 185, 207.

And the Americans would: Nathaniel Philbrick, *Bunker Hill: A City, A Siege, A Revolution* (Viking, 2013), 174; Kevin Phillips, *1775: A Good Year for Revolution* (Penguin Books, 2013), 300; *BAA*, 43.

"Parliament actually prohibited the exportation of arms": *RPT*, 1: 159.

Virginian was "ignorant": *RPT*, 1: 236.

What he found when he: Rick Atkinson, *The British Are Coming: The War for America, Lexington to Princeton, 1775–1777* (Henry Holt, 2019), 127; *BAA*, 44.

The need to arm at all costs would lead Americans abroad: *RPT*, 1: 239; 2; 273. Note that Warren didn't always appreciate the success of the smuggling—probably because so much of it was clandestine and wasn't widely reported on at the time.

sulfur and saltpeter were not commonly mined: Philbrick, *Bunker Hill*, 62; *SSP*, 41.

"one necessary thing": Adams to James Warren, September 26, 1775, FO.

expedition to the Bahamas: Atkinson, *The British Are Coming*, 306; *SSP*, 97.

the Dutch island of Sint Eustatius: *SSP*, 41–42; Barbara Tuchman, *The First Salute: A View of the American Revolution* (Knopf, 1988); Marion Huibrechts, "War Supplies from the Low Countries," in *The American Revolution: A World War*, eds. David K. Allison and Larrie D. Ferreiro (Smithsonian Books, 2018), 160–166; *BAA*, 37–39; Kevin Phillips, *1775*, 32–33.

90 percent of gunpowder: *SSP*, 45; *WFA*, 98; Andrew Jackson O'Shaughnessy, *An Empire Divided: The American Revolution and the British Caribbean* (University of Pennsylvania Press, 2000), 213.

"a people of a different religion, language, habits, and manners"..."ancient prejudices": *RPT*, 2: 107.

Quebec Act: Mark Anderson, *The Battle for the Fourteenth Colony: America's War of Liberation in Canada, 1774–1776* (University Press of New England, 2013), 12–13; Atkinson, *The British Are Coming*, 15, 143.

CHAPTER TWO: THE ALLIES THAT WEREN'T

The main one, under Generals Philip Schuyler: *RPT*, 1: 257–258.

A somewhat smaller force under Benedict Arnold: *RPT*, 1: 260–261.

a typewritten monograph: "Fort Chambly During the Revolutionary War" by Margaret Duffert in *Fort Chambly: Interpretive Papers*, by Pierre Nadon, David Lee, Antonio Jurkovich, Margaret Duffert (Parks Canada, Department of Indian and Northern Affairs, 1966).

"conquered into liberty": Anderson, *Battle for the Fourteenth Colony*, 42. In 1774, Congress meant that when Britain took Canada from France in the Seven Years' War, Quebec had been conquered into British liberty—but the phrase is also an apt one for what America sought to do in 1775.

"the acquisition of Canada": GW to Philip Schuyler, November 5, 1775, FO.

"to arrange themselves under the banners of liberty": *RPT*, 1: 258.

Several hundred Canadians did so: Anderson, *Battle for the Fourteenth Colony*, 104, 133.

"gates were thrown open": *RPT*, 1: 259.

"held in equal contempt both danger and principle": *RPT*, 1: 200.

"a hideous wilderness": *RPT*, 1: 261.

ran out of food: Atkinson, *The British Are Coming*, 157–160.

"almost exhausted by hunger and fatigue": *RPT*, 1: 262.

"The term of their enlistments was nearly expired": *RPT*, 1: 264.

"under the cover of a violent snow storm": *RPT*, 1: 265–266.

divided their forces: Anderson, *Battle for the Fourteenth Colony*, 194.

"gained intelligence of these movements": *RPT*, 1: 266.

Montgomery led his men: Atkinson, *The British Are Coming*, 209–210.

as Washington wrote in a letter to Schuyler: GW to Phillip Schuyler, April 19, 1776, FO.

Here in this château: Atkinson, *The British Are Coming*, 273–274; Anderson, *Battle for the Fourteenth Colony*, 303–304.

arrested priests: Atkinson, *The British Are Coming*, 277.

Guy Fawkes Day: Anderson, *Battle for the Fourteenth Colony*, 173.

"cannot be done so effectually by conquest": GW to John Hancock, April 19, 1776, FO.

"Words and professions are of little avail": *RPT*, 1: 257.

rescue mission: *SSP*, 72–73; Anderson, *Battle for the Fourteenth Colony*, 312–315, 328–331.

"Our misfortunes in Canada": John Adams to Abigail Adams, June 26, 1776, FO.

dissected the defeat: John Ferling, *Shots Heard Round the World: America, Britain, and Europe in the Revolutionary War* (Bloomsbury, 2025), 61, 63, 64; Anderson, *Battle for the Fourteenth Colony*, 332–337.

"alliances with foreign states": John Adams to Abigail Adams, July 3, 1776.

reached Crown Point: Anderson, *Battle for the Fourteenth Colony*, 331.

CHAPTER THREE: SENDING OUT AN SOS

Sending out an SOS: Stacy Schiff described the Declaration as an SOS in her *A Great Improvisation: Franklin, France, and the Birth of America* (Henry Holt, 2005). Larrie Ferreiro called it a call for help.

undercover agents: *BAA*, 21–28.

In late November 1775: *BAA*, 52–53; *HFSA*, 1–9; Joel Richard Paul, *Unlikely Allies: How a Merchant, a Playwright, and a Spy Saved the American Revolution* (Riverhead Books, 2009), 118–125; John Ferling, *Winning Independence: The Struggle to Set America Free* (Bloomsbury Press, 2011), 208–211.

"Pomp and Parade": John Adams to Abigail Adams, July 3, 1776, FO.

"America had been little known among the kingdoms of Europe": *RPT*, 1: 140.

In his research: *BAA*, 21–23.

"piddle at the threshold": Stuart, *Muse of the Revolution*, 98.

frigates...an ally with a powerful fleet: *SSP*, 1, 87–89.

"safety of America"..."bloody summer": Edward G. Lengel, *General George Washington: A Military Life* (Random House, 2002), 129, 133.

Washington assembled a force...two fortresses: Atkinson, *The British Are Coming*, 357–359.

the Patriots had gunpowder: Atkinson, *The British Are Coming*, 306.

The largest of the readings: Edwin G. Burrows and Mike Wallace, *Gotham: A History of New York City to 1898* (Oxford University Press, 2000), 232; Atkinson, *The British Are Coming*, 348–350; Ferling, *Winning Independence* ("melted majesty" quote).

Redcoats began to arrive off New York: Philbrook, *Bunker Hill*, 5–6; *SSP*, 120–123.

One noted British historian: *WFA*, 70.

seized Fort Washington: Atkinson, *British Are Coming*, 454–459.

"at so low an ebb": *RPT*, 1: 338.

"our generals were outgeneraled": John Adams to Abigail Adams, October 8, 1776, FO.

"the pains of anxiety, disappointment, and want": *RPT*, 1: 325.

"All was at stake": *RPT*, 1: 360.

the brig *Reprisal*: Schiff, *Great Improvisation*, 7; *BAA*, 61; Atkinson, *The British Are Coming*, 465–466.

CHAPTER FOUR: SIGNS OF HOPE: THE FIRST SALUTE AND THE CROSSING

Netherlands' military power had declined: Ronald Hurst, *The Golden Rock: An Episode of the American War of Independence* (Naval Institute Press, 1996), 52.

Sint Eustatius was...a free port: Hurst, *Golden Rock*, 1.

trade and wealth "beyond any calculation": *RPT*, 3: 119.

warehouses: Along with the exhibits in Statia's excellent museum, good background on this topic includes Tuchman, *First Salute*, 20–22; Hurst, *Golden Rock*, 1–2.

Misha led us past a flaming-red: To supplement Misha's story, you can look at Tuchman, *First Salute*, 13–14, 20–22; Hurst, *Golden Rock*, 2; *BAA*, 37–38; O'Shaughnessy, *Empire Divided*, 215–216.

"the *Andrew Doria*, came flying the American flag": Tuchman, *First Salute*, 6, 48; O'Shaughnessy, *Empire Divided*, 214.

were not amused by his gesture: Tuchman, *First Salute*, 16; Hurst, *Golden Rock*, 2.

the governor threw a party: Tuchman, *First Salute*, 15–16.

On Christmas Eve 1776, Congressman: Robert Morris to GW, December 23–24, 1776, FO (see also notes on the *Andrew Doria*'s trip home).

General Washington dashed off a reply: GW to Robert Morris, December 25, 1776, FO.

"motley mercenaries": *RPT*, 1: 298.

"The surprise was complete": *RPT*, 1: 347.

"fugitive army": *RPT*, 1: 352.

In December 1776, Benjamin Franklin landed: Schiff, *Great Improvisation*, 13–15; 25–28; 71.

CHAPTER FIVE: THE FRENCH CONNECTION

"Yes, because it used to be": Schiff, *Great Improvisation*, 31.

The seventy-year-old Franklin wore: Bruce Lancaster, *The American Revolution* (American Heritage Press, 1985), 233; Schiff, *Great Improvisation*, 89–90.

The foreign minister Vergennes: Orville T. Murphy, *Charle Gravier, Comte de Vergennes: French Diplomacy in the Age of Revolution, 1719–1787* (State University of New York Press, 1982), 345; Paul, *Unlikely Allies*, 109–110; Schiff, *Great Improvisation*, 87.

Franklin had brought a copy of the Declaration of Independence: *BAA*, 91–92.

But not all the other ministers: *HFSA*, 41; *WFA*, 103.

all Franklin did: Schiff, *Great Improvisation*, 31–32.

In 1776, France had only: Jonathan Dull, "France and the American Revolution Seen as Tragedy," in Ronald Hoffman and Peter J. Albert, eds., *Diplomacy and Revolution: The Franco-American Alliance of 1778* (University Press of Virginia, 1981), 94.

Vergennes had to swear: Schiff, *Great Improvisation*, 60–61.

"the universe is going to fall on me": Paul, *Unlikely Allies*, 111.

Unfortunately, Spain rejected Vergennes's: *BAA*, 89–93.

The company's head, Pierre Caron de Beaumarchais: *BAA*, 54–61; *HFSA*, 48; Paul, *Unlikely Allies*, 176–186.

Vergennes's "original mind": Murphy, 95.

"dreaded the rising glory of the United States": *RPT*, 2: 133.

To find out: Murphy, *Charle Gravier*, 3–6; Jean François Labourdette, *Vergennes, Ministre Principal de Louis XVI* (Paris: Editions Desjonquères, 1990), 9–21.

Constantinople: Murphy, *Charle Gravier*, 63.

In the course of his work, Vergennes: Labourdette, *Vergennes*, 41–46; Murphy, *Charle Gravier*, 171, 257.

community of French traders: Labourdette, *Vergennes*, 49–50; Murphy, *Charle Gravier*, 63.

He was sent to Stockholm: Labourdette, *Vergennes*, 57–90.

crowded to see his bust: Schiff, *Great Improvisation*, 97.

"a theatrical show": John Adams to Benjamin Rush, June 21, 1811, FO.

Recent scholarship has uncovered: Labourdette, *Vergennes*, 100.

In the spring, with Vergennes's: Paul, *Unlikely Allies*, 219, 246.

dockyards...cod fishing fleet: Dull, "France and the American Revolution Seen as Tragedy," 95–96; Schiff, *Great Improvisation*, 97.

"help her courageously and effectively": *BAA*, 95.

CHAPTER SIX: FIRST ALLIES

July 4, 1777...the "most splendid illumination": Len Travers, *Celebrating the Fourth: Independence Day and the Rites of Nationalism in the Early Republic* (University of Massachusetts Press, 1997), 17–18.

The first campaign: Nathaniel Philbrick, *Valiant Ambition: George Washington, Benedict Arnold, and the Fate of the American Revolution* (Viking, 2016), 108; Kevin J. Weddle, *The Compleat Victory: Saratoga and the American Revolution* (Oxford University Press, 2021), 51–53, 59–65.

British general Howe embarked his force: Philbrick, *Valiant Ambition*, 120.

"to traverse a forlorn wilderness": *RPT*, 2: 55.

the village of Kanowalohale: Joseph T. Glatthaar and James Kirby Martin, *Forgotten Allies: The Oneida Indians and the American Revolution* (Hill and Wang, 2006), 65–66.

"savages": There are unfortunately numerous references to Indigenous peoples using this word in *RPT*.

fed the Patriots information and served as scouts: Glatthaar and Martin, *Forgotten Allies*, 130, 139–140.

visited Washington's camp: Glatthaar and Martin, *Forgotten Allies*, 142.

invading fighters: Weddle, *Compleat Victory*, 182–183; William Kidder, *Defending Fort Stanwix: A Story of the New York Frontier in the American Revolution* (Three Hills, 2024), 92.

"On August 2, 1777": Weddle, *Compleat Victory*, 189–190; Glatthaar and Martin, *Forgotten Allies*, 155–159.

The ambush: Glatthaar and Martin, *Forgotten Allies*, 163–169; Weddle, *Compleat Victory*, 195–218.

The Native warriors on the side: Glatthaar and Martin, *Forgotten Allies*, 176–177, 186–187.

a masterful ruse: Philbrook, *Valiant Ambition*, 134–136; Weddle, *Compleat Victory*, 213–215; Glatthaar and Martin, *Forgotten Allies*, 173–176.

America's first allies: Glatthaar and Martin, *Forgotten Allies*, 179, 186, 192.

In August, Burgoyne sent: Philbrick, *Valiant Ambition*, 133; Weddle, *Compleat Victory*, 243–254.

In the spring of 1777, Beaumarchais's five ships: *BAA*, 70–71; Paul, *Unlikely Allies*, 220.

Another European import had arrived: *BAA*, 124–125.

He wound up giving: Weddle, *Compleat Victory*, 264.

The first of the two battles: Philbrick, *Valiant Ambition*, 146–150.

reinforcements poured into the Patriots' camp: Philbrick, *Valiant Ambition*, 156.

Some 150 Native American: Glatthaar and Martin, *Forgotten Allies*, 183.

"Sooner should a fond mother forget": Colin Calloway, *The American Revolution in Indian Country* (Cambridge University Press, 1995), 286.

beneath Bemis Heights: Weddle, *Compleat Victory*, 318–323.

"hills and forests": Erick Trickey, "The Polish Patriot Who Helped the Americans," *Smithsonian Magazine*, March 8, 2017.

Burgoyne surrendered: Weddle, *Compleat Victory*, 339–342.

"So many thousands of brave men": *RPT*, 2: 51.

secret weapon: *BAA*, 92–93; Nathan Miller, *Sea of Glory: A Naval History of the American Revolution* (Naval Institute Press, 1974), 193.

"Thus, to the consternation of Britain [and] to the universal joy of America": *RPT*, 2: 39.

News of the victory: *SSP*, 200; *HFSA*, 113; Dull, "France and the American Revolution Seen as Tragedy," 94.

a carriage clattered north: Louis Gottschalk, *Lafayette in America, 1777–1783* (Arveyres, France: L'Esprit de Lafayette Society, 1975), Book Two, 11. Lafayette abandoned his carriage at some time near this date and continued on foot, then later by boat.

CHAPTER SEVEN: THE EUROPEAN AVENGERS

The American cause...the perfect opportunity: Gottschalk, *Lafayette in America*, Book One, 10, 50, 54; Mike Duncan, *Hero of Two Worlds: The Marquis de Lafayette in the Age of Revolution* (Public Affairs, 2021), 8, 40.

"promising offices of rank": *RPT*, 2: 133.

letting Lafayette go would be too risky: Gottschalk, *Lafayette in America*, Book One, 79, 98; Duncan, *Hero of Two Worlds*, 42.

Defying the order: Gottschalk, *Lafayette in America*, Book One, 106–109.

making his way up to the American capital: Duncan, *Hero of Two Worlds*, 47–50.

"men of real merit, military experience, and distinguished rank": *RPT*, 2: 134.

Louis Duportail...wise strategist: *BAA*, 134, 155, 158–159; *HFSA*, 70–71, 84, 104, 138, 140.

Francois De Fleury, the Tech Man: Philbrick, *Valiant Ambition*, 182–183; *HFSA*, 56, 101–104.

Thaddeus Kosciuszko...the Artiste: *BAA*, 124–125.

Casimir Pulaski...cavalryman: Schiff, *Great Improvisation*, 54; *BAA*, 139.

The last to arrive was: *BAA*, 151–155; Philbrick, *Valiant Ambition*, 197–198.

the Howe Brothers were sailing south: John Ferling, *Almost a Miracle: The American Victory in the War of Independence* (Oxford University Press, 2007), 242–245.

"The eyes of all America and of Europe": Philbrick, *Valiant Ambition*, 157.

"the fortune of the day declared against the Americans": *RPT*, 1: 374.

One bright spot: *BAA*, 144–145.

the title was meant to be for show: Duncan, *Hero of Two Worlds*, 56.

Lafayette rallied the American: Gottschalk, *Lafayette in America*, Book Two, 44–47; Philbrick, *Valiant Ambition*, 139–140; Harlow Giles Unger, *Lafayette* (John Wiley and Sons, 2002), 43–46; Duncan, *Hero of Two Worlds*, 58–59.

"distinguished gallantry": *RPT*, 1: 375.

"determined to be in the way of danger": Sarah Vowell, *Lafayette in the Somewhat United States* (Riverhead Books, 2015), 137.

While the Battle of Germantown: Ferling, *Shots Heard Round the World*, 142–145.

"nearly destitute of tents": *RPT*, 1: 387–391.

De Fleury's genius: *BAA*, 147.

new quartermaster general, Nathanael Greene: Philbrick, *Valiant Ambition*, 197.

"The Oneidas have manifested": Glatthaar and Martin, *First Allies*, 194–196, 203–205.

"never more critical": Bob Drury and Tom Clavin, *Valley Forge* (Simon and Schuster, 2019), 120.

a "powerful friend": General Orders, May 5, 1778, FO.

encouraging France to join in: Gottschalk, *Lafayette in America*, Book Two, 176.

On May 2, a rider arrived at Valley Forge: *BAA*, 97–100; Schiff, *Great Improvisation*, 132, 141–142.

The entire army came: Thomas Fleming, *Washington's Secret War: The Hidden History of Valley Forge* (Smithsonian Books/Collins, 2005), 248–252; Wayne Bodle, *Valley Forge Winter: Civilians and Soldiers at War* (Pennsylvania State University Press, 2002), 221–222.

PART TWO: THE WORLD WAR

CHAPTER EIGHT: LOST IN TRANSLATION

"Nothing can justify": *BAA*, 97.

acting like Don Quixote: Schiff, *Great Improvisation*, 134.

Vergennes didn't like these demands: *BAA*, 96–97.

sixty-six ships of the line to France's fifty-two: Dull, "France and the American Revolution Seen as Tragedy," 94.

one quick campaign in 1778: *SIUS*, 78.

training exercise in Normandy: *HFSA*, 93; *BAA*, 186.

the *Belle Poule*: *SSP*, 2–5, 210–213; *BAA*, 111.

"the discharge of a whole broadside": *RPT*, 3: 106.

In the pageant feast: *SSP*, 220–229; *WFA*, 209–211; *BAA*, 111.

"to strike at the trade": *RPT*, 3: 108.

"controlling the nations and defying the universe": *RPT*, 3: 114.

commanded by the Comte d'Estaing: *BAA*, 103; *SSP*, 231–233.

gifted me a copy of a book: Dider Bonvouloir, "Julian de Bonvouloir," in *Le Camp de Vaussieux et le Bassin en 1778, une etape dans la guerre d'Independance americaine*, ed. Gregory Pique (Orep Editions, 2023).

"The object of the war being now changed": *WFA*, 186.

London ordered the Redcoats: O'Shaughnessy, *Empire Divided*, 208; *WFA*, 185.

"Our islands must be defended": Matthew Lockwood, *To Begin the World Over Again: How the American Revolution Devastated the Globe* (Yale University Press, 2019), 136.

On May 20, 1778, Washington: Glatthaar and Martin, *Forgotten Allies*, 209–215.

Monmouth Courthouse: Ferling, *Almost a Miracle*, 300–306.

"Houra, my good friend": Fleming, *Washington's Secret War*, 248.

"There may still be business enough": Philbrick, *Valiant Ambition*, 199.

"plain and easy road": Schiff, *Great Improvisation*, 166.

"a series of disappointments": *RPT*, 2: 179–180.

The first came when he: *SSP*, 233–238; Philbrick, *Valiant Ambition*, 216–218.

The admiral promised: *SSP*, 241–245; Philbrick, *Valiant Ambition*, 218–219; *BAA*, 174–178; *HFSA*, 157–161.

The First Rhode Island: Michael Lee Lanning, *African Americans in the Revolutionary War* (Citadel, 2000), 74–78; Christian McBurney, *The Rhode Island Campaign: The First French and American Operation in the Revolutionary War* (Westholme, 2011), 47–48, 187–192, 199.

"a most rascally manner": *SSP*, 246.

"This disappointment occasioned some temporary murmurings": *RPT*, 2: 104.

Meanwhile, tensions rose: *SSP*, 248–251; *HFSA*, 162–164; Christian McBurney, "Why Did a Boston Mob Kill a French Officer?", *Journal of the American Revolution* (October 23, 2014).

"first impressions are long remembered": Robert L. O'Connell, *Revolutionary: George Washington at War* (Random House, 2019), 216.

One well-meaning American: Schiff, *Great Improvisation*, 170; Norman Desmarias, "A Frog Feast," *Journal of the American Revolution* (August 22, 2023).

He arrived in December 1778: *SSP*, 258–265; *WFA*, 232–232.

the Chasseurs-Volontaires de Saint-Domingue: *BAA*, 200; Robert Scott Davis, "Black Haitian Soldiers at the Siege of Savannah," *Journal of the American Revolution* (February 22, 2021).

failed to give them the bounties: Lanning, *African Americans in the Revolutionary War*, 103.

"seldom a favorite of fortune": *RPT*, 2: 163.

would far outnumber: Dull, "France and the American Revolution Seen as Tragedy," 94.

"cannot struggle long": *SIUS*, 88.

the Spanish treasure fleets: *BAA*, 103, 113.

CHAPTER NINE: NOBODY EXPECTS THE SPANISH INTERVENTION

Aranjuez, his spring palace: *BAA*, 78; Carlos Gómez-Centurión, "La Corte de Carlos III," in *Carlos III y su Epoca*, Luis Miguel Enciso Recio, ed. (Century Publishers, 2021), 378–379.

compel the British "to abandon America": *SSP*, 280.

Even if he didn't bring: *BAA*, 78.

modernize his country's economy: *SIUS*, 7; *BAA*, 77.

The king was a creature: Carlos Gómez-Centurión, "La Corte de Carlos III," 369–374.

"the spirit of freedom might be contagious": *RPT*, 3: 328.

What they really wanted: *BAA*, 112.

Spain took Gibraltar: Roy Adkins and Lesley Adkins, *Gibraltar: The Greatest Siege in British History* (Penguin Books, 2017); 1–8; James Falkner, *Fire over the Rock: The Great Siege of Gibraltar, 1779–1783* (Pen and Sword Military, 2009), 1–11.

In 1778, Spain even: *BAA*, 112–113.

"this pile of rocks called Gibraltar": *BAA*, 113.

"more strongly tinctured with insanity": GW to John Jay, August 16, 1779, FO.

the fleet had reached Spain safely: *BAA*, 103, 113.

an aggressive plan of attack: *BAA*, 114.

ships of the line: Dull, "France and the American Revolution Seen as Tragedy," 94.

Spain signed a treaty with France: *SSP*, 282; *BAA*, 115, 182.

José de Gálvez wrote secret letters: *BAA*, 115.

"droops like a withering flower under a declining sun": *SSP*, 283.

the Neutral Ground: Adkins and Adkins, *Gibraltar*, 15–19.

Back in 1779, Gibraltar was a melting pot: Adkins and Adkins, *Gibraltar*, 11–12; Falkner, *Fire over the Rock*, 26.

"impregnable strength": *RPT*, 3: 157.

"against the most tremendous attack": *RPT*, 2: 292.

The British cleverly blasted these tunnels: Adkins and Adkins, *Gibraltar*, 277–278, 284–287.

depressing carriage: Adkins and Adkins, *Gibraltar*, 261–262.

"torrents of fire and brimstone": *RPT*, 3: 158.

a two-hour long siesta each day: Adkins and Adkins, *Gibraltar*, 191, 212.

"The awful play of the artillery of death": *RPT*, 3: 154.

working on the Sultan of Morocco: *SIUS*, 145; Falkner, *Fire over the Rock*, 24.

"a few worm-eaten biscuits": *RPT*, 2: 291–292.

"Let us now rest a little from the roar of cannon": *RPT*, 3: 158.

escorting a huge convoy: *WFA*, 311; Adkins and Adkins, *Gibraltar*, 98–99; Falkner, *Fire over the Rock*, 43.

The Portuguese got the message: *SIUS*, 43; *BAA*, 92–93.

the League of Armed Neutrality: *BAA*, 247, 285; *SIUS*, 145; *SSP*, 401–402.

"Admiral Rodney, determined to pursue his success": *RPT*, 2: 292–293.

The old gambler: Adkins and Adkins, *Gibraltar*, 101–105; Falkner, *Fire over the Rock*, 45–51; *SSP*, 359–361.

"One reason for his speed": *BAA*, 195–196.

"The Spanish ship San Domingo": *RPT*, 2: 293.

Gibraltarians were overjoyed: *SSP*, 362–264; Adkins and Adkins, *Gibraltar*, 105–114.

"the end of the siege": Jabez Bowen to GW, March 20, 1780, FO.

CHAPTER TEN: THE BRITISH INVASION

assembled a fleet of some 186 warships: A. Temple Patterson, *The Other Armada* (University of Manchester Press, 1960); *BAA*, 185.

the "mistress of the seas": *RPT*, 1: 247.

"humble the pride and power of Britain": *RPT*, 1: 400.

troops would cross the Channel: *WFA*, 279; GW to Henry Laurens, September 29, 1779 (note), FO.

"brew or provide small beer": Patterson, *The Other Armada*, 154.

Thus, in relative sobriety: Patterson, *The Other Armada*, 14, 49–50; *WFA*, 279–280.

a French prince put together a fleet: States of Jersey, *The Battle of Jersey* (Jarrold and Sons, Ltd., States of Jersey, 1984).

"greatly apprehensive": James Lovell to GW, August 25, 1779, FO (enclosure and notes).

Among those who: Patterson, *The Other Armada*, 152–153; *HFSA*, 184–186.

The French fleet was supposed: *BAA*, 183–184; *WFA*, 281.

None of the Spanish ships: *WFA*, 281; *BAA*, 183–185; *HFSA*, 185.

"improvise their signals": *BAA*, 285.

"I foresee a fatal outcome": *SSP*, 286.

"the wide field of conjecture": GW to Lafayette, September 30, 1779, FO.

Britain's worst fears came true: Patterson, *The Other Armada*, 217; *SSP*, 290; *WFA*, 287–292.

"Since the time of the Invincible Armada": *SSP*, 293.

Yet even as the fear: *SSP*, 291; *HFSA*, 188; *WFA*, 294; *BAA*, 186–188.

One of those forms: *BAA*, 189–192; *HFSA*, 189–191.

"The *Bonhomme Richard* was reduced to a wreck": *RPT*, 3: 112.

"causes a universal depression": Thomas Digges to Benjamin Franklin, October 8, 1779, FO.

Baron de Rullecourt, returned in 1781: States of Jersey, *The Battle of Jersey*.

"The design was so secret and the attack so sudden": *RPT*, 3: 149.

Rullecourt was mortally wounded: States of Jersey, *The Battle of Jersey*.

"the resultant alarm and despondency": *HFSA*, 175; Patterson, *The Other Armada*, 226.

"as a leopard over his prey": *SSP*, 293.

"exhausted England": *HFSA*, 189.

"checks to their pride": *RPT*, 2: 204–205.

They sent additional troops: *RPT*, 2: 211.

the worried British kept a huge Home Fleet close to their shores: Dull, "France and the American Revolution Seen as Tragedy," 99.

CHAPTER ELEVEN: A DAY IN THE LIFE OF A WORLD WAR

Old St. Mary's Church: George W. Boudreau, *Independence: A Guide to Historic Philadelphia* (Westholme Publishing, 2012), 122.

"dwelling of Satan": "dispersed impiety": Atkinson, *The British Are Coming*, 143–144.

The mass had been sponsored: *BAA*, 104–109; "The First Catholic Celebration of the Fourth of July," *The American Catholic Historical Researches* 17, no. 2 (April 1900): 60–63.

three states even voted: Len Travers, *Celebrating the Fourth: Independence Day and the Rites of Nationalism in the Early Republic* (University of Massachusetts Press, 1997), 24–25.

Then came the toasts: Toasts at an Independence Day Banquet (July 5, 1779), FO; Schiff, *Great Improvisation*, 212–215.

thirty-three modern nations: The countries are the Bahamas, Barbados, Belize, Canada, Cape Verde, Cuba, Dominica, the Dominican Republic, France, Haiti, Ghana, Grenada, Guatemala, Guyana, Honduras, India, Indonesia, Ireland, Jamaica, Malaysia, Mexico, the Netherlands, Nicaragua, Portugal, Senegal, Spain, South Africa, St. Kitts and Nevis, St. Lucia, St. Vincent and the Grenadines, Sri Lanka, Suriname, Trinidad and Tobago, and the United Kingdom. And, oh yes, the United States of America.

"When, my dear Marquis?": GW to Lafayette, July 4, 1779.

Miralles was a particularly: Juan de Miralles to GW, May 22, 1779, FO.

"destroy their settlements": GW to Lafayette, July 4, 1779.

scorched-earth campaign: Glatthaar and Martin, *Forgotten Allies*, 240–256.

a regiment of Canadians: Holly Mayer, *Congress' Own: A Canadian Regiment, the Continental Army, and American Union* (University of Oklahoma, 2021), 166–182.

After France entered the war: *WFA*, 252, 258, 266–272; *BAA*, 212: Ferling, *Almost a Miracle*, 387–388.

battle was being fought on the island of Grenada: *WFA*, 273–274; *SSP*, 306–310.

"attempted to storm the town": *RPT*, 2: 178.

The losses included the gallant Count Pulaski: *BAA*, 202.

The Chasseurs took on: *BAA*, 200; Robert Scott Davis, "Black Haitian Soldiers at the Siege of Savannah"; Marlene L. Dant, *The First and Last King of Haiti: Henri Christophe* (Knopf, 2025), 48–52.

some seven to ten American ships: Robert Patton, *Patriot Pirates: The Privateer War for Freedom and Fortune in the American Revolution* (Pantheon Books, 2008), 235.

Bernardo spent July 1779: John Walton Caughey, *Bernardo de Gálvez in Louisiana, 1776–1783* (Pelican Publishing, 1972), 149–153.

the guns of Gibraltar: Falkner, *Fire over the Rock*, 26–27.

"The American war had become very unpopular in England": *RPT*, 3: 181.

Unrest was increasing in Ireland: Lockwood, *To Begin the World Over Again*, 84–90.

CHAPTER TWELVE: THE FAR SIDE OF THE WORLD

It started as a small: Shashi Tharoor, *Inglorious Empire: What the British Did to India* (Scribe, 2016) 2–8; William Dalrymple, *The Anarchy: The East India Company, Corporate Violence, and the Pillage of an Empire* (Bloomsbury, 2019), 13–20; 54–64.

"The British began further north, near Calcutta": Several of the Indian cities I refer to have since changed names; Madras has become Chennai, Calcutta has become Kolkata, and Pondicherry has become Puducherry. I will mostly be using their historic names here.

"The Europeans came to trade in cloth": Dalrymple, *The Anarchy*, 20, 64.

"wash their bottoms?": Tharoor, *Inglorious Empire*, 5.

"a strange absurdity": Dalrymple, *The Anarchy*, 202.

In 1772, with the business: Dalrymple, *The Anarchy*, 228–233; Richard Sambasivam, "British Global Ambitions and Indian Identity," in *The American Revolution: A World War*, eds. Allison and Ferreiro, 97; Dalrymple, *The Anarchy*, 228–233.

"catalogue of cruelties": *RPT*, 2: 223.

learned of France's 1778 entry into the war: *SSP*, 269–270.

a musty old book: Pierre Bourdat, *Eighteenth Century Pondicherry* (Pondicherry Museum, 1995). I thought it was even older when I first unwrapped it, since the cover was so faded from the heat and humidity!

With the loss of that port: Lockwood, *To Begin the World Over Again*, 245.

CHAPTER THIRTEEN: BATTLE OF THE BAYOU

exhausted by "the great heats of the weather": Juan de Miralles to GW (encl.), February 18, 1780, FO.

British forces were to simultaneously sail: Caughey, *Bernardo de Gálvez*, 149–150; *SIUS*, 166.

Gálvez's officers counseled caution: Caughey, *Bernardo de Gálvez*, 150–151.

advance notice of Spain's declaration of war: Caughey, *Bernardo de Gálvez*, 149; *SIUS*, 135.

"prepared themselves for a rupture": *RPT*, 2: 290.

"overcome storms, dangers, disappointments": *RPT*, 2: 291.

"go and find our enemies": Gonzalo M. Quintero Saravia, *Bernardo de Gálvez: Spanish Hero of the American Revolution* (University of North Carolina Press, 2018), 146.

To find out: The talk was in conjunction with the excellent New Iberia Spanish festival, an event I will introduce in the next section.

France gifted its Louisiana province...unhealthy climate: Caughey, *Bernardo de Gálvez*, 4–6.

acting governor: Quintero Saravia, *Bernardo de Gálvez*, 6.

Oliver Pollock...George Rogers Clark: Quintero Saravia, *Bernardo de Gálvez*, 139–142; Caughey, *Bernardo de Gálvez*, 85–88, 98–99; *BAA*, 134–136; *SIUS*, 97–98, 113–117.

"grateful sense of the favors": Thomas Jefferson to Bernardo de Gálvez, November 8, 1779, FO.

"proceed immediately to surprise": *RPT*, 2: 290.

"the land flooded, and everything drowned": Quintero Saravia, *Bernardo de Gálvez*, 147.

"Don Bernardo de Gálvez, Governor of Louisiana": *RPT*, 2: 290.

"I shall defend the province": Caughey, *Bernardo de Gálvez*, 152–153.

They carried Gálvez...raised sunken ships: Caughey, *Bernardo de Gálvez*, 151–152; Quintero Saravia, *Bernardo de Gálvez*, 148.

"set off in search of adventure": Quintero Saravia, *Bernardo de Gálvez*, 148.

founded this town: Quintero Saravia, *Bernardo de Gálvez*, 120, 123.

Havana wanted no part: *SIUS*, 168.

settlers to come: Quintero Saravia, *Bernardo de Gálvez*, 91, 120–121; Caughey, *Bernardo de Gálvez*, 78–81, 137–38.

the Spanish population never made up more than 15 percent: Quintero Saravia, *Bernardo de Gálvez*, 110.

The French residents were an unruly bunch...Marie Félicité de Saint-Maxent d'Estrehan...Creole elite: Caughey, *Bernardo de Gálvez*, 14–16, 84; Quintero Saravia, *Bernardo de Gálvez*, 94–95, 131–134.

free Blacks...slave laws: Quintero Saravia, *Bernardo de Gálvez*, 94, 113–117.

"One hundred and sixty Indians undertook the march": Juan de Miralles to GW (encl.), February 18, 1780, FO.

"600 [men] of all kinds and colors": Juan de Miralles to GW (encl.), February 18, 1780, FO; *BAA*, 161; *SIUS*, 170.

"in total command of the troops": Quintero Saravia, *Bernardo de Gálvez*, 156.

Fort Bute: Quintero Saravia, *Bernardo de Gálvez*, 150; *SIUS*, 171.

The fort at Baton Rouge: Quintero Saravia, *Bernardo de Gálvez*, 151; Juan de Miralles to GW (encl.), February 18, 1780, FO.

"infest and ruin our trade": Patrick Henry to GW, March 13, 1779, FO.

Captain William Pickles: *SIUS*, 171; *BAA*, 161; Quintero Saravia, *Bernardo de Gálvez*, 153; Caughey, *Bernardo de Gálvez*, 159–160.

"lack of anything else to conquer": Quintero Saravia, *Bernardo de Gálvez*, 154.

a hero's welcome: *SIUS*, 171–173; Juan de Miralles to GW (encl.), February 18, 1780, FO.

a "Sea Tortoise": Juan de Miralles to GW, October 2, 1779, FO.

"United with the arms of France": GW to Juan de Miralles, October 16, 1779, FO.

The next spring, Washington got: *SIUS*, 174–176; *BAA*, 137, 163; Quintero Saravia, *Bernardo de Gálvez*, 161–175; Caughey, *Bernardo de Gálvez*, 172–186.

"keys to the Gulf of Mexico": *BAA*, 161.

Following a brief siege: *BAA*, 163; *SIUS*, 174–176.

"Mobile, Pensacola, Galvez, and Spain": General Orders (Second General Orders), June, 8, 1780, FO.

CHAPTER FOURTEEN: WHEN THE AMERICAN REVOLUTION WAS MEXICAN

the captain-general of Guatemala: *SIUS*, 14, 119–125.

British loggers set up: *SIUS*, 14, 39, 151; *BAA*, 86.

London had developed: *SIUS*, 152; *BAA*, 169.

On a fine day in September 1779: *SIUS*, 152; David Morley, *Wars of the Americas: A Chronology of Armed Conflict in the New World, 1492 to the Present* (ABC-CLIO, 1998), 323–324.

Fort St. George: *SIUS*, 152; Morley, *Wars of the Americas*, 324.

the "key and outer wall of the kingdom": *SIUS*, 151.

the Spanish regained San Fernando: *SIUS*, 153.

"arms of Spain": *RPT*, 2: 290.

contributed their money: *SIUS*, 153, 214–215.

***pulquerias*, the speakeasies of the day:** *SIUS*, 213–214.

He spun out the fantastic: For more on the San Juan campaign, see *SIUS*, 150–158; *BAA*, 162; *WFA*, 318, 335–336.

On September 15, 1779: Substance of a Conversation with La Luzerne, September 16, 1779, FO; Nathaniel Philbrick, *In the Hurricane's Eye: The Genius of George Washington and the Victory at Yorktown* (Viking, 2018) 3, 7; *BAA*, 209–210; *SIUS*, 173.

as "humiliating" as he admitted that it was: *RPT*, 2: 232.

CHAPTER FIFTEEN: WHOM CAN WE TRUST?

But many of the French ships: *BAA*, 219.

the *Expedition Particulière...Hermione*: *BAA*, 210–211; *SSP*, 378.

frigates...desperate plea for help: Carl Borick, *A Gallant Defense: The Siege of Charleston, 1780* (University of South Carolina Press, 2012), 45, 94.

Alarmed, Washington sent: Borick, *A Gallant Defense*, 200–213; *BAA*, 213–215; *SSP*, 345–355.

Lafayette arrived..."a day of universal joy": *SSP*, 380; *BAA*, 211; Duncan, *Hero of Two Worlds*, 106.

"France and Spain must save us": Alexander Hamilton to John Laurens, June 30, 1780, FO.

the Special Expedition left Brest: *BAA*, 219.

"a few sad and frightened faces"...The next day: Richard M. Ketchum, *Victory at Yorktown: The Campaign That Won the Revolution* (Henry Holt, 2004), 25; Lee Kennett, *The French Forces in America, 1780–1783* (Greenwood Press, 1977), 48.

"[w]e are now, sir, under your command": *BAA*, 220.

By the end of August: Kennett, 55, 80–81.

a "very embarrassing question": Arnold Whitridge, *Rochambeau: America's Neglected Founding Father* (The MacMillan Co., 1965), 111–112; Ketchum, *Victory at Yorktown*, 82–83.

sent Lafayette as an intermediary: Ketchum, *Victory at Yorktown*, 29–30.

They finally did so in September 1780, in Hartford: Ferling, *Winning Independence*, 237–238; Ketchum, *Victory at Yorktown*, 37–38.

"his troops were totally routed": *RPT*, 2: 243.

"Picture it as bad as you possibly can": Edward Stevens to Thomas Jefferson, August 20, 1780, FO.

Spanish defenders in St. Louis: *SIUS*, 178–180.

"worth more than 50 Mobiles and Pensacolas": *SIUS*, 174.

continued to fight the British in Nicaragua: *SIUS*, 155–156.

As for Rochambeau: Philbrick, *Hurricane's Eye*, 20–21; Ketchum, *Victory at Yorktown*, 38–39.

Rochambeau reluctantly agreed..."more ships, more men, and more money": *BAA*, 224–225.

gushing with admiration: Whitridge, *Rochambeau*, 101; Ketchum, *Victory at Yorktown*, 43–45; Harlow Giles Unger, *Lafayette* (Trade Paper Press, 2003), 122.

"Whom can we trust now?"...Arnold had betrayed the cause: O'Connell, *Revolutionary*, 245–246; Philbrick, *Valiant Ambition*, 311.

"Providence is for us": O'Connell, *Revolutionary*, 252; Ketchum, *Victory at Yorktown*, 78–79.

the Great Hurricane swept through the Caribbean: *WFA*, 381; Philbrick, *Hurricane's Eye*, 17; *SSP*, 412; Tuchman, *First Salute*, 217.

changed France's strategic thinking: Philbrick, *Hurricane's Eye*, 18.

Bernardo de Galvez had just taken to sea: *BAA*, 243–244; *SIUS*, 182.

"A very severe storm": Lt. Gen. Rochambeau to GW, October 8, 1780, FO.

the *Amazone* made a beeline for France: *BAA*, 225; Ketchum, *Victory at Yorktown*, 137; Philbrick, *Hurricane's Eye*, 21.

PART THREE: ALL FOR THE COMMON CAUSE

CHAPTER SIXTEEN: THE TIGER OF MYSORE

Yet continuing on: Dalrymple, *The Anarchy*, 242.

his own small navy: *SSP*, 272–273; Dalrymple, *The Anarchy*, 242.

Hyder attacked the East India Company: Mohibbul Hasan, *The History of Tipu Sultan* (Delhi: Aakar Books, 2022), 8–9; Kate Brittlebank, *Tiger: The Life of Tipu Sultan* (Juggernaut Books, 2019), 28–31.

the neighboring Maratha Confederacy launched an attack: Hasan, *History of Tipu Sultan*, 10–11; Brittlebank, *Tiger*, 31–32; Lockwood, *To Begin the World Over Again*, 245.

"all-powerful in India": Dalrymple, *The Anarchy*, 318.

Hyder sent some ninety thousand troops: Hasan, *History of Tipu Sultan*, 12; Dalrymple, *The Anarchy*, 246.

The British belatedly sent troops: Hasan, *History of Tipu Sultan*, 12–13; Dalrymple, *The Anarchy*, 258.

Tipu ordered his artillery: Hasan, *History of Tipu Sultan*, 14–15; Dalrymple, *The Anarchy*, 252–253.

The Mysoreans pioneered: Hasan, *History of Tipu Sultan*, 12–13; Dalrymple, *The Anarchy*, 243; Richard Sambasivam, "The Tiger Aids the Eaglet," *Journal of the American Revolution* (April 26, 2016).

"hideous roaring of elephants": Dalrymple, *The Anarchy*, 253.

Pollilur..."the severest": Hasan, *History of Tipu Sultan*, 15; Dalrymple, *The Anarchy*, 253–255.

"rather live a day as a tiger than a lifetime as a sheep": Dalrymple, *The Anarchy*, 257.

the harsh conditions: Lockwood, *To Begin the World Over Again*, 259–260; Dalrymple, *The Anarchy*, 256; Brittlebank, *Tiger*, 5–6, 117.

story of Tipu killing: *RPT*, 3: 242–243.

forced Christian prisoners to convert: Dalrymple, *The Anarchy*, 321; Brittlebank, *Tiger*, 46–47.

Enlightenment philosophy...silkworms: Dalrymple, *The Anarchy*, 319, 321; Brittlebank, *Tiger*, 30, 56.

"common cause": Philbrick, *Hurricane's Eye*, 143; *BAA*, 116.

John Adams, serving: Edmund Jennings to John Adams, April 4, 1781, FO.

"severed from them, perhaps forever": James Madison to Edmund Pendleton, October 30, 1780, FO.

the *Hyder Ally*: Lockwood, *To Begin the World Over Again*, 258; Louis Arthur Norton, "Joshua Barney, the *Hyder-Ally's* Triumph, and Its Aftermath," *Journal of the American Revolution* (October 17, 2019).

"India and America are alike escaping": Dalrymple, *The Anarchy*, 258.

"the preservation of India": Richard Sambasivam, "The Tiger Aids the Eaglet," *Journal of the American Revolution* (April 26, 2016).

the British ordered a squadron: *WFA*, 391–393; 495; *SSP*, 429; *BAA*, 283.

CHAPTER SEVENTEEN: THE EMPIRE STRIKES BACK

Here in the church's cemetery: Hurst, *Golden Rock*, 6, 109–117, 122–124.

In late 1780, the Netherlands was preparing to join too: Hurst, *Golden Rock*, 54–55.

And so, right before the League: Hurst, *Golden Rock*, 59, 107; O'Shaughnessy, *Empire Divided*, 216.

"has done England more harm": O'Shaughnessy, *Empire Divided*, 221.

"take care [of] this nest of thieves": Hurst, *Golden Rock*, 133.

"The storm burst on the Dutch West India islands": *RPT*, 3: 119.

The Dutch had posted only: Hurst, *Golden Rock*, 109.

"appeared to me as a dream": Hurst, *Golden Rock*, 133.

"[t]he loss of one half of it": Tuchman, *First Salute*, 137, 218.

"Hunger will compel them to surrender": Hurst, *Golden Rock*, 117.

the laws of war: O'Shaughnessy, *Empire Divided*, 219.

a scene of "general pillage": *RPT*, 3: 122.

"acted like robbers": Miller, *Sea of Glory*, 465.

"wickedly rapacious": *SSP*, 417.

filed their petitions away in "a special place": Hurst, *Golden Rock*, 137.

the island's thriving Jewish community: Hurst, *Golden Rock*, 6–7, 63; O'Shaughnessy, *Empire Divided*, 218.

"deeply concerned in supplying the enemy": Miller, *Sea of Glory*, 465.

"The garments of the aged and respectable": *RPT*, 3: 123.

"One rascal of a Jew"...Jewish men were deported: O'Shaughnessy, *Empire Divided*, 221; Hurst, *Golden Rock*, 129, 133, 141–142.

keep the spoils of the war: Hurst, *Golden Rock*, 137.

"Not a night [goes by]": Miller, *Sea of Glory*, 464.

had the goods...sold at auction: Frank Moya Pons, *History of the Caribbean: Plantations, Trade, and War in the Atlantic World* (Markus Weiner Publishers, 2007), 141; Tuchman, *First Salute*, 13, 56, 99, 100; O'Shaughnessy, *Empire Divided*, 216, 219, 224; Hurst, *Golden Rock*, 147–150.

seize the state capitol in Richmond: John E. Selby, *The Revolution in Virginia, 1775–1783* (Colonial Williamsburg Foundation, 1988), 221–224.

In February 1781, Washington: John R. Maas, *The Road to Yorktown: Jefferson, Lafayette, and the British Invasion of Virginia* (The History Press, 2015), 42–50; Philbrick, *Hurricane's Eye*, 46–72.

"We fight, get beat, rise, and fight again": O'Connell, *Revolutionary*, 271.

Cornwallis too would cross into the Old Dominion: O'Connell, *Revolutionary*, 272.

denounced in Parliament...lawsuits: *WFA*, 417; O'Shaughnessy, *Empire Divided*, 226.

"poverty, desolation, and every species of misery": *RPT*, 3: 120.

only a halfhearted attempt to prevent de Grasse's arrival: Hurst, *Golden Rock*, 153; Miller, *Sea of Glory*, 467.

CHAPTER EIGHTEEN: OUR DELIVERANCE MUST COME

"Now or never...our deliverance must come": GW to John Laurens, April 9, 1781.

"surely ruin France": Ketchum, *Victory at Yorktown*, 137; *BAA*, 235.

sent the *Concorde* back with orders...the Comte de Barras...the Comte de Grasse: *WFA*, 413; *BAA*, 236.

"a crisis of expectation": *RPT*, 3: 2.

might strike a deal at the bargaining table: GW to Thomas Jefferson, June 8, 1781; John Ferling, *Setting the World Ablaze: Washington, Adams, Jefferson, and the American Revolution* (Oxford University Press, 2000) (in context of the summer of 1780).

an emergency meeting in Wethersfield: *WFA*, 413; Philbrick, *Hurricane's Eye*, 114–119.

evacuate his entire force to the West Indies: Philbrick, *Hurricane's Eye*, 112.

Rochambeau also had to: Philbrick, *Hurricane's Eye*, 154.

Rochambeau marched the Special Expedition south: *BAA*, 239; Kennett, *French Forces in America*, 109.

Washington knew Yorktown well: Philbrick, *Hurricane's Eye*, 152.

James Armistead: Encyclopedia Virginia, "James Lafayette, ca. 1748–1830"; Duncan, *Hero of Two Worlds*, 160.

Thousands of African Americans: Philbrick, *Hurricane's Eye*, 120–121.

the First Rhode Island regiment...began marching south: Lanning, *African Americans in the Revolutionary War*, 78.

St. Vincent..."maroons": O'Shaughnessy, *Empire Divided*, 174.

Senegal: *BAA*, 181; *HFSA*, 183.

CHAPTER NINETEEN: INDEPENDENCE IN THE BALANCE

Saint Martin was half-French: Hurst, *Golden Rock*, 61, 68–69, 116.

King George III insisted: Lockwood, *To Begin the World Over Again*, 136.

"sweeten his tea for breakfast"...Tobago: O'Shaughnessy, *Empire Divided*, 49, 170.

Born in his family castle: Jean-Jacques Antier, *l'amiral de Grasse: héros de l'indépendance américane* (Rennes: Editions de la Cité, 1991), 19–23, 43–49; *BAA*, 256.

the "world in miniature," one observer wrote, with 110 guns: Philbrick, *Hurricane's Eye*, 198; O'Connell, *Revolutionary*, 279. Philbrick has a slightly lower estimate of the guns.

the direct ancestor of astrophysicist Neil deGrasse Tyson: *BAA*, 326.

"[T]he Americans are at the end of their resources": Philbrick, *Hurricane's Eye*, 139.

Rochambeau was also running out of cash: Tuchman, *First Salute*, 231.

Back in Spain, he had: *SIUS*, 12, 178, 183; *BAA*, 249.

"reproached by all in case of failure": Philbrick, *Hurricane's Eye*.

Spain would guard the French island by sea: *SIUS*, 201, 204.

He sent collectors out into: For more on Saavedra's fundraising efforts, see *SIUS*, 201–203; *BAA*, 258–259; Barbara Mitchell, "Bankrolling the Battle of Yorktown," HistoryNet (November 28, 2012).

"take everything on myself for the common cause": Philbrick, *Hurricane's Eye*, 143.

take a dangerous route between the Bahamas and: Tuchman, *First Salute*, 240; Philbrick, *Hurricane's Eye*, 144, 149.

Washington got the news of de Grasse's departure: O'Connell, *Revolutionary*, 275.

CHAPTER TWENTY: SEAS OF GLORY

"everything honorable and glorious": GW to Lafayette, November 15, 1781, FO.

Preoccupied with his plunder: Harold Atkins Larrabee, *Decision at the Chesapeake* (C.N. Potter, 1964), 170–180; *BAA*, 257–259; Philbrick, *Hurricane's Eye*, 145–146, 160–161; *SSP* 454.

"the noblest ship in the world": Larrabee, *Decision at the Chesapeake*, 178.

The combined British fleet set sail... de Barras: Larrabee, *Decision at the Chesapeake*, 182–184.

"most noble and majestic spectacle": *SSP*, 453.

De Grasse stationed twenty-four of his ships...disembarking: Larrabee, *Decision at the Chesapeake*, 185.

the British could only counter with nineteen: Larrabee, *Decision at the Chesapeake*, 188.

the "line of speed": *BAA*, 261; Philbrick, *Hurricane's Eye*, 184.

Yet here the horticulturalist was: Larrabee, *Decision at the Chesapeake*, 191–193; *BAA*, 261; Philbrick, *Hurricane's Eye*, 190–191.

The British were ready first...the *Terrible* started leaking: Larrabee, *Decision at the Chesapeake*, 185, 194–196.

"the most violent naval concussions": *RPT*, 3: 2.

"those few testing moments": *HFSA*, 262.

the Count de Barras had slipped into the Chesapeake: Larrabee, *Decision at the Chesapeake*, 221.

a "grand sight": *Hurricane's Eye*, 198.

"To this inferiority": *WFA*, 429.

a huge fleet of twenty-nine British ships of the line was uselessly patrolling: Dull, "France and the American Revolution Seen as Tragedy," 99.

a Dutch fleet in the North Sea: *SSP*, 437.

while the commander in Jamaica had refused: *WFA*, 423.

a squadron to reinforce India: *WFA*, 391–393; 495; *SSP*, 429; *BAA*, 283.

landed troops on the British-held island of Minorca: *SSP*, 441.

all for the common cause: Philbrick, *Hurricane's Eye*, 143.

CHAPTER TWENTY-ONE: THE WORLD TURNED UPSIDE DOWN

keeping their final destination a secret: Tuchman, *First Salute*, 247.

a great show of assembling landing craft...brick ovens: Ketchum, *Victory at Yorktown*, 151.

"The deception was so complete": *RPT*, 3: 9.

marched for weeks...a logistical challenge: O'Connell, *Revolutionary*, 246; Philbrick, *Hurricane's Eye*, 157–159; Tuchman, *First Salute*, 244.

wade through the waters upriver: Philbrick, *Hurricane's Eye*, 165.

marched through Philadelphia: Ketchum, *Victory at Yorktown*, 161–166.

Rochambeau had generously loaned Washington...silver dollars: *HFSA*, 258; Philbrick, *Hurricane's Eye*, 174–175; Ketchum, *Victory at Yorktown*, 163.

"catch a grand flock of vultures": *SSP*, 447.

In mid-September, following: *HFSA*, 264; Philbrick, *Hurricane's Eye*, 195.

"my dear little general": O'Connell, *Revolutionary*, 279.

de Grasse...agreed to stay: *BAA*, 266.

He personally rode off: *HFSA*, 183; Kim Burdick, "A Look at Lauzun in l'Expédition Particulière," *Journal of the American Revolution* (October 5, 2016); *BAA*, 219; Schiff, *Great Improvisation*, 168–169; Ketchum, *Victory at Yorktown*, 164; Tuchman, *First Salute*, 246.

the Battle of the Hook: *HFSA*, 271; *BAA*, 268; Ketchum, *Victory at Yorktown*, 215–217.

the engineer Louis Duportail: *HFSA*, 270.

delegation of Oneida warriors... Other Oneida fighters were back in New York State: Glatthaar and Martin, *Forgotten Allies*, 279–283.

The First Rhode Island Regiment: Lanning, *African Americans in the Revolutionary War*, 78.

since Spain still wasn't: Instead, Gálvez received the grateful thanks of American sea captains who had docked in Havana that fall—they threw him a great party to recognize his contributions to the cause.

a barrage of bombs...white flag of surrender: O'Connell, *Revolutionary*, 282–283; *HFSA*, 279–282; *BAA*, 271–272.

"*Vive le Roi!*": Ketchum, *Victory at Yorktown*, 259.

In the City of Brotherly: Ketchum, *Victory at Yorktown*, 265–266.

"the instruments of their salvation": *RPT*, 3: 32–33.

gave "thanks to almighty God": William Hallahan, *The Day the Revolution Ended: 19 October 1781* (John Whiley, 2004), 220; Ferling, *Almost a Miracle*, 541.

have enough money to reimburse: Ketchum, *Victory at Yorktown*, 266.

Rochambeau gave the honor: Ketchum, *Victory at Yorktown*, 259.

The French were already: Schiff, *Great Improvisation*, 290; *HFSA*, 283.

"'Oh God! It is all over!'": *BAA*, 272.

CHAPTER TWENTY-TWO: THE LAST BATTLE

"fall into a state of languor": GW to Nathanael Greene, November 16, 1781, FO.

King George gave a rousing speech: Ferling, *Almost a Miracle*, 542; Glickstein, *After Yorktown*, 22.

And so, Washington marched: *BAA*, 292–293.

Rochambeau received orders to move north: *BAA*, 294; Ferling, *Almost a Miracle*, 549; Michael Cecere, "The French Army in Williamsburg, Virginia, 1781–1782," *Journal of the American Revolution* (December 13, 2022).

"as much in the dark as ever": GW to Nathanael Greene, July 9, 1782, FO.

He spent our nation's: GW, General Orders, July 4, 1782, FO.

begged de Grasse to provide naval support: Ferling, *Almost a Miracle*, 546.

"the greatest man in the world": Joseph Ellis, *His Excellency George Washington* (Alfred A. Knopf, 2004), 139.

Washington giving a belt: Glatthaar and Martin, *Forgotten Allies*, 284–285.

Even as late as 1782: Ferling, *Almost a Miracle*, 548.

On Independence Day, after: *BAA*, 294; Merv O. Ahrens, "Revolutionary Revenge on Hudson Bay, 1782," *Journal of the American Revolution* (May 7, 2020).

a "paltry little skirmish": Glickstein, *After Yorktown*, 111.

One window would show: John D. Garrigus, "Saint-Domingue's Free Men of Color," in *The American Revolution: A World War*, eds. Allison and Ferreiro, 190.

Rodney attacked de Grasse: *SSP*, 465; *BAA*, 277; *SIUS*, 207.

"saved Jamaica from its impending fate": *RPT*, 3: 132.

"England is so giddy": John Adams to Robert Livingston, June 9, 1782, FO.

Noticing how overstretched: Hurst, *Golden Rock*, 191.

a combined Spanish and American fleet took the Bahamas: *SIUS*, 207–208; *BAA*, 278–280.

Jamaica Invasion 2.0, this time to be led: *SIUS*, 210–211.

Meanwhile, Mathías de Gálvez: *SIUS*, 157–165.

In August 1781, the French: *BAA*, 286–288; *SIUS*, 146–148.

"All the powers of invention were called forth": *RPT*, 3: 153.

floating artillery batteries... Grand Assault: Adkins and Adkins, *Gibraltar*, 317–329; Falkner, *Fire over the Rock*, 105–119; *BAA*, 288–291.

"the unceasing blaze of the other": *RPT*, 3: 156.

The French suffered some: Adkins and Adkins, *Gibraltar*, 338; Falkner, *Fire over the Rock*, 120.

a large allied fleet sailed into the English Channel: *SSP*, 466.

Suffren..."full of audacity and lust for action"...Admiral Satan: *SSP* 429; *BAA*, 282; Roderick Cavaliero, *Admiral Satan: The Life and Campaigns of Suffren* (I.B. Tauris, 1994).

Suffren spent July 4, 1782, maneuvering his ships... More clashes: *WFA*, 496–500; *SSP* 467; *BAA*, 283.

On February 27, 1782: *HFSA*, 285; *WFA*, 461–462; *SIUS*, 206.

The last shot: Hasan, *History of Tipu Sultan*, 48–51; *BAA*, 283–284; *WFA*, 500.

The British captain boarded: Hasan, *History of Tipu Sultan*, 51–53; *BAA*, 284; Lockwood, *To Begin the World Over Again*, 270.

Among the dead: *BAA*, 284.

EPILOGUE: AN AMERICAN FOURTH

the "common cause," as both Washington and Admiral de Grasse put it: Philbrick, *Hurricane's Eye*, 143; *BAA*, 116.

"to the Memory of those Heroes": Fraunces Tavern Museum, "George Washington's Farewell to His Officers," https://www.frauncestavernmuseum.org/washingtons-farewell.

"I have lost the only friend": Murphy, *Charle Gravier*, 473.

one hundred thousand soldiers and sailors: *BAA*, 305.

Not only were France's own military operations costly: *BAA*, 335.

By 1786, over half the national budget: *BAA*, 316.

The Americans had done: *BAA*, 299; *SSP*, 468.

By contrast, France didn't: *BAA*, 302; *HFSA*, 302.

"The American war seems first to have awakened": Thomas Jefferson to Richard Price, January 8, 1789, FO.

"missionary of liberty": Lafayette to GW, March 17, 1780, FO. The Marquis even took a lead role in drafting the French Declaration of the Rights of Man, with some passages modeled after the American Declaration of Independence. No wonder—he had help behind the scenes from a ghostwriter, Ambassador Jefferson himself.

"seldom a favorite fortune": *RPT*, 2: 163.

Even Lafayette's wife Adrienne: *HFSA*, 308–313; *BAA*, 319; Duncan, *Hero of Two Worlds*, 305–308.

"History is not the province of the ladies": John Adams to Elbridge Gerry, April 17, 1813, FO.

Larrie Ferreiro, the professor: Larrie Ferreiro, "Rewriting the American Revolution," in *The American Revolution: A World War*, eds. Allison and Ferreiro, 224–236.

Washington had coveted: *SIUS*, 1–2, 219; GW to Robert Townsend Howe, July 18, 1784, FO; *BAA*, 313.

"my thanks for the Jackasses": GW to Floridablanca, December 19, 1785, FO.

American Mammoths: *BAA*, 313.

treaty with Britain: Ferling, *Shots Heard Round the World*, 375; *BAA*, 300–301.

Relations with Spain remained: Murphy, *Charles Gravier*, 382–385; *BAA*, 320; Gordon Wood, *Empire of Liberty: A History of the Early Republic, 1789–1815* (Oxford University Press, 2009), 112–114, 201.

Although the Spanish put down these uprisings: *SIUS*, 204; Lockwood, *To Being the World Again*, 155–170.

Many of the leaders explicitly drew from the Declaration: David Armitage, *The Declaration of Independence: A Global History* (Harvard University Press, 2007), 108–109, 146–148; *BAA*, 323–324.

Hardly any of the Spanish: *SIUS*, 217–219.

Saavedra...came out of retirement: *SIUS*, 221.

The United States never paid its debts from the war to Spain: *SIUS*, 221.

Their peace treaty gave: David J. Hancock, "Crafting the Peace" in *The American Revolution: A World War*, eds. Allison and Ferreiro, 202–203.

"all the subsequent disasters": *SSP*, 470.

In 1787, Jefferson left: Derek Baxter (Sourcebooks, 2022). This remains one of the two best books that I've written.

"pomp and ceremony": Thomas Jefferson to John Jay, August 3, 1788, FO.

"took advantage of my youth": Labourdette, *Vergennes*, 104.

Cornwallis mounted a fierce campaign: Hasan, *History of Tipu Sultan*, 167–169; 239–263; Brittlebank, *Tiger*, 65–72.

the British preemptively attacked them: Hasan, *History of Tipu Sultan*, 296–315; Brittlebank, *Tiger*, 75–76.

tiger-striped uniforms: Dalrymple, *The Anarchy*, 348; Brittlebank, *Tiger*, 89.

The British laid siege: Hasan, *History of Tipu Sultan*, 316–317; Brittlebank, *Tiger*, 76.

For many Blacks: Lockwood, *To Begin the World Again*, 376; Glickstein, *After Yorktown*, 351–358.

"Devourer of Villages": Colin Calloway, *The Indian World of George Washington: The First President, the First Americans, and the Birth of the Nation* (Oxford University Press, 2018), 25.

"almost fatal to the nation": Kidder, *Defending Fort Stanwix*, 255.

Many Oneida villages: Glatthaar and Martin, *Forgotten Allies*, 300; Kidder, *Defending Fort Stanwix*, 256; Calloway, *The American Revolution in Indian Country*, 286.

The Canandaigua agreement: Glatthaar and Martin, *Forgotten Allies*, 310.

Han Yerry, the leader: Kidder, *Defending Fort Stanwix*, 255; Glatthaar and Martin, *Forgotten Allies*, 312.

New York State leaders: Glatthaar and Martin, *Forgotten Allies*, 295–296, 306–311.

In 1825, as he toured: Glatthaar and Martin, *Forgotten Allies*, 3–5.

The pressure on the Oneida: Glatthaar and Martin, *Forgotten Allies*, 314.

"solemnized with Pomp and Parade": John Adams to Abigail Adams, July 3, 1776, FO.

Warren died in 1814: Stuart, *The Muse of the Revolution*, 267–268.

Telling "the complete history": John Adams to the Abbé de Mably, January 15, 1783, FO.

Index

Note: Page numbers in **bold** indicate photographs.

C

D

E

F

G

H

M

S

T

About the Author

Derek Baxter is the author of *In Pursuit of Jefferson: Traveling Through Europe with the Most Perplexing Founding Father,* in which he recounts his journeys through six countries, armed with a guide written by Jefferson in 1788. This is his second book. He lives with his family in northern Virginia. Follow his adventures at derekbaxterbooks.com.